Ferdinand Vandeveer Hayden, Printers C. Sherman & Son

Contributions to the ethnography and philology of the Indian tribes of the Missouri Valley

Ferdinand Vandeveer Hayden, Printers C. Sherman & Son

Contributions to the ethnography and philology of the Indian tribes of the Missouri Valley

ISBN/EAN: 9783337057152

Printed in Europe, USA, Canada, Australia, Japan

Cover: Foto ©Thomas Meinert / pixelio.de

More available books at **www.hansebooks.com**

CONTRIBUTIONS

TO THE

ETHNOGRAPHY AND PHILOLOGY

OF THE

INDIAN TRIBES

OF THE

MISSOURI VALLEY.

By DR. F. V. HAYDEN,

MEMBER OF THE AMERICAN PHILOSOPHICAL SOCIETY, OF THE ACADEMY OF NATURAL SCIENCES OF PHILADELPHIA, ETC. ETC.

PREPARED UNDER THE DIRECTION OF CAPT. WILLIAM F. RAYNOLDS, T. E. U. S. A.,
AND PUBLISHED BY PERMISSION OF THE WAR DEPARTMENT.

PHILADELPHIA:
C. SHERMAN & SON, PRINTERS.
1862.

CONTENTS.

PAGES

CHAPTER I. Introduction, 231–234

ALGONKIN GROUP, A.

II. Knisteneaux, or Crees—Ethnographical History, . 231–248
III. Blackfeet—Ethnographical History, ... 248–256
IV. Remarks on the Grammatical Structure of the Blackfoot Language, 257–266
V. Vocabulary of the Sik-si-ka', or Blackfoot Language, . . . 266–273
VI. Shyennes—Ethnographical History, ... 274–282
VII. Remarks on the Grammatical Structure of the Shyenne Language, . 283–290
VIII. Vocabulary of the Shyenne Language, . 294–320

ARAPOHO GROUP, B.

IX. Arapohos—Ethnographical History, and Remarks on the Grammatical Structure of their Language, . . 321–327
X. Vocabulary of the Arapoho Language, . . 328–339
XI. Atsinas—Ethnographical History and Vocabulary, 340–345

PAWNEE GROUP, C.

XII. Pawnees—Ethnographical History and Vocabulary, . 345–351
XIII. Arikaras—Ethnographical History and Vocabulary, . 351–363

DAKOTA GROUP, D.

XIV. Dakotas—Ethnographical History and Vocabulary, 364–378
XV. Assiniboins—Ethnographical History and Vocabulary, . . . 379–391
XVI. Aub-sa'-ro-ke, or Crow Indians—Ethnographical History, with Remarks on the Grammatical Structure of their Language, . 391–402
XVII. Vocabulary of the Aub-sa'-ro-ke, or Crow Language, . 402–420
XVIII. Minnitarees—Ethnographical History and Vocabulary, 420–426
XIX. Mandans—Ethnographical History, ... 426–435
XX. Observations on the Grammatical Structure of the Mandan Language, . 435–439
XXI. Vocabulary of the Mandan Language, ... 439–444
XXII. Sketch of the Oma'-ha, and Iowa or Oto Indians, with Vocabularies, 444–456

ARTICLE III.

CONTRIBUTIONS TO THE ETHNOGRAPHY AND PHILOLOGY OF THE INDIAN TRIBES OF THE MISSOURI VALLEY.

BY F. V. HAYDEN, M.D.

CHAPTER I.

INTRODUCTION.

THE materials which compose the following chapters have been accumulated since the summer of 1855, and I now for the first time venture to present them for publication. They are named "Contributions," because they by no means exhaust the subjects treated, and also because they convey but little more than a glimpse of the beauty and fulness of the various Indian languages spoken in the Northwest. No opportunity will be left unimproved in the future to verify or add to the materials already secured, although no effort has been spared to render the present memoir as accurate as possible. A very full *Grammar and Dictionary of the Dakota Language* has been published by the Smithsonian Institution, which it is but just to pronounce the most important contribution to Indian Philology ever made in this country. To this work I am very much indebted for many valuable suggestions during the latter part of my researches. It can hardly be regarded as necessary to perform an equally laborious task for all the native languages of our continent, neither could it be done except by intelligent missionaries, who have spent their lives with the Indians, and acquired a great degree of familiarity with their modes of expression. With the Dakotas, who occupy so vast an area of our Northwestern country, educated missionaries have resided many years, and have become able to converse with fluency in their own tongue, but this can be said with regard to very few of the Northwestern tribes. In the spring of 1860, some Lutheran missionaries attempted to establish a mission school and farm in the Crow district, near the eastern base of the Big Horn Mountains, but they had been in that country but a few months before the principal man of the enterprise, Rev. Mr. Brauninger, was killed by a roving war party of Dakotas, and thus the attempt to civilize the Crows was abandoned. Among the Blackfeet, at the present time, are some Catholic priests, who are laboring to instruct the youth in the English language, but as yet nothing has been done toward acquiring a knowledge of the native tongue. No permanent mission station has ever been established among the Assiniboins, Minnitarees, Mandans, Arickares, Shyennes, Arapohos, or Dakotas of the Missouri, and with the exception of the latter, only brief vocabularies of the languages spoken by these nations have been published.

The tribes enumerated in this work have been separated into four distinct groups, and it is believed that a more careful study and comparison of their different dialects will only tend to confirm this division.

I.	KNISTENEAUX, OR CREES,	Algonkin Group, A.
II.	BLACKFEET,	
III.	SHYENNES,	
IV.	ARAPOHOS,	Arapoho Group, B.
V.	ATSINAS,	
VI.	PAWNEES,	Pawnee Group, C.
VII.	ARIKARAS,	
VIII.	DAKOTAS,	Dakota Group, D.
IX.	ASSINIBOINS,	
X.	CROWS,	
XI.	MINNITAREES,	
XII.	MANDANS,	
XIII.	OMAHAS,	
XIV.	IOWAS,	

Belonging to the last group are the Ponkas, Otos, Missourias, Kansas, Osages, Inapaw, Winnibagos, whose languages have not yet been studied to any extent.

I am well aware how incomplete these Contributions are, and would not at this time suffer their publication, did I not believe that there is contained in them much useful information which ought to be given to the world in advance of a more elaborate work. In stating the definitions of many of the words, I have often used the peculiar idioms of those Far-Western men, which they have derived from long intercourse with the Indians, and an acquaintance with their peculiar modes of expression.

In obtaining words from the native Indian, the object is not to labor with any preconceived opinion in regard to their meaning or their grammatical structure, to which the mind of the Indian must bend in giving his replies, but to let him answer freely, and then by a variety of cross questions, arrive at an approximation to the truth. It has often been a matter of much surprise to me, how much of the grammatical structure of a language may be obtained from a wholly uneducated but intelligent native by judicious management. I have found it of great advantage to enlist the aid of the chiefs and leading men in my labors, from the fact that they, in almost all cases, take great pride in being regarded as the censors of the purity with which their language is spoken. They have not unfrequently told me that all the words obtained from certain of the more common men of the tribe were useless, inasmuch as they did not speak their own language correctly. Among all the tribes with which I have been acquainted, physical and mental superiority have always taken the lead in the affairs of the nation, without regard to birth, and this is a result growing out of the nature of their nomadic and precarious life. Life to them is, to a great extent, a struggle for existence, and therefore the position of an Indian in his tribe is an almost certain index of his mental status. For this reason, in securing information or in acquiring the language of a tribe, it will be found most advantageous to consult only the chiefs and leading men, and this is the course that I have endeavored to pursue in collecting the materials for this memoir. Whenever I have been obliged to accept the aid of women or ordinary men, I have always submitted the results to a chief to be verified or rejected.

In these preliminary papers, the orthography employed by Mr. Riggs and Professor Turner in the Dakota Grammar and Dictionary published by the Smithsonian Institution, has been adopted in part. It is to be hoped that the Smithsonian Institution, which takes the deepest interest in all researches relating to the aboriginal inhabitants of our country, will recommend some uniform system, and reduce all the Indian languages to a single standard of pronunciation. In the following vocabularies, the consonants are used with their common English sounds, when it could be done, and this is understood when not expressly mentioned.

a is sounded as in ah, father; when followed by a consonant, ä* is used, otherwise it is short, as a in fat.

e has the sound of a in face, or e in they; short when followed by a consonant, as in met.

i, as in marine; i short as in pin.

o, as in note, or short o as in got.

u as oo in food; short as in hut.

ai has the sound of i in line.

au, as in now, how.

ć has the aspirated sound of ch in chin, church.

g always the hard sound, as in go, give.

ḣ represents a strong guttural sound, like that of ch in the Gaelic word *Loch*, or the German *ich*; also resembling the Arabic kha.

ŋ denotes the nasal sound, similar to the French *n* in *bon*, or the English *n* in *drink*.

ks has the sound of *x* in *maxim*.

ts is sounded as in Betsy.

wh as in what, when.

ź has the sound of *z* in *azure* or *s* in *measure*.

* As a rule, a vowel is long when ending a syllable, and short when followed by a consonant. The exceptions to this rule are indicated thus: ā, long; ă, short.

Any additional sounds that may be needed, will be noted at the bottom of the page in succeeding portions of the work.

All the syllables are separated, for greater distinctness, and accented when it could be done with certainty. The accents of some words are omitted, from neglect when securing them in the country, and I dare not trust to my memory to remedy the matter now.

In all my researches in the Northwest, most important aid has been rendered to me by the different members of the American Fur Company. All their stores of knowledge of Indian life, language, and character, which they had acquired by years of intercourse with the different tribes, were freely imparted to me, only a small portion of which is given in the following pages. I am especially indebted to Mr. Alexander Culbertson, the well-known agent of the American Fur Company, who has spent thirty years of his life among the wild tribes of the Northwest, and speaks several of their languages with great ease. To Mr. Andrew Dawson, Superintendent of Fort Benton, Mr. Charles E. Galpin, of Fort Pierre, and E. T. Denig, of Fort Union, I am under great obligations for assistance freely granted at all times.

To the Smithsonian Institution, and to Professor Henry, I am indebted for rooms, books, and every facility that could be afforded, for the prosecution of my studies. The memoir was written within the walls of the Institution.

I wish also to acknowledge my indebtedness to the veteran author, Mr. H. R. Schoolcraft, for the loan of many rare books, and especially to Col. Peter Force for the free use of rare books in his magnificent collection, without access to which the present work would have been far less complete.

The Indian reservations were located on the map under the direction of Hon. Wm. P. Dole, the Commissioner of Indian Affairs. This map represents the latest information of that Bureau.

CHAPTER II.

ETHNOGRAPHICAL HISTORY.

I. KNISTENEAUX, OR CREES.

A GREAT difficulty occurs at the commencement of the history of any of these prairie tribes, in discovering anything of ancient date of a reliable character. Among people where no written records exist, and whose only method of preserving their national history is oral tradition, this, after being handed down through several generations, becomes usually so confused and fabulous by the additions and fanciful embellishments of the several narrators, that but little can be extracted worthy to be considered of historical value. In regard to the Crees, all appears obscure farther back than 1760.* At any rate, events said to have happened prior to that period, narrated by different persons, differ so materially as to be unworthy of note. From 1760 down to the present time the history of the Crees can be traced with a fair degree of certainty.

So much has already been written in regard to the literature of the Cree language with its cognate Algonkin dialects, that I have thought it unnecessary to present a resumé of its bibliography at this time, but pass on at once to a sketch of this nation, condensed from information obtained from some of the most intelligent men of the tribe. I will, however, call attention to a rare work† on the Cree language, by Mr. Joseph Howse, which I regard as a very important contribution to Indian philology. It appears to be a thorough and philosophical analysis of the grammatical structure of the language, with copious illustrations from the Chippewa, which show the close affinity of the former to the latter.

The Cree nation was originally a portion of the Chippewa, as the similarity of language proves; and even now they are so mingled with the latter people as with difficulty to be considered a distinct tribe, further than a slight difference in language and their local position. Their name for the tribe in their own tongue is Né-a-ya-óg, which means, "those who speak the same tongue." They are called by the Assiniboins Shi-é-ya, by the Dakotas Shi-e-á-la, and by other neighboring tribes, as the Crows, Blackfeet, and Gros Ventres of the prairie, nearly the same, only differing a little in the pronunciation of the word Shi-é-ya. This word has very nearly the same signification among the Assiniboins as that of Né-a-ya-óg among the Crees. Indeed, the word Shi-é-ya being Assiniboin, could have no other meaning as a derivation among other tribes, except as an appellation of the native Cree, received from the Dakotas and Assiniboins where it originated.

Prior to the year 1700 the Crees say they inhabited a district much farther north than at present. Their range at that time was along the borders of Slave and Athabasca Lakes,

* Since writing the above I have had access to an interesting collection of voyages, recently published under the editorial direction of Mr. J. G. Shea, of New York. In the account of Le Sueur's voyage up the Mississippi, 1699–1700, there is an allusion to the Crees and Assiniboins. Le Sueur seems to have been an Indian trader, and had erected a trading post on the Mankato, or Blue Earth River, a tributary of the St. Peter's River. These tribes are called by him Christinaux and Assinipoils, and he remarks that they "live above the fort on the east, more than eighty leagues up the Mississippi." We are thus able to ascertain very nearly the geographical location of these two tribes more than one hundred and sixty years ago. The Indians themselves, however, can give no definite information of their movements farther back than the period mentioned in the text.

† A Grammar of the Cree Language, with which is combined an analysis of the Chippewa Dialect, by Joseph Howse, Esq., F.R.G.S., twenty years a resident in Prince Rupert's Land, in the service of the Hon. Hudson's Bay Company; pp. 324. London, 1844.

the northern end of Lake Winnipeg, and stretching along the Saskatchewan by a chain of small lakes, in the direction of Hudson's Bay, though never reaching the latter place. The Chippewas, on the other hand, spread out towards Lake Superior, Lake of the Woods, and extended as low down as Lakes Huron, Michigan, and Prairie du Chien.

The time when and the cause why the Crees separated from the Chippewas and formed themselves into a distinct nation are now lost; most probably the division was of very ancient date, and arose from some family feud, so frequent in their former patriarchal and primitive condition. The reason may have been that they were induced by superior hunting advantages presenting themselves in that district, where even yet the woods abound with game, and the rivers and lakes are well stocked with beaver, fish, and wild fowl. Whatever the cause of the separation was, it is now not remembered; and after long and bloody wars with nations still farther north, they were obliged to retreat south-westwardly, where, in the year 1760, we find them along the shores of Red River and the lower end of Lake Winnipeg, living at peace with the Assiniboins, who then joined them and entered into a league, offensive and defensive, against all the surrounding nations except the Chippewas.

About the year 1800 most of their Assiniboin allies left and migrated to the Missouri and Yellowstone Rivers, though even yet some two hundred to two hundred and fifty lodges live with the Crees. The present boundary of the Cree nation is nearly as follows: On the north and northwest by Red River and Riviere du Parc; on the south and east by Pembina River; thence west to the Coteau de Prairie, or divide; thence along the Coteau through Woody, Cypress, Tinder, and Prickly Pear Mountains, nearly to the bank of the Saskatchewan; thence to Lake Winnipeg and Red River. This is the section claimed by them as their own, though in their hunting excursions they do not confine themselves to these limits, but are as frequently found west of their boundary, in the country of the Assiniboins, especially if buffalo are not numerous in their own district. Occasionally they sell their robes to the traders on the Missouri, but most of the fine furs they collect they carry to the posts of the Hudson's Bay Company established in their territory.

The Crees are surrounded on the east by the Chippewas, on the southeast and south by the Dakotas, on the west by the Assiniboins, and on the north and northwest by the Gros Ventres of the prairie and Blackfeet. With the Assiniboins and Chippewas they have always been at peace, but with the Blackfeet and Dakotas they have waged an inveterate war beyond the recollection of any one now living, varied only by a transient peace with a portion of the former nation, whom they sometimes meet and hunt with near the Fort de Prairie of the Hudson's Bay Company.

Before the small-pox made its appearance among them in 1776 or '77, the Crees numbered about eight hundred lodges, one-half of whom, it is estimated, died of that disease.

Since that time they have gradually increased, particularly those bands that are too remote to suffer from invading foes. At this time (1856) they number about ten or eleven hundred lodges, averaging four souls to a lodge, making a total of between four and five thousand persons. Like most of the tribes in the Northwest Territory, they are separated into clans or bands, and live in different districts for greater advantages in hunting. The names and number of these bands are as follows: Co-káh, or band of "Eyes Open," bearing the name of the chief who governs it, consists of one hundred lodges and upwards, who reside in the neighborhood of Lac Qu'apelle; live in skin lodges; hunt and trade their skins at the posts of the Hudson's Bay Company. Pe-i-sí-e-kau, or "Striped," is composed of forty or fifty lodges; rove and hunt near Tinder Mountains; live in skin tents, and trade with the same Company. Pis-ka-káu-a-kis, or "Magpies," are about thirty lodges; are stationed at Tinder Mountain; live in dirt lodges and log-cabins; cultivate the soil to some extent, and raise considerable quantities of corn and potatoes; hunt buffalo during the winter, and trade also with the Hudson's Bay Company. Ki-á-sku-sis, "Small Gulls," reside around the fourth lake from Lac Qu'apelle; live in skin tents; were formerly numerous, but are now nearly all killed off by the Blackfeet, they being nearest of all the bands to this large and fierce nation of enemies. At this time the number is thought not to exceed thirty or forty families.

1. Wik-yu-wám-ka-mus-e-nái-ka-ta,—"The Painted Lodge."
2. Mus-kwoi-ká-ke-nut,—"He who shoots bears with arrows."
3. A-pis-te-kái-he,—"The Little Eagle."
4. Mus-kwoi-káu-e-pá-wit,—"Standing Bear."

The above are the names of four chiefs who govern each a small band which takes the same name as its leader. These bands live near each other in the country about Fort de Prairie, and trade at that place. They number in all about one hundred and thirty to one hundred and forty lodges, and live in skin tents.

Ma-tái-tai-ke-ók, or "Plusieurs des Aigles," known among the traders as "Le Sonnant," is chief of about three hundred lodges, who roam and hunt the country along the Montagnes des Bois, and sometimes trade at the American Fur Company's trading post on the Missouri River near the mouth of the Yellowstone, but more frequently at some of the Hudson's Bay Company's forts on Red River. The band of She-mau-káu, or "La Lance," hunt near and in Cypress and Prickly Pear Mountains; live in skin tents; occasionally visiting the Missouri for the purposes of trade, especially if opposition runs high and goods are cheap, otherwise they prefer dealing with the English traders in their country. This is the largest band, and contains three hundred and fifty lodges. Several smaller bands of from thirty to forty lodges each are found every winter near the Woody Mountains. They generally trade their robes on the Missouri, and carry their fine furs, wolf-skins, dried meat, and tallow, to the traders of the Hudson's Bay Company.

Besides the foregoing there are about two hundred lodges more who are not formed into bands, but scattered along Lac de L'Isle Croix, and live by hunting reindeer, moose, fish, and wild fowl. They live in skin tents in the summer, but sometimes build log and bark huts in winter, and seldom more than one cabin is found in the same place. These are the poorest of the Crees.

These Indians are of the same opinion in common with other prairie tribes, that the Master of Life, the sun, intended all hunting lands for the sole use and occupation of the Indians, but do not think that he parcelled out distinct portions to each nation. Land, as far as their knowledge of it extends, is regarded as a common whole, which any nation (of Indians) has a right to live upon and retain possession of as large a district as they are able to defend. Their right to their own territory is in accordance with this general principle, contending that they have been forced back from superior grounds to those they now inhabit, and consequently they have the right in turn to dislodge others for their own welfare. All nations feel and acknowledge the expediency and necessity for seeking a subsistence any and everywhere, as long as they are dependent solely on the chase for support; hence the deadly struggles on the borders of each to prevent approximation. Each nation feels that it must make war to prevent others from settling near them, and the result is, that between each nation there is a large extent of neutral ground, seldom if ever traversed except by passing war parties.

The Crees do not seem to possess any idea, either by tradition or otherwise, from which we should judge that whites or any other civilized race had occupied the country previous to the Indians; nor have they any knowledge of quadrupeds foreign to America, or differing from those now hunted and domesticated by them. They have no name for the entire continent, neither are they aware of its extent. They will mention American lands, English possessions, &c., but these terms only extend to those parts with which they are acquainted.

None of these wild tribes have any just idea of the form of the earth, nor of its natural divisions into seas, continents, islands, &c. The earth they regard as a great plain, and they know that there are many lakes that contain islands, for the Cree country abounds with them. All the nations are well enough acquainted with the natural features of their own lands, but they have no idea of the extent of other territories. They have no notion of the earth as a whole, and the ocean they think is a large lake, from the description given them by the voyageurs of that body of water. Indeed, they have a very faint idea of any lands or waters outside of the boundaries of the district over which they range; and when the voyageurs, who have been sent out by the Hudson's Bay Company to the sea-coast, describe to them the great ocean, they are not generally disposed to place any confidence in their statements.

The principal river in the Cree country is the Riviere du Parc, which takes its rise from springs in the Rocky Mountains, east of the Missouri, and, running in a northeastern direction, empties into Lake Winnipeg. In regard to its length, our informant, who has frequently travelled from its mouth to its source, states it to be sixty-seven days' travel up in Mackinaw boats; which, averaging eighteen miles per day, would make its whole navigable length about twelve hundred miles, and from the head of navigation to its source one hundred and fifty miles farther. Small boats are taken up this river at all times, when it is free from ice, to within one hundred and fifty miles of its source, where the Hudson's Bay Company have erected a fort, called "Fort Cassepierre," at which point goods are landed for the trade with the Crees in that vicinity. This is the highest post on the river, though there are other trading-houses at different points lower down the stream. The middle portion of this river is about three hundred yards in width; at its mouth it is nearly a mile wide, and generally from ten to fifteen feet deep, and contains one hundred and sixty rapids and falls of various heights; at all of which the goods which are taken up, or the packs of furs which pass down, are carried round by portage. On this account, all packages are made to weigh ninety-five pounds each. These are transported on the backs of voyageurs around the falls, and at large or dangerous rapids the boats are also carried, otherwise they are let gently down after having been unloaded.

Assiniboin River takes its rise on the north side of the Woody Mountains, and after running through several lakes, empties into Lake Winnipeg. Its entire length, including the lakes, is estimated at four hundred miles. There are no rapids in this river, and it is navigable throughout with Mackinaw boats, in which the goods and peltries of the Hudson's Bay Company are carried to and from the different posts along its banks.

Red River is a branch of the Assiniboin River, emptying into it about forty miles above the junction of the latter with Lake Winnipeg. This is called "The Fork," and on it is established one of the largest forts belonging to the Hudson's Bay Company. The principal branch of Red River rises in Red Lake; it is from fifty to sixty yards wide, with a deep and slow current. The other branch heads in Lake Traverse, and joins the first about one hundred miles above the mouth of Pembina River. This is called the "Plat Cote" branch, and is not navigable for boats except during spring freshets, and even then it is attended with much danger.

Pembina River rises in Turtle Mountain, its sources soon forming a lake; after which it passes through four other lakes. It is a long, crooked stream, full of rapids, and is not navigable by any craft larger than a bark canoe. It empties into Red River, eighty miles above the junction of that river with the Assiniboin. Nine miles above its mouth, and spread along its banks, is a settlement of the Cree half-breeds.

La Riviere aux Souris owes its origin to springs rising in the Coteau de Prairie, or "divide." This is a long and very crooked stream; so much so, we are informed, that after seven days' travel down it, a distance of not more than thirty miles in a right line has been gained. Its length is estimated at six hundred miles; it is from one hundred to one hundred and fifty yards wide, but very shallow, and is not navigable except when swollen by the spring thaws, when it may be descended with loaded Mackinaws. It joins Assiniboin River ninety miles above the mouth of Red River, and there are five trading-posts of the Hudson's Bay Company along its banks.

These are the principal rivers in the Cree country, although there are many others running into these. Along the banks of all, and indeed throughout the whole of this immense district, are a great many springs of excellent water, many of which might afford power for machinery; others are impregnated with salt, from which an abundant supply of this article is obtained by the inhabitants. Nearly all the lakes of the larger class are deep enough for good-sized steamers, and are stocked with incredible quantities of fish and wild fowl.

All the territory claimed by the Crees, with the exception of a few square miles near its southeastern boundary, is beyond the parallel of 49°, and consequently in the English possessions. The general surface of the country is what may be called rolling, though there are extensive level prairies in some parts of it. As a whole it forms a gradual descent from the base of the Rocky Mountains east of the Missouri, including several mountains of smaller note, which give rise to the rivers and creeks running in every direction through the interior, thus cutting up the surface. At the base of many of the hills and mountains from which springs flow are found marshes, or what are called by the inhabitants "muskegs," of various extent, from a few miles to a day's travel across, depending upon the supply of water by which they are fed, or whether the surface of the ground is level and without any indented outlet. These swamps are, for the most part, covered with tall, strong grass, growing very thick, six or eight feet high, sometimes with rushes intermingled; but the ground, though humid, is not miry, and can in most places be traversed on horseback. All the rivers are well wooded along their margins, and groves occur on the adjoining bluffs and for some distance beyond, often extending several miles when the soil is moist and adapted to the growth of trees. On the level plains patches of timber are to be met with, being more numerous and larger in the northern than in any other part of the district. Although there is more prairie than woodland, it is by no means a barren country, and differs materially in quality of soil and appearance from the Dakota lands, which continue on the east and southeast, where all the plains are dry and unfruitful.

The soil of the whole Cree district is of a good quality, as has been shown by the agriculturists settled along the banks of Red and Pembina Rivers, and the small band of Cree Indians who raise maize and other vegetables at Tinder Mountain. The half-breed settlement on Red River contains at this time over eight thousand persons, many of whom cultivate the soil and raise live stock to a great extent; but owing to their locality being subject to inundations from Red River during the spring thaws, sweeping off their stock and other property, many of them have been induced to remove and settle on Pembina River within the American boundary, where they live by hunting and cultivating small portions of land. Many more of these people will follow, and soon a village will spring up in this place. There are at the present time a Catholic and a Presbyterian church, schools, grist and saw mills, several stores and trading establishments, &c.; indeed, the country presents many advantages which cannot fail to attract the attention of numerous restless emigrants in search of lands flowing with milk and honey. Wheat, oats, barley, and corn grow well; also potatoes and all kinds of garden vegetables are produced abundantly; but as yet, no market being created for their surplus grain and stock, the attention of settlers on the American side has not been directed to farming on a large scale. Those on the English side dispose of a portion of their produce and stock to the Hudson's Bay Company, who ship it to other parts farther north, where breadstuffs are not raised; but only a small part is thus disposed of, the greater portion being consumed among themselves.

It is believed that the whole Cree district is arable and fit for tilling or grazing purposes, both prairie and woodland, though the latter perhaps is not as good as the low prairie, on which the spontaneous grasses of the most nutritious character grow. But the small rushes, common to the low grounds in this country, are said to be more nutritious for animals than any kind of grain. A very poor horse will become fat if allowed to range among them twenty-five or thirty days. Notwithstanding the high latitude of the country the domestic animals are not usually housed during the severe cold winter; and those left to run at large are said to be invariably in a better condition in the spring than those kept in stables and fed on grain. Indeed, this region is known to be one of the best grazing and grain-growing countries in North America. Horned cattle and horses are raised in numbers, with a few sheep, but the latter are not much attended to.

Where springs and streams are not convenient, water can be obtained by digging from ten to thirty feet in level places, and the water thus found is free from any mineral taste, and suitable for culinary purposes. The portions designated as marshes are not useless or irreclaimable; on the contrary, the waters accumulating in these swamps could be collected and made subservient to agricultural uses. The soil in these places is of the richest quality, and would soon repay the expense of draining did the increase of population demand it.

In most places where the country is thickly timbered, the ground underneath is covered with moss and bushes, but with little or no grass. It is only in such places and for that reason that the soil sustains any damage from the burning of the prairies. The moss forming the sod being reduced to a cinder by the fire, the roots are destroyed, and several years must elapse before another coat of green adorns it; which, like the preceding, is destined to be burned when the fire passes in that direction. The vegetation of the prairie, however, receives no such damage; being deeply rooted the stalk only burns, and the heat is swept away by the winds; the roots retain their life; and soon after another crop springs up more lively and thick than the former, owing to the surface being cleared, by the fires, of the decayed vegetation. The large timber, however, suffers greatly on these occasions. Vast forests are thus completely destroyed, and centuries will be required to replace them.

The burning of the prairies is not a custom resorted to by the Indians to facilitate hunting, as is generally supposed. Nothing offends them more, and their laws among themselves are very severe in this matter, as it effectually destroys their hunting by driving away all game, and renders the country unfit for pasturage during the winter when burnt late in the fall. These fires originate, for the most part, in the carelessness of hunters and travellers, by the malice of individuals, or passing war parties of other nations. Sometimes these fires are very destructive, and sweep over districts hundreds of miles in extent; on other occasions they are extinguished by rains, snow, or the wind blowing in the contrary direction. A few years ago a large party of half-breeds camped near a frozen swamp and let their horses loose among the tall grass. Their camp fires by some accident communicated with the grass, and the wind being very strong, all their horses, to the number of two hundred or more, were surrounded by the flames and destroyed.

The climate may be considered variable, not in regard to heat and cold, but moisture and dryness. Cold and constant northeast winds in the spring bring rain, and from May until the last of June may be called the wet season. In July and August there are no settled rains for days at a time, but violent thunderstorms come from the west and southwest, which in a few hours swell the smaller streams to the top of the banks, though seldom to overflowing. Red River, being the grand reservoir of all the others, is the only stream that inundates the surrounding country. This inundation is seldom caused by rain, but only by the sudden thawing of the deep snow in the spring. Severe thunderstorms seldom last more than an hour or two, when the clouds pass away, the sun shines out fiercely, and soon the prairies are as dry as before. These storms are of frequent occurrence in the summer months, but the autumn is dry and pleasant. About the tenth of September the evenings and mornings become cool and frost appears. October ushers in the winter with snow; the rivers close up about the first of November, and remain frozen over until the middle of April. The snow is deep, the months of December, January, and February very cold, the thermometer seldom rising above zero, but ranging from that point to 40° below it. During the winter north and northwest winds prevail, which always bring snow, while at that season south and west winds indicate clear weather. All travelling and hunting by the Indians and half-breeds in the winter season is done with dog-sleds, horses not being able to wade through the deep snow. The hunters travel about on snow-shoes. The snow is never permitted when it falls to lie quietly on the ground, but is soon drifted by the winds into immense banks, and every valley and ravine becomes almost impassable. Thus large areas are left bare, exposing the grass to the animals. The climate is quite healthy; fevers are almost unknown, but exposure for a long time in the cold air brings on catarrh, rheumatism, quinsy, and diseases of the lungs.

On one of the branches of Red River, and near the new settlement of Pembina, is a small lake, from which two hundred barrels of salt have been obtained by the inhabitants. Lignite occurs quite abundantly over a large portion of the Cree country, and may at some future period be employed for the purposes of fuel.

These immense plains and forests are alike silent as to their having been anciently the abode of any race differing from the present occupants. Nothing is ever seen that would indicate that this country had ever been the residence of other nations of savages, much less any works of human industry of civilized beings at a remote period. The only objects worthy of attention in this respect, are the mounds of earth raised by the interments of the dead; but these have been formed within the last century, and are known to contain the bodies of those Indians who died of the small-pox in 1776 or 1777.

Hundreds of bodies have been buried beneath them, or, rather, the mounds are composed of many separate burials, alongside, and over each other; and persons are yet living who contributed to their structure, by interring their parents or friends. During the second visitation of this disease in 1838, several smaller depositories of this kind were made by the Crees; a comparatively small number of people having died at that time. These facts may throw light upon the origin of these formations in other parts of our country. Ordinarily, Indians are not buried in heaps; because, when not visited by severe maladies, they rove in quest of game, are a healthy people, and seldom more than one or two graves are seen near any one of their transient encampments; and even where large villages have wintered, the interments do not often exceed ten or a dozen. But, when a pestilence like the small-pox prevails, attacking the whole nation at the same time, they are disabled from travel, obliged to remain stationary until the disease abates, and thus hundreds are consigned to the same burial-ground. In former years, the Indians could not excavate to a sufficient depth, for want of proper tools; and, therefore, as each individual died, he was interred near the surface, and the spot covered with a large quantity of rock and earth to protect the body from birds and beasts of prey. The disposition of all the Indians is to have their bodies deposited near those of their deceased relatives, or even on the top of them; and this would, in process of time, build up a large mound-like cemetery, which would also become covered with grass and trees. It is evident, that the extensive mounds found in different parts of this continent, have been formed in this manner, where large villages of Indians have been located for years, and selected a spot for their burial-ground. The size of these mounds is not remarkable, since they took, perhaps, a century or more to accumulate; but where a numerous population existed, and were swept off by pestilence, each interment contributing its quantity of earth and rock, a mound of large size would soon appear. As it has always been the custom, and still is, for the North American tribes to bury with their dead, if a man, his implements of war, if a woman, her domestic utensils, these depositories, if carefully opened, and the different strata of burial examined, would exhibit the different stages of advancement, providing they had made any. The only change we now know anything of, is the abandonment of their stone implements, as soon as they were able to obtain metallic ones. The Cree nation always inter their dead, in preference to placing them in the forks of trees, as is the custom with other tribes. The grave is scarcely of sufficient depth to cover the body, which, with the envelopes and implements, is of considerable bulk. A pile of earth and stone is raised, around and on the top, in the form of a cone, fifteen to twenty feet in circumference, and two to four feet in height. The arms and utensils used by this tribe in ancient times, were, pots of stone; arrow-points, spear-heads, hatchets, and other edged tools, of flint; knives of the buffalo hump rib; fish-hooks from sturgeon-bones, and awls from the bones of the moose; the fibres of the root of the pine tree, called by them wa-táh, was, and is still to some extent, used as twine for sewing together their bark canoes; a kind of thread is also made out of a weed called shá-a-sup, which they use for making nets; stone axes and mallets were made of various sizes, and used for different household purposes; spoons, called mi-kwói-yis, and pans, were made out of the horns of the moose. Of all these, there yet remain a few, but most of them have been laid aside for more convenient ones obtained from the traders. Bone fish-hooks and awls, with lines made of the aforementioned root and plant, are still in use, and preferred by the Indians to those of European manufacture. They also cling with great tenacity to the horn spoon; perhaps for the reason that it is larger, and better adapted to serve their capacious stomachs. The process of manipulation by which these things were wrought, was chiselling one stone with another, until the flint knife was made, with which other instruments were formed; a process, doubtless, long and tedious. The art is now lost, or, at least, discontinued; but we are informed that it was not confined to separate individuals, as a trade: each warrior or hunter made his own arms, or employed some old man to make them, whose time was of less value.

The amount of their knowledge on this subject is small, even less than that of the surrounding nations. They believe the earth to be an extensive territory of the same figure as their own country, intersected by rivers, mountains, lakes, and surrounded by oceans, the whole forming, as it were, a flat circle, joined around the edge to the sky, which is a solid mass of blue earth supporting the entire universe. The sun, they say, is a body of light and heat, and is the great master of life, gives life, heat, and light to all things, and is a country inhabited by departed spirits. The moon also they regard as another world, but not a hot body, deriving its light from the sun and stars, and in the sun and moon is located the Indian paradise. Stars are small lights attached as by a cord to the sky, and are not supposed to be other worlds, but ornaments and luminaries to the upper regions. The Milky Way is called the "Chief's Road," and is thought to be a line of division separating the sky into two portions. This was done by their Great Spirit Chief for purposes set forth in their traditions, which are too lengthy to be recounted here. The sun is thought to go round the earth, which remains stationary; and every effort proves abortive to make them understand that the apparent motion arises from the diurnal revolution of the earth. When the sun is in an eclipse, they say a portion of the material is burned up,—dead,—and this is what is meant by a "dead sun," but they entertain no superstitious fears of eclipses being the forerunners of great evil, as other nations, and look upon the extinction of a part as the natural result of a burning body, which, as it exists of itself, has the power to burn again. The North Star is called the stationary star; the Ursa Major, the "tail of stars." These are all that have particular names attached. They are also aware of the revolution of the Ursa Major around the Polar Star, and can tell the watches of night by this with tolerable certainty. The Aurora Borealis is called the "dance of the dead," who are supposed to be enjoying themselves in these regions. Meteors are stars falling out of their places by having the cords burned that attach them to the sky, and go out as they fall. In regard to comets they have no clear idea, neither have they any superstitious belief attending their appearance. Indeed, these Indians do not seem to fear any natural phenomena except thunder, which is supposed to be the screaming and flapping of the wings of a large bird, which they represent on their lodges as a great eagle. Wind is supposed to be produced by its flying, and flashes of lightning are caused by the light of the sun reflected from its white and golden plumage, and when strokes of lightning are felt, they are thunder-stones cast down by this bird. All storms, tornadoes, &c., are caused by its wrath, and fair winds, calm and fine weather, are regarded as tokens of its good humor.

The Crees have no word signifying a year, neither is there any stated number of days forming that period of time. Each month begins when the new moon appears, and ends when it is no more seen. During the few days the moon is invisible, it is said to be dead. They cannot even tell how many days make a moon, and all subdivisions of time are denoted by the different phases of the moon, as "moon on the increase" (first quarter), "half moon" (second quarter), "more than half round" (third quarter), "full or round moon," "decreasing moon," "small moon," "dead moon." Every moon is named after some fruit ripening, or other invariable annual occurrence, as follows, beginning with the spring some time in March, when the snow begins to disappear.

1. Is-ke-pé-sim, Duck month or moon.
2. A-ik-e-pé-sim, Frog moon.
3. Sha-ke-pá-ka-o-pe-sim, Leaf moon.
4. Mé-ne-sa-ká-tik-tuk-e, Service berries ripe.
5. Nó-tse-hi-kó-pe-sim, Buffalo-rutting moon.
6. Wa-ke-pa-kán-o-pe-sim, Leaves-changing moon.
7. Wa-sta-o-pa-ká-wo-pe-sim, Leaves entirely changed.
8. Pin-pa-kán-o-pe-sim, Leaves off the trees.
9. Na-ma-pí-ne-kais, Fish-catching moon.
10. Pa-pa-ke-sé-kin-o kis, Moon that strikes the earth cold.
11. Kis-ki-pá-pa-ke-ték-e-num, Coldest moon.
12. Ka-mák-e-tuh-pe-sim, Ice-thawing moon.
13. Me-ke-sŭ'-e-pe-sim, Eagles-seen (moon).

The other divisions of time are as follows:

Pa tak-páw, Daybreak.
Pe-e-sim-sák-o-ta-o, Sunrise.
A-pe-ták-e-se-káu-o, Midday.
Pa-kis-e-mó, Sunset.
Wa-wa-ne-ná-kwon, Twilight.
Te-pis-ká-o, Night.
A-pis-tá-te-ka-o, Midnight.
We-pá-a-sta-o, Moonlight.

Any intermediate period of time would be indicated by pointing with the finger to the place where the sun is supposed to be at the time referred to.

One, pe-ét.
Two, ni-shí.
Three, ni-sto.
Four, na-ó.
Five, ne-un-ún.
Six, gú-to-wa-shik.
Seven, ta-pa-kó.
Eight, a-ha-ná-ne-o.
Nine, ka-ká-we-ta-tat.
Ten, mí-ta-tat.
Eleven, pa-á-kwo-sap.
Twelve, né-so-sap.
Thirteen, nísh-to-sap.
Fourteen, ná-o-sap.
Fifteen, ne-á-nun-sap.
Sixteen, gu-to-wá-she-sap.
Seventeen, me-tá-ta-ta-ŭ-wá-ta-pá-ko.
Eighteen, me-ta-ta-ta-ŭ-wa-a-a-na-ne-o.
Nineteen, me-tá-ta-ta-u-wá-ka-ka-we-tá-tat.
Twenty, né-si-ta-no.
Twenty-one, ne-si-ta-nó-pe-ét-o-sap.
Thirty, ni-stó-mi-ta-nó.
Forty, na-mí-ta-no.
Fifty, ne-a-nú-na-mí-ta-no.
Sixty, gu-to-wá-se-mí-ta-no.
Seventy, ta-pa-o-ta-te-mí-ta-no.
Eighty, a-a-ná-na-tá-ta-mí-ta-no.
Ninety, ka-ká-me-ta-tá-te-mí-ta-no.
One hundred, me-tá-ta-sta-mí-ta-no.
Five hundred, ne-a-nún-me-tá-tas-ta-mi-tá-no.
One thousand, kis-éé-me-ta-tás-ta-mi-tá-no.
Ten thousand, me-tá-tat-kis-ée-me-tá-tas-ta-mi-tá-no.

It is seen by the above that the Crees, as is the case with most if not all the Northwest tribes, count entirely by tens. From one to ten, each number has a separate name, but afterwards the word "sap" is added, meaning beyond, as, pa-á-kwo-sap, one beyond ten,= eleven; né-so-sap, two beyond ten,=twelve; and so on until we reach seventeen, when the name for ten and for seven is mentioned, as me-tá-ta-ta-ñ-wá-ta-pá-ko. This continues to twenty, which becomes né-si-ta-no, and to it are prefixed the names of the first ten numerals in their order up to thirty, &c. They can count with correctness as far as a thousand, but farther than this, they have very little occasion to enumerate. Should it become necessary, they use small sticks as counters, to prevent confusion. They have no number representing a million, nor do they add, subtract, or divide, without the use of counters to aid their memory.

It is customary with the traders of the Hudson's Bay Company to facilitate hunting by crediting the Indians for small amounts, varying according to the character of the person credited. Indians that have always paid their debts promptly can get advances to the amount of thirty plues, while others of more doubtful reputation are credited with an amount sufficiently large to enable them to hunt, say five to ten plues. A plue is an imaginary amount placed on the value of skins, equal to about two shillings sterling. The proceeds of all hunts are reckoned in plues, and the prices of merchandise are fixed to conform to this standard, by which the Indians are able to calculate with certainty how much of each article they will receive for furs collected. The traders' accounts are kept in the following manner.

Dr.			*Le Chef du Tonnérre.*	*Cree.*	Cr.
1854.			1855.		
Aug.	To 6 feet blue cloth, ...	8 plues.	March.	By 10 muskrat skins, ...	2 plues.
	" 1 foot scarlet cloth, . . .	3 "		" 1 large beaver skin, . . .	4 "
	" 1 white blanket, 3 points, .	7 "		" 1 small " " . . .	2 "
	" 20 loads ammunition, . . .	1 "		" 10 otter skins, average 2 p., .	20 "
	" 3 feet N. W. twist tobacco, .	1 "		" 6 cross fox skins, " 4 " .	24 "
	" 1 N. W. gun, ...	15 "		" 2 silver " " " 5 " .	10 "
	" 1 horse, ...	30 "		" 1 buffalo robe, ...	3 "
		65 "			65 "

Now although a plue has a nominal value of about two shillings sterling, it is not to be inferred that the actual value of that amount of money is paid in merchandise, at prime cost, with expenses of transportation and a fixed per cent. added. All articles of trade are reduced to a standard price, and made proportionally higher or lower as they are necessary or indispensable to the Indians. Care is taken, however, not to rate too high such articles as guns, ammunition, horses, traps, and other things absolutely required for hunting purposes, for in that case, the Indians not being able to procure them, would fail in their hunts, and the trade thereby suffer. But such articles as tobacco, cloth of gay colors, ornaments, beads, &c., bear very high prices in comparison with their actual cost. Thus we see in the foregoing bill that a Northwest gun, the prime cost of which in England is seldom less than two pounds sterling, sells for fifteen plues, while half a pound of tobacco worth sixpence is sold for one plue.

The Indians themselves keep no accounts either pictorial or otherwise, nor can we learn that any devices are used by them in trade, except that they sometimes aid the memory by notches on a stick, or the memory is refreshed by the trader when they have the means to pay. The Crees sometimes use strokes in successive lines of ten each, until they arrive at the required amount, as

1 1 1 1 1 1 1 1 1 1 . . .	10	34
1 1 1 1 1 1 1 1 1 1 . . .	10	
1 1 1 1 1 1 1 1 1 1 . . .	10	
1 1 1 1	4	

CHAPTER III.

II. Blackfeet.

ETHNOGRAPHICAL HISTORY.

It has usually been understood that the history, traditions, and customs of Indians have been handed down from generation to generation by the principal men of each tribe with a fair degree of certainty by means of oral tales. Each tribe, it is true, has its traditions, which are very numerous, but they are for the most part fabulous; and I have never yet met with an Indian nation that could give its history with any degree of accuracy farther back than one hundred years. Even then it is so mingled with fable that it becomes quite a difficult matter to sift out the truth from so much chaff. It becomes, therefore, a matter of great ethnological interest to place on record as much of the present history of these wild, changing tribes of the prairie, as can be secured of a reliable character. From the different members of the American Fur Company, many of whom are intelligent, well-educated men, I have obtained a large mass of information in regard to the Blackfeet, which I think is reliable, and in a future publication I hope to present it in full.

The Indians usually known under the general name of Blackfeet, are the Piegans, Blood Indians, Blackfeet, and the Gros Ventres of the prairie, or, as they are sometimes called, Fall Indians. Of these, the first three speak the same language, and are sprung from the same stock, but the last belong to quite a different group, and use a dialect entirely distinct from the others. The Gros Ventres, or, as they call themselves, Atsinas, are a branch of the Arapohos, who, from some feud, so common among savages, became separated from their friends, crossed the Rocky Mountains and associated themselves with the Blackfeet. When this division took place is not now correctly known, though it seems not to have been at a very remote period, most probably within the last century. When treating of that group in a subsequent sketch, I shall present all the information that can be obtained in regard to that matter. Their former hunting grounds, as indeed those of the whole Blackfoot nation, were on the tributaries of the Saskatchewan, in which region buffalo and other game abounded. Previous to the opening of the trade with these Indians on the Upper Missouri, they sold all their skins to the Hudson's Bay Company, seldom visiting the headwaters of the Missouri, except for marauding purposes.

The Blood Indians range through the district along Maria, Teton, and Belly Rivers, inclining west and northwest far into the interior. In this section, wood is more abundant, pasturage excellent, and, consequently, buffalo almost always abound there.

The Blackfeet inhabit a portion of country farther north than the Bloods, extending to the banks of the Saskatchewan, along which they often reside.

They have never altogether abandoned their English friends, and more frequently dispose of their furs to them than to the American traders on the head branches of the Missouri.

The Piegans roam through the Rocky Mountains on the south side of Maria River, on both banks of the Missouri. They often extend their travels as far as St. Mary's Valley, where the Flatheads are stationed, with whom a precarious peace has been in existence for many years back, though often interrupted by the other bands of Blackfeet. They also hunt as far down the Missouri as the Mussel-shell River, and up that stream to the borders of the Crow country.

The three divisions last mentioned constitute the Blackfoot nation proper, whose name has become notorious for their fierce and deadly struggles with all the neighboring tribes, and in former times struck terror to all white men who travelled in any district from the Saskatchewan to the Yellowstone, and from the Yellowstone to the Columbia.

The Blackfeet are such a nomadic people that it is a difficult task to obtain a perfectly accurate statement of their numbers. The following estimate, given in one of the United States Indian agent's reports,* is probably an approximation to the true number:

Bands.	Lodges.	Men.	Women.	Children.	Total.
Blackfeet, ...	150	260	400	540	1200
Bloods, ...	300	500	800	1100	2400
Piegans, ...	460	900	1200	1600	3700
Total, ...	910	1660	2100	3240	7300

* Report of the Commissioner of Indian Affairs, 1858.

In Volume I of the Pacific Railroad Reports, by Gov. I. I. Stevens, Mr. James Doty has given an estimate of the numbers of the Blackfeet, from information obtained under the most favorable circumstances.

Bands.	Lodges.	Population.	Warriors.
The Bloods, ...	350	2450	875
The Blackfeet, ...	250	1750	625
The Piegans, ...	360	2520	900
Total, ...	960	6720	2400

These bands all live in skin tents, like the rest of the prairie tribes, follow the chase for a subsistence, and in former years were famous for their war excursions against neighboring tribes.

The country they inhabit varies in its natural features from the broad plains east of the Missouri to the highlands and undulating hills as we approach the western barrier of the Rocky Mountains. That part of it reaching towards the Saskatchewan is a level plain, many days' travel in extent, and nearly destitute of timber. There is an abundance of good grass, however, and small lakes supply water to the immense herds of buffaloes that are found there in the summer season. These animals seem to prefer the level plains in warm weather, approaching the timbered sections in the fall and winter to obtain the shelter of woods and hills during the severe cold and deep snows of that season. On this account the Indians can provide themselves with food and clothing at all times; for if the buffalo remained in the plains during the winter season, they would not be able to procure fuel, and certain death would ensue from the intense cold and terrible winds that sweep over these broad, naked prairies.

On the south side of the Missouri, up the Mussel-shell, Judith, or any of the streams which take their rise in the mountains in that direction, the face of the country is more broken, hilly, and better timbered. Travelling over this district is quite difficult, on account of the exceeding ruggedness of the surface, called by the Indians and Canadian voyageurs "Bad Lands." Very good grass is found in this portion in many places, and it is a favorite resort for game, on account of the facilities for concealment. Near the mountains there is an abundance of wood, water, and grass, for the wild animals, or for the horses of the Indian and voyageur.

The timber of the several rivers running through the Blackfoot country, is chiefly cottonwood, and on the hilly portions, several kinds of pine and cedar, with a few quaking asps and stinted elms. Along most of the ravines springs up a thick growth of bushes, such as osier (*Cornus*), rose, and bluewood, with patches of cherry, plum, and service-berry shrubs. On the eastern side of the Missouri, berries are not abundant, but along the base of the mountains, they are very plentiful. Plums and cherries are the most abundant, and are eagerly sought after by the Indians, and regarded as great delicacies. Gooseberries, wild currants, and grain de bœuf can also be found, but not in large quantities. None of the trees bear nuts that can be eaten, and in consequence, the supply of fruit cannot be considered a safe resource, should game become scarce.

The soil of this portion of the western territory is not generally more than three or four inches in depth, and in the "Bad Lands," or more rugged portions, there is comparatively little grass, and the rocks are composed mostly of clays, sands, and sandstones. The valleys and level plains are quite well clothed with the short, curly buffalo grass, and other prairie grasses. None of these grasses grow more than eighteen inches or two feet in height, but they are very nutritious. No great variety of flowers adorns these endless plains, and we look in vain for the beautiful display so often seen along the lower portion of the Missouri. The whole extent of country presents a dreary, desolate aspect, especially when parched up by the hot sun of midsummer, or covered with the deep snow of winter. There is nothing inviting to the eye of the traveller, except, perhaps, the herds of buffalo, some one of whom may furnish him a repast, after he has spent the day traversing the prairie in search of wood and water sufficient to cook his meal.

The climate near the mountains is much milder than that lower down the Missouri; the rivers close later, and open much sooner than at the mouth of the Yellowstone. Leaves put forth from two weeks to a month earlier in the spring, and sometimes the vegetation exhibits the full bloom of spring at the Blackfoot Fort, while the hills around Fort Union are covered with snow, and the trees show no sign of leaves. Snow-storms are not so violent and cold, nor of so long duration, and in the level country, the snow rarely falls more than eighteen inches in depth, but it is soon blown into the ravines, leaving the tops of the hills bare, and the valleys impassable on horseback.

The degree of cold at the Blackfoot trading post is seldom lower than 20° below zero; usually above that point, while at Fort Union, the thermometer ranges from 25° to 40° below zero for three or four weeks at a time. War parties of Assiniboins, going to the Blackfeet from the latter place, have travelled as far as Milk River on snow-shoes, over three feet of snow, and above that point, found the surface scarcely covered. Ducks and geese pass the winter at the foot of the mountains, in springs and streams which are never frozen over. On the summits of the mountains, snow often continues the year round, while that collected on their sides and in the valleys, melts away about the middle of May, which causes the annual rise of the Missouri. It is said by the Indians and voyageurs, that this rise almost invariably occurs about the time when the roses are in bloom.

In the summer of 1855, a treaty was concluded with the Blackfeet, by Commissioners on the part of the United States, having for its object the entire cessation of hostilities between them and neighboring tribes. Other stipulations were made with regard to depredations on white persons, either resident in, or travelling through their country. About $50,000 worth of goods of various kinds were sent to their country by the Government, and distributed among them, and a number of other tribes who were present at the treaty. Since that time, the Blackfeet have become more and more peaceable, and at the present time, they are considered the best disposed Indians in the Northwest. Their head chief has adopted, in part, the costume of the white man, and is setting the example to the remainder of his tribe, of settling down for a portion of the year, and cultivating the soil; and as the game becomes scarce, others will follow.

In regard to the early history of the Blackfoot nation, we know very little, except from brief allusions of various writers, and a few scanty vocabularies. They have always been considered a bloodthirsty, cruel, and treacherous race, a terror to white men as well as Indians. As far as their present condition is concerned, the contrary is the case. There is now no more peaceable, honorable, and prosperous Indian nation in the West than the Blackfeet. The impression in regard to their ferocity was doubtless derived, to a great extent, from the glowing accounts which have been given from time to time of their sanguinary conflicts with the trappers, a class of people, many of whom were scarcely less savage than themselves, and who always gave them ample cause for attacking them, when they found them the weaker party. From my own experience among them, and from information derived from intelligent men, who have spent the greater portion of their lives with them, I am convinced that at the present time, they are among the most peaceable, honorable Indians in the West, and in an intellectual and moral point of view, they take the highest rank among the wild tribes of the plains. They are also more flexible and teachable in their natures, and the head chief, a man who has attained his position by his prowess and success in war, has laid aside the Indian costume, put on that of the white man, located his family permanently on the Government farm, and commenced the cultivation of the soil, thus setting a noble example to his tribe. I have never met with Indians who appeared so susceptible to the influences of civilization as the Blackfeet, providing they are rightly applied. It is true that they have been brave and fond of war, which they have waged with relentless zeal against the Crows, and other hereditary enemies, from time immemorial. Their superior intelligence and energy have rendered them successful against an equal number of whites, and superior numbers of the neighboring tribes, until they became a terror to both. The writer has travelled much in their country, and when within the limits of the district claimed by them, he has felt safe, but when white men are found by them in their enemies' country, they are regarded as giving aid and comfort to their foes, and are liable to be treated accordingly; at least, this was the case until after the treaty with the United States Government in 1855. Since that time, they have been, for the most part, at peace with all nations.

Very little reliable information has ever yet been given to the world in relation to this tribe, and it is only within a comparatively recent period, that the true affinity of their language was known, some supposing them to speak an independent language; others a remote dialect of the Dakota stock. In the Transactions of the American Ethnological Society, Vol. II, Gallatin proved conclusively that they belonged to the great Algonkin Group. So far as I can ascertain from the books within my reach, I desire to present a brief account of the statements of travellers, who have noticed them, and to allude to the different vocabularies of their language, which have already been given to the world.

So far back as 1789, Mackenzie, in his "General History of the Fur-Trade," says: "On the head waters of the South Branch (Saskatchewan), are the Picaneux, to the number of twelve to fifteen hundred men. Next to them, on the same water, are the Blood Indians, of the same nation as the last, to the number of fifty tents, or two hundred and fifty men. From them downwards extend the Blackfeet Indians, of the same nation as the two last tribes; their number may be eight hundred men. Next to them, and who extend to the confluence of the South and North Branch, are the Fall or Big-bellied Indians, who may amount to about six hundred warriors." Again, he says, "The Picaneux, Blackfeet, and Blood Indians are a distinct people, speak a language of their own, and I have reason to think, are travelling northwest, as well as the others just mentioned, nor have I heard of any Indians with whose language that which they speak has any affinity."

Umfreville, in a well-written work, published about 1791, says (on page 200) that the three bands, Blackfeet, Piegan, and Blood Indians, all speak the same language, and have the same laws and customs. They were the most numerous and powerful nation with which he was acquainted. In this work he gives a list of forty-four words of their language, which, so far as I know, was the first ever published of their tongue. He also mentions the occurrence of the small-pox in 1781, which spread generally throughout the Indian country. It proved very destructive, not one in fifty of those attacked surviving, and it seriously injured the trading interests.

In Lewis and Clarke's Journal, quite extended and interesting accounts are given of their intercourse with this tribe, but nothing definite in regard to their former history, and no vocabulary of their language. It would appear that at the time of their visit to the West, in 1804, '5, and '6, these Indians had taken up their abode near the sources of the Missouri.

Brackenridge, in his "Voyage up the Missouri River, in 1811,"* merely alludes to the Blackfeet. "They wander on the heads of the Missouri, Maria River, and along the Rocky Mountains; they are also Sioux. They trade at the same establishments with the Assiniboins, and are at war with the Crow nation. They have been very troublesome to our traders, to whom they have conceived a deadly hatred. Their country the most abundant in beaver and other furs."

Mr. Morse, in 1822, speaks of the Blackfeet as inhabiting the headwaters of the Missouri, of whom very little is known.†

In the Transactions of the American Antiquarian Society, Vol. II, Mr. Gallatin has summed up in the most able manner, all the knowledge that had been previously obtained in regard to the Blackfoot nation, and their language. Mr. Gallatin's memoir was published in 1836, and at that time, he says: "We have as yet no other vocabulary of those two nations (Blackfeet and Gros Ventres of the prairie), and of the Assiniboins, but the scanty one of Umfreville. It is sufficient, however, to show that the Assiniboins are, as they have been uniformly stated, a branch of the Sioux family, and that the languages of the Rapid Indians and of the Blackfeet are distinct from each other, and different from any other known to us."

Again, in 1848,‡ Mr. Gallatin published a second memoir on the American Aboriginal Languages, in which he proves most conclusively the affinity of the Blackfoot language with the Algonkin stock. Out of 180 words of which the vocabulary was composed, 54 have clear affinities. The vocabulary, as well as much information in regard to the Upper Missouri tribes, was furnished to Mr. Gallatin by Mr. Kenneth Mackenzie, an intelligent Scotchman, and for many years one of the principal partners of the American Fur Company, in charge of Fort Union, at the mouth of the Yellowstone.

A vocabulary of the Blackfoot language is published in Vol. VII of the United States Exploring Expedition, Ethnography and Philology, by Horatio Hale, Philadelphia, 1846. From what source Mr. Hale obtained this vocabulary, I could not ascertain.

In a work by George Catlin, "Letters and Notes on the Manners, Customs, and Condition of the North American Indians," London, 1841, 2 vols. 8vo., may be found a very good vocabulary of the language under consideration, and it is remarkable as being the second one ever published of these Indians. Mr. Catlin did not visit the Blackfoot country, however, inasmuch as he did not ascend the Missouri higher than the mouth of the Yellowstone. The Blackfeet not unfrequently visited this post in former times for trading or marauding purposes.

* Journal of a Voyage up the Missouri River, in 1811, by H. M. Brackenridge, Esq. Pittsburg, 1814.

† Report to the Secretary of War on Indian Affairs, by Rev. J. Morse, D.D. New Haven, 1822.

‡ Transactions of the American Ethnological Society, Vol. II. New York, 1848.

But the most reliable information in regard to the Indians of the Upper Missouri is given in that magnificent work of Maximilian, Prince of Wied.* He visited that country in the years 1832, '3, and '4, and spent considerable time among the Blackfeet, under circumstances which were favorable for obtaining an accurate knowledge of them. He also procured a brief but very correct vocabulary.

There is also a vocabulary of the Blackfoot language in the "Proceedings of the Philological Society of London," Vol. IV, 1850, but I was unable to gain access to it.

A good traders' vocabulary was made by J. B. Moncrovic, who was for a long time a trader among the Blackfeet Indians on the Upper Missouri. This is published in Schoolcraft's "Indian Tribes of the United States," Vol. II, pp. 494–505.

A few words, about twenty-three in number, and the Lord's Prayer translated into the Blackfoot language, is given in the latter part of a work entitled, "Oregon Missions, and Travels over the Rocky Mountains, in 1845 and '46, by Father P. J. De Smet, of the Society of Jesus."

The above comprises, as far as I can ascertain, the entire literature of the Blackfoot language, and it will be seen that it consists only of rather brief vocabularies. Nothing of the grammatical structure has ever been secured, and thus my brief sketch may be considered as the first attempt toward a grammar of this language.

An interesting sketch of the Blackfoot nation may be found in Part V of Schoolcraft's great work. The materials were supplied by the late Col. D. D. Mitchell, of St. Louis, Missouri, who spent many years among these Indians, as one of the partners of the American Fur Company. It may be well in this place to discuss the origin and meaning of the names of the different bands of the Blackfeet. Col. Mitchell relates the origin of the term Blackfoot in the following manner. These Indians originally inhabited the region of country drained by the Saskatchewan and its tributaries, and only visited the valley of the Missouri on hunting excursions or marauding expeditions. They became distributed over a wider range of country on account of the claims of two ambitious chiefs, each one of whom desired the sole command of the nation. Thus a separation took place, and the followers of one chief retired southward to the headwaters of the Missouri, where game is plenty and all the luxuries of a savage life are abundant. The remainder continued in the valley of the Saskatchewan, where they roam at the present day, trading, for the most part, with the Hudson's Bay Company. Prior to the separation, however, bloody battles ensued, in one of which the parties fought "three days and three nights. The sun and moon was made red by smoke of the hot blood which flowed through the ravines, and the rocks along the banks of Belly River remain red to this day." The black chief was at length defeated,

* Reise des Prinzen Maximilian zu Wied, Coblentz, 1839–1841. 2 vols. 4to. Vol. II, pp. 589 *et seq.*; Vol. II, pp. 480–486. There is also an English translation of the narrative in 1 vol. 4to. London, 1843.

and he and his followers retired to the Missouri, where they arrived in the fall, when the prairies are burnt by the autumnal fires. In their travels their moccasins and leggins became blackened by the burnt grass, and in this condition they were first seen by the Crows and other neighboring tribes, who at once gave them the name they now bear. This account undoubtedly forms a part of their mythology, but how much of truth there is in it, it is impossible to determine. So far back as 1789, before any of the nation roamed so far southward as the sources of the Missouri, we know that the same three divisions, bearing the same names as at the present time, constituted the Blackfoot nation. The name is derived from sik-si-nim', black, and probably at-si-kin', a shoe or moccasin, which could be easily abbreviated into sik-si-ka', the name not only for a band or division, but also for the whole tribe.

The name of the second band has been spelled in a variety of ways, as, Kahna, Kaenna, &c.; but as given to me by the best interpreter in the country, and approved by the chief, it is Kai'-e-na, people who counted a plenty of "coups," that is, people who took in war a great many scalps and arms; and this appears to me to be the true interpretation. The meaning given by the Prince of Neuwied is essentially the same. "Before the Blackfeet divided into separate bands, they were encamped in the neighborhood of five or six tents of the Kútonas or the Sarcees, I believe the former. The Siksikai and the Kahna desired to kill the Kútonas; and though the Pickanns declared against it, a part of those Indians attacked the few huts during the night, killed all the inmates, took the scalps, stained their faces and hands with the blood, and then returned. Disputes ensued in consequence of this cruel action; the Indians separated from each other, and the murderers received the name which they have ever since retained. They have always manifested a more sanguinary and predatory character than the others, of whom the Pickanns have always been remarked as the most moderate and humane of this nation."

The name of the third band has also been spelled in a variety of ways, as, Picaneux, Pickan, Pickanns, Piegan, &c. From the best authority, the interpreter before-mentioned gave the name to me as, Pi-kun'-i, people with badly dressed robes.

In the following grammatical sketch and vocabulary, I have presented only an abstract of the materials in my possession, and have made the whole as brief as possible. Farther researches will render much of the information not included in these papers more complete and reliable, and on that account it is omitted.

CHAPTER IV.

REMARKS UPON THE GRAMMATICAL STRUCTURE OF THE BLACKFOOT LANGUAGE.

I. Parts of Speech.

1. The parts of speech are the noun, adjective, adverb, preposition, conjunction, interjection, pronoun, and verb. Of all these, the verb is the most complex, and the most important.

II. Nouns.

2. No change is made in the termination of a noun to indicate its case: this is known by its position in the sentence. In nouns indicating possession, the name of the possessor usually comes first; as, mus-ŏp-ski′-o-yis′, a muskrat's lodge.

3. Nouns have two numbers, singular and plural, which are shown by difference of termination. In the Blackfoot language all nouns, with few exceptions, have variable but distinct terminations, indicating the plural number, and a portion possess two plural endings; as, pō′-ksa-ćis, a hammer; plural, po′-ksa-ćiks; second form, po′-ksa-ći-sa′-wa, the word a-ku′-a-wa, meaning "a good many," being incorporated into the noun. Examples:

	Singular.	Plural. 1st form.	Plural. 2d form.
Spring,	mu-tu′,	mu-tu′-isć,*	mu-tu′-a-wa.
Summer,	ni-pu′,	ni-pu′-isć,	ni-pu′-a-wa.
Autumn,	mu-ku′,	mu-ku′-isć,	mu-ku′-a-wa.
Winter,	stu′-yi,	stu′-yisć.	
Star,	ko-ka′-tos,	ko-ka-to′-siks.	
Antelope,	a-wa′-kos,	a-wa-ko′-siks.	
Tongue,	ma-tsi-ne′,	ma-tsi-ne′-īks,	ma-tsi-ne′-a-wa.

4. So far as I have yet observed, gender is distinguished by the use of different names; as, stum′-ik, a buffalo bull; ski-ni′, a cow; pu-no-ka′-mi-ta, a horse; ski′-am, a mare.

III. Adjectives.

5. Adjectives usually follow the nouns which they describe; as, mis′-tis-ŏh′-o-tŏk, petrified wood. But to this rule there are an unusual number of exceptions in the Blackfoot language; as, pi-wah′-o, bad lands, from pi′-wa, rough, rugged, and ah′-o, land; ba-kap′-sa-ko-ma′-pi, a lazy boy.

6. Adjectives have the same numbers as nouns (see Remark 3); as,

* Last syllable pronounced as istch.

	Singular.	Plural. 1st form.	Plural. 2d form.
Good,	ah'-si-o,	ah'-si-iks,	ah'-si-a-wa.
Lazy,	ba-kaps',	ba-kap'-sïks,	ba-kap'-si-a-wa.
Bad,	ma-kaps',	ma-kap'-siks,	ma-kap'-si-a-wa.
Dreadful,	ko-ma'-pi,	ko-ma'-pisé.	
Ugly,	muh-si-num',		muh-si-num'-i-a-wa.
Hot,	kris-tu'-yi,	kris-tu'-yisé.	

7. Degrees of comparison in adjectives are not shown by inflection, but their signification is increased or diminished by means of adverbs; as, ki-nai'-ah'-si-o, all good; i-tai-mah'-si-o, there are none so good; mis-ti-pöks'-ah'-si-o, beyond good, the best of all.

8. Adjectives are sometimes formed from nouns by the addition of a syllable; as, öh'-o-tök, a stone, öh-o-tök'-sku, stony; mis-tek', a rock, mis-tek'-sku, rocky. A more thorough knowledge of the language would doubtless multiply these examples.

9. The cardinal numbers are as follows:

One, nis'-i.
Two, na-tök'.
Three, nöh.
Four, ni-su'-i.
Five, ni'-si-to.
Six, na'-au.
Seven, ih'-it-sih.
Eight, na-nis'-o.
Nine, pih-su'-a.
Ten, ki-pu'-a.
Eleven, nit'-si-ko-put'-o.
Twelve, nat'-si-ko-put'-o.
Thirteen, ni'-ko-put'-o.
Fourteen, ni'-si-ko-put'-o.
Fifteen, ni-sit-si'-ko-put'-o.
Sixteen, na-a'-ko-put'-o.
Seventeen, ih-it'-si-ko-put'-o.
Eighteen, na-ni'-si-ko-put'-o.
Nineteen, pih'-si-ko'-put'-o.
Twenty, na-tsi'-po.
Twenty-one, na-tsi'-po-nit'-si-ko'-put'-o.
Thirty, ni-hip'-o.
Forty, ni-sip'-o.
Fifty, nis-it'-sip-o.
Sixty, na'-ip-o.
Seventy, kit-si'-kip-o.
Eighty, na-na'-sip-o.
Ninety, pih'-sip-o.
One hundred, ki-pip'-o.

IV. Adverbs.

10. Adverbs precede the verbs which they qualify, as, ma-töh'-si-po-ksi-po'-at, he came afterwards. The following is a list of the principal adverbs known:

e-sum'-o, a good while.
a-sto-ko'-ki, near by.
na-to'-tsi, so, likewise, in like manner.
ma-töh'-si, afterwards.
ma-to-ko'-tsi, never.
mats-ta'-nis-tsit, again, once more.
a-me'-töhs, above.
seh'-ta, it may be, perhaps.
ai-sum'-o, long ago.
ah-o-tsi'-ma, in exchange.
skna'-to-nis, early, soon in the morning.
a-pin'-o-kös, to-morrow.

pi-ih'-tsi, far off, at a distance.
nōh, now.
kin'-i, enough.
nun'-u-wa, at last.
nun'-u-wa-po-ksi-po'-at, he came at last.
ai-pis-tskai'-kum-o, a little while ago, lately.
mi-im', over yonder.
kin-i'-nai, there.
u'-no-mai, here.
e-ka'-pa-nis-tsi, after.
spoh'-tsi, above.
a-kai'-im, much, plenty.
sa-nis'-tsi, when, at what time?
tsi-ma', where, in what place?
ta'-ni-sto-tu'-yi, how? how have you done it?
to-tōh'-tsi, on this side.
a-pum'-ōts, on the other side.
pi-na-pōh'-tsi, down, as down the river.
sa-ōh'-tsi, out of doors.
na-kōh'-tsi, a little.
pa-ki-tsi'-ku-im, with great difficulty.
ka-tets', none.
ka-nis'-i, smoothly.
ma-ta'-kai-im, not enough.
is-ći'-ka, more.
ma-tu'-ni, yesterday.
ah sah'-ta, why?

V. Prepositions.

11. As a general rule, prepositions follow the nouns which they govern, as:

sa-toh'-si, beyond.
pau-ah'-u-i-sa-toh'-si, beyond the ridge.
u-ni'-mai, at.
mu-yis'-u-ni'-mai, at the house or lodge.
pi-sto'-tsi, in.
mu-yis'-pi-sto'-tsi, in the house.
se-to'-ko, through, between.
kai-e'-ksi-se-to'-ko, through a gap or pass.
se-to-ko'-ksin, between or among.
a-pa-toh'-si, behind.
sai-a'-ni-sōts, down.
it-si'-o, in.
sa-ko'-mi-it-si'-o, in the ground.

VI. Conjunctions.

12. Conjunctions are few in number, as:

i-yo'-pi, if.

VII. Interjections.

13.

e-ku'-ta-nis-ći'-wats! is it possible!
at-sto mat'-sa! oh dear!
a-e'! oh! yes! is it so!
at-sto'-ma-ki-ni'-sa! pity! poor fellow!

VIII. Pronouns.

14. The pronouns are of two kinds, the simple and the fragment pronoun. The simple pronouns are complete in themselves, but the fragment pronouns are either prefixed or inserted into verbs, adjectives, and nouns. The simple pronouns are as follows:

ni-stu'-a, I.
ki-stu'-a, you or thou.
u-stu'-i, he or him.
ni-stu'-nan, us or we.
ki-stu'-wa-wa, you.
u-stu'-wa-wa, they or them.

nit-si-nan', mine.	nit-si-na'-nan, ours.
kit-si-nan', thine.	kit-si-na'-nan, yours.
u-tsi-nan', his.	u-tsi-nan'-wa'-wa, theirs.
nin-i-ći'-tup-i, I myself alone.	nin-i-ći'-tup-i-nu'-ni, we ourselves alone.
kin-i-ći'-tup-i, you yourself alone, or thyself.	kin-i-ći'-tup-i-nu'-ni, you yourselves alone.
u-ni-ći'-tup-i, he himself alone.	u-ni-ći'-tup-i-wa'-wa, they themselves alone.

15. The fragment pronouns are connected with nouns, adjectives, adjective verbs, and verbs. Those prefixed to nouns denote possession; as,

no-tōs', my horse.	no-to'-sīks, my horses.
ko-tōs', thy horse.	ko-to'-sīks, thy horses.
o-tōs', his horse.	o-to'-sīks, his horses.
nōh'-u-a, my son.	nōh'-u-īks, my sons.
kōh'-u-a, thy son.	kōh'-u-īks, thy sons.
ōh'-u-a, his son.	ōh'-u-īks, his sons.
nōh-u-i'-ksi-nan, our sons.	no-kōs', my child.
kōh-u-i'-ksi-nan, your sons.	ko-kōs', thy child.
ōh-u-i'-ksi-nan, their sons.	o-kōs', his child.
ni-tun'-a, my daughter.	no-ko'-sīks, my children.
ki-tun'-a, thy daughter.	kit-o-ki'-man, thy wife.
i-tun'-a, his daughter.	u-no'-i, his father.
no-ko'-si-nan-sa'-ko-ma'-pīks, our children, boys.	no-ko'-sīks'-ni-tun'-īks, our children, girls.

16. These fragment pronouns are also incorporated into adjective verbs and adjectives; as,

ni-ta'-ats, I am well.	ni-ti'-o-to'-kōs, I am sick.
ki-ta'-ats, thou art well.	ki-ti'-o-to'-kōs, thou art sick.
a-a'-tsu, he is well.	i'-o-to'-kōs, he is sick.
	ni-ti'-o-to-ko'-spin, we are sick.
i-a-tsōp', i-a-tsi-a'-wa, } they are well.	ki-ti'-o-to-ko'-spin, you are sick.
	i'-o-to-ko'-ksi-a, they are sick.
ni-tut'-si, I am brave.	nit-o-kaps', I am bad.
ki-tut'-si, thou art brave.	kit-o-kaps', thou art bad.
ma'-tsi, he is brave.	nit-o-ka'-spin, we are bad.

17. The following is a list of the principal adjective pronouns:

Singular.	Plural.
a-mo', this.	a-mōks', these.
o'-ma, that.	o'-maks, those.
ta-ka', who.	ta-ki'-ksan.
ah'-sats, what.	ah-sa'-i-ksan.
sa-kah'-ta, what person?	

SINGULAR.	PLURAL.
kris-ta'-pi, something.	kris-ta'-pi-au-a.
mah-tsi'-tsi, nothing.	
it-sin'-a-ka, all.	
sta-nis'-čis, when, at what time?	
tsa-ni-ta'-pi, how, in what way?	
tsim'-a, where, at what place?	

IX. VERBS.

18. To the verbs belong mood, tense, number, and person. The indicative, imperative, and infinitive moods are well marked, and also the present, past, and future tenses. The verbs are conjugated as follows:

a-ko-mim', to love, loving.

nit-a-wa'-ko-mim, I love, or am loving.
kit-a-wa'-ko-mim, thou lovest, or art loving.
a-wa'-ko-mim, he loves, or is loving.
nit-a-wa'-ko-mi'-mi-nan, we love, or are loving.
kit-a-wa'-ko-mi'-ma, you love, or are loving.
a-wa'-ko-mi'-mi-o, they love, or are loving.

ni-ti'-a-ka'-ko-mim, I will love.
ki-ti'-a-ka'ko-mim, thou wilt love.
i'-a-ka'-ko-mim, he will love.
ni-ti'-a-ka'-ko-mi'-ma-nan, we will love.
ki-ti'-a-ka'-ko-mi-mo-wa'-wa, you will love.
i'-a-ka'-ko-mi'-mi-o, they will love.

ni-kai'-a-kris'-ta-ko-mim, I have loved.
ki-kai'-a-kris'-ta-ko-mim, thou hast loved.
i-kai'-a-kris'-ta-ko-mim, he has loved.
ni-kai'-a-kris'-ta-ko-mi'-ma-nan, we have loved.
ki-kai'-a-kris'-ta-ko-mi'-ma-wa, you have loved.
i-kai'-a-kris'-ta-ko-mi'-mi-a, they have loved.

a-ko'-mi-mis (imp. sing.), love.
ka-na'-wa-ko'-mi-mis (pl.)

nit-a-ko'-mi-mo'-tsi, I love myself.
kit-a-ko'-mi-mo'-tsi, you love yourself.
a-wa-ko'-mi-mo'-tsi, he loves himself.
nit-a-ko'-mi-mo-tsih'-pi-nan, we love ourselves.
kit-a-ko'-mi-mo-tsih'-pu-wa'-wa, you love yourselves.
a-wa-ko'mi-mo'-tsiks, they love themselves.

o'-yi, eating, to eat.

ni-to'-yi, I am eating.
ki-to'-yi, thou art eating.
o'-yi, he is eating.
nit-o-yih'-pi-nan, we are eating.
kit-o-pih'-pi-nan, you are eating.
o-i'-yiks, they are eating.
n'se-mi'-sto-yih'-pi-nan, we both are eating.
se-mi'-sto, both or two.

ni-ta'-kso-yi, I am going to eat.
ki-ta'-kso-yi, thou art going to eat.
i-a'-kso-yi, he is going to eat.
ni-ta'-kso-pih'-pi-nan, we are going to eat.
ki-ta'-kso-yih'-pu-a, you are going to eat.
i-a'-kso-yiks, they are going to eat.

ni-ta'-kse-mi-sto-yih'-pi-nan, we two are going to eat.
ki-ta'-kse-mi-sto-yih'-pu-a, you two are going to eat.
i-a'-kse-mi-sto-yi'-waks, they two are going to eat.

nit-e-kris'-o-yi, I have done eating.
kit-e-kris'-o-yi, thou hast done eating.
it-e-kris'-o-yi, he has done eating.
nit-e-kris'-o-yih'-pi-nan, we have done eating.
kit-e-kris'-o-yih'-pu-wa'-wa, you have done eating.
it-e-kris'-o-yi'-waks, they have done eating.
nit-e-kris'-e-mi-sto-yikh'-pi-nan, we both have done eating.

ni-ta'-wa-to'-to-pi-a, if I eat.
ki-ta'-wa-to'-to-pi-a, if thou eatest.
o-yīh'-to-pi-a, if he eats.
a-yo-pi-nit-so-yīkh-pi-nan, if we eat.

a-yo'-pi-kit-so-pīkh'-pu-wa-wa, if you eat.
a-yo'-pi-at-so'-pi-waks, if they eat.

na'-ksi-kum'-o-yi, perhaps I will eat.
ka'-ksi-kum'-o-yi, perhaps thou wilt eat.
a'-ksi-kum'-o-yi, perhaps he will eat.
na'-ksi-kum'-o-yīh'-pi-nan, perhaps we will eat.
ka'-ksi-kum'-o-yīh'-pu-wa'-wa, perhaps you will eat.
a'-ksi-kum'-o-yi'-waks, perhaps they will eat.

o'-yīt (imp. sing.), eat.
ka'-kso-yīh'-pu-wa (imp. pl.), eat.
a'-ni-i-so'-yīks, let them eat.

a'sim-i, to drink.

ni-tai'-sim-i, I drink, or am drinking.
ki-tai'-sim-i, thou drinkest, or art drinking.
a-tai'sim-i, he drinks, or is drinking.
ni-tai'-sim-īh'-pi-nan, we drink, or are drinking.
kit-ai'-sim-īh'-pi-nan, you drink, or are drinking.
a-tai'-sim-īh'-pi-nan, they drink, or are drinking.

ni-tai'-ak-sim'-i, I will drink.
ki-tai'-ak-sim'-i, thou wilt drink.
a-tai'-ak-sim'-i, he will drink.
ni-tai'-ak-sim-īh'-pi-nan, we will drink.
ki-tai'-ak-sim-īh'-pi-nan, you will drink.
a-tai'-ak-sim-īh'-pi-nan, they will drink.

ni-tai'-kris-im'-i, I have drunk.
ki-tai'-kris-im'-i, thou hast drunk.
a-tai'-kris-im'-i, he has drunk.
ni'-tai-kris-im-īh'-pi-nan, we have drunk.
ki-tai'-kris-im-īh'-pi-nan, you have drunk.
a-tai'-kris-im-īh'-pi-nan, they have drunk.

sim-it' (sing. imp.) drink.
ak-sim'-i-ŏp (pl. imp.) drink all of you.

a-i-mi, to laugh.

ni-tai'-im, I laugh.
ki-tai'-im, thou laughest.
ai-im'-i-o, he laughs.
ni-tai'-im-pīh'-pin, we laugh.
ki-tai'-im-pīh'-po, you laugh.
ai-im'-i-a, they laugh.

ni-tai'-a-kim, I will laugh.
ki-tai'-a-kim, thou wilt laugh.
ai-a-ksim-i-o, he will laugh.
ni-tai'-a-ksim-pīh'-pin, we will laugh.
ki-tai'-a-ksim-pīh'-po, you will laugh.
ai-a-ksim-i-a, they will laugh.

ni-tai'-kris-tsim, I have laughed.
ki-tai'-kris-tsim, thou hast laughed.
ai'-kris-tsim'-i-o, he has laughed.
ni-tai'-kris-tsim'-pīh-pin, we have laughed.
ki-tai'-kris-tsim'-pīh-po, you have laughed.
ai'-kris-tsim'-i-a, they have laughed.

ai-im'-it (imp.) laugh.

nit-i-a'-sto, I come, or am coming.
kit-i-a'-sto, thou comest, or art coming.
i-a'-sto, he comes, or is coming.
nit-i-a-stŏkh'-pi-nan, they come, or are coming.
kit-i-a-stŏkh'-pi-nan, you come, or are coming.
i-a-sto'-yīks, they come, or are coming.

nit-i-pi-o'-ksa-po, I am coming here.
kit-i-pi-o'-ksa-po, thou art coming here.
i-pi-o'-ksa-po, he is coming here.
nit-i-pi-o'-ksa-pŏh'-pi-nan, we are coming here.
kit-i-pi-o'-ksa-pŏh'-pi-nan, you are coming here.
i-pi-o'-ksa-po'-īks, they are coming here.

ni-ti'-a-ko'-to-me-po'-ksa-po, I will come here.
ki-ti'-a-ko'-to-me-po'-ksa-po, thou wilt come here.
i'-a-ko'-to-me-po'-ksa-po, he will come here.
ni-ti'-a-ko'-to-me-po'-ksa-pŏh'-pi-nan, we will come here.

ki-ti'-a-ko'-to-me-po'-ksa-po-pu'-wa-wa, you will come here.

a-ti'-a-ko'-to-me-po'-ksa-po'-īks, they will come here.

ni-kai'-a-po'-ksa-po, I have come here.

ki-kai'-a-po'-ksa-po, thou hast come here.

a-kai'-a-po'-ksa-po, he has come here.

ni-kai'-a-po'-ksa-pōh'-pi-nan, we have come here.

ki-kai'-a-po'-ksa-pōh'-pu-wa'-wa, you have come here.

a-kai'-a-po'-ksa-po'-īks, they have come here.

po-ksa-po'-at (imp. sing.), come here.

po-ksa-pōk' (imp. plu.), come here.

ni-ko'-ta-me-po'-ksa-po, have I come here.

ki-ko'-ta-me-po'-ksa-po, hast thou come here.

ko'-ta-me-po'-ksa-po, has he come here.

ni-ko'-ta-me-po'-ksa-pōh'-pi-nan, have we come.

ki-ko'-ta-me-po'-ksa-pōh'-pu-wa'-wa, have you come.

ko'-ta-me-po'-ksa-po'-īks, have they come here.

seh'-ta-i-a'-kso-po'-ksa-po, perhaps he will come.

kit-a'-ni-sta, I told you.

kit-a'-ni-ku'-a, he told you.

ni-ta'-nik, he told me.

ta-ni-ki'-nan, he told us.

ma-to'-ki-nan (imp.), take us.

mis-ta-pīkst' (imp.), throw away.

e-a'-kse-ni, he is going to die.

e-a'-kse-ka-mi'-ta, I think he will live.

sput'-se-ko-i-ta'-po, he has gone to the sandhills,—a common expression, meaning, he is dead.

sput'-se-ko-i-ta'-pi-ki'-mi-taps, he, poor man, has gone under, is dead.

ke-ai'-yo-nit-si-nu'-a, I saw a bear.

ke-ai'-yo-kit-si-nu'-a, you saw a bear.

ke-ai'-yo-u-tsi-nu'-a, he saw a bear.

ke-ai'-yo-nit-si-nu'-a-nan, we saw a bear.

po-ksi-pip'-i-no'-tōs, bring my horse.

pōk-sup'-sko-no'-tōs, drive my horse here.

pōk-sup'-sko-o-mo'-ksim-po-no-ka'-mi-toks, drive those horses here.

si-mi'-a-pi-so-mo'-ksim-po-no-ka'-mi-tōks, water those horses.

sa-pīk'-si-mait, light the pipe.

kah-o'-ćis, come and smoke.

kit-o'-ta-tsi-wa'-ni-nte-a-ka'-ksi-te-ke, when I meet you, I shall be happy.

e-a'-kso-tau, it is going to rain.

ni-tes'-tau-e-a'-kso-tau, I think it is going to rain.

ma-ti-a'-kso-tau, it is not going to rain.

ni-ma'-tis-tah-pa-a'-kso-tau, I do not wish it to rain.

is-tah'-si-a'-kso-tau, I would like to see it rain.

so'-tau, it is raining.

ah-po'-tau, it snows.

e-a-kah'-po-tau, it is going to snow.

ma-ti'-a-kah'-po-tau, it is not going to snow.

ma-tah-po-tau, it is not snowing.

ah-sats'-kit-a'-pa-sum'-i, for what are you searching?

i-mi'-wa-ne-he-tah'-tai, the river is high.

ma-tsi'-wa-ne-he-tah'-tai, the river is not high.

ni-pe'-po-tat-a-pin'-a-ku, it is daylight, I will make a fire.

po-ći'-ći-mi-ni, stir up the fire.

to-kōh'-i-tsa-tso-pats', give me some powder.

ni-pis-ći'-o-koh'-it, give me a blanket.

tsi-mak-tu'-i-ta-po, where has he gone?

a-mi-to'-ksai-ta'-po, gone up the river.

ki-a'-pi-te-ksi-na-pu'-is, there are a few houses there.

nit-ai'-is-ći'-nit, I cut it off.

kit-ai'-is-ći'-nit, you cut it off.

et-ai'-is-ći'-nit, he cuts it off.

nit-ai'-is-ći-nih'-pi-nan, we cut it off.

kit-ai-is-ći-nih'-pi-nan, you cut it off.

et-ai-ći-nih'-pi-nan, they cut it off.

as-ći'-nit, to cut off.

nit-au'-a-sen, I cry.

kit-au'-a-sen, you cry.

nit-eh'-pi, I dance.

kit-eh'-pi, you dance.

i-a'-ksa-kris'-ta-ku, it is approaching daylight.

a-ni-stis'-ko-ksa-po'-a, tell him to get up.

NAMES OF BANDS OF THE BLACKFOOT NATION, AND PRINCIPAL CHIEFS.

pi-kun'-i,* Piegans.
kai'-e-na, Blood Indians.
sik-si-ka', Blackfeet.

1. a-pi-kai'-yiks, The Polecat Band.
2. ko-te'-yi-miks, The Band that do not laugh.
3. si-kōh'-i-tsim, The Band with black doors.
4. a-mīks'-eks, Little Robes.
5. e-pōh'-si-mīks, The Band that fries fat.
6. sus-kso'-yiks, The Band with hairy mouths.
7. mo-ta'-tōts, The Band that are all medicine men.
8. is-ksi'-na-tup-i, The Worm people.
9. kai'-it-ko-ki'-ki-naks, White-breasted Band.
10. a'-pe-tup-i, The Blood people.
11. e-ka-to'-pi-staks, The Band that have finished packing, as bales of anything.
12. si-ka'-tsi-po-maks, The Band with black patched moccasins.
13. ne-ta'-ka-ski-tsi-pup'-iks, People that have their own way, that listen to no one.

1. ko-te-tsi'-tsi-man, The man who cannot overtake the buffalo.
2. i-tut'-tsi-ki'-o-pi, The man who sits in the middle.
3. im-i-te'-sko-mah-an, The dog that goes back.
4. ni-nai'-po-a-ksin, The man who rises in the morning.
5. ni-na-kai'-i-yo, Bear chief.
6. kit-si-po'-ni-sta, This name indicates any animal that has an unnatural color, and lives on the side of a hill or mountain, as a white buffalo, white skunk, &c.
7. i-muh'-se-ko-kau, Large painted lodge.
8. sta-tsi-stum'-ik, Underneath the bull.
9. pu-no-ka'-it-si-ni'-na, Elk tongue.
10. ni-na-sta'-ko-i, Mountain chief.
11. stum'-i-ko-tu'-kan, Bull's head.
12. im-e-te'-ko-en, Little Dog.
13. o-ni-ste'-po-ka-o, Young white calf.

NAMES OF SOME OF THE BANDS OF THE KAI'-E-NA.

i-ni'-po-i, Buffalo rising up,—meaning rather obscure.
sik-si-no'-kai-iks, Black Elks.
ni-tet'-ska-iks, They that fight by themselves.
mum-i'-o-yiks, Fish-eaters.

NAMES OF PERSONS AND NEIGHBORING TRIBES.

kut-e-se'-pi-a, They did not rush, as upon an enemy.
e-sta-po'-a-wah'-au, Walking off.
ma-kris'-kum, Spring of water.
ah'-se-i-ni'-ki-o, She that did not kill.
pah-tōk'-sai-ki-o, The woman of the pine.
ai-ki'-o-pi, The sitting squaw, a Gros Ventres chief.
ku'-ti-na-a'-pi, Old Kootenay, a Blackfoot chief.
ni-te'-na, The only chief.
he-ka'-ske-ne, Low horn.
ni-na'-i-sta'-ko, Mountain chief.
pu-no-ka'-ni-na, Elk chief.
o-ni-sta'-a-kōp, The sitting calf.

o-ni-sta'-sa-nu'-ku-en, The calf out of sight.
stum-i-ko'-sak, Bull's back fat.
na-to'-so-o-ni-sta', The medicine calf.
sa-ku'-i-stum'-ik, Hindmost bull.
noh'-ska-stum'-ik, The three bulls.

i-sa-po'-a, The Crow Indians.
ko-tōh'-spi-tup'-i-o, The Flathead Indians.
ko-mun'-i-tup'-i-o, Green Paint Indians, Nez Percés.
ni-he-ta-te-tup'-i-o, Pend Oreilles.
pi-ći'-kse-ni-tup'-i-o, Snake Indians.
mum-i'-tup-i-o, Fish Indians.

NAMES OF MAMMALS.

stum'-ik, a buffalo bull. *Bos Americanus.*
ski-ni', a cow.
o-ni-stah's', a calf.
pu'-no-ka-o, a general term for elk. *Cervus Canadensis.*
pu'-no-ka-stum'-ik, a male elk.

* See page 256.

pu′-no-ka-pu′-ka, a young elk.

i-si′-ko-ti, black-tailed deer. *Cervus macrotis.*

o-muk-i′-ki-na, big-horn. *Ovis montana.*

a-wa′-to-yi, white-tailed deer. *Cervus leucurus.*

so-ki′-a-wa′-kos, antelope. *Antilocapra Americana.* (so-ki′, a prairie, and a-wa′-kos, deer.)

a-pu′-muk-i-na, a white big-horn. *Aplocerus montanus.*

kai′-yo, a grizzly bear. *Ursus horribilis.*

kai-yi-pu′-ka, a young bear.

si′-ko-kai′-yo, a black bear. *Ursus Americanus.*

sik-so-so′, a moose. *Alce Americanus.*

kris-tuk′-i, a beaver. *Castor Canadensis.*

kris-tuk′-i-pu′-ka, a young beaver.

i-si′-tsi, a wolverine. *Gulo luscus.*

mi-sin′-sku, a badger. *Taxidea Americana.*

a-pi′-sin, large wolf. *Canis occidentalis.*

sna′-o, medicine wolf. *Canis latrans.*

o-ta′-to-yi, red fox. *Vulpes macrourus.*

si-no-pa′, small kit fox. *Vulpes velox.*

pi-no-tu′-yi, a fisher. *Mustela Pennanti.*

au′-mo-nis, an otter. *Lutra Canadensis.*

so′-yi-kai′-yi, a mink. *Putorius nigrescens.*

mus-öp′-ski, a muskrat. *Fiber zibethicus.*

u-muk′-u-ka-ta, a large prairie dog. *Cynomys ludovicianus.*

kit-si′-su-mu-ku′-ka-ta, a small prairie dog. *Cynomys Gunnisonii.*

kai′-ska, a porcupine. *Erethizon epixanthus.*

a-pi′-a-kai-yi, striped back, a skunk. *Mephitis mephitica.*

a′-pa, a weasel in winter pilage.

o-mu′-ka-pa, a large weasel.

o′-ta, summer weasel.

si-ka-ći′-sta, sage rabbit. *Lepus artemisia.*

o-muk′-a-ći′-sta, jackass rabbit. *Lepus campestris.*

i′-kais, a pine squirrel. *Sciurus Hudsonius.*

i-a-tsi′-ki, thirteen-lined squirrel. *Spermophilus tridecem-lineatus.*

ka′-na-skin, a wood mouse.

o-muh′-a-ka′-na-skin, a wood rat. *Neotoma cinerea.*

so-yi′-ka′-na-skin, a water mouse.

NAMES OF BIRDS.

pi-ta′-o, the war eagle.

si-kit-si-nai′-aks, a black eagle.

i-si-sun′-i-kim, the bald eagle.

si-kai′, a buzzard.

a-pe-ta-pun′-i-ki-mi, a fish hawk.

si-ke-ta-pun′-i-ki-mi, a brown fish hawk.

si-kup′-e-ta-pun′-i-ki-mi, a gray hawk.

kse′-ni, a cow bunting.

o-muk-sa′-kse-ni, a crow blackbird.

a-pi-a-ksa′-kse-ni, a brown blackbird.

so-yi′-ksi-ni, a water blackbird.

mi-e-kut′-si, a kind of duck.

mi-e′-sa, a fish duck.

ap-spi′-ni, the common wild goose.

kai′-yi, a kind of gull.

o-muk-sa′-kai-yi, a large gull.

a-pit-so′-to-yi, small prairie plover.

a-muk′-o-pit-so′-to-yi, large prairie plover.

kit-se-pit-′se-ku′-yi,

ni-a′-tsi, a killdeer plover.

o-muk′-a-tsi, a large killdeer.

sik-se-kun′-i-ki-su′-yi, a black woodpecker.

mi-ki′-ma-ta, a kind of small speckled woodpecker.

o-muk-si-ki′-ma-ta, red-headed woodpecker.

ōh′-u-mi, the domestic hen, or the bird that screams.

a-pin′-a-ku-sis-tse, the morning bird.

i-si-kau′-kai-yi, the lark.

ni-pu′-ma-ki, tomtit.

ma′-sto, a beaver.

ki′-to-ki, the common prairie hen.

o-muk′-si-ki′-to-ki, large prairie hen, sage cock.

kit′-si-it′-sim, pheasant.

pi-ksi-ka′-ći, teal duck.

pi′-ksi, a fish hawk.

ma′-ma-a-ći′-kim, the magpie.

pi-ći′-ksin, a small snake.

o-muk′-si-ći′-ksin, the rattlesnake.

mu-ći′-e-ku-ći′-man, a frog.

o-muk′-i-ći-o-ku-ći′-man, a large toad.

ma-ni′-ski (pl. -skiks), water lizards.

sko'-pi (pl. -piks), tortoises.
ma-to'-is-ći, a hair worm.
i-ski-se'-na (pl. -naks), worms.
a-po'-ni (pl. -nīks), butterflies.
tse-ka'-a-tse (pl. -tse-īks), grasshoppers.
tup-i-kai'-nim, a large cricket.
si-ki-tup'-i-kai, a common cricket.
at-si'-na-ko, a mosquito hawk.
sūs-kris'-i, a mosquito.
o-muk-sūs'-kris-i, a large horsefly.
ut-si'-mo-sūs'-kri-si, a stinking fly that swarms about meat.
u-sko'-kin, a large ant.
o-ko'-ma, a body louse.

a-tse'-tsi-ksim, cottonwood.
ka-po'-ksim, the ash.
pah'-tōk, pine.
sik-si-no-kōk', cedar, or blackberry pine, so called from its black fruit.
o-tōh'-o-tsist. *Opuntia Missouriensis.*
ōt-sta'-tsi-man. *O. Nuttalli.*
ak-spīs', gummy weed. *Grindelia squarrosa.*
mas, pomme blanche. *Psoralea esculenta.*
ōts-će'-nist, strawberry. *Fragaria Virginiana.*

CHAPTER V.

VOCABULARY OF THE SIK-SI-KA' OR BLACKFOOT LANGUAGE.

A.

across, a-pum'-ōts.
Adam's apple, i-to-kits'-kris-tun.
after a while, ni-ta'-tum-i; I will come after a while, ni-ta'-tum-i-tup'-o.
air, a-mi-pūk'.
alive, e-te'-pi.
all, it-si'-na-ka; the whole, ki'-na; all, entirely, mo-tu'-sa; all icy, mo-tu'-sa-ko-ku'-to.
ankle, ki-tah'-o-kin-a'-ki.
annoying, ska'-aps.
arm, o'-ćis; right arm, i-tōh'-si; left arm, i-a-kris'-o-ōks.
armpit, ōh-ris'.
around or **about**, a-ko'-kats; around about the village, ko-na'-to-ka'-to-a-ko'-kats.
to arrive, ma'-no-tu.
arrow, aps, or ap'-si; an arrow point, sa'-ku-pun; who owns these arrows? ta'-ka-mi-a-psi'-wa.
ashamed, ne-tu'-yis.
ashes, muks-kit'-si.
asleep, o'-kau; sleeping, i-yo'-kau.
to be astonished, ki-o'-to.
at, u-ni'-mai; at the house, mu-yis'-u-ni'-mai.
autumn, mu-ku'.
axe, ko'-ksa-kin.

B.

back, as the back part of the head or body, na-ka'-kin-i; back, backward, ah-pa-to'-tsi; back, in past time, mi-sam'.
bad, ba-kaps', ba-ka'-psu, me-ska'-psu; a bad boy, ba-ka'-psa-ko-ma'-pi.
bank, of the river, at-siks'; the bank is near by, it-sat'-siks.
bark, of a tree, o-tōk'-skris.
barrel, su'-i-in.
beads: red beads, a-mank'-sku; black beads, si-ksi'-no-ku; white beads, about the size of pigeons' eggs, used in the Indian trade, ćik'-sku.
beak, of a bird, pi-kso'-kris-is.
beans, o-to'-ksi-nu'-tsi.
beard, mo-yo'-yi.
bed, sa'-a-kan.
behind, a-pa-toh'-si.
belly, o-ku'-a.
belt, or sash, me-pis; pl. me-pisé'.
to bend, ta-wa'-ksi-pin'-a-ki; bent, a-ksi-kin'-o-tuks.
better, su-kaps'.
between or among, se-to-ko'ksin.
beyond, sa-toh'-si; beyond the ridge, pau-ah'-u-i-sa-tōh'-si.
black, sik-si-nim'.

bowels, pi-stum′-i.

bowl, or plate, su-iħ′-ta-ćis.

box, ai-i-su′.

boy, sa-ko′-ma-pi; a boy without finger or toe nails, sa-ko′-ma-pi-e-kai′-sa-na.

brains, o′-pi.

blanket, na-pis′-ći; a green blanket, ut-skai′-pis-ći.

blisters, arising on the skin from burning, a-moħ′-sa-wa-nit′-si.

blood, a-pau′-ni.

blow the nose, i-mi-ći′-kin-i, to blow the nose.

blue, ōt-ku′-e-nut′-se.

boat, or canoe, a-ki′-ōħ-sa′-ćis; steamboat, a-ki-ōħ-sa′-ćis-a-mi′-to; also, is-ći′-a-ki-ōħ-sa′-ćis, fire-boat; is-ći′, fire; ferry-boat, the boat that crosses people over the river, i-maħ′-ta-pa-to-ći′-wa.

bog, low wet ground, paħ-si-kaŋ′-ku-i.

boil, i-kiħ′-an; a sore containing pus, i-ta′-ćis; the pus of the sore, a-ćis′-i-o.

bone, oħ′-in; collar-bone, i-sa-mi′-kan.

book, a pile of folded leaves, sa-pa′-ko-tsi-na′-ksi.

both, or two, sem-is′-to.

bottle, so-ko′-ka-tōs.

bow, spe′-kin-a-ma.

brass, ko-te-ke′-me; also, o-tai′-kim; small brass bells, used in the trade, mo-sōħ′-i-ki-ni; small brass nails, e-tus′-ta-kai′-ōp.

brave, ma′-ći, also ma′-tsi.

to break, si′-nit.

breechcloth, oħ-e′-a-ksa′-ćis.

brother, elder brother, nis′-a; younger brother, ni′-skum.

broom, na-mu′-ki-ma-ćis.

broth, o′-pis.

to brush, as clothes, ta-sa-tsi′-ni ōks.

buffalo, in a mass, i-ni′-wa; a mad bull, ma-ni-kris′-stum′-ik; a mad cow, ma-ni-kris′-ski-ni′; the dried excrement of the buffalo, "buffalo chips," kaħ′-piħ-ta.

to burn, e-nit′-se; burnt, it′-sin-it′-se.

butterfly, a-po′-ni.

to buy, pum′-at.

by, passing by, stut-sko′-a; by the house, or passing by the house, stut-sko′-a-mu-yis′.

C.

to call, mu-ta′-ui-stis.

to carry, a-wa′-se-ni.

circingle, for a horse, is-ksi′-si-pi-staue′.

chair, so-pats′.

cherries, puħ′-i.

chief, nin′-a; pl. nin′-aks.

child, po′-ka; pl. po′-kīks; o-kōs′ is also used; po′-ka, denotes an infant.

chin, ōp-ski′-na.

claw, of a bird, pi-kso′-ki-ćis.

to climb, a-mis′-o.

cloth, nai-pis′-ći; blue cloth, si-kai′-pis-ći; black cloth, sik-si-nuts′; red cloth, maħ′-ai-pis′-ći.

cloud, so-kris′-te-ko-is; far beyond the clouds, so-kris-te-ko′-is-mi-sto-po′-ats; cloudy weather, a-su′-kris-te-ku′-i.

coat, su′-kōs; chief's coat, ni-ni′-o-su′-kōs.

coffee, ai-sik-si-ki′-mi; a coffee-pot, kri-su′-yi.

cold, stu′-yi; I am not cold, mis-ći′-stu-yi; I am cold, nis-tu′-yi; you are cold, kis-tu′-yi.

come, quickly, in a hurry, a-ke′-po-kse-po′-at.

to cook, ap′-sat; to cook different kinds of food in a pot together, a-yo′-sit.

copper, me-ko-ti′-ke-me.

cord, a-pis′; a rope made of hemp, a-pis′-ta-pi′-kin.

cough, ses-ki′-na.

coulée, sau-auħ′-tai.

cow, ski′-ni; domestic cow, a-pōt′-ski-ni.

crazy, mat′-saps.

to cry, au-a-sen′.

crooked, yu-mo′-ki-o.

to crumble, as food, si-si-ki′-a.

cup, kūs.

curious, pi-si-ta′-pi; a curious dog, pi-si-ta′-pi-im′-i-ta′o.

to cut or split the feather from a quill, te-a-kris′-ta-ta-nin′-im.

D.

to dance, eħ′-pi; I dance, nit-eħ′-pi; you dance, kit-eħ′-pi.

darkness, ske-nut′-si.

daughter (my), ni-tun′-a.

day, kris-te-ku′-e.

to die, a'-ni; dead, a-ni'-wa; I die, ni-ta'-ni; you die, ki-ta'-ni.
deer, a-wa'-kŏs; a white-tailed deer, a-wa'-to-yi; prairie deer, antelope, so-ki'-a-wa'-kŏs.
deep, mi'-a.
to destroy, mo'-tsa.
dog, im-i-ta'-o; a young dog, im-i-te'-ku-en; you are a dog, im-i-te'-ta-pi.
door, kit'-sim.
down, na-po'; gone down the river, wai-na-po'.
dreadful, ko-ma'-pi.
to drink, a-sim'-i.
dry, o-ki'-ksi-o; it is dry, o-ki-ksu'-yi; dried apples, a'-pa-sta-mi-na'-tsi,—so called because they look like rotten wood.
dust, sis-će'; dust flying, sis-će'-pu-ka.

E.

eagle, pi-ta'; pl. pi-teks'.
ear, oh'-to-kis; the external ear, ŏh'-o-ŏh'-to-kis.
earth, suh'-um.
easily, ki-na'-pi.
to eat, o'-yi.
egg, o'-wa.
elbow, o-kin'-stis.
enemy, ni-kuh'-to-ma.
enough, ki'-nai-e.
evening, o-to-ku'.
every, each, ki-nai'; everybody, ki-nai-tup'-i.
eye, a-waps'-pits; eye winkers and brows, u-mi-a'-pi-nan; eyelids, ko-wap'-spi.

F.

face, o-sto'-ksis.
to fall, e-ni'-si; falling, e-ni'-si-wa.
far off, at a distance, pi-oh'-tsi; a little way, a little distance, o-te'-stsi; near by, a-stsi'.
fat, o-tsi-nau'-a.
father, ni-i-na', or ni-na'.
feather, pi-kso'-ku-is.
fear, ko'-pum.
to feel, ti-e'-nim.
few, ki-a'-pi, scattered.
fine, ma-tso'-waps; a fine horse, ma-tso-wa'-psi-no-ko'-mi-ta-o; also, ma-tsi'-no-ko'-mi-ta-o.
finger, o-ki'-ćis; thumb or large finger, o-ma-ki'-ćis; little finger, o-tsa-na'-ki-ćis; finger-rings, sa-pe'-ki-ćo-sa'-ćis; the finger nails, ta-wa-ka'-no-ki'-ćis; the joints of the finger, i-ta-ku'-yi-kit-si'-pi.
to fight, it-skan'.
fish, mum'-i; a fish-line, mih'-a-tsis.
fire, is-ći', also, is-ći'-wa; a plenty of fire, a-kau'-is-ći.
flame, pa-ku'-is.
flint, kris-a'-ki-ta.
flood, i-ka-ku'-yi.
flour, ai-ki'-ta-tŏp.
flower, ki-ni'-wa.
to fold the arms, a-ne'-i-kin-sak.
fool, mat-saps'; foolish, a-wa-tsaps'.
foot, ŏh'-ats.
forehead, o'-mis.
forest, ut-si-wat'-sku-i.
forever, es-ksa'-a-ni'-ste.
friend, nit-sih'-i-wa.
frightful, sku-ni'-ta-pi.

G.

garnishing, on a robe, a-to-nus'-i.
get up (imp.), ni-pu'-uk.
to give, ko'-ćis; give me, ko'-kit; I give it to you, ki-to'-ko-ta-o; you give, ki-ta'-kum.
girl, a-ke'-ku-en.
glove, o-tsĕć'.
glue, tek-spo'-te-ku.
gold, same name as brass.
to go, a'-ma-to; go (imp.), po-ko'-mis; go with them, po-ko'-mi-sa-o; go away, mi-sto-po'-at; to go ahead, a-ma'-tup-i-isé'.
good, ah'-si-o; a good house, ah'-si-mu-yis'; a good boy, ah'-si-sa-ko-ma'-pi; all good, ki'-nai-ah'-si-o; beyond good, best of all, mis-ti-pŏks'-ah'-si-o; he alone is good, i-tai-ah'-si-o; there are none so good, i-tai-mah'-si-o.
good while, wai-sa'-mo; he is gone a long time, wai-sa'-ma-ma'-to.
grass, ma-tu'-yis.
grease, po-mis'.

great, sku′-na-taps.

green, ut-sku′-i.

ground, sa′-ko; in the ground, sa-ko′-mi-it-si′-o; ground, the surface of which is covered with little butes, or hillocks, pi-kaň′-o.

grove of trees, u-tso′-a-sku-yi.

gum of the pine, a-wa′-ksis.

gun, na′-ma; to miss fire, to snap a gun, na-mi-ka′-kis; where is my gun? a-na′-ni-mo.

H.

hail, kris-i′-ki-ni.

half, or a part, a-no-kŏhts′.

hallo! i′-ya.

hair, tu-ko-iň′-in-i-pi; long-haired, i-nu′-spi; hair on the upper lip, ma-ta′-ksi-wa′-tsi.

hammer, po′-ksa-ćis.

hand, mo-ćiň′-so-ku′-ist.

handsome, ba-tsi′-num, also, aň-waps′.

happy, a-ksi′-ti-ke.

hard, mi-wa; hard wood, mi-wa-mis-ćis′.

hat, i-ći′-mo-kain.

head, o-to-kan′; a kind of shell, of the genus *Dentalium*, used by the Indians as ornaments for the head, a-pi-ksis′-ćim-a-o-ksu′-is.

to heal, a-ki′-o.

to hear, ai-ōň′-sim.

heart, ōň-it′-sa-pa′-pi.

heavy, so-ku′ and so-ke-sim′; both words are in use.

heel, ōň-tu-tun′-i.

here, in this place, un-i′-ma, u′-no-mai.

to hesitate, hold back, pe-i-tsiň′-tan.

high, spi; a high animal, spi-mi′-o.

hill, pa-waň′-u.

hip, ōň-i′-ni-sak.

to hold, e-i-ni′-o.

hole, aň-a′-ni-ka.

honest, ko-mo′-tsi; an honest man, ko-mo′-tsi-tup′-i.

horn, ōt-ski′-na.

horse, pu-no-ka′-mi-ta, literally elk dog, from pu-no-ka′-o, an elk, and im-i-ta′-o, a dog; mi-o′-mi-ta (pl. mi-o′-mi-tōks), pack horses; another form is in use in declension denoting possession: my horse, no-tōs′; your horse, ko-tōs′; his horse, o-tōs′; his horses, o-to′-siks; a white horse, a-pi′-wa-no′-tōs; a gray horse, si-ka-pi′-wa-no′-tōs; a horse with black ears, i-sik′-sta-ki-no′-tōs.

hot, kris-to′-tsūs; kris-tu′-yi.

house, of the white man, na-pu′-is, mu-yis′.

how, in what way? tsa′-ni-ta-pi; how many? sa-na′-tsim.

husband, o′-ma.

I.

ice, ko-ku′-to.

if, i-yo′-pi.

in, pis-toňs′; in company with, ti-a-koň′-po-ko′-mau; in company with my son, ti-a-kōň′-po-ko′-mau-nōň-o′-a.

Indian, ni-i′-tsa-ta′-pi.

intestines, o′-ćis; manifolds, or large intestines of an animal, i-si′-stōn.

island, mi-ni′-wa.

iron, miks′-kim; an iron frying-pan, miks-kim′-i-kūs; iron horse, locomotive, miks-kim′-o-nu-ka′-mi-ta; iron wire, sik-si-ak′-skim.

J.

joint, i-tōň′-o-ki′-na-ki.

joke, ka-saps′.

jug, sa-ku′-ko-tus-ko.

to jump, eň-pa′-sto.

K.

kettle, i′-ski; isk.

kidneys, o-to-ko-to′-kisć; also o-tōk′.

to kill, i-ni′-ki-o.

kiss, so-nau′-ski-pi.

kinnic-kinnic, a-pi′-ni-kim.

knee, o-to′-ksi.

knife, stu′-un; a sheath for a knife, a-so′-tu-un; a two-edged knife or sword, sa-ma-kin′.

L.

lake, o-muň′-si-ki-mi.

land, aň′-o; a country, sa′-ko; the whole country, ki′-na-sa′-ko.

large, a-pa′-ki; a large quantity, o-muň′-u; a heap, a-kau′-i, also a-ku′-a-wa.

lately, i'-so.

to laugh, a-i'-mi.

lazy, buh-aps' or ba-kaps'; a lazy fellow, good for nothing, pah'-i-kah'-si-o.

lead, o-wak'-shu-pa.

leaf, nips; also so-yo'-po; dry leaves, so-yo'-po-kist.

leg, o-kuts'; leg below the knee, a-tse'-na; calf of the leg, ōh-ki'-nan; an instrument for dressing robes, made from the leg-bone of the antelope, ma'-ski.

leggins, a'-tsi.

lengthwise, i-kum'-o; splits lengthwise, i-kum'-o-i-sta-to'-ksi.

less, o-wa'-tu-ksi.

level plain, mi-ni-stah'-wah-u.

light, kris-ti-ku'-e-nut'-si.

lightning, i'-pa-pum.

like, ni-tu'-i; he is like my son, ni-tu'-ni-i-tso-ōh-u'-i; just like, as he is just like his father, a-ye'-ko-no-tse; like, applied to any object but persons, ni-tum'-a-nis'-tsi-num'-i-a.

limb, of a tree, o-ku'-niks.

to listen, kris-to-ći'-si.

little, small, a-nuks'; a small man, a-nuk-si'-na; a little or small quantity, no-tse-nah'-o; give me a little, no-tse-nah'-o-kōh'-it.

to live, e-ta'-pi; I live, nit-se-ta'-ta-pi; you live, kit-se-ta'-ta-pi.

lodge, mu-yis'; a beaver lodge, kris-tuk-u-o-yis; a hole or rent in the lodge, ah'-un-ih-a; pins driven into the ground, to fasten down the bottom of the lodge, i-sto-ka'-ćis; the holes in the lower edges of the lodge where the pegs are inserted, pi-ki'; pins to fasten the side of the lodge-skin, after it is erected, sa-pi'-ki-na-na-ma'-ćis; the act of tying the lodge-poles at the top, a-tu'-ksi-pi'-stan; the hole in the top of the lodge to let out the smoke, ma-o-to'-tsi-man; lodge-poles, ma'-ni-stam.

long, i-nu'-ye.

long ago, a-ka'-a; I was displeased with you long ago, a-ka'-a-o-ki'-ma-su-ki.

look (imp.), sum'-is; look at me, i-sum'-o-kit; look at me, I am ugly, sum'-o-ki-tun'-i-to-kaps; look! he looks ugly, sum'-is-sum'-o-kaps.

lost, a'-tsa.

louse, tut-se-po'-kōk; I am bitten by lice, ni-tai-sik'-si-pūk.

to love, a-ko-mim'.

low, e-kuk'.

M.

maiden, a-ki'-a-ko'-a, (pl.) a-ki'-a-ko'-aks.

maize, or corn, bes-ka'-ta, a word derived from the Arapoho language.

mammæ, un'-i-kis, breasts.

man, or person, ma-ta'-pi; a young, unmarried man, a-si'-ta-pi; also ma-ni-ka'-pi; a white man, na-pi'-ku-un; a black man, sik-sa-pi'-ku-un.

mare, ski'-am.

marrow-bone, i-nun'-i.

mean, as a mean fellow, ma-ksi-num'.

measure, e-ska'-ki.

meat, kai'-yis; meat in small fragments, pi-i'-wa.

medicine, drugs, sa'-am; a medicine man, or doctor, i-su'-ki-wa'-ke; medicine, or mystery, na-tu'-yi.

midday, tut'-se-ka-kris-ta-ku'; midnight, tut'-se-ka'-ku-ku.

middle, as in the middle of the river, tut'-se-kuts.

milk, u-ni'-kis.

mirror, tsa-pi'-a-tsis.

to mix, pa-so'-ko.

moccasins, at-si'-kin-i; top of the moccasins, ntuk'-o-to'-to-nan; shoestrings, sa-pi'-ne-ka'-ats; to tie up the shoes or moccasins, nta'-ksi-naus.

moon, ke-sum'.

more, stik'-i, is-ći'-ka.

morning, ma-to'-nis; early in the morning, ska-na'-to-nis.

mosquito, sūs-kris'-i.

mother (my), ni-krist'.

mould, a-pi-su'-yi; mouldy, a-pi-su'-yi-wa; it will be mouldy, i-a'-ka-pi-su'-yi; to smell mouldy, a-pi-su'-yi-e'-mo.

mountain, mi-stah'-u.

mouth, a-o'-yi; my mouth, na-o'-yi; your mouth, ka-o'-yi.

much, a heap, a-ku'-im, a-kai'-im.

mud, miry, pa-kse'-kah'-u-a.

mule, long ears, o-muk'-sto-ki.

N.

name, nin-ik-ōs'; his name, sin-ti-kōs'.

narrow, e-ki'-o.

navel, o-to'-yis.

near, close, o-tsūst'.

neck, ōh-o'-kiu-i; back part of the neck, oh-tun'-is.

needle, large needles, o-muk-o'-to-nau'-ksi-čis; small needles, o-to-nau'-ksis.

new, ma'-ni; a new arrow, ma-no'-psi.

night, ko-kūs'; the same night, a-nu'-ko-kūs'.

no, sa; also a-ni'-yi.

noon, tut-si-ke'-a-kris'-te-ku'; (pl. -ku-isé).

nose, ōh-kris'-is; my nose, noh-kris'-is.

nostril, o-pis'-ki-sa.

nothing, ma-tsi'-tse, and kris-ta'-pi.

O.

old, na'-pe; a white man, na-pe'-ku-un, literally old people; applied to a female, ki-pi'-ta; an old woman, ki-pi'-ta-a-ki'-wa.

open (imp.), kau-a-pi'-sta; open the door, kit'-sim-kau-a-pi'-sta; open out, spread out, o-po'-tōs.

opinion, plan, se-ni'-stan.

outside, sa-ōhs'.

over, i-sōk'.

P.

paddle, it-i-ah'-e-o-kso-pe; to paddle, as a boat, mai-a'-ki-ōks.

pail, su-yen'.

parfleche, ko-to-ki'-a-no-ko.

pepper, pi-stup'-o-ku.

perhaps, ah-si-kum'; seh'-ti; perhaps he will come, ah-si-kum'-a-sto.

pins, spin-o-to'-nauks.

pine tree, pah'-tōk.

pipe, ah-o-i'-ni-man.

plain, prairie, so-ka', so-ki'.

to play, e-ku'-e-ni.

plenty, a-kai-im'; a plenty of people, a-kai'-tup-i.

pole, i-ne'-stam; a long pole, i-ne'-ni-stam.

pork, ai'-ksin-i, a grunter, hog.

post, a-kun'-iks.

potatoes, in-su'-mōn.

powder, sa-tso-pa'-ats.

prairie, so'-ki, sometimes so-ka'.

puzzle, ōh'-pi-ska.

pumpkin, ōh'-to-ki-nut'-si, so called when cut and dried.

Q.

quickly, ki-pun'-is-tsi.

quill, ma'-min.

R.

rain, i'-so-ta; rainy, so'-tau; to clear away, as clouds after a rain, ai'-e-pun'-i; the rain has passed away, so-te'-ai-pun'-i.

rattles, on the tail of a rattlesnake, se'-tsi-ko'-to.

ravine, ka-wah'-u-a.

raw, uncooked, ko-te'-tsi.

red, mōh'-si-nut'-si; a red blanket, mōh'-o-pe'-pist; vermilion red paint, mōh-i'-san.

relation, kso'-qua.

rest, sik-si'-ste-ku.

rib, pi-kis'.

river, ni-i-tuh'-ta; a stream or creek, a-se-tuh'-ta; a little run, wa-wa'-ku-a.

road, mo-ksa'-ku-yi; path or road, pa-tōt'-sku-yi.

rock, mis-tek'; rocky, mis-tek'-sku.

rosebuds, ki-nīks'.

rope, a'-pis, a lariat for a horse.

rough, rugged, pi'-wa; bad lands, pi-wah'-o, and si-na-tah'-o.

to rub off, or brush, ta-sa'-tsi-ni-ōk'-sto.

to run, o-ma'-ka; aks'-kas; to run quickly, ka-mōks'-kas; run (imp.), aks-ka'-sit, and, mah-at'; run away, mis-ta-pi'-mah'-at; ni-to-mah', I run; ki-to-mah', you run.

rusty, a-psu'-yi.

S.

sacred, holy, kse'-maps.

salt, stik-se-po'-ko.

sandbar, sput'-se-ko; the great sand pile where the dead go, o-muks'-sput'-se-ko.

sash or belt, ma'-pis.

scabbard, a-sto'-tu-wa.

scabby, a-pe'-kris; a scabby bull, a-pe'-kris-stum'-ik.
scalp, sa-o-to'-mu-a.
scattered, ki-a'-pi.
to scratch, ta-ksi-ki'-na-to'-he.
sea, mo-toh'-i.
seat, nu'-o-sa.
searching, a-pa'-su-mi.
to see, na-mu'-i-nu.
seed, e-ni-si'-man.
selfish, avaricious, a-kum-i'-tup-i-o.
sharp, kris-e'-kim; a sharp knife, kris-e'-ki-sto'-a.
to shave off with a knife, ksi-kit-si'-ni-aks.
shears, ste-si'-so-yōp.
shells for earrings, po-kun-um'; to the fossil shells, which occur in that country very abundantly, the Indians give the name o-ćis'-he.
shirt, stah-ti-so'-kaus.
shooting, sku-ni'-ke.
shot, kit-si-ko'-pun-i.
shot-pouch, su-i-a'-tsi-man.
shoulder, o-kut'-si-kin.
sick, ōh-to-ko'-ksi.
sinew, hai-si-pi'.
to sing, e-ni-ki'-o; I sing, ni-tai'-ni-ki; you sing, ki-tai'-ni-ki.
sister, i-sa'-ki-mi.
sit down (imp.), pi'-it.
skin of an animal, to'-kis, and, o-to'-kis; a cow-skin dressed, pakh'-i; undressed, i-ni'-o-to'-kis.
sky, spōhts.
sleep, wai-yo-ka'.
slow, e-tse-tse'-kris-to.
small, ōh-po'-ki-o, and, na-ko'-tsi-o.
smart, active, ku-waps'.
smell, a-mas'; a bad smell, mes-ka'-pa-mas.
smoke, sa-tsi'-wa; smoky, se-nu'-tsu.
to sneeze, a-si'-i-si.
snow, kōn; kōn'-sko; snowing, ōh'-po-ta-o.
soap, sis-ki-o-sa'-tsis.
soft, ki'-ni, also, ih-i-ni'-si.
to soil or dirty, po-mis'.
something, ki-sta'-pi.
sometimes, ni-ta'-tum-i.
son, ōh-u'-a.
soon, skun'-i; come soon, skun'-i-o-po-ksa-po'-at.
soup, o-ko'-pis; goose soup, ap-sin'-i-o-ko'-pis.
sour, eh-i-mu'-i.
to speak, a-pu'-i.
spear or lance, sa-pa-pi'-sta-ćis.
spirit or ghost, o-ni-stan'; Great Spirit, the Great Medicine Man above, na-to'-yi-tup-i'-spo-ma'-pi.
spot, e-na'-ki-o; a yellow spot, o-tōh'-u-i-na'-tsi-o.
spoon, i-nōh'-si-o.
spring, mu-tu'; (pl. -tu-ist.)
spring of water, ma-ki'-kum.
spurs, ta-wa'-wa-ka-piks.
stand up (imp.), ne-pu'-yi-pu-yit.
star, ka-ka'-tōs.
to steal, ka-mōs.
stingy, it-si'-ki-ma'-ats.
stockings, a-to-wa'-ksin.
stomach, no-kin', o'-ku-un.
stone, ōh'-o-tōk; stony, oh'-o-tōk'-sku.
stop! hi-ka'-o.
straight, kum-o'-e-sim.
to stretch, or yawn, se-pi'-is; I stretch, ni-tai-se'-pi-is; you, &c., ki-tai-se'-pi-is; he, &c., e-tai-se'-pi-is.
to strike, a-wa'-a-ki; I strike, nit-a-wa'-a-ki; you strike, kit-a-wa'-a-ki.
strong, mi-ska'-pi.
to suck, sta.
summer, ni-pu', (pl. -pu-isé.)
sun, na-tōs', na-to'-se; sun's rays, se-ki'-so-au.
sweet, me-ne-po'-ko; sometimes, ma-tse'-pu-ku.
swelled, kah'-pi.
swift, e-kum'-i-si; a swift dog, e-kum'-i-si-im-i-ta'-o.

T.

tail, ōh-su'-yis.
take it, mat'-sit.
temples, ōt-skup-u'-na.
tooth, ōh-pi'-a-kin.
then, i-tek'-si; then, in that place, un'-i-it-si'-o.
thigh, u-wa'-pi-sak.
thin, stōh'-i; a thin leaf, stōh'-so-yo'-po-ki.
to think, a-ah-ska'-to-ki.
thread, thread made of sinew, e-si'-pis; cloth thread, ne-pi-stai'-si-pis.

throat, ŏh-kris′-tun-i.
thunder, kris-te-kum′.
to tickle, si-kus′-i-ta′-ki, and e-ko′-i-ni-sto′-to.
to tie, isk′-si-ni-stuk′-sim; tie (imp.) sksi′-nit.
tobacco, pis-ta′-kan; Indian tobacco of the best quality, *Lobelia inflata*, ne-ets′-ti-nis; common Indian tobacco, both kinds used in the religious ceremonies of the Indians, e′-nis; cutting-board for tobacco, su-pi′-ksis-tsi-ma′-ćis; a garnished tobacco sack, a-su′-a-ći′-man.
to-morrow, a piu′-o-kōs; I will go to-morrow, a-pi-nuk′-si-ta-ko′-ma-ta.
to-night, ko-kūs′.
tongue, ma-tse′-ne.
tooth, ōh-pi′-a-kin.
top, or summit, si-ko′-ki-tōhs.
to touch, ksi′-nit.
towards, pit-si-ōh′-to.
towel, ste′-sis-ki-o.
travail, ma-nis′-ći.
tripe, o-ku′-un.
true, truth, kit-si′-ma; you are not a man of truth, ki-ma-to′-ma-nīh′-pa.
trunk, or box, a-so′-kai-is; a wooden trunk, mis-ćis′-o-kai′-is.
to twist, a-niks′-ka-pi-kris′-ta-kis.

U.

ugly, muh-si-num′.
under, stahs; it is under something, stahs-mi-it-si′-o; there is something under the stone, ōh-o′-to-ki-stahs-mi-it-si′-o.
up, a-mi-tōks′.

V.

valley, pi-i-stah′-wah-u′-mi-ni-stah′-u-i.
vein, ōs-ći′.
verdigris, ōh-o-mo′-ni-nut-si; ko-na′-no is sometimes used.
very, e-a′, sku-nuts′, e-ku′-i; this very night, a-nu′-ke-a-ksa′-ko-kus-e-ku′-i; a very old man, e-ku′-i-na′-pi-o; very cold, sku-nuts′-tu-yi.
village, a-ki′-ta-pi-sko′; a plenty of lodges, o-ki′-o-kum-i.
villain, ma-kse-tup′-i.
to vomit, o-kit′-skum.

W.

wagon, or cart, a′-na-kaus.
to walk, sik-so′-o; I will walk, nit-a′-ksi-ksi-ni; you will walk, kit-a′-ksi-ksi-ni; he will walk, ta′-ksi-ksi-no.
war, kah′-to-ma; a war-club, ko′-ksa-kin.
warm, kris-to′-yi.
warrior, tsu′-a-pits.
wasp, na′-mo.
water, oh′-i.
weak, ma-tse-kut′-saps.
weeds, ki-sta′-po-tu′-yis; dried grass, ki-pi-ta′-tu-yis.
well, it′-ksu; he got well again, at′-ai-it′-tsu.
wife (my), nit-o-ki′-man.
wind, i′-so-pu; sometimes pronounced, su-po; a strong wind, a-muk′-sa-pu′-yi.
windpipe, o′-ku-stun.
wing, of a bird, o-min′-stra-kin.
winter, stu′-yi; sto′-yi.
within, pi-sto′-tso; without, su-ōh′-so.
wise, mo-ku′-ki-aps.
to wish, te-tsih′-ta.
what? ah-sats′; what more? what else? akh-sas′-ći-ki; what do you say? sa-wa′-ni; when? at what time? sta-nis′-ćis; where? at what place? ći′-ma.
whip, is-ći′-pi-si-ma′-ćis; to whip, is-ći′-pi-sis′.
whiskey, na-pi′-ōh-i, white water.
white, ći-ksi-num′; white cloth, ći-kai-pi′-ći.
who? ta-ka′.
woman, a-ki′-ma; (pl. a-kiks′.)
wood, mis′-tis; stone wood, petrified wood, mis′-tis-oh′-o-tōk; all kinds of hard wood, tsa-si′-ksa; rotten wood, bi′-a-kuk′-si-ksi; split wood, ni-sta′-to-ksaks; a pile of drift-wood in the river, ka-ćis′-ko.
word, e-pu′-o-ksin.
to work, a-po′-to-ki; work (imp.), a-po′-to-kit; I am going to work, nta-ka-po′-to-ki.
to wrap up, a-mo-pit′.
wrist, i-tah′-o-ki-wis-tsi′-pi.
to write, a-sin′-a-ki; write (imp.), sin′-a-kit; writing, sin′-a-ki; books, a-sin′-aks.

Y.

yellow, o-tōh′-u-i.
yes, a.
yesterday, ma-tun′-i-ye.
yet, sa′-ki; he is living yet, sa′-ki-ai-to′-pi-wa.
yonder, o′-mim.

CHAPTER VI.

III. SHYENNES.

ETHNOGRAPHICAL HISTORY.

COMPARATIVELY little has been published in regard to this tribe of Indians, and their former history is quite obscure. The few facts already recorded seem to render it very probable that they emigrated from the north and northeast to their present location, but I can find no reliable account of their movements or their history, in any works within my reach. How so important and interesting a tribe of Indians has escaped the notice of travellers, is a matter of some surprise. Even the indefatigable Schoolcraft was unable to obtain any extended account of them. From my own personal observations, and from all the sources within my reach, I have constructed the following brief sketch of this tribe.

This nation has received a variety of names from travellers and the neighboring tribes, as Shyennes, Shiennes, Cheyennes, Chayennes, Sharas, Shawhays, Sharshas, and by the different bands of the Dakotas, Shai-én-a, or Shai-é-la, the meaning of which is not known. On the Missouri River, near latitude 45° and longitude 101°, is the entrance of the Great Shyenne River, one of the most important branches of the Missouri. It takes its rise in the divide between the valley of the Yellowstone, and that of the Missouri, and is called by the Dakota Indians, Wash-te'-wah-pa, or Good River. About thirty miles below the eastern base of the Black Hills, is the junction of two important branches, called the North and South Forks of the Shyenne. The South Fork rises far to the northward of the Black Hills, in the arid, tertiary hills which form the dividing ridge between the waters of the Yellowstone and those of the Missouri, and flows around the southern base of the Black Hills, receiving numerous tributaries from the mountains. The North Fork rises in the same dividing ridge, making a flexure around the northern base of the Black Hills, likewise receiving numerous branches, fed by springs in these hills. Uniting, they form the Great Shyenne, as before mentioned. The country bordering this river, from its mouth to the junction of the two forks, is underlaid by the black, plastic, saline clays of the cretaceous system, and is, consequently, for the most part, quite arid and barren. The bottoms, however, forming the immediate valley, are clothed with grass, and furnish a supply of fuel sufficient for all the wants of the Indian. Game is also quite abundant, as elk, deer, and antelope, and in former years, vast herds of buffalo roamed over this region, though at the present time, only now and then a stray bull is seen along this river from mouth to source. In the vicinity of the Black Hills, the clear, beautiful streams that flow from the mountains, swarm with beaver, the prairies are covered with antelope, and the wooded valleys and hills are favorite resorts for elk and deer, the whole rendering this country one of the most delightful spots to the Indian. We will not at this time describe the country in detail, inasmuch as we shall dwell more at length upon it in our history of the Dakota bands which now roam over it. We now allude to it, from the fact that it seems to be the starting-point in our knowledge of the Shyennes. A little farther up the river, a small stream flows into the Missouri from the north, which is called the Little Shyenne. These streams evidently derived their names, from the fact that they drain the country once occupied by this tribe of Indians.

Those enterprising travellers, Lewis and Clarke, give us no extended account of the Shyennes, and simply allude to them in their Journal.* On their map attached to their report, they locate them near the eastern base of the Black Hills, in the valley of the Great Shyenne River, and state the number at fifteen hundred souls. They also speak of the remains of their old villages along the Missouri (vol. i, p. 149), which seem to show the course of their migrations. Near the mouth of a little stream, named by them "Chayenne" Creek, they observed "a circular work or fort, where the Sharsha or Chayennes formerly lived." There are, also, on one of the banks of the Red River of the North, the remains of an old village of the Shyennes, with an important stream bearing their name. All these forts show quite clearly that the Shyennes either gradually and slowly migrated from the far north to their present location, in search of better hunting grounds, or were driven by the superior strength of their more numerous neighbors. We have the statements of persons now living in that country, that the Dakotas drove them from the Missouri to their present position.

Brackenridge in his Journal of a tour up the Missouri River, in 1811,† says of these Indians that they are a "wandering nation on the heads of the Shyenne River; trade with the Arikaras; speak a different language from any nation I know; their complexion very fair. They trade also with the Spaniards, and have a great number of horses, &c."

During the time of Long's expedition to the Rocky Mountains, in 1819 and 1820, a small portion of the Shyennes seem to have separated themselves from their nation on the Missouri, and associated themselves with the Arapohos, who wandered about the tributaries of the Platte. On page 367, vol. ii: "The Shyennes associated with those wandering tribes (Arapohos, &c.), are a small band of seceders from the nation of the same name, residing upon the Shyenne River. They are said to be daring and ferocious."‡

* Travels up the Missouri, during the Years 1804, '5, and '6, by Captains Lewis and Clarke. London edition, in three volumes.

† Views of Louisiana, together with a Journal of a Voyage up the Missouri River, in 1811. By H. M. Brackenridge, Esq. Pittsburg, 1814.

‡ Account of an Expedition from Pittsburg to the Rocky Mountains, performed in the Years 1819 and 1820, by order of the Hon. J. C. Calhoun, Secretary of War, under the command of Major Stephen H. Long, compiled by Edwin James, Botanist and Geologist to the Expedition. 2 vols., with an Atlas. Philadelphia, 1823.

According to Mr. Morse, in 1822, "this tribe, of 3250 souls, dwell and hunt on the river of this name, a western tributary of the Missouri, a little above the Great Bend."*

We have no means at hand for determining the exact time when these Indians took up their abode in the Platte country. We only know that at the present time they claim, in connection with the Arapohos, the country bordering upon the North and South Platte Rivers. They range, however, in their war excursions and in their search for buffalo, far into the Crow country, along the various branches of Powder River, along the Sweetwater, and even as far to the west and north as the Black Hills, south to the Arkansas, and west to the valley of Green River. Owing to the rapid immigration of white settlers into that region for a few years past, the Indian Bureau has attempted to place these Indians upon a reservation; but they must be taught to cultivate the soil before they will become a contented or a prosperous people.

The writer, attached to a United States Exploring party, under the command of Capt. William F. Raynolds, spent the winter of 1859 and 1860 at the base of the mountains, about a hundred miles above Fort Laramie, on the North Platte. The Indian Agent, who resided at the same place, had several very intelligent Shyenne hunters, from whom much information was obtained. The following extracts are taken from the writer's journal kept at that time.

"There are many instances of Indians possessing several wives, from two to fifteen, but jealousies are constantly arising, and are kept in check only by force on the part of the husband. Every woman rejoices when she finds she is the only lawful wife; and when she suspects that her husband meditates the taking of a second, she throws every obstacle in the way, first by renewed attentions and kindness to her husband, and then by creating difficulties with the intended wife. When an Indian takes several wives, he usually selects one as his favorite. She may be a young woman, or the first wife and the mother of his children. The remainder are intended more as slaves, to dress robes and to perform the drudgery of the lodge.

"Rib, our excellent Shyenne hunter, has been out in pursuit of game for several days, and although one of the best Indian hunters in the country, he has had very poor success. He is very superstitious, like all his tribe, and says it is the moon that is in fault. It is now full moon, and he says that when the moon dies his luck will return again. Thus these people are continually impeded in their efforts by their superstitious notions. The first time he went out hunting during this moon he wounded an antelope; it escaped, and many other chances occurred, yet he returned without meat, to receive the angry looks of the wife, who would give him no supper. Having rested himself he started out again,

* A Report to the Secretary of War of the United States on Indian Affairs. By Rev. Jedediah Morse, D.D. New Haven, 1822.

wounded an elk, and pursued it into the mountains, until it became buried in a snowdrift, from which place it was impossible for him to carry away the meat. The next day he started out again, and found a deer asleep near a little creek: then, too, his gun missed fire. Again he took deadly aim at a deer, and the ball stopped within a few feet of the muzzle of the gun. He now waits patiently for the next moon, when, he says, he will kill an abundance of game.

"Rib has a Dakota wife, one quarter white. She presents the only instance that I have met with among the Indians, in which the woman ruled the man directly. It is very seldom that an Indian allows his wife to gain any power over him, though she may quietly influence him; yet any disobedience of his orders is punished, oftentimes with great severity. In their domestic affairs each one has his or her duty to perform, and there is no interference the one with the other, though the tastes and wishes of the man are consulted, and have the preference. His is the first or principal place in the lodge, usually the farthest from the door. On one occasion Rib ventured to punish his children for some act of disobedience. His wife turned him out of the lodge, and threw all his things out after him. He went away alone quite crestfallen. When rallied for his want of heart, and asked why he did not whip her, he replied that he loved his wife, and did not wish to strike her. So he waited patiently until her wrath cooled, and all was made right again. He says that if he were to punish his wife every time she conducted herself badly, he would be compelled to stand with his whip in his hand all the time, and could not use his gun.

"The Shyennes are a proud race, large and well formed, more like the Dakotas than any tribe I am acquainted with on the Missouri. They are at peace with the Dakotas, and have become so intermarried now, that it is hardly probable that they will ever break their friendly relations. So many of them speak the Dakota language, that their own language is not used at the present time in diplomatic affairs. I have never heard of but one white interpreter for these Indians, and he has long since left them, his knowledge of their language being of no pecuniary benefit to him.

"The Shyennes, like the Dakotas, are quite rigid in regard to the fidelity of their women. When a woman proves false to her husband, which is not common, she is punished with great severity, and not uncommonly with death. When a young man sees a woman fair to look upon, and one which his heart desires, he at once commences to apply his arts. If he succeeds in seducing the woman to elope with him, he immediately escapes to another tribe or band, and if he remains away, nothing is said or done about the matter; but if he returns, in some instances the injured husband kills him, though usually the man who decoyed away the wife gives to the former husband a horse and other presents, and he and a number of their mutual friends gather together at the lodge of the first husband, who hands the latter a pipe, and they all smoke together. The injured husband then says that his heart was bad, but has now become good, and the past is forgotten. Among the Blackfeet it is not uncommon for a lapse from virtue on the part of the woman to be visited with the worst form of punishment, the cutting off of the nose. A few rare cases have occurred among the Shyennes, but, as Rib says, only bad men do so. In a few cases the women have been killed.

"There is at this time (January, 1860), a serious warlike feeling existing between the Shyennes and the Crows. Each tribe accuses the other of having broken the peace, but, as near as I can ascertain, the Crows are in the wrong. About one year ago, one of the head chiefs of the Crows came to the Platte and stole from the Shyennes about thirty horses. In endeavoring to get them back the latter lost some men and the former some. About a month ago, the Shyennes, in considerable numbers, were encamped on Powder River. The Crows surprised the camp one morning, killed five persons and wounded several others, taking five children prisoners. The Crows being mounted, took the children in front of them on their horses. Being hard pressed by the Shyennes, who were in pursuit, the Crows drew their knives and stabbed the children, and threw them from their horses. The Indians at once removed from the interior to the Platte, near our winter quarters, bringing their wounded with them, most of whom died. One old woman was scalped alive, and though she was not otherwise injured, soon after died. It is considered the greatest insult to a tribe to scalp one of its members in that way. A lad about sixteen years of age, is now with his parents near our camp, with a bullet lodged in his thigh. It is quite uncertain what the result will be. The Dakotas and Shyennes have united against the Crows in a war of extermination. It would seem as though the country which the Crows have so long possessed, and regarded as the finest region in the world, would soon be taken from them. They are surrounded on all sides by enemies.

"At this time (January 25th, 1860), there are several lodges near the Agency. One of the old men has a daughter about sixteen years of age. Near his tent there is a small temporary hut, which is occupied by the girl during her menstrual period. During this time she is not permitted to touch anything, not even a horse, if so, it is considered bad 'medicine,' and unclean. This is a universal custom among all Indians with whom I am acquainted.

"Rib gives me the following information in regard to the religious belief of the Shyennes. He says that they all believe that when a person dies a portion returns to the earth, and another part, the spirit, goes to the Great Spirit, from which it had its origin. It then enters a child again and returns to this world; and should that being at any period during its lifetime walk over the dust of the former body, it also dies. 'Grass, an unusually intelligent Indian, a hunter for the Agent, says, that the Indians are aware that there is a Great Spirit who made the heavens and the earth, but farther than that they know nothing. They mourn for the dead because they are lost to them, and they know they cannot return. They place food and articles of clothing on the grave, because they think that the spirit continues with the body after death a short period, and then departs for the place where all spirits are gathered together. Grass says that the Indians often hear the spirits of the dead, and know their presence by various noises, but that he himself never saw them, though he has looked for them many times. His own belief is, that when an Indian dies that is the last of him: his body goes to the ground, his flesh to feed the worms, and his bones to form earth. He says also that the other Indians are fools for having any different belief. Is he not an infidel? None of the prairie Indians originally believed in a bad spirit, but have derived that idea from the whites. To sum up the religious belief of the Indians, it is simply an indefinite idea of a great Creator of all things; and farther than that they know nothing.

"The Great Spirit made half of the country for the whites, suitable for raising all kinds of grain, &c. He made the other half for the Indians, mostly prairie, and placed upon it an abundance of game; but that the white men were continually intruding upon them, and would soon drive them into the sea. He illustrates his remark in this way,—that the whites are like ants, and desire to have the whole world for an ants' nest.

"There are no special ceremonies connected with the birth of a child. As soon as a child is born, it is dipped in cold water and wrapped in a blanket. Presents are made to the old woman who acts as midwife. The father desires that the child shall be a boy, to aid him in herding the horses and in the hunt, while the mother prefers it to be a girl, to assist her in carrying wood and in making moccasins. There is considerable ceremony in piercing the ears of the child when it has attained a certain age, say four years. Liberal presents are given to the person who performs the act.

"There is great regularity in the operation of smoking the pipe. The Indians always pass around the pipe, the first man puffing a few whiffs, and then handing it to the one next to him. One person takes hold of the pipe-stem at a certain place, the next one above, and the next below alternately. Should any one fail to observe this order, whether white man or Indian, he cannot get the pipe until he takes hold of it in the proper way. The reason given is, that it is their 'medicine;' that no two men, sitting side by side, shall handle the pipe in the same way. It is also very common for a man, on receiving the pipe, to point the bowl toward the ground, and the stem toward the heavens. There is, perhaps, no more interesting ceremony than that of smoking. It is to them a great luxury, and as they sit in groups around, puffing out large volumes of smoke, and conversing in a low, quiet tone of voice, they present the most perfect picture of happiness and contentment.

"The Indians, both male and female, arrive at the age of puberty at from fifteen to seventeen years, occasionally, though rarely, at thirteen or fourteen. Rare instances are known of females being married at thirteen years of age."

Abortion is produced, to a greater or less extent, among all the Indians. When a woman does not wish to give birth to a live child, she takes a stick which is used for digging the *pomme blanche*, or prairie turnip, and presses the end of it against the abdomen, causing the death of the child in utero. It is very seldom that there is any fatal result to the mother from this operation.

I can find no reliable evidence that any of the prairie Indians are especially neglectful of their aged people. When they become so old that they cannot walk, they are not left to perish, but are provided with horses or a travais, and cared for until they die. There may be cases in which there is a want of filial affection, but the contrary is the general rule. So long as a chief can hunt and go to war, he can maintain his influence in his tribe, but as soon as he fails through age to lead his people to battle, his son takes his place, or some other man who, by acts of bravery, may have elevated himself to the position of chief.

It is not so uncommon for the Indians to have deformed children as one would suppose at first glance. The vicissitudes of a nomadic life usually destroy such children very soon after birth. They are usually cared for in time of plenty, but when food is scarce they are allowed to starve. I was told by the Indians themselves, that many are born deaf and dumb, and blind. An instance occurred of a woman giving birth to four children at a time, two of which were blind. I saw a very pretty half-breed girl among the Crows, who had been deaf and dumb from her birth, otherwise she apppeared bright and intelligent.

There are a great number of dances among the Indians, the most important of which is the sun dance. The names of a portion are given below. Oh-i'-om, the Sun Dance, "to dance and look at the sun." The principal medicine-man gathers all the warriors in the village together at a certain place, and each one makes an offering to the sun, and then they all dance and beat the drum from two to four days, or as long as they can endure without eating or drinking. They do not sing, but whistle a continuous note on a bone instrument, tap the drum, and dance. They also fold the skin in different parts of the body, piercing a hole through it with a sharp knife, insert a stick, and fasten the stick with a cord to a pole above their heads, or the limb of a tree. They then endeavor to break the stick or cord by the pressure of their weight, at the same time giving away a horse, or some other equally valuable present. The fold of skin sometimes tears away, producing a most painful wound. They do this that they may be successful in all their undertakings, have plenty of buffalo, kill numbers of their enemies, have no sickness, &c.

The commencement of this ceremony is brought about by some one in the village having a dream, which informs him that the sun controls all the affairs of life. He then bids all the people to prepare for its performance. The same dance occurs among the Dakotas, and is called by them Wi-wai'-aŋ-i-wa'-ći.

E-a-ćis-to, Scalp Dance. When a war party goes out against the enemy, and returns with plenty of scalps, all the village, men, women, and children, join in dancing and singing, sometimes for half a day or all night. They also build large fires. The same dance occurs among the Dakotas, and is called by them I-wa'-ki-ći-pi. As the description will apply to the ceremony among both tribes, I quote from the Dakota Dictionary. "This dance follows the bringing home of the scalps of their enemies. A circle is formed, on one side of which stand the young men, with their bodies painted, with their feathers in their heads, and their drums, rattles, and other instruments of music in their hands, while on the other side stand the young women, in their best attire, carrying the scalp or scalps stretched on a hoop. The war song commences, and the women dance around, sometimes advancing towards the men, who are stationary, and then again retreating, and responding at intervals to the music in a kind of chorus. If the scalp is taken in the winter, the dance is kept up, frequently by day and night, until the leaves grow in the spring. If it is taken in the summer, they dance and rejoice over it until the leaves fall off, when it is buried."

O-ta'-mi-mi-sa'-o, Strong Heart Dance. The young men only join in this dance. The Dakotas call it ćaŋ'-te-su-tai'-wa-ći.

E-wŏk-si'-hi-wa-to: Dakota, To-ka'-la-wa-ći'-pi, the Fox Dance. The Indians make a large kettle of soup, and dance for good luck. Only the young, unmarried women, that is, virgins, join in this dance.

Ho-tum'-i-ta'-ni-o, Dog Dance; Dakota, I-haŋ'-shi-wa-pa'-wa-ći, the Big Owl Dance. The manner of performance is the same in both tribes. In this dance, all the male sex, and all the virtuous wives join. It is said that not more than four or five women dance.

O-ho-mi-no'-toh-i-o, Soldier Dance; Dakota, Wi'-ćis-ka, the White Belt Dance. Among the Dakotas, the belt that holds all their hunting apparatus is white. Only the young men join in this dance.

O-tu'-a-ta'-ni-o, Bull Head Dance; the same meaning in Dakota, Ta-taŋ'-ka-pa-wa-ći. They perform the most violent gesticulations in this dance. The men form a ring, wearing a bull's head in the shape of a mask, imitating the grunt of a bull. Two women stand inside the ring. It is the most picturesque and exciting of all their dances.

Mo'-he-ta'-ni-o, the Elk Dance; Dakota, He-ĥa'-ka-wa-ći. This is a sort of Medicine dance. All join, men, women, and children.

Na-ko-yo-su'-is-to, Bear Dance; Dakota, Ma-to'-wa-ći-pi. A man dreams of having a fight with a bear; he awakes in the morning, and if he overcame the bear in his dream, he tells his friends, and they all have a dance. Only the males join. The motions and grunt of the bear are imitated.

As we have before remarked, our previous knowledge of the Shyennes and their language is very limited. A brief list of the "Words and Vocabularies" of the Shyenne language is given in Ludwig's "Literature of American Aboriginal Languages," to which nothing has been added up to this date. In the Archæologia Americana, vol. ii, p. 379, is a list of the names of the Shyenne chiefs who signed the treaty of July, 1825. It so happens, that all the names were given in the Dakota, and are, therefore, no contribution to the Shyenne.

Reise des Prinzen Maximilian zu Wied, Coblenz, 1839–1841, ii vols., 4to. On pp. 487–489, about sixty-seven words of the Shyenne are given, apparently very correctly taken.

The vocabulary secured by Lieut. Abert, U. S. A., is, perhaps, the most valuable one ever taken, though quite brief. Great use was made of this by Mr. Albert Gallatin, in his Comparison of the Indian Languages. See Transactions of the American Ethnological Society, vol. ii, pp. cxvi–cxviii. It was first published in Abert's Report of his Examination of New Mexico, in the years 1846 and 1847, pp. 467–518, forming a part of Emory's Notes of a Military Reconnoissance, &c., Washington, 1848, 8vo. It seems that it was from Lieut. Abert's vocabulary, that Gallatin first detected the affinity of the Shyenne to languages of the Algonkin stock. "Out of forty-seven Shyenne words for which we have equivalents in other languages, there are thirteen which are indubitably Algonkin, and twenty-five which have affinities more or less remote with some of the languages of that family."*

A vocabulary of nearly three hundred words is published in Schoolcraft's "History and Prospects of the Indian Tribes of the United States," Part III, pp. 346–459. John S. Smith, to whom the credit is given for this vocabulary, is the only white man who ever claimed to have anything like a thorough acquaintance with the Shyenne tongue. He was interpreter and trader for that tribe for many years. He at this time (1860) keeps a trading-house near the mouth of Cache la Poudre creek, on the South Platte.

So far as we can ascertain, the above list comprises everything of an original character, published in regard to the Shyenne language, up to this date.

The following grammatical notes and vocabulary, were obtained during the winter of 1859 and '60, at the Indian Agency on the South Platte, about one hundred miles west of Fort Laramie. I was fortunate in securing the services of a very intelligent Shyenne Indian, who spoke, in addition to his own tongue, the Dakota with almost equal fluency. His wife was a very intelligent Dakota woman, who understood the English language quite well. With the aid of a Dakota interpreter, I would pronounce the words from the Dakota Dictionary, published by the Smithsonian Institution, and the Indian would then give the corresponding words in the Shyenne language. I, therefore, feel much confidence in the accuracy of the materials thus obtained.

* Gallatin, Transactions American Ethnological Society, vol. ii, p. cxi. Langue des Indiens Cheyennes (numerals), Bulletin de la Société de Géographie, Paris, 1846, 8vo. Third series, tome vi, pp. 381–386.

CHAPTER VII.

REMARKS ON THE GRAMMATICAL STRUCTURE OF THE SHYENNE LANGUAGE.

I. Nouns.

1. In the Shyenne language no change is made in the terminations of nouns to indicate their case. The nominative and objective cases are inferred from the position of the nouns in a sentence, and the idea of possession is denoted by fragment-pronouns, which are usually prefixed, and sometimes, though rarely, inserted into the nouns.

2. Nouns have two numbers, singular and plural; and these are usually distinguished by difference of termination, as: (sing.) o'-he, a river; (pl.) o-he'-ist; (sing.) wiḧ'-pōts, a leaf; (pl.) wiḧ'-po-tots; (sing.) mu'-i-no, a horse; (pl.) mu'-i-no-ham; (sing.) na'-e, otter; (pl.) na'-in.

a. There seem to be two forms of the plural number, one of which denotes a moderate number of individuals, and the other a great many; as, (sing.) ho'-ma, a beaver; (1st pl.) ho-ma', several beavers; (2d pl.) ho-ma-e'-yo, a great many beavers.

b. The plural of some nouns is formed by simple change of accent from one syllable to another; as (sing.) ho'-tum, a dog; (pl.) ho-tum'; (sing.) ho'-ma, a beaver; (pl.) ho-ma'; (sing.) no'-man, a fish; (pl.) no-man'.

3. The gender of nouns is denoted by the use of different words; as, o-to-a', a bull; mi, a cow; o-tu'-a-mu, a male elk; mi'-i-mu, a female elk; wo-stun', a man; hi, a woman.

II. Adjectives.

4. In the Dakota, Blackfoot, Crow, and other Indian languages of the Northwest, the adjective usually follows the noun which it qualifies; but in the Shyenne it most commonly precedes, though examples of both cases occur; as, e-ku'-si-si'-o-tum, a sharp-nosed dog; mōḧ-ta'-o-hum, a black horse; mai-is'-ći, a red shirt. In the following instances, the adjective follows the noun: ho'-i-av-si-wa', bad lands; wo-i'-ha-i-nōt, thick clouds; i-shi'-ni-pit'-siv, a snowy day.

5. Adjectives have two numbers, singular and plural, the same as nouns. There are also two plural forms; as,

Singular.	Plural. 1st form.	Plural. 2d form.	
na-tōs,	na-to-si-o,	na-to'-sis-to,	cold.
no-mōḧ'-ta,	no-mōḧ'-tai-yo,	no-mōḧ'-tas-to,	well.
i-ha'-i-yōm,	i-ha-i-yo'-mi-o,	i-ha-i-yo'-mis-to,	fat.
e-ho'-ni-ćist,	e-ho'-ni-ćis'-ta-o,		lazy.
e-wo'-kōm,	e-wo-ko'-mi-o,	e-wo-ko'-mo-nist,	white.

6. The cardinal numbers are as follows:

one, nŏh.
two, nih.
three, na'-a.
four, ni-pa.
five, nŏn.
six, na-su'-tu.
seven, ni'-so-tu.
eight, na-nŏh'-tu.
nine, sŏh'-tu.
ten, ma-tŏh'-to.
eleven, ma-tŏh'-to-o-ta-nŏh'.
twelve, ma-tŏh'-to-o-ta-nih'.
thirteen, ma-tŏh'-to-o-ta-na'-a.
fourteen, ma-tŏh'-to-o-ta-ni'-pa.
fifteen, ma-tŏh'-to-o-ta-nŏn'.
sixteen, ma-tŏh'-to-o-ta-na-su'-tu.
seventeen, ma-tŏh'-to-o-ta-ni'-so-tu.
eighteen, ma-tŏh'-to-o-ta-na-nŏh'-tu.
nineteen, ma-tŏh'-to-o-ta-sŏh'-tu.
twenty, ni-so'.
twenty-one, ni-so'-o-ta-nŏh'.
thirty, na-no'.
thirty-one, na-no'-o-ta-nŏh'.
forty, ni-pu'.
fifty, no-no'.
sixty, na-so'-to-nu.
seventy, ni-so'-to-nu.
eighty, na-nŏh'-to-nu.
ninety, sŏh'-to-nu.
one hundred, ma-tŏh'-to-nu.
two hundred, nih'-a-ma-tŏh'-to-nu.
three hundred, na'-a-ma-tŏh'-to-nu.
four hundred, ni'-pa-ma-tŏh'-to-nu.
five hundred, nŏn'-ma-tŏh'-to-nu.
six hundred, na-su'-tu-ma-tŏh'-to-nu.
seven hundred, ni-so'-tu-ma-tŏh'-to-nu.
eight hundred, na-nŏh'-tu-ma-tŏh'-to-nu.
nine hundred, sŏh'-tu-ma-tŏh'-to-nu.
one thousand, ma-tŏh'-tu-ma-tŏh'-tu-nu.

7. Other forms occur, either as numeral adjectives or adverbs.

i-o-ni'-so-wah'-si-o, twice, in two ways.
nih'-ut-si-na'-wo, a double-barrel gun.
ni-ni-shish', you two.
e-no'-ka, one pair.
e-nih-anst', two pairs.
e-na-hanst', three pairs.
na-sŭh'-ta-tsi'-na-wo, six mouths, a revolving pistol.
i-na-sŏh'-to-yŏs, six toes, a man with six toes.
e'-ni-wo'-wa-tanst', in four ways, four times.

III. Adverbs.

8. Adverbs usually precede the verbs which they qualify; as, po-no-i-wo'-no-o-ist, to throw anything down; i-hav'-siv-i-mi'-i-ŏts, to smell badly.

IV. Prepositions.

9. Prepositions generally follow the nouns which they govern; as, ho-ev', on the ground.

V, VI. Conjunctions and Interjections.

10. Of conjunctions and interjections there are but few. Most of the former are connected with other words, though a few are separate; as, ma'-tu, and, also.

VII. Pronouns.

11. The fragment or incorporated pronouns are prefixed to, or inserted into nouns, adjectives, and verbs.

ma, an arrow.
ma-hŏts', pl. arrows.
na-ma', my arrow.
ni-ma', thy arrow.
ho-ist', a fire, or his fire.
na-to'-ist, my fire.
ni-to'-ist, thy fire.
ho-i'-stats, pl. fires, or their fires.
na-to'-is-tam, our fires.
ni-to'-is-tam, your fires.
ma'-ćĭk, a bow, or his bow.
ma'-takst, pl. bows.
na-ma'-ćĭk, my bow.
ni-ma'-ćĭk, thy bow.
mo'-ćĭk, a knife.
na-mo'-ćĭk, my knife.
ni-mo'-ćĭk, thy knife.
i-mo-ćĭk, his knife.
mo-takst', knives.
na-mo-takst', our knives.
ni-mo-takst', your knives.

12. The following are the words that denote kindred, and changes are made to denote the person of the relationship affirmed, by prefixing to the nouns the fragmentary personal pronouns; as,

na-ho-e', my father.
na-ko-e', my mother.
na'-a, my son.
na-tŏn', my daughter.
na-nih'-a, my grandchild.
ni-nih'-a, your grandchild.
nih'-a, a grandchild.
na-e-ih'-a, my great grandchild.
na-ni'-a, my elder brother (spoken by a male).
na-ta'-ta-nim, my elder brother (said by a female).
nam'-ham, elder sister (said by a male).
hin'-i, elder sister (said by a female).
i'-he-mi-ŏts, she is an elder sister.
na'-he-mi-ŏts, she is my elder sister.
ni'-he-mi-ŏts, she is your elder sister.
nah'-a-him, my younger sister (said by a male).
ni-ah'-a-him, your younger sister (said by a male).
i-ah'-a-him, his younger sister (said by a male).
is'-i-ma, younger sister (said by a female).
na-is'-i-ma, my younger sister (said by a female).
ni-is'-i-ma, your younger sister (said by a female).
na-hi'-ni-hi'-nŏts, my brothers.
na-e'-ka-e'-ni-nŏts, my sisters.
ni-to', brother-in-law.
ni-tam', sister-in-law (wife's sister).
na-wi'-si, a woman's husband's brother's wife.
him'-shim, a father-in-law.
na-nim-shim', my father-in-law.
ni-nim-shim', your father-in-law.
na'-him-shim'-i-nŏt. (?)
ni'-him-shim'-i-nŏt. (?)
i'-him-shim'-i-nŏt. (?)
na'-him-shim'-i-no. (?)
ni'-him-shim'-i-hu. (?)
ni'-him-shim'-i-no. (?)
na-han', his aunt.
na-na-han', my aunt.
ni-na-han', your aunt.
it-sin'-ŏt, nephew, his nephew.
na-tsin'-ŏt, my nephew.
ni-tsin'-ŏt, your nephew.
na-it-sin'-o-ta, our nephews.
ni-it-sin'-o-ta, your nephews.
na-ham', his niece.
na-na-ham', my niece.
ni-na-ham', your niece.
na-na-hai'-ha-mi-nuts, our nieces.
na-hai'-ham-i-wo, our nieces.
e-mi-shim', his stepfather.
na-mi-shim', my stepfather.
ni-mi-shim', thy stepfather.
nish'-ki-e, mother-in-law (said by male and female).
hi-hum', a husband.
hi-hum'-i-wo, pl. husbands.
na-i-hum', my husband.
ni-i-hum', thy husband.
e-is'-tsi-im, his wife.
e-is'-tsi-im'-i-o, his wives.

na-tsi-im', my wife.
ni-tsi-im', thy wife.
ni-sis', a man's male cousin.

13. The single pronouns are divided into separate or incorporated, or those which form separate words, or those which are prefixed to or inserted into verbs, adjectives, and nouns. The following is a list of the principal separate pronouns, personal or otherwise:

na-ni'hu, I.
ni-ni'-hu, thou.
i-ni'-hu, he or it.
na-ni'-hu-in, we.
ni-ni'-hu-in, you.
in-i-hu-wi'-o, they.
na-tsi'-ōts, mine.
nis-tsi'-ōts, thine.
is-tsi'-ōts, his, hers, its.
nat-so-tan', me, myself.
nit-so-tan', thou, thyself.
is-tso-wiv', they, themselves.
ne'-wi-shi'-wōs, both, they two.
ni-wa'-as, who.
ni-wa'-si-o, pl.
hi'-nu-wa'-it, what.
to'-nish, when.
tas, which.
to-nist', how many.
no'-tsi-to, this.
nis'-i-wo, that.
he-to', these.
he-to-is'-ta-nuts, those.
no-nis'-to-whews, those.

VIII. Adjectives.

14. Adjectives and adjective-verbs are declined, by prefixing the fragment-pronouns, in the following manner:

na-pi'-wa, I am good.
ni-pi'-wa, thou art good.
i-pi'-wa, he is good.
na-pa'-wan, we are good.
ni-pi'-wan, you are good.
i-pi'-wa-na'-no, they are good.

na-tai'-pa-wan, I will be good.
ni-tai'-pa-wan, thou wilt be good.
e-tai'-pa-wan, he will be good.
na-tai'-pa-wa'-na-nōn, we will be good.
ni-tai'-pa-wa'-na-nōn, you will be good.
e-tai'-pa-wa'-na-no, they will be good.

*na-shi-pau'-a, I am already good or handsome.
ni-shi-pau'-a, thou art already good or handsome.
i-shi-pau'-a, he is already good or handsome.
na-shi-pau'-av, we are already good or handsome.
ni-shi-pau'-av, you are already good or handsome.
i-shi-pau'-av, i-shi-pau'-a-na-no, } they are already good or handsome.

na-pau'-hai, na-pe'-whai, } I am handsome or pretty.
ni-pau'-hai, thou art handsome or pretty.
i-piv'-hai, he is handsome or pretty.
na-pau'-haim, I am handsome or pretty.
ni-pau'-haim, you are handsome or pretty.
i-pau-hai'-yo, i-pau-hais'-to, i-piv-hais'-to, } they are handsome or pretty.

na-pi'-wi-e-wi, I am well, or in good condition.
ni-pi'-wi-e-wi, thou art well.
i-pi'-wi-e-wi, he is well.
na-pi'-wi-iv'-nim, we are well.
ni-pi'-wi-iv'-nim, you are well.
i-pi'-wi-iv'-ni-o, i-pi'-wi-iv'-nis-to, } they are well.

* The adverb nish is inserted, meaning now, already, quickly.

na-na'-tŏs, I am cold.
ni-na'-tŏs, thou art cold.
i-na'-tŏs, he is cold.
na-na'-to-sim, we are cold.
ni-na'-to-sim, you are cold.
i-na'-to-si'-o, } they are cold.
i-na'-to-sis'-to, }
na-sa'-na-to-sin, I am not cold.
ni-sa'-na-to-sin, thou art not cold.
i-sa'-na-to-sin, he is not cold.
na-sa'-na-to-si'-him, we are not cold.
ni-sa'-na-to-si'-him, you are not cold.
i-sa'-na-to-si-hi-o, they are not cold.

na-shi-na'-tŏs, now I am cold.
ni-shi-na'-tŏs, now thou art cold.
i-shi-na'-tŏs, now he is cold.
na-shi-na'-to-sim, now we are cold.
ni-shi-na'-to-sim, now you are cold.
i-shi-na'-to-si-o, } now they are cold.
i-shi-na'-to-sis-to, }

There is a form in frequent use among the Shyennes, which expresses future time by prefixing an adverb; as:

nŏh'-a-na-na'-tŏs, I will be cold.
nŏh'-a-ni-na'-tŏs, thou wilt be cold.

na-no-mŏh'-ta, I am well (not sick).
ni-no-mŏh'-ta, thou art well.
e-no-mŏh'-ta, he is well.
na-no-mŏh'-tam, we are well.
ni-no-mŏh'-tam, you are well.
e-no-mŏh'-tai-yo, } they are well.
e-no-mŏh'-tas-to, }

i-mŏh-tan', black.
na-mŏh-tan'-wa, me black, I am black.
ni-mŏh-tan'-wa, thou art black.
i-mŏh-tan'-wa, he is black.
i-mŏh'-ta-whai'-yu, black-black (emphatic), like the Dakota sap-sap'-pa.

IX. Verbs.

15. Shyenne verbs have three moods, indicative, imperative, and infinitive; three tenses, present, past, and future; three persons, first, second, and third; two numbers, singular and plural. There are two forms of the plural; the common form meaning a number or several, and the other is probably caused by the addition of a-is'-to, a great many, like the similar form in the Blackfoot verbs, by the addition of a-ku'-a-wa.

na-wi'-ats, I am.
ni-wi'-ats, thou art.
i-wi'-ats, he is.
na-wi'-at-sim, we are.
ni-wi'-at-sim, you are.
i-wi'-at-si'-o, they are.
i-wi'-at-sis'-to, they are.

na-pau'-i-mit, I give liberally.
ni-pi'-wi-mit, thou givest liberally.
i-pau'-i-mitst, he gives liberally.
na-pi'-wi-mi-tain, we give liberally.
ni-pi'-wi-mi-tain, you give liberally.
i-pi'-wi-mi-ta, } they give liberally.
i-pi'-wi-mi-tai'-yo, }

By inserting the word *nish*, now, at once, quickly, we have the other forms of this verb, conjugated as follows:

na-shi-pau'-i-mit, I give liberally now.
ni-shi-pi'-wa-mit, thou givest liberally now.
i-shi-pi'-wa-mi'-o, he gives liberally now.
na-shi-pi'-wa-mi'-tain, we give liberally now.

ni-shi-pi'-wa-mi-tain, you give liberally now.
i-shi-pi'-wa-mi'-a-to, they give liberally now.

SECOND FORM.

na-pi'-wi-i-shi, I give liberally now.
ni-pi'-wi-i-shi, thou givest liberally now.
i-pi'-wi-i-shi, he gives liberally now.
na-pi'-wi-i-shi'-im, we give liberally now.
ni-pi'-wi-i-shi'-im, you give liberally now.
i-pi'-wi-i-shi'-i-o, } they give liberally now.
i-pi'-wi-i-shi'-is-to, }

na-mis'-a, I eat.
ni-mis'-a, thou eatest.
i-mis'-a, he eats.
na-mis'-em, we eat.
ni-mis'-em, you eat.
i-mis'-i-o, they eat.

na-shi'-i-ni-mis'-a, I eat quickly now.
ni-shi'-i-ni-mis'-a, thou eatest quickly now.
i-shi'-i-ni-mis'-a, he eats quickly now.
na-shi'-i-ni-mis'-em, we eat quickly now.
ni-shi'-i-ni-mis'-em, you eat quickly now.
i-shi'-i-ni-mis'-i-o, they eat quickly now.

na-mis'-a-tun, I will eat.
ni-mis'-a-tun, thou wilt eat.
i-mis'-a-tun, he will eat.
na-mis'-a-tun-öm, we will eat.
ni-mis'-a-tun-öm, you will eat.
i-mis'-a-tun-öh'-to, they will eat.

mis'-a (imp. sing.), eat. (Dakota, wo-ta-wo'.)
wi'-na-mis'-a (imp. pl.). (Dakota, wo-ta-po'.)

This verb may also be negatively conjugated by the insertion of the negative particle *sa*.

na-sa'-mis-a-tun, I will not eat.
ni-sa'-mis-a-tun, thou wilt not eat, &c.

na-pi'-o-si-man, I think badly of some one secretly in the heart.
ni-pi'-o-si-man, thou thinkest badly, &c.
i-pi'-o-sim, he thinks badly, &c.
na-pi'-o-si-ma'-nim, we think badly, &c.
ni-pi'-o-si-ma'-nim, you think badly, &c.
i-pi'-o-si'-mi-o, } they think badly, &c.
i-pi'-o-si'-mo-ći'-sto, }

e'-wi-ist (infinitive), to beg.

na-wi-is'-to-mo, I beg.
ni-wi-is'-to-mo, thou dost beg.
i-wi-is'-to-mo, he begs.
na-wi-is'-to-mo'-in, we beg.
ni-wi-is'-to-mo'-in, you beg.
i-wi-is'-to-mo'-i-o, they beg.

mi'-ta-nut, to remember.

na-mi'-ta-nut, I remember.
ni-mi'-ta-nut, thou dost remember.
i-mi'-ta-nut, he remembers.
na-mi-ta'-nut-a-nu, we remember.
ni-mi-ta'-nut-a-nu, you remember.
i-mi-ta'-nut-o, they remember.

na-o'-mo-töm, I breathe.
ni-o'-mo-töm, thou breathest.
i-o'-mo-töm, he breathes.
na-o'-mo-to-mim, we breathe.
ni-o'-mo-to-mim, you breathe.
i-o'-mo-to'-mis-to, they breathe.

o'-mo-töm (imp. sing.) breathe.
o'-mo-to-mist (imp. pl.)

na'-no-mats, I steal.
ni'-no-mats, thou stealest.
e'-no-mats, he steals.
na-no-ma'-tsim, we steal.
ni-no-ma'-tsim, you steal.
e-no-ma'-tsi-o, } they steal.
e-no-ma'-tsi-to, }

na-tai'-no-mats, I will steal, I am going to steal.
ni-tai'-no-mats, thou wilt steal.

e-tai'-no-mats, he will steal.
na-tai'-no-ma'-tsim, we will steal.
ni-tai'-no-ma'-tsim, you will steal.
e-tai'-no-ma'-tsi-o, } they will steal.
e-tai'-no-ma'-tsi-to, }

na-ni'-no-mats, I have stolen, I am done stealing.
ni-ni'-no-mats, thou hast stolen.
e-ni'-no-mats, he has stolen.
na-ni'-no-ma'-tsim, we have stolen.
ni-ni'-no-ma'-tsim, you have stolen.
e-ni'-no-ma'-tsi-o, } they have stolen.
e-ni'-no-ma'-tsi-to, }

no-ma'-tsi-ŏst (imp. sing), steal thou.
no-ma'-tsi-o (imp. pl.)

na-ŏh-to', I trade or barter.
ni-ŏh-to', thou dost trade or barter.
e-ŏh-to', he trades or barters.
na-ŏh-to'-wam, we trade or barter.
ni-ŏh-to'-wam, you trade or barter.
e-ŏh-to'-wa-o, } they trade or barter.
e-ŏh-to'-wa-to, }

na-tai'-ŏh-to, I will trade or barter.
ni-tai'-ŏh-to, thou wilt trade or barter.
e-tai'-ŏh-to, he will trade or barter.
na-tai'-ŏh-to-wam', we will trade or barter.
ni-tai'-ŏh-to-wam', you will trade or barter.
e-tai-ŏh-to-wa'-o, } they will trade or barter.
e-tai-ŏh-to-wa'-to, }

na-i-nŏh'-to, I have traded or bartered, or I have done trading.
ni-i-nŏh'-to, thou hast traded, &c.
e-nŏh'-to, he has traded, &c.
na-i-nŏh'-to-wam, we have traded, &c.
ni-i-nŏh'-to-wam, you have traded, &c.
e-nŏh'-to-wa-o, } they have traded, &c.
e-nŏh'-to-wa-to, }

na'-am, I shoot.
ni'-am, thou dost shoot.
i'-a-mo, he shoots.
na'-a-mŏn, we shoot.
ni'-a-mŏn, you shoot.
i'-a-mŏv, they shoot.

na-ta'-am, I will shoot.
ni-ta'-am, thou wilt shoot.
i-ta'-a-mo, he will shoot.
na-ta'-a-mŏn, we will shoot.
ni-ta'-a-mŏn, you will shoot.
i-ta'-a-mŏv, they will shoot.

na'-ni-am, I have shot.
ni'-ni-am, thou hast shot.
i-ni'-a-mo, he has shot.
na-ni'-a-mŏn, we have shot.
ni-ni'-a-mŏn, you have shot.
i'-ni-a-mŏv', they have shot.

am (imp. sing.) shoot.
ta'-mi (imp. pl.)

na-na'-i-yŏts, I am dead.
ni-na'-i-yŏts, thou art dead.
i-na'-i-yŏts, he is dead.
na-na'-i-yo'-tsim, we are dead.
ni-na'-i-yo'-tsim, you are dead.
i-na'-i-yo'-tsi-o, they are dead.

na'-to-isé, I wrap up anything.
ni'-to-isé, thou wrappest up anything.
i'-to-isé, he wraps up anything.
na'-to-is'-ći-nŏn, we wrap up anything.
ni'-to-is'-ći-nŏn, you wrap up anything.
i'-to-is'-ći-no, they wrap up anything.

nah'-ai-im, I cry.
ni-ah'-ai-im, thou criest.
i-ah'-ai-im, he cries.
nah'-ai-a-mim, we cry.
ni-ah'-ai-a-mim, you cry.
i-ah'-ai-a-mi-o, they cry.

e-ah'-ai-a-mi (imp. sing.), cry.

na-sa-ah'-ai-im, I do not cry.
ni-sa-ah'-ai-im, thou dost not cry.

nah-po-o'-isé, I bind or tie.
ni-ōh-po-o'-isé, thou dost bind or tie.
e-ōh-po-o'-isé, he binds or ties.
na-ōh-po-o'-is-ći-nōn, we bind or tie.
ni-ōh-po-o'-is-ći-nōn, you bind or tie.
e-ōh-po-o'-is-ći-no, they bind or tie.

e-ōh-po-o'-inst (imp.)

na-ta'-mit, I give.
ni-ta'-mit, thou givest.
i-ta'-mit, he gives.

mi'-tsi (imp.), give.
ni-mitst (imp.), give me.
tsi'-vi-mit (imp.), not give.
nu-ha'-na-ta'-mit, hold on, I give.

i-shi-mansé', to be done or finished.

na-shi-mansé', I am done or have finished.
ni-shi-mansé', thou art done or hast finished.
na-shi-man'-séi-non, we are done or have finished.
ni-shi-man'-séi-non, you are done or have finished.
i-shi-ma'-ni-o, they (a moderate number), are done or have finished.
i-shi-man'-séi-no, they (a great many), are done or have finished.

NAMES OF TRIBES, PERSONS, AND RIVERS.

o-e'-tun'-i-o, the Crows.
so'-so-ni and so'-so-i-ha'-ni, Snakes.
i-tun'-i-wo, the Skymen, Arapohos.
o-o'-ho-mo-i'-o, Dakotas generally.
o-tōh'-sōn, Little Stars, Ogallalas.
mōh-ta'-wa-ta-ta'-ni-o, Blackfeet Dakotas, the Blackfeet people.
ma'-i-sin-as, Sansarcs, No-bows, same meaning as with the Dakotas.
wo-ni-to'-na-his, Brulees, Burnt Thighs.
nih'-a-o-ćih'-a-is, Two Kettle band.
ho-tum'-mi'-hu-is, the Band that eat no dogs.
mi'-sis: one half of the Shyenne tribe call themselves mi'-sis; same name as the Platte River.
po-no-i'-ta-ni-o, the name of the other portion of the Shyennes. Different nations with whom they have been at war, gave them the name, shai-en'-a, shai-e'-la, &c.
na'-to-wo-na, the Mississippi Dakotas.
ho-he'-i-o, Assiniboins.
mōh-tau-hai'-ta-ni-o, the Blackmen, Utes.
ka-ko'-is-tsi'-a-ta'-ni-o, people who flatten their heads; the Flatheads.
po'-o-mas, blankets whitened with earth, Blackfeet.
his-tu-i'-ta-ni-o, Gros Ventres of the prairie, Atsínas. The Shyennes say that the Atsínas call themselves, "men" or "people;" hence, they have another name for them, e-ta'-ni-o, which means a people.
wi-tup-a'-tu, Comanches.
shish-i-nu'-wut-tsit'-a-ni-o, the Rattlesnake people, Kiowas; shish-i-nu'-wut, a rattlesnake.
o-ni'-ha-o, the Drum-beaters, Omahas.
ho-ni'-i-ta-ni-o, the Little Wolf people, Pawnees.
o-no'-ni-o, Arickaras.
mo-no'-ni o, Mandans.
ma-wi'-o, Red-bodied people, Mormons.
mish-i-si'-wi-o, people with hairy noses, Spaniards.
ka-he'-ta-ni-o, people with white ermines, some people who accompanied the Spaniards to trade with the Shyennes, and tied their hair with strips of white ermine skin.
hev'-hai-ta-ni-o, the hairy people, a band of the Shyennes.
is-is-i-wi'-ho-niv, head chief of the mi'-sis band.
tsi-wi'-o-nirst, the name of a chief.
he-o-ma'-ast, the Red Body, a woman's name.
ni-ni-i'-o-he, the Platte River.
wa-at'-si-wa'-i-yo-he, Deer Creek.
hi-na-i-yu'-he, Laramie Fork.
tsin'-o-o-no, Box Elder Creek, Bad-wood Creek.
ha-ha'-o-he, Very Windy Creek.
nah-o-i-yo'-he, Bear Creek.
ōh-i-i'-o-he, Lodge Pole Creek.
a-wo'-a-na-tsi'-o-he, the creek where the Pawnees cry.

The Pawnees went to war with the Shyennes, and had several of their number killed; on their return, they stayed four days on this creek, and cried for revenge, without eating or drinking.

wi-ta-ni'-o-he, Fat River, South Platte.

mah-i-mi'-no-i-o-he, Plum Creek.

i'-o-mit, Turbid or Muddy Water, Missouri River.

mo-e-i-o'-he, Elk River, Yellowstone.

NAMES OF THE PRINCIPAL MAMMALS.

o-to-a', a male buffalo. *Bos Americanus.*

mi, a female, a cow.

mŏk-si-ai', a calf.

is'-i-wan, a herd of buffalo.

o-tu'-a-mu, a male elk. *Cervus Canadensis.*

mi'-i-mu, a female elk.

mu-ki-his', a young elk.

mu-e', a herd of elk.

o-tu'-a-kŭs, mountain sheep, male. *Ovis Montana.*

mi'-i-kŭs, female sheep.

ku-sai'-i-su, young sheep.

ku-sun', a flock of sheep.

o-tu'-o-wo-ka, white-tailed deer. *Cervus leucurus.*

mi'-i-wo'-ka, female deer.

wo-ka-hais', young deer.

wo-ka'-i, a herd or flock.

mŏh'-ta-wi-wast-wa-wo'-tsi-wa, black-tailed deer. *Cervus macrotis.*

mŏh'-ta-wi-wast-wo'-tsi-wan, black-tailed deer, (pl.)

wa-ko-tsi-wai-is, small or young black-tailed deer.

wo'-ka, antelope. *Atilocapra Americana.*

wŏh-o'. *Lepus artemisia.*

ai'-ni-wo. *Lepus campestris.*

wŏh-is', swift fox, kit fox. *Vulpes velox.*

ma-ta-i'-wŏh-is', large red fox. *Vulpes macrourus.*

ha'-o, a skunk. *Mephitis mephitica.*

mŏh'-ta-wi-na'-ku, a black bear. *Ursus.* Na'-ku, a bear.

mi'-ni-wa-ka'-o. *Spermophilus tridecem lineatus.*

mi-ni-wa-ka'-tsi-po-ast. *Tamias quadrivittatus.*

no-e', red squirrel of the pines.

he-ko'-wit, a porcupine. *Erethizon epixanthus.*

NAMES OF BIRDS, SERPENTS, ETC.

mo (sing.), mo'-e (pl.), magpie. *Pica Hudsonica.*

ma-ka-i-tai'-wi-kis, a humming bird, iron bird.

ni'-po-tats-pi, nighthawk. *Chordeiles popetue.*

ai'-sto-mo-pi, poorwill. *Antrostomus Nuttalli.*

a-o-tsi'-mis-taé, prairie owl. *Athene hypugæ.*

si-wa'-ni-shish, fish-duck. *Mergus Americanus.*

po-pai'-ki-ta-nais, sandpiper. *Tringa.*

mih'-a-is, chickadee. *Parus septentrionalis.*

e-it', Maximilian's jay. *Gymnokitta cyanocephala.*

a-ka-wo'-i-tu is', sap-sucker.

ma-i-shi'-o-nun, robin-redbreast. *Turdus migratorius.*

sus'-ki-wat, a small, gray, winter sparrow.

ko-nah-tum', gray-crowned finch. *Leucosticte tephrocotis.*

mah-e-mis'-ta-a, large eared owl. *Otus Wilsonianus.*

mis-ta-kis', small gray owl. *Nyctale acadica.*

mai'-ya-tak, spatula-billed duck. *Apatula clypeata.*

sis-ta-to'-wi-kis, Say's flycatcher. *Sayornis Sayus.*

o'-i-na, small woodpecker, with a red band on back of the neck.

o-ba'-mi-shish', green-winged teal. *Nettion Carolinensis.*

ha-ma-shish', blue-winged teal. *Querquedula discors.*

mo-he-nuh, a rusty yellow hawk.

hau'-no-wa-wi-kis, butcher bird.

ho-i-no'-si-wi-kis, common snowbird. *Junco hyemalis.*

ha-ćin, mud-hen. *Fulica Americana.*

wŏh-a, bald eagle. *Haliætus leucocephalus.*

ai'-e-no, a kind of hawk.

o'-ko-um, a small screech owl. *Scops asio.*

mo-e'-a, domestic pigeon.

mah-e-min', wild pigeon. *Ectopistes migratoria.*

he-mi-ni'-su, turtle-dove. *Zenaidura Carolinensis.*

shish-to-tu'-wi-kis, cedar bird. *Ampelis cedrorum.*

mai'-e-sai'-e, cheewink. *Pipilo arcticus.*

mat-si'-ni. *Tyrannus Carolinensis.*

o'-e-ni, little nuthatch. *Sitta Canadensis.*

ma-e-wis', red-breasted grosbeak. *Guiraca melanocephala.*

sus-ki'-wat, a brown bunting.

mi-wa-wi'-kis, butcher bird. *Collyrio excurbitoides.*

e-a-wo-ći-mo-pa, a cuckoo. *Coccygus Americanus.*

mah-ta'-he-in, white-winged blackbird. *Dolichonyx oryzivorus.*

e-nis'-ko-na'-wi-wo-to'-nats, martin. *Progne purpurea.*

shih-o-to'-ne, banded-tailed hawk.

no-man'-to-ki-si-wa'-nōs, a kind of hawk.

mo-ta'-wo-is-tōm, a kind of hawk.

po-pa'-ki-ta-no'-i-sun, a sandpiper. *Tringoides.*

he-i'-mi-e. (?)

shi'-ish, a heron. *Ardea herodias.*

wi-i-e', bittern. *Botaurus lentiginosus.*

mo-o-ko', whooping crane. *Grus Americanus.*

wo'-a, a swan. *Cygnus buccinator.*

he'-na, a brant goose.

wo-ko-mi'-na, a white goose.

mai-a-tauh, a goosander.

shi-wa-ne-shish', red-breasted teal. *Querquedula cyanopteris.*

o-wish', long-billed curlew. *Numenius longirostris.*

pa'-wi-wi-kis, wax wing. *Ampelis garrulus.*

shish-to-to'-wa'-hi-yis, ruffed grouse. *Bonasa umbellus.*

shi-shi-noh'-uts, a rattlesnake. *Crotalus confluentus.*

sas-ko'-wi-tan, a striped water-snake. *Eutainia Haydeni.*

ni-e', large prairie snake. *Pituophis Sayi.*

o-ho'-i-tsi-mim, a green snake. *Bascanion flaviventris.*

ka-ko'-i-mim, a bull snake. *Heterodon nasicus.*

ma'-i-min. (?)

moh'-ta-wi-min, water moccasin. *Nerodia sipedon.*

nis'-tōh'-an, a round turtle that sits on the prairie, looks like a "buffalo chip," and if undisturbed, watches the sun, and turns with it.

ha-ta'-o-wis, a swift, or lizard, found in the sand-hills. *Plestiodon.*

ho'-o-ma, a musquito.

hah'-nōm, a horse-fly.

minst'k-so-ni, small insects, ants, lice, &c.

mi'-shi-min, caterpillars.

NAMES OF PLANTS.

ho-i-nai'-i-mo-i, a plant found near the summits of the high mountains, growing on the rocks in thick masses, like moss.

wih-ći-wa-no, *Sarcobatus vermicularis*, called by the traders "grease-wood." It is a chenopodiaceous plant, grows in thick clumps, three to six feet high, and is often used for fuel by the Indians and voyageurs in their travels over the treeless prairies. It is very abundant throughout the saline clays of the cretaceous and tertiary formations of the Upper Missouri, but more especially abundant in the valleys of the Yellowstone and Missouri near their sources.

tōh-to-i-wih'-i-wa'-no, a shrub somewhat similar to the last.

mah'-i-wa'-no, *Artemisia trifida*, a very abundant shrub along the bottoms of streams, as well as the uplands on the Upper Missouri. It grows sometimes to the height of ten feet, with stems six inches in diameter, and is also useful for fuel.

he'-i-wa-nost', *Artemisia frigida*, wild sage.

kōk-si-wa'-no, a species of *Artemisia* like *A. trifida*, growing on the Big-horn Mountains.

wa-ni'-tsi-pa-i-me'-i-its, a low sage; herbaceous.

mah-i-mi'-ka-ist, *Linosyris graveolens*, a shrub associated with the grease-wood and sage, and used as fuel.

o-i-nai'-i-ko-wōst, *Phlox Hoodi*, a low species; looks like gray, rigid moss.

ha-ma-mih'-a-ist, *Gutierrizia euthamiæ.*

wōh-pi-wih'-i-wa-no, *Eurotia lanata.*

ći-hōs-ći'-a-wo'-e-ist, a *Solidago*, named from its large yellow flowers.

mi-mi'-a-tōn, spruce pine. *Abies.*

wa'-no-wan, *Frasera*, a tall plant growing in the mountains.

ha-ma-sis'-ti-to, *Pinus.*

he-yo-wo'-ist, all kinds of moss.

mah-i-no-a-ni'-o-nuts, *Chimaphila umbellata.*

shi-ni-wa'-tsi-wa-mo'-e, *Potentilla Norvegica.*

ma-ōst', a tall, fine species of *Eriogonum.*

he-ho-wa-nis'-tōts, a yellow moss like lichen, used for dyeing porcupine quills.

he-si'-i-yo-tsi'-mo-ist, *Marchantia polymorpha*, used as a medicine.

tsiħ-i-wŏp-tsa'-a-wo-ist, *Achillea millifolium*.

wo-ko-mi-si'-i-ōts, *Entoca sericea*.

tōħ'-to-i-wa-nōst, a gray shrubby plant, like *Linosyris*.

tōħ-to-i-ćiħ'-i-wo-yast, a common ground lichen.

tsi-waks-tsi'-a-wo-ist, a fire-weed growing on the tops of the mountains. *Erechthites*.

tōħ-to-e'-o-pais, a fungus, a small puff-ball.

ćiħ-ća-e'-o-ni'-o-wist, a shrub growing abundantly in the Shyenne country.

mish-kim', box elder. *Acer negundo*.

hais-taħ-pa-nis'-to-tuts, "white grass or weeds;" a low species of *Eriyonum* growing among the rocks.

eħ'-o-wo-ist, "jagged seeded." *Atriplex*.

i-a-kis'. *Spirea*.

o-ta'-tōn-wi-si'-i-ōts, "green medicine;" a plant growing on the Big-horn Mountains.

ma-ko'-ist, "red-weed." *Epilobium effusum*.

we'-si-wo, a kind of grass, the stem of which is used to clean out the pipe-stem.

na-si'-tsi-wo, "pipe-tail grass," a species of grass.

ho-i-nōs, "bunch-weed;" a species of *Erigeron*, growing in bunches.

hai'-ku-ni-ka-maħ', "strong or hard wood;" a bush growing in the mountains.

si-wōpst-ći'-a-wo-ist, "gray grass with white blossoms." *Antennaria plantaginifolia*.

ais'-to-mi-wa-nōst, "white weed of the prairie," a woolly plant.

tseħ-e'-wo-nist, "rattling weed." *Penstemon*.

he-e-wa-nōst', "woman-weed;" so called because it is used by the women during the period of their menses as a tea. *Artemisia frigida*.

mōħ-ta'-wi-wa-nōst, "black-gray grass." *Artemisia ludoviciana*.

so-so'-ni-wa-nōst, "snake-weed;" a kind of *Artemisia*.

wi-ōħ'-i-wa-nōst, "bad-weed." It is called "bad-weed" because it catches the clothes with its thorns.

ksa-ma-tum-ōts, "bush that the big-horn eats;" grows in the mountains; looks like a *Smilax*.

hai-i-so', "prairie-water weed." *Polygonum ramosissimum*.

wis-ki-e'-mi-nōst, "sweet blueberries;" a large-leaved plant growing in the mountains.

mi-ni-mi-nōtst, "rattlesnake bush;" so called because the rattlesnake is supposed to eat the leaves. *Berberis aquifolium*.

shi-sto-to', a spruce pine.

ma-pi'-mo-ist, "weeds that the water flows through." *Parnassia*.

na-ko'-is-ta'-tsi-mi-nu, "bear berry," black haw; so called because the bears eat the fruit.

si-uħ-i-i'-si-o-te-si'-ist, fox-tail grass; named from the beards which get in the mouth, and work down the throat, and excite coughing.

hōn-ski-wi'-si-wo, "grass with a small stem," a species of grass.

i-ta'-ni-wa-nōst', "man's weed," *Artemisia Canadensis*.

mo-i-ać', "milk-weed," *Lygodesmia juncea*.

mo-tōć', "bitterwood," *Populus*, bitter cottonwood.

ais'-to-mi-mōħ'-shin, "sweet-smelling prairie weed," *Scrophularia nodosa*.

ais'-to-mis-ta'-si-mi-nu', "the prickly berry," *Ribes Missouriensis*.

o-i-nōs', "wood that grows in the prairie," *Helianthus giganteus*.

mōħ'-ta-wi-si'-i-ōtst, "black medicine-weed," *Liatris*.

ho-e-tōħ'-o-nōst, "gummy weed," *Grindelia squarrosa*.

miħ-a-haist', "bird-weed," same as the name of a bird.

o'-ta-mi-mi-nōst', "dog bush," *Acer Pennsylvanicum*.

wi-ski-e'-mi-nu, "very sweet berry," *Rubus strigosus*.

wi-ski-e'-mi-nuć, red raspberries.

ma-ćai'-no-was, the burrs of *Glycyrrhiza lepidota*.

ma-ćai'-no-wa-si-wu', the stalk of the last.

wish-ke', *Populus*, sweet cottonwood.

ma-pi'-mōħ-shin, "sweet-smelling water-weed," *Mentha Canadensis*.

miħ-ni-mi-nust', so called because the animals crush the fruit with their teeth, *Celtis crassifolia*.

na-ko-is-ta'-tsi-min "bear-killer," *Crategus coccineus*. It received its name from the Indians, because they say that when the bears eat the fruit, it causes them so great pain, that they try to tear out their bowels.

CHAPTER VIII.

VOCABULARY OF THE SHYENNE LANGUAGE.

A.

above, e-am′, above, overhead.

abominable, si′-e-to-wa′-no, very mean, abominable.

abreast, e-mo-no′-i-o-tsi-o, abreast, in a row.

abstain from, e-ni-ni-ta′-mi-ōts, to abstain from, to leave off when one has eaten enough.

accept, e′-i-stan, to accept or take.

acid, tsi-wi-ki′-i-nu, acid.

acquaint, e-ōh′-ta-han, to relate or acquaint.

acrid, e-wi-ōh′-i-i-no, acrid, sharp to the taste.

across, i-ta-ta′-o-mi, across, by a near way, a cut-off.

adhesive, e-pa′-o-yōts, sticky, adhesive.

adulteress, he-im′-i-sa-ni, an adulteress.

afar off, ta′-a-is, i-ha′-is, ha′-ish, at a great distance, afar off, far away, a long distance.

after, ho-oh′, following after, immediately after.

afraid, shi′-i-pais, to be afraid, to be astonished.

i-mo′-si-o-tōh′-ta, to be scared or afraid secretly.

ni-i-e′-yo, to make afraid by talking to.

na-a′-hi-yo, I am afraid.

na-sa′-a-hi-yo, I am not afraid.

e-e-po-no′-ma-au, to have fear, to be afraid.

ago, o-o-mi′-shi-iv, long ago.

all, ni-ta′-o, all, the whole.

ni-ta-a′, all over, all around.

ho-i-ni′-ta-o, all the world over.

alone, e-ho-wa′-a-haiv, alone, single, unmarried.

always, ho-wōh′-po-nit, at all times, at any time, always.

and, ma′-tu, and, also.

annoyed, in-ha-stun′, bothered, annoyed.

any, nasts-mih′-o-yats, any one, no matter who.

appear, i-mi′-i-ōts, to be visible, manifest, appear.

tsi-me′-i-nis, to appear occasionally, as one passing under a hill, or as the sun through clouds.

arm, he′-ats, an arm; na′-ats, my arm.

ni′-ats, thy arm.

he-a-tsi-ni′-wōts (pl.), arms.

ma-i-tsi′-nōts (dual?), both arms.

e-tsi-nōn′, the armpit.

e-wōh′-ći-ōn, the bend of the arm.

i-ći-na′, the part of the arm above the elbow.

ni-hi′-sta-tan, within arm's reach.

e′-e-wo-ni, an armful of wood.

arrive, i-nih′-o-yōts, to arrive at a place.

e-tam-sto′-i-yōts, to arrive, and remain at home.

arrow, ma, an arrow.

ma-hōts′ (pl.), arrows.

na-ma′, my arrow.

ni-ma′, thy arrow.

ascend, e-i′, to ascend, as a hill.

ashes, pa′-a, ashes.

pa-isé′, (pl.)

o-sta′-pa-a. (?)

ask, ni-midst′, to beg, or ask of any one.

nih′-o-mist, to ask for anything.

assembly, i-mo-hi′-no-is-to, an assembly of men.

astride, i-tsi′-o-i-ta′-ho, straddling, astride.

i-ni′-sko-na, to sit astride of anything.

at, nai′-nu, at or to.

attack, e′-min-hau, to charge on, to attack.

i-ta′-min-ho-wa′-to, to make an attack.

audibly, mah′-i-hast, audibly, with a loud voice.

aunt, e′-ha-hi-sto, to have for an aunt.

awake, tōst, to awake from a sleep, to be awake.

awl, he′-ōn, an awl.

he-o-ninst′, pl. awls.

na′-tsi-ōn, my awl.

ni′-tsi-ōn, thy awl.

axe, ho-ak′, an axe.

ho-ōksé′, pl. axes.

ho′-to, axe-handle.

ho-to′-ist, pl.

B.

back, i-to′-to-nas, a crooked back.

he-na-ōn′, upper part of the back, across the shoulders.

tau-ta-ma-inst′, at or on the back.

bad, av-si-wai', sing.
av-si-wai'-yo, pl.
ho'-i-av-si-wa', bad lands.

ball, e'-hu-a-si-wa'-to, to play ball with the foot.
o-ho-ni'-wo-ŏh, a ball club, with a hoop at the end to hold the ball as it is thrown.

bare, i-ŏks'-ti-a, to be bare of anything, as a bald head.
na-i-kŏs'-ti-a, I am bare or bald.
ma-i-ni'-a-si-tak, bare, as an open prairie without thickets, or a tree without leaves.
i-ma'-tau, to become bleak or bare, as the ground when the snow disappears.

beads, o-ni'-a-wŏkst, beads.
wŏh-pi'-o-ni'-a-wŏkst, white beads.
ma-e-ni'-a-wŏkst, red beads.
o-ta'-ta-wi-o-ni'-o-wŏkst, blue beads.
mŏh-ta'-wi-ni'-o-wŏkst, black beads.
i-yu-wi-o-ni'-o-wŏkst, yellow beads.

bean, mo'-nisk, (sing.)
mo-ni'-ski (pl.), beans.

bear, nah'-u, and na'-ku.
nah'-u-yo, (pl.)

beat, e-po'-po-no, to beat on, as a drum.

beaver, ho'-ma.
ho-ma' and ho-mà-e'-yo, both plural forms, are in use.

beard, i-mi'-ats, the beard.
i-mi-a'-tsi-nah'-to, beards.
na-mi'-ats, my beard.
ni-mi'-ats, thy beard.
ni-mi-a'-tsi-num, dual, both your beards.
e-hu'-i-mi-ats, yellow beard.
mŏh-ta'-i-mi-ats, black beard.

bend, ih-a-ma'-i-yuts, to bend, as the body, forward.
i-to'-to-na, to bend backwards.
e-hi-a-ma'-i-yuts, to bend the head to one side.
i-sta-wŏn', outside of a bend.
mo-mi'-ka-na-nuts, to bend into or around, as a piece of iron.
e-a-wo'-i-yu-ha, to bend away with the foot, as the grass on the prairie.

beyond, a-stu', beyond, over.
ta-sit-sinst', more, beyond, farther.

black, i-mŏh'-tau, black.
i-mŏh'-tau-o-nist, (pl.)
i-mŏh'-ta-wa, to make anything black or dirty.
na-mŏh'-ta-wa, I make anything black or dirty.
ni-mŏh'-ta-wa, thou dost make anything black or dirty.
i-mŏh'-ta-wa'-a-no, they make anything black or dirty.

bind, e-ŏh'-po-o, to bind or tie.
nah'-po-o'-isé, I bind or tie.
ni-ŏh'-po-o'-isé, thou dost bind or tie.
e-ŏh'-po-o'-isé, he binds or ties.
na-ŏh'-po-o'-is-ći-nŏn, we bind or tie.
ni-ŏh'-po-o'-is-ći-nŏn, you bind or tie.
e-ŏh'-po-o'-is-ći-o, they bind or tie.

bird, wi-kis', a bird.
wi-ksi'-o (pl.), birds.

birth, i-sta'-ŏts, the birth of a child.
no-to-mo'-i-nŏtst, first-born, if a son.
ma-kŏs', the first-born, when a daughter.

bite, e-i'-wo-ŏht, to bite off.
e-wo'-wo-sŏht, to bite notches.
i-ku'-ku-ni-mo, to bite or tear anything in pieces.
i-yo-stai'-yu-stŏt, to bite a hole in anything.

bitter, i-av'-si-vi-e'-no, it is bitter.
nav-si'-vi-at, mine is bitter.
ni-av-si'-vi-at, thine is bitter.

bladder, ih-ai-no'-kuts.

blanket, wŏp'-shi-un, a blanket.
wŏp-shi'-u-non, pl.
na-wŏp'-shi-un, my blanket.
ni-wŏp'-shi-un, thy blanket.
na-wŏp'-shi-u-no'-nam, my blankets.
ni-wŏp'-shi-u-no'-nam, thy blankets.
mai-wŏp'-shi-un, red blanket.
e-tai'-i-wŏm, dark blue blanket.
mŏkh'-ta-wŏm, black blanket.
mo-ku-ta'-wi-ka-ku'-i-shi-ŏn, a blanket of fine blue cloth.
o-ta'-ta-wi-ka-ku'-i-shi-ŏn, a blue striped blanket.
mai'-ka-ku'-i-shi-ŏn, a blanket of fine scarlet cloth.
o-ta'-ta-wi-is'-ći, a blue coat.
nis-ko'-ŏm, a blanket of all colors, Spanish.

wŏp-shi'-un-o-nis, a small, one-point blanket.

blaze, eh'-o-as, a blaze, burning, prairie fire.
eh-o-a-su'-mi, pl.

blind, i'-ok-ćim, to be blind.

blow, i-ha'-a, to blow, as the wind.
i-wo'-na-a, the wind blows, it blows.
ih-tai'-na-a, the wind blows long and steady.
i-sto-woh'-tŭts, to blow, as wind, or with the mouth.
i-a-mi-ni'-to-a-o, to blow into, as wind into a lodge.

blue, e'-hi-wah-so, to become blue or green.

blunt, e-nih-ap', blunt, dull, bruised up.

boat, sim, a boat.
sim'-o-nōts, pl.
o-i-sta'-sim, a fire-boat, a steamboat.

body, nan'-sti-ni'-to-wa, he-wi'-to-wa-ni'-to, } the whole body.
he-wi'-to, the body, or principal part of anything.
ta-yōh', one side of the body.
po-to-ma', in the body.

bone, ho'-ni-ku.
ho'-ni-sta-ta-mo, shoulder bone or blade.
his-ćis-to'-o, underjaw bone.
his-ćis-to'-o-nin, pl.
e-ko-ni'-wo-was, the tail-bone.

borrow, is-ći-ŏć-na-no'-o-ćisé, to borrow.

both, no'-ni-shi-wŏs, both, they two.
i-ta'-i-sto-we, both together.

bottom, in'-ma-si, bottom upwards.

bow, ma'-ćik, a bow.
ma'-takst, pl.
na-ma'-ćik, my bow.
ni-ma'-ćik, thy bow.
ho-tai-wo', a bow lined on the back with sinews.

boy, kai-kŭn', a small boy.
kai-ku'-ni, pl.
na-kai-kŭn', my boy.
ni-kai-kŭn', thy boy.
na-kai-kŭn'-ham, my boys.
ni-kai-kŭn'-ham, thy boys.

braid, e'-sto-tun-a, to plat or braid.

brains, his-ta'-pi, brains of animals.
e-shi-sta'-pi, to brain a robe or skin.
na-shi-sta'-pan, I brain a robe.
ni-shi-sta'-pan, thou dost brain a robe.

branch, kam-hi'-ōts, the branches of a tree.
kam-hi'-o-tsi-o'-e-nats, to break off the branches of trees.
hi-si'-o, branching, or having many roots, as a tree.

bread, ma-ha'.
na-mi'-si-tun-a-ma-ha', I eat bread.
ko-ku'-ko-no, a kind of bread.

break, o-ni'-so-wan, to break in pieces, to divide as bread.
e'-po-i-yōts, to break or tear in pieces.
ta'-mi-i-sa, to break off, as the nose.
e-o-ni'-yu-ha, to break a string with the foot.
o-i'-u-ha, to break anything with the foot.
su-a-o-mi'-uts, to break through, as the ice.
i-yo-si'-o-sto, to break out of the shell, as a bird.
i-ōh'-i-wo-he, broken off, as a spoon-handle, or a glass flawed.
i'-yo-ōh, to break in two by striking.
na'-yo-ōh, I, &c.
ni'-yo-ōh, thou, &c.
e'-i-yōts, to break with the hand, as a stick, but not entirely off.
na'-i-yōts, I, &c.
ni'-i-yōts, thou, &c.

breast, e-ta-nun', a woman's breast, the udder of a cow.
e-ta-nai'-wo, pl.
na-ta-nun', my breast.
ni-ta-nun', thy breast.
he-in', the breast and neck of an animal.

breath, he-o-mi-to'-mi-stōts, the breath of life.
i'-o-mo-tōm, to breathe on.
e-i'-si-i-i'-mas, to breathe hard through the nose.
i'-ha-ha-o-tōm, to pant, to breathe hard after severe exercise.
i-ha-o-to'-mi-ōts, to be out of breath, and in a great perspiration.
na-he'-o-na-a'-sto-wōt, to make the fingers warm by breathing or blowing upon them.

bridle, ōh-ut'-si-na'-si-o, a bridle for a horse.

bring, ih-u-yatst', to bring wood for a fire.
si-mo-i'-no-mo-i, to bring a boat to shore, or over the river.

brood, ni-si-ća', a litter, a brood.

broom, maȟ'-i-wo-ma-o'-yi.

brother, e-ni'-sŏn, a brother.
e-ni'-so-ni-wo (pl.), brothers.
na-ni'-sŏn, my brother.
ni-ni'-sŏn, thy brother.
na-ni', a man's elder brother.
na-ta'-ta-mim, a woman's elder brother.
na-si-ma', younger brother.
na-hi'-ni-hi'-nŏts, my brothers.
e'-to, a brother-in-law.
ni-to', your brother-in-law.
he'-wi-to, his brother-in-law.
ni-a-wi'-to-wi'-to-wats, you are my brother-in-law.
ni-sa'-he-wi-to-he-nits, you are not my brother-in-law.
he-wi'-tŏst, to have for a brother-in-law, to sustain that relation.

bubble, e-hi'-si-wŏt, to bubble up in boiling, as water.
i'-a-niv-si-wŏts, to bubble, or flow along with a noise, as water over rocks.
ma-pe-e'-hi-ni-o, to make water bubble up, as water when a stone is thrown in.

buckle, e-o'-we-me-kait, brass buckle.

bud, ho-o'-tsi-si'-mi-nŏts, the buds of the trees in the spring.

build, pa-yo'-na-o-we, to build a house, or pitch a tent.
ći-na'-no-is-to-he-ni-to, to build a fence around a corn-field.

buffalo, o-to-a', a male buffalo. *Bos Americanus.*
mi, a female.
wŏk-si-ai', a calf.
is'-i-wan, a herd of buffalo.
e-mas', bois de vache, "buffalo chips."
i'-yo-iv, an old, scabby, buffalo bull.

bulky, ta-sis'-to-wo, to be bulky, to hinder or impede, by putting on too many clothes.

bunch, e-po-pis'-tai-i-na, bunches, knots, excrescences, on trees; the Indians make dishes of them.

burn, i-si-to-wa-o, to burn or smoke, as incense, with a smell.

burst, e'-ni-sta-ni-wa'-wŏt, to make pop or burst.
e-ŏȟ'-i-wo-yat, to burst, as a boiler or a gun.

bush, mi'-no-ći-a, willow bushes.

button, o-ni-kŏm'.
o-ni-ko'-mo-nŏts, (pl.)

C.

call, wi-hu-in'-i-min, to call to a meal.
o-no'-o-mi, to call to a feast, to invite.
i-a-no'-ma-ći'-sto, to call each other to a feast.

calm, e'-he-kut, calm, still, without wind.

callous, e'-wo-wi, any hard place formed by a burn or cut on the skin.

candle, wa-ksi'-na-nis-to, a torch or candle.

cap, wi-ŏȟ'-ća.
wi-ŏȟ'-ća-ist, (pl.)

carry, e-mo-he'-he-nŏȟ'-to, to carry or draw.
e'-ni-a-mi-ŏts, to carry or bring anything.
maȟ-pe-i'-nŏt, to carry or take on the shoulder.

cat, ka-e-si'-o-tum, a cat, a short-nosed dog. The plural is formed simply by changing the accent from the third syllable to the last.

catch, i-no-ŏȟt', to catch in the mouth, anything that is tossed.

cause, ta-no-ŏnst', to cause to see.

chair, taȟ-i-si'-is-tŭts.
taȟ-i-si'-is-to-tŭts, (pl.)

champ, ma-kai'-i-ta-i'-ko-nŏt, to champ, as a horse his bit.

chapped, i-mo-o'-a, smarting, chapped by the wind.

cheap, e-he'-ya-na, cheap, easily purchased.

cheek, e-wo-ta'-nŏts.
e-wo-ta'-no-tse-hik, cheek-bone.

cherries, maȟ-ŏt-sta'-min, fruit of *Cerasus pumila.*

chewed, pe-nŏȟ'-tŏts, anything chewed fine, like musk-rats' food.

choke, i'-o-hŏć, to choke, to be choked in eating.
na'-o-hŏć, I was choked in eating.
ni'-o-hŏć, thou wast choked in eating.

clearly, o-ha-ći'-stŭts, clearly, conspicuously.
in-sis'-to-wa-a, clear and cold, with particles of snow in the air.

climb, e'-i-wo-ni, to climb, as a tree.

close, ho'-o-sist, to be close to, to press on.

ke-kas′,
kać,
im′-a-e-kas′, } near by, close.

cloth, ni-na-wo′-i-stūts, clothing of all kinds.

clouds, e-wo-iv′, to cloud over, to be cloudy.
e-wo-iv′, clouds, sky, heaven.
i-mŏkh′-tau-wo′-i-yōts, black clouds.
wo-i′-ha-i-nōt, thick clouds.
wo-e-e-he-ni′-wo-ist, broken clouds.
wo-e-e′-a-si-ta, scattering clouds.
en′-i-wo-iv, the sky becoming black with clouds.

coffee, mōh-ta′-whōp, black water, or medicine coffee.
ma-ta′-o-ki-mi-nuts, coffee-grains.

coil, o-ni′-mo-ta′-o-to-nōts, to coil or knot by twisting.
mo-me′-ka-no-ni-a′-nuts, to coil up, as a rope.
e-o-ni′-sta-ćis, to lie coiled up on one's side.

collect, i-ho′-sun, to collect together.

cold, i-to-nit′, to be cold.

come, ni′-ni-o-tsi-o, come (imperative mood).
o-hum′, come close.
ni-ni′-o-ist, come towards, come this way, (imp.)
na-ni′-o-tsitst, I come in a hurry.
ni-ni′-o-tsitst, you come in a hurry.
e-ni′-o-tsitst, he comes, or to come in a hurry.
ni′-ni-ats, come on, let it be so, (imp.)
ni-is′-taks, come in, (imp.)
nin′-shi-wi-ōst, come here quickly, (imp.)
ni-wa′-i-si′-ni-i-ko, to come and peep in and then draw the head back.
he-wi-no′-wo-tau-ūtst, to come towards one.

comb, tsi-i-ni′.
tsi-i-ni′-he-yo, (pl.)
i-tsi-i-ni′-a, to comb the hair.

commit, he-wi-no′-nun-o-ho′-ni, to commit murder.

comrade, ni-si-ma-ha′, my comrade.
he-wi′-so-no, thy comrade.

concave, i′-wo-wōs, hollowed out, concave.

concealed, ni′-ha-mōs, out of sight, behind something, concealed.

cook, i-ho-mōh′-to-wo, to cook, as food.
e′-hat, to be cooked or roasted, as meat.

copper, ma-i-ma-kai′-it, copper, red metal.

corn, ma-mi′-nūts.
ho-o′-tsi-mi-nu, cornstalk.
ho-ōts′, an ear of corn.
ho-ōtsts′ (pl.), ears of corn.
ma′-mi-nu-tsi-o-i′-mi-nist, to shell off as corn with the hands.

corral, ni-ma-i′-nuts, the circle or corral formed by wagons at a camp.

covering, e-wi′-shi-main, covering, as clothes or a sheath.
ah-to-ho′-ma-i-nats, to be covered up with earth.
i-a′-to-ho, to cover over with earth, as a grave.
in-i-in′-i-ōht, to be covered with frost, as grass in the morning.

cough, i′-hi-a, he coughs, or to cough.
na′-hi-a, I cough.
ni′-hi-a, you cough.

count, o-is-to′-nist, to count.

court, e-sta-ni-e′-wa, to court a woman.
e-sta-ni-e′-wah-to, (pl.)

cousin, ni-sis′, your male cousin.

crack, a′-po-at, a crack or hole, as in a lodge.
i-o′-sin, to crack a louse.

crawl, he-ći′-a-mist, to crawl up carefully on anything.

creak, he-ni′-to-e-ni′-sto-ni-wun, to creak or grate, like a door.

creep, i-a-mi′-wo-minst, to creep or crawl.
ta-mi′-wo-minst, " "
i-a′-me-wu′-ne-ots, to creep on.

crisped, e-hi′-se-maut, crisped or drawn up.

crooked, e′-wōh, to be crooked, arched.
e-wo-wo′-kit-si-an, crookedly, in an arched manner.

cross, i-ōh′-o-ho, to cross a river.
i-ta′-ko-ho, to wade across a stream.
a-mi-sta′-nōts, crosswise, across something else.

crumbs, mo-es′-te-pih-pi-ots, crumbs or fragments.

crupper, hōh-i-si′-ni-o.
hōh-i-si′-ni-o-nōts, (pl.)

crush, i-so′-so-is, to mash, or crush.
mih′-ni-min, to crunch, crush, grind, champ, to make a noise with the teeth.

i-po-i-ha', to break or crush in pieces, as meat or tallow.
na-po-i-ha', I break, &c.
ni-po-i-ha', thou breakest, &c.
i-po-i-ha'-o, they break, &c.

cry, ni-ōh'-ai-im, to make cry, by talking to.

cup, to-i-ni'-o.
to-i-ni'-o-nōts, (pl.)
to-i-ni'-o-ni-wi-tōk, a cup with a handle, dipper.

curl, im'-a-ma-kai, to curl, as hair.
ma-mah-ai-e', curly.

currants, he-sta-tsi'-min', black currants, *Ribes floridum.*

curtain, ni-i'-psi-no'-i-nuts, to curtain, or cover with a curtain.

cut, e-ih', to cut.
e-wo-ih', to cut off a string from a skin.
e-pi-ih', to cut in pieces, to destroy with a knife.
e-po-ih', to cut off, as a piece of meat.
i'-o-tah, to cut holes in anything with a knife.
i-o'-sis, to cut or rip open.
i-o-ta'-o-mo, to cut a hole into, as in wood.
e'-i-so, to cut in the middle.
ho-o-i-ninst', to cut tobacco.
pi-nōhts', to carve, to cut.
e-mi-ko'-yo-kah, to cut or shear off the hair.

D.

damp, e-hi'-ko-o, damp.
e-yo'-i-yats, to be moist or damp.

dance, e-mah'-ta-a, a dance.
e-mah'-ta-o, to dance.
ma-mah'-ta-o, I dance.
ni-mah'-ta-o, you dance.
i-mi-tah'-to, they dance.
i-o-so'-i-to, to dance on anything.
i-ma-yun'-i-so'-i-sto, a sacred dance.
e-ho'-i-o-ći'-sto, a scalp dance. When the Indians arrive at the camp with scalps, they come in dancing.
e-a'-ćis-to, a regular scalp dance. This dance is conducted among the Shyennes, the same as with the Dakotas.

dark, i'-a-no-nit, to be dark, darkness.
in-sta-e'-wi-ōts, to become dark.
i'-shi-ta-e'-wi-ni, to darken, to shadow as clouds.

daughter, he'-mi.
na-tōn', my daughter.

day, i'-shi-i-wa.
i-shinst' (pl.), days.
i'-shi-iv, all day.
si-to'-shi-iv, the middle of the day.
e-pa-wi-i'-shi-o, } a good day.
i-hav'-si-vi-i'-shi-o, } a good day.
i-shi-ni-pit'-siv, a snowy day.
i-shi-i-wai'-i-hi-ko, a rainy day.
i-shi'-hi-kōt, a mild, calm day.
e-i-to'-iv, dusk, between sunset and dark.
in-i-wo'-o-ni-yōts, day breaking, daylight.
e-ho-so'-wo-ma-no, broad daylight, full light.

dead, ho-wa-tsi'-e-wish.
i-na'-i-yōts, to be dead.

debilitated, i-ha-mu'-ta, sick, debilitated.
i-ha-mu'-ta-yo, (pl.)

December, e-po-iv'-si-o, the month when the animals shed their horns.

deep, i-ha'-o-tum, deep as water, dense as foliage, thick as hair.
ho-i-ta'-is, deep, far within.

deer, mu-ksa', young deer or fawn.
mu-ksa'-o-iv, a fawn or deerskin.

defecate, he-mats', to defecate.

defective, wi'-shi-to-nōst, to be defective, wanting.

deformed, e-nōh-ni-ka, deformed, deficient in any part.

demijohn, i-shi-i'-wi-to, a large bottle.
na-niv'-sit, a glass bottle.

descend, e-ha'-ni-wo-ni, to descend from a tree.

desert, tōh-to'-a, a desert place where no one dwells.

destitute, i-sa-a'-i-nu, to be destitute, to have nothing of.
na-sa-a'-i-nu, I am destitute.
ni-sa-a'-i-nu, thou art destitute.
i-sa-a'-i-nu'-i-nu (pl.), they are destitute.

dew, e-hi-ko-wi'-ni-o.
i-ma-hi'-ko-wi'-ni-o, dewy everywhere.

diaphragm, he-to'-nish, the diaphragm of a deer.

die, ni-in'-a, to die.

na-ni'-na, I die.
ni-ni'-na, you die.
i-na'-tsa-ta-no'-ats, to die of fright, to faint from alarm.

different, i-ni'-ta, he is or to be different, another.
na-ni'-ta, I am different.
ni-ni'-ta, thou art different.
i-ni'-tai-yo, they are different.
na-ni'-tam, we are different.
ni-ni'-tam, you are different.

difficult, i-ho'-wa-nat, hard to do, difficult.
i-ho'-to-wa'-na-tōn, to think anything hard or difficult.

dig, ma-a'-ko, to dig, as a bear, in the earth.

diminished, sik-sta'-ōts, less, diminished.

dip, ni'-hi-a-ta-i-na'-nūts, to dip food out of a kettle with a ladle.

dirty, im-a-si'-a-hōt, to be dirty, as a gun that needs cleaning.

disagreeable, e'-wo-ev, unpleasant, disagreeable, as the appearance of the weather or country.

dish, e-tōk', a dish or plate.
e-to'-ko-nōts, (pl.)

disposition, nōh-to-wi'-ta-no-tūts, mind, will, disposition.
shu-mi'-a-tu-a, a good disposition.
shu-mi'-hav-sūs, a bad disposition.
i-ta'-ko-wi-ni-hav'-siv, to be of a surly disposition.

displeased, e-av'-si-vi'-tan, to be sorry, displeased, sad.

dispute, i-hi'-si-ta'-tsi-no, to dispute about anything.

dissatisfied, o-wa-no'-isé, not pleased with.

distribute, wo-tsi'-no-o-wa, to distribute.
wo-tsi'-no-ho-ma-kis, the distributor of presents.

disturbed, i-ha'-i-sta, disturbed in mind.
i-ha'-i-sta'-ha-ōts, (pl.)

dog, ho'tum.
ho-tum' (pl.), only change of accent to form the plural.
ho-tum'-i-na-tōts, my dog.
ho-tum'-i-nis-tōts, your dog.

domestic, wi-o-i-o'-to-a, domestic cattle.
ko-ku'-yah, domestic fowls.
e-nis-tōn', to tame, to domesticate animals.
na-nis-tōn', I tame, &c.
ni-nis-tōn', thou dost tame, &c.

door, he-ni'-to, a door, that which covers the entrance of the lodge.
ći-hi'-to-hi'-o-niv, at the door.
ho'-a-nōts, shut the door.
o-ni'-sta-nūts, open the door.

double, mo-mi'-ka-nōts, to double up with the teeth.

draw, e-nih-o'-ta, to draw tight, as a belt around the waist.
e'-si-a-nōt, to draw in anything with the breath, as dust or smoke.

dream, e'-o-wah, to dream.
na'-o-wah, I dream.
ni'-o-wah, thou dreamest.
i'-o-wah, he dreams.
na-o-wah'-i-nam, we dream.
i-o-wah'-i-nam, you dream.
i-o-wah'-i-na-to, they dream.
e-o-wah'-i-na-o, " "

dress, ho'-is-tōts, a woman's dress.
he-i-wo'-is-tōts (pl.), all dresses.
ho-i-ma-ni-he-wo-is-tōts, dresses of an hermaphrodite.

dried, ho-ōh'k', dried, hard.

drive, a-ma'-o-me, to drive along, as cattle.

drop, e'-hi-ōts, to drop, like rain.

drowned, im-im-stan', to be drowned.

drunk, in-o-no'-to-wa-sish, to be drunk.

dry, i'-o-un, to make dry, to wipe dry.

dull, e'-nih'-ap, to be dull or blunt.

dumb, i-sa'-no-to-wins'-ći, to be dumb.

duodenum, his-tatst', the duodenum of ruminating animals.
his-ta'-tōts, (pl.)

dust, hi'-i-pin, dust, powdered earth.

E.

each one, i-ta-shi'-wa-i-no, each one, every one.

ear, sto-wo'-ats, external ear, ear of animals.
i-sto-wo'-ats, his ear, or an ear.
na-sto-wo'-ats, my ear.
ni-sto-wo'-ats, your ear.

ni-nih'-a-ist-na-to-wo'-ats, my two ears, both my ears.
na-sa'-to-wo'-ats, not my ears.
ni-sa'-to-wo'-ats, not thy ears.
i-sa'-to-wo'-ats, not his ears.
e-o-ma'-ōts, to prick up the ears, as a horse at a sound.
e-ći'-ći-ist, to move the ears, as a horse.
i-nis-kis-ta'-ōts, to put the ears forward, as a horse.
i'-o-ta-ist, the orifice of the ear, the touchhole of a gun.

eat, i-na'-so-i-no, to be full from eating.
na-na'-so-i-no, I am full from eating.
ni-na'-so-i-no, thou art full from eating.
i-na'-so-i-na'-sto, they are full from eating.
e-tsi-ti'-mi-o, to eat or gnaw wood, as a horse.
stah'-o-mats (imp.), give to eat.
nih'-o-nist (imp.), give me to eat.

earth, i-ho'-wo-ni, brown earth.
ho-i-tsi-wōh'-po-mau, sweet earth, alkaline earth.
ho-i-tsi'-si-to'-wa-o, smoking or burning earth, from the ignition of the lignite beds.
ish-i-ći'-wi-to, an earthen pot, vessel, jug.

egg, wo'-wōts.
wo'-wo-tōts, pl.

eldest, e-nu'-ći-ma-ait, eldest, firstborn.
na-ni'-ći-ma-ait, my eldest.
ni-ni'-ći-ma-ait, thy eldest.
ni-ni'-ći-ma-ai'-tum, pl. your eldest.

elope, i-a'-si-ta-e'-wi, to elope, to run away with a woman, or another man's wife.

eloquent, i-pi'-wi-ist, to be eloquent, to speak well.

empty, i-ma'-tōh-i-yōts, to become empty, to decay, as the inside of a tree.

encampment, mōh-tanst', an old encampment, after the lodges have left.

enemies, i-no'-tsi-to-wa-ći'-sto, those who are at variance with each other.

equal, ćit'-ski, not equal.

escape, i-ha'-o-mi-ni, to be unable to escape, to be unable to extricate oneself.

evacuate, i-tam'-si-ka, to evacuate, to ease oneself.
e-mi-si'-to, to evacuate on any one, a term of reproach.

evaporate, e'-po-no-i, as when a creek becomes dry.

even, i-si'-i-sto-to, even, just, exactly.

explain, tah-ti-i'-a-mo-un, to unfold, explain, to make bare, as a falsehood.

eye, e-ih-anst', the eye.
na-ih-anst', my eye.
ni-ih-anst', thy eye.
e-ih'-ai-i-wōts, pl.
e-we'-e-nōt, eyebrow.
e-ih-a'-e-wi'-a-nūt, eye-winker.
e-ih-a'-e-wi-a-ni'-a-stūts, eyelids.
e-po-pi-ih'-a-nist, the ridge bone above the eye.
is-ćik'-o-niv-ih'-a-nist, projection formed by the ridge above the eye.
shi'-ta-sho-tōh, as far as the eye can reach.
i-o'-ki-ni-o-sti'-no, to strike and put out the eye.
i-o'-i-nu-na'-wi-ma'-tsin, to grow blind.
i'-ha-i-ma'-tsi-ni-ōts, to wink the eye.
i-o-o'-in, to be blind, having the eyes put out.
e-we-hin', to be blind, with the eyeball white.
i-o-ni'-mi-i-kan, to be squint or cross-eyed.
i-nōh-ta'-wi-o-in, to be nearsighted.
i'-na-ko-o, to be clearsighted.

F.

fail, e'-wa-ni-ōts, to come to nothing, to fail.

fall, e'-o-hain, to let anything fall.
in-so'-ta-mo, to fall out with, not to be on speaking terms with.

falsifier, i-a-sto-mōh'-ta-un, a great liar.
in-i-ći-hi'-o-niv, to fabricate a lie, to falsify about one.

fat, i-ha'-i-yōm.
i-ha-i-yo'-mi-o, (pl.)

father, he'-hu; ih is sometimes used.
na-ho'-i, my father.
ni-ho'-i, thy father.
ni-ho'-he-nuts, to have a father, to be the child of any one.
he-nim-shim, his father-in-law.
na-nim-shim, my father-in-law.
ni-nim-shim, thy father-in-law.
he-ni'-sa-na-mōn, a man's stepfather.

feast, ma-ho-yun'-hōp, a sacred feast.
ma-he-yun'-haist, to make a sacred feast.

fence, i-ni-po-o', to fence as a field, to fasten or bolt.
na-ni-po-o', I fence, &c.
ni-ni-po-o', thou dost fence, &c.
ferment, po-a-ha'-i-nis-tŭts, to ferment, as yeast.
field, i-na-no'-is-tŭts-tsi-mo'-na, a new field, one in which there is a new crop.
no-ni-na-no'-is-tŭts, an old field, where the crop has been removed.
fight, pi-so-mi'-o-tats, to fight over anything.
file, wi-o-yo-ksi'-im, a file.
finger, na-ni'-so-to-yŏs, the fore finger.
na-no'-to-yŏs, the second finger.
na-so'-to-yŏs, the third finger.
na-to-oh'-i-yŏs, the fourth or little finger.
na-to'-a-no-ni-mo'-i-yŏs, finger nails.
finished, i'-shi-ma-nisé, to be done, finished.
fire, ho-ist'.
ho-i'-stats, (pl.)
na-to'-ist, my fire.
ni-to'-ist, thy fire.
na-to'-is-tam, my fires.
ni-to'-is-tam, thy fires.
his-to-is-ta'-mi-wo, different fires of other people.
e'-no-si-sto'-wo, burning coals.
ho-sta'-wi-no, a firebrand.
ho-i-sta'-wa, in the fire.
i-ha-ha'-i-si, sparks of fire.
i-no-to-wa'-ŏtst, to extinguish the fire.
e'-nu-to, there is no fire.
ai-sto-a-si-na-nis'-tŭts, a fireplace, a chimney.
ma-kai'-tai-sto-a-si'-na-nis-tŭts, a stove or iron fireplace.
ih-o-wa', to draw near and warm oneself by the fire.
first, ni-ĭ-ni'-ta, at the first.
fish, no'-man.
no-man', pl.
no-no-no', a fish-line.
no-ma'-he-mĭk, fish-head.
no-maik'-sŭn, small fish.
no-ma'-he-hĭk, fish-bones.
ma-i-tsa-nŏn', red-fin, a kind of fish.
he-to-to', a crayfish.

fit, i-tai'-ist, to cause to fit; to fit well, as a bullet in a gun.
na-i-tai'-ist, I make it fit well.
flank, his-tsi-to'-ni, the flank of an animal.
flat, i-kah'-o-no, to make flat, like a board.
flesh, he-ma'-e, flesh that clings to a skin.
flimsy, e-hi'-sis, flimsy, not firm; elastic.
e-hi'-si-so-ni'-o, pl.
float, e'-i-wo-it, to float along, as on the water.
in-o-mo'-i, to float down a stream, to drift by the wind as a leaf.
i'-pi-no, to rise to the surface and float, as on water.
flood, i-ya-mi-ŏh-whit' (last syllable pronounced strongly), to flood with water.
flow, in'-shi-wit, to flow or run, as water.
fly, i-ya'-mi-ha-ŏts, to fly, as birds.
foam, e'-ta-wo-niv-ŏm', to froth or foam, as when anything is thrown into the water.
fog, ma-i-ni'-ni-po-is, to become foggy, as when a white fog arises, and obscures the sky.
fold, e'-i-mits, to fold up the arms.
foliage, i-ha-i-wih'-pŏt-siv, dense foliage.
follow, e-ta-ni'-hi-ŏt, to follow after anything.
ta-ni-he-whi' (the last syllable strong), to follow after one is gone, to pursue an enemy.
food, e-mi'-sa.
foolish, im-a-sa'-ni-o, foolish, to be foolish.
foot, ma'-is, a foot.
na'-is, my foot.
ni'-is, thy foot.
ma-hai'-sŏts (pl.), feet.
no'-tsi-ma-is, another man's foot, the foot of a man of a different nation.
mo-mah'-a-ta, a large foot.
ha-po'-si-wa, a crooked foot.
wa-ni-sa'-ta, the feet turn out.
wo-wŏh'-éa-ta, feet with the toes turned in.
po-pe'-ha-ta, the ball of the foot.
to-tam'-ha-ta, foot with no toes.
hau-o-no'-is-éist, big-heeled foot.
tŏts-ki-éis'-to-na, small-heeled foot.
o-iv'-ha-ta, scaly foot.

forbid, he-wi'-no-e'-wi-ho-ist, to forbid one's house, to prevent persons from coming in.

forget, e-wa-ni'-ta-nūt, he is, or to be forgetful, to forget.
na-wa-ni'-ta-nūt, I forget.
ni-wa-ni'-ta-nūt, thou dost forget.

forked, i-ni'-so-wa-ats, forked, as a stream.
i-ni'-sko-nat, forked, as a stick; a stream double or forked.
i-ni-sko-na'-wi-wo-tōn, a forked tail, as of a fish or martin.

foundation, i'-wa-ha, a foundation, a place to stand on.

fracture, e-o-ta'-ni-ōs-to-no, a fracture, wound, rent.

freeze, i-o-ma'-o-mōt, to freeze over, as ice on the river.
e'-ko-nōht, stiff, hardened, frozen.
o-tse'-to-e'-ko-no-si-o, wood when hardened by frost, frozen.

friend, ho'-wa.
he-wi'-so-nist, to have for a special friend.
e-na'-no-wa-ćis'-tōm, to be friendly, to be friends.
nis-in', your friend.

full, i-o-to'-mo-in (adjective).
i-o'-to-mōt, to be full.
i-na'-so-i-no, to be full or satisfied, as with food.
i-sa-i-na'-su-i-nōn, not full, empty as to the stomach.

G.

gap, i-to-wo'-i-yo'-i-sats, to gap, to break out a piece from the blade of an axe.

gather, ma-i-ni'-nūts, to gather up.

gentle, i-o-wan'-ha (adjective).

girl, he-i'-kai-kūn, a small girl.
he-i'-kai-ku'-ni, (pl.)

girth, o-tu tai'-shi-o, a girth.

give, i-ta'-mit, to give.
o-wa-he'-wi-i-stūts (imp.), give it to me, let me have it.

glad, i-a'-i-yo, to be glad, thankful.

glisten, i'-o-ha-se, to glisten.

glove, na-to'-a-e-ni'-wo-a-na'.

gnaw, ih'-i-wa-nōts, to gnaw on.

go, tai'-i-mōnst, to go off on a journey.
ta-no-inst', to go together.
ta-mi-o-nanst'-st, to go before to break the road.
tau-akst', to go out of doors.
he-um', to go up, to ascend.
wi-tsin', to go directly to anything without a medium.
ōh-ta'-tau-wo-wo'-ist, to cause to go before.
e-ho-i-wi'-o-ći-sto, to go on a war party.
e-ni-so-wa'-o-hi-yo, to go different ways, separately.
a-stu'-ta-tsi-ōtst, to go beyond, or over a hill, or any place.
ta-ōt'-sti-ta'-no-ōtst, to go home and lie down to sleep.
no-no'-to-ha-ninst, to take one's all and go away and live in another place.
ta-si'-ōsé, go, (imp.)
i-tau', go out, (imp.)
tau-wakst, go away, or go out, (imp.)

gold, wi-ho'-ni-ma-kai'-i-ta-tsi'-i-ho, yellow iron.

good, e-pi-whai'-sto, a "heap" good, very good.
e-po'-pi-wha'-e-wi-sōn, goodness, kindness.

grab, i-si-va'-i-ni, to grab at, to catch at, as at a person.
i-ći'-o-si-ōts, to seize or grab at, as a fish in water, or a fly.

grandchild, nih'-a.
na-nih'-a, my grandchild.
ni-nih'-a, thy grandchild.

grass, mo-isé', grass, herbs, hay.
e-si'-i-ho-nūts, grass, roots, &c.
wa-nōt', gray grass or herbs.
mah'-e-wa-ma-ōts, clear of brush or long grass.
o-ōh-o-si'-o-ta-tau, green, like grass.

graze, e'wi-nōts, to graze, as cattle.

grease, um (noun).
e'-ko-ma-nōts, to grease over anything.

great, tsi-ma-ha'-a, great, large.
tsi-ma-ha'-o-ist (pl.)

ground, ho-ev', on the ground.

grouse, wa-ko-yis', a sharp-tailed grouse.
wa-ko-yis'-i-ma'-is, the feet of the sharp-tailed grouse.

wa-ko-yis'-is-ći-wa-to-nisé, the tail of the sharp-tailed grouse.

wa-ko-yis'-e-min, the wing of the sharp-tailed grouse.

wa-ko-yis'-i-mi-k, the head of the sharp-tailed grouse.

gun, ma-ai-tun, a single-barrelled gun.

ma-ai-tun-o'-ist, (pl.)

na-ma-ai'-tun-o, my gun.

ni-ma-ai'-tun-o, thy gun.

nih'-ut-si-na'-wo, a double-barrelled gun.

to-no-wo', a rifle-gun.

mah-i-mai'-i-tun-o, a long, iron gun, a cannon.

no-tah'-i-wo, a musket, a soldier's gun.

tsi'-ma-ha-is-ćis-to-nōt, breech of a gun.

e'-to-i, loaded as a gun.

II.

hair, he-i'-wa, also he-i'-wōs, hair of the head, scalp.

mi'-ko-nōts, the whole scalp with the hair.

nōh'-pa-e, white head of hair.

he-ho'-wa-e, yellow hair.

ma'-o-wi-sa, red hair.

ōk'-ći-a, thin hair.

ma'-ma-ka-e, curly hair.

ha'-is-ta-e, long hair.

ćik'-sta-e, short hair.

wo'-his-ći-a, to be bald on the front part of the head.

e-ki-i'-wo-to-na, hair braided with strips of otter skin.

e'-wa-wo-to'-nu-stōts, scalp-lock, on the back of the head.

i-o-ko'-tak, to cut hair.

na-o-ko'-tak, I cut hair.

ni-o-ko'-tak, thou dost cut hair.

i-o-ko-ta'-ki-o, they cut hair.

e'-ni-mo-iv, a lock of the hair on the side of the head tied up.

e'-a-no-no-ish, to hang over, as the hair over one's face.

eh-o-wa'-ōts, to take the hair off by rubbing or shaving.

i-ha-wa'-wi-ōt, a bunch of hair growing on the inside of a deer's leg.

half, ōh, ta-yōh'.

hallo, nōh-a', hallo, look here.

hammer, tōn'-ho-i-nis-tōts.

handsome, i-pi'-wi-wi-to, he is handsome.

na-pi'-wi-wi-to, I am handsome.

ni-pi'-wi-wi-to, thou art handsome.

i-pi'-wi-to-wah'-to, they are handsome.

hand, o-wo-si'-to-yi, to raise the hand to strike.

handful, e-to'-si-ōh-i-ćis'-i-ōts, a handful, what can be held in the hand.

hang, e-ho-is'-ćin-ōts, to hang from, to be suspended from, as a tree.

haul, e-mo-he'-na-ninst, to haul or transport, as a cart.

i-tam-han', to haul wood from a great distance.

haw, na-ko-is-ta'-tsi-min, "bear-killer," red haws. The Indians say that this fruit causes the bears so much pain when eaten, that they attempt to rip open their bellies.

e-ta-ni-mi'-nuts, black haws.

head, mik'k.

mi'-ko-nōts, (pl.)

na-mik'k, my head.

ni-mik'k, thy head.

wo-ka-he-mik'k, a deer's head.

si-to-sta', top of the head.

e'-i-ho-wa, yellow head.

e'-ta-pes-ći'-a, a big head.

i-to-i-no'-hiv-tsi-a, a line running over the middle of the head, caused by the parting of the hair.

heap, ha'-is-tu, a heap, a great deal, a great many.

healthy, na-sa-ha'-ma-to, healthy, sound in body, not sick.

hear, i-ni'-sto-mōn, to make one hear, or he makes one hear.

na-ni'-sto-mōn, I make one hear.

ni-ni'-sto-mōn, thou makest one hear.

i-a'-to-mōn'-sto, they make one hear.

na-sa-ni'-sto-mōn, I do not hear, or make one hear.

ni-sa-ni'-sto-mōn, you do not hear.

i-sa-ni'-sto-mōn, he does not hear.

heart, hais-ćist'.

hais-ćis'-ta-wōts, (pl.)

heavy, i-ha'-a-nun (adjective).

heel, hes-ćist', the heel.

ma-ćist'-to-nōts, (pl.)

na-ćist', my heel.

ni-ćist', thy heel.

no-tsi'-ma-ćist, the heel of a person of a strange nation.

helpmeet, his-to-tsi'-o-nam, a helper, helpmeet, laborer.

hew, e-kah-o-no, to hew a long log on one side, and then on the other.

hermaphrodite, he-i'-ma-ni.

hiccough, a-i-so'-wa, to hiccough.

na-i-so'-wa, I hiccough.

ni-i-so'wa, thou dost hiccough.

i-so-nih'-to, pl.

hide, no'-o-ist, to hide or conceal.

high, ha'-shi-um, high, very high, lofty.

hill, o-ha-ni-no', piled up as a hill or a mound of stone.

o-si'-wa-ta-ōtst, at the hill.

e'-ta-tak, country with many hills, like Bad Lands.

hi-na-it'-sit-a'-wi-o-tum', what did you see on the hill?

hipbone, ai-si'-tsi-o, ilium.

his, his-ći'-ōts, his, her, its.

hiss, wi-ho-i'-shi, to hiss at, as a dog.

hog, e-ku'-si-si'-o-tum, a sharp-nosed dog, pork, bacon.

hold, i-ho-ist', to hold back, to withhold, to retain.

hole, woh, a deep hole.

ho-i-i'-o-ta-o, a hole in the ground.

i'-o-ta-in, to bore or make a hole in anything.

i'-o-ta-i-sta, to make a hole, to bore or pierce the ear.

e-pin'-o-ist, full of holes, as cloth.

e-wih'-pi-o-in, holes in an animal's head, communicating with the nostrils.

hollow, i-ha'-o-nōn, the hollow in the leg behind the knee.

honor, i-pa'-wo-e, to honor, respect, reverence.

hop, i-ku-ka'-ak, to hop as a grasshopper.

horse, mu'-i-no.

mu'-i-no-hum, pl.

mōh-ta'-o-hum, a black horse.

mōh-ta'-o-hum-i, pl.

wōh'-po-am, a white horse.

wōh'-po-a-mi-i'-o, pl.

i-san'-stai, a wild, prancing horse.

ma'-o-wai, a bay or dun horse.

ma-o-wai-i'-yo, pl.

mo-e'-i-hai-tu, a yellow or sorrel horse, with hair like that of an elk.

mōh-ta'-wi-wo'-a-si, black and white spotted horse.

mo-ći'-nu-a-mis', a colt.

e-ho'-wo-hum, a red-haired horse.

ha-ma'-no-wa, a chestnut bay horse.

i-ta-ni'-hum, a stallion.

i-i'-hum, a mare.

i-i-ham', pl.

house, i-ha'-i-no-no, a village, or cluster of houses or lodges.

hai-sta-nūh', council-house.

wi-i-tsi-ma'-yu-nim, a church, a sacred house.

i-nōh', at the house, at home.

i-no-ći'-o-mi-nu, away from any house.

ho-to-ma'-ni-ta-o, household, including persons and things.

wih'-po-tsi-mai'-yo, to make leaf houses or booths.

wih'-po-tsi-mai'-yo-na-to, pl.

na-wih'-po-tsi-mai'-yo, I make, &c.

ni-wih'-po-tsi-mai'-yo, thou dost make, &c.

how, i-to'-ni-ta'-i-ni-ōt, how far round, how extensive.

howl, e'-ho-pits, to howl, as a dog or wolf.

hunt, i-o-mo'-o-ni'-sto, to hunt buffalo, to surround and kill, as in a buffalo hunt.

husband, hi-hum', a husband.

hi-hum'-i-wo, pl.

na-i-hum', my husband.

ni-i-hum', thy husband.

I.

ice, ma'-ōm.

ma-o-minst', (pl.)

illiberal, i-mi'-o-ta-nūć, to be stingy or illiberal.

immediately, e'-i-sak, suddenly, immediately.

inconstant, sći-wi-i'-o-si-vi-ōn, inconstant, unchaste.

ink, is-ta-ni'-i-hōs.

intestines, ih-ai'-i-man, the large intestines of animals.

iron, ma-kai'-it.

ma-ka'-i-tai'-wi-kis, iron bird, humming bird.

wi-ho'-ni-ma-kai'-it, white iron, silver.

wi-ho'-ni-ma-kai'-i-tai'-wo-at, silver medal.

moh'-ta-wi-ma-kai'-it, black metal, iron.

itch, i-si-si'-i-nats, to have one's body to itch all over.

J.

jealous, e-o'-si-wi'-o-ni, to be jealous, envious.

joint, ći-hu'-na-i'-o-na-as, joints of animals.

journey, i-ōh'-o-wi-stan, to be journeying or travelling.

ni-wa'-is-ti-ōh-o-wi'-stan, who is that journeying?

jump, e-ko'-ka-an, to jump.

i'-ka-ak, to jump over, as a horse.

in-ha', to frisk or jump about, like a spirited horse.

i-no'-i-tsi, to make a jump, prance about, wild.

o-na-is'-i-an, to plunge or jump into water, as a frog.

K.

kettle, ma-ai'-ta-to, a kettle.

ma-ai'-ta-to'-o-nōts, (pl.)

mōh-ta'-wi-to, a black kettle, iron kettle.

e-ho'-ni-to, yellow iron, brass kettle.

ma'-i-to, red iron, a copper kettle.

wo'-ni-wi-to, white iron, a tin kettle.

ka-e'-wi-to, a kettle with a spout, a coffee-pot.

o-wah'-i-ni-to, frying-pan, "pan with a tail."

tsi-ōh-i-wi'-sho-is-to, gridiron, cooking-iron.

is-to'-wo-kats, the ears of a kettle.

o-ni'-o-na-ti-ni'-ma-o-i, the rim of a kettle.

key, wi'-o-i-mah, a wooden key.

ta-ta-ho'-i-yo, to turn a key, to unlock, as a trunk.

ta-ta-ho'-i-nis-tōts, turning a key.

kick, ōh-ta'-o-wi, to kick.

i-ōh-ta'-o-wo, to kick one or something.

i-o-ni'-nih-an, to kick in pieces.

kidneys, ist-si'-tat, kidneys of a buffalo.

kill, e-ha-na'-e-wo, to kill by pressing or lying on.

kindle, e-natst', to build or kindle a fire.

kinnic-kinnic, ma-ko'-mi-his, a mixture of one-fourth tobacco and the remainder the bark of red osier (*Cornus*), or the leaves of the bear-berry (*Arctostaphylos uva-ursi*), dried and made very fine; used by the Indians for smoking.

kiss, e'-wo-sim, he kisses, or to kiss.

na'-wo'-sim, I kiss.

ni'-wo'-sim, thou dost kiss.

e'-wo-sim-a-tsi'-o, they all kiss.

knee, en-stan', kneepan, patella.

nan-stan', my kneepan.

nin-stan', thy kneepan.

en-sta'-nio, en-sta'-ni-i-wo } (pl.)

is-tsi'-ma-ni-wa', between the knees or feet.

knock, i-ha'-ni-o-sto'-no, to knock on the head, to kill or stun by striking.

he-siv', the fleshy part of the leg below the knee of an animal.

knife, mo'-ćik, a knife.

na-mo'-ćik, my knife.

ni-mo'-ćik, thy knife.

i-mo'-ćik, his knife.

mo-takst' (pl.), knives.

na-mo-takst', our knives.

ni-mo-takst', your knives.

knob, to'-ni-a-hu'-yo, a knob, button, head of a pin or nail.

know, i-ho'-ni-in, to know.

ni-tōn'-shi-wi, to make oneself known, to tell one's name.

L.

lake, tsi-ma'-o-mo-i, a lake.

lame, i-no'-ni-kai'-yūts, to go lame, to limp.

i-no'-ni-ka, lameness.

large, im-a-ha'-o, large, great in any way.

na-ma-ha'-it, I am large.

ni-ma-ha'-it, thou art large.

im-a-ha'-it, he or it is large.

im-o'-ma-ha-i-ta'-o, they are large.

i-to'-ni-ta'-o, how big? how large?

last, hi-stōh'-is, the last.

lately, e'-kas, lately, very near, very soon.

laugh, i'-ho-hats, to laugh at, to make fun, to ridicule.

i'-ha-na'-tum-a-o, to laugh immoderately.

lay, i-na'-nŭts, to lay anything aside or down.

lazy, e-ho'-ni-ćist, lazy, laziness.

e-ho'-ni-ćis'-ta-o, pl.

lead, wi'-ho-i-ma.

leaf, wiħ'-pŏts, a leaf.

wiħ'-po-tŏts, pl.

e-ho-wi'-wiħ-po-tsi-wat, when the leaves are falling, dead.

league, no-taħ'-i-o, league, covenant, communion, fellowship, a church, society, community.

no-taħ'-iv-sto, pl.

lean, in-o-wo'-i-yo, to lean, as one tree against another.

e-ni'-mi-ŏt, leaning, or not perpendicular.

e-wiħ'-pu-na, to become poor or lean, as cattle in the spring.

leave, wi-hŭħ'-i-a-no, to leave the lodge, said when the women and children leave the tent, for the men to partake of a feast.

leech, wiħ'-o, a leech.

leeks, ħa-o'-i-taħ'-i-wŏts, leeks, onions.

leggins, e-wŏħ'.

e-wŏħ'-to-iv, and e-wŏħ-to'-i-wŏts, pl.

lend, i-ta'-ho-ho, to lend, as a horse.

length, e-a'-i-sta.

lie, e-he'-ni-o, to lie flat on the side, as animals do.

ho-ta-mi-pau'-o-nast, to lie with one's back to the fire.

i-ŏħ'-tai-in, to lie in wait, to spend the night out, while hunting or killing deer.

lightning, i-o-i'-tsi-ŏts.

limber, e-ći-kŏht', to make limber or pliable by biting, as leather.

lip, hists; nats, my lips; nists, thy lips; mats, his lips.

his-ći'-ni-o, } pl.
his-ći'-ni-wŏts, }

i-to'-no-wats, pouting lips.

i-to'-no-wa-tsi'-na-o (pl.)

listen, i-a'-to-wo, to listen.

na-a-tŏħ', I am listening.

ni-a-tŏħ', thou art listening.

na-sa-a'-to-wa, I am not listening.

ni-sa-a'-to-wa, thou art not listening.

a-ha-sći'-ŏts, to listen, to hearken to or for any one.

ni-ha'-to-wŏts, } you listen to or for any one.
ni-ha'-to-mo-ni, }

live, e-wa-wo-sta'-niv, to live again, to return to life, to revive.

im-a-yu'-nim, to live or dwell apart, as a woman in her menses.

liver, he, liver of animals.

lodge, we'-e; na'-no-wan, our lodge; ni'-no-wan, your lodge.

wi'-e-nŏts (pl.), a good many lodges.

i-to'-wo-ni-sto, to build, pitch, or put up a lodge.

ho-ha'-mi-wi'-e, sides and roof of a lodge or house.

wi-e-no'-tsi-ne-shi'-tanst, on both sides of the tent.

wi'-i-he-wi-no', that one's lodge.

he-wi-no'-tsi-nŏts, those lodges.

ći-ma'-mo-o-no-wi'-e, top of the tent or lodge, hole where the smoke goes out.

si-ma'-mo-wa'-e-hum, top of a tent, ridge of the house, the crossing of the top of the poles of the lodge.

he-wi'-no-e'-wi-nŏt, the pole of a tent left standing, the skeleton of a tent.

ai-to-wi-mi'-o-niv, between houses.

na-tai'-wa-si-ŏts, from a place or lodge.

ni-ni-wa'-si-o-tsi, to be in a place or lodge.

e-shi'-yu-nit-hu'-a-tu'-wa-o, hole in the lodge for the smoke to escape.

siħ-pa-te'-i-ho-nŭts, the place in front of the lodge, which is fastened with pins.

tsi-wi'-sto-na'-ta-ŏts, to a place or lodge.

ći-sti'-i-naus, household, or all the things in a lodge.

waħ-tum', place opposite the door.

ho-whi', lodge-poles.

no-taħ'-i-um, a soldier's lodge.

no-taħ'-i-um-mi-to'-i-ni-sto, to make a soldier's lodge.

look, to-to'-ats, to look, to look at.

no'-tsi-wi'-tŏts, to look into.

i-ko'-o-tŏts, to look with a spy-glass, to reconnoitre.

o-no'-e-yo-tōts, to look upon, to have an oversight.

e'-i-ko, to look into a house.

a-mo'-o-ma-ćis'-tōts, a looking-glass.

lose, e'-ho-nist, to lose, to have lost.

ha'-shi-e-wa'-ni-ōts, to be lost, disappear.

i-sa'-wo-nish, not to be lost.

louse, s-ta'-im.

s-ta'-im-i-wo, (pl.)

mi-shin, a wood louse.

M.

maid, mah-i-e'-ne, an old maid. There is one old woman among the Shyennes, who never has had a husband.

mallet, to'-o, an Indian stone mallet.

man, wo-stūn'.

wo-stūn'-i-o, (pl.)

e-wo'-stu-ni-wa-o, to have attained one's growth, to have reached manhood.

si-vi-o-nivst-'sh, a chief, a great man.

e-si'-i-o'-tsi-tan, medicine-man.

ksu-wa', a young, unmarried man.

ksu-wa'-i-hē, (pl.)

ma-a'-kis, an old man.

ma-ak'-si, (pl.)

ai-ta'-ni-kai-kūn, a boy 12 or 14 years of age.

mane, e-ma-ta'-o-in-o-to'-un, mane of a horse.

many, to-nist', how many.

e-tōnst'-tanst, how many? how much?

e'-ni-sta-nist, only so many, only so much.

mark, to-tōh-tsih'-wōts, to mark, to cut gashes in mourning.

marry, e-wi'-stōm, he marries, or to marry.

na-wi'-stōm, I marry.

ni-wi'-stōm, thou dost marry.

na-wi'-sto-mōn, we marry.

ni-wi'-sto-mōn, you marry.

e-wi'-sto-o'-mo, they marry.

i-tais'-tsi-im, he desires to marry, or wishes a wife.

na-tais'-tsi-im, I desire to marry.

ni-tais'-tsi-im, thou desirest to marry.

i-tais'-tsi-im-i-o, they desire to marry.

na-tais'-tsi-im-im, we desire to marry.

ni-tais'-tsi-im-im, you desire to marry.

im-a-yun'-i-wi-sto-i-ma'-tsin, to be married according to the customs of the whites, a sacred marriage.

i-sa-mai'-yun-i-wi'-sto-i-ma'-tsin, to be married after the manner of the Indians.

he-na-tau-hai'-nōts, to be old enough to be married.

matches, o-ha-si-ha'-si-o-nōts.

meat, o-e'-wōh-ōts, fresh meat.

o-no-wōh', dried meats.

o-no-wōh'-o-nōts, (pl.)

i-ho'-so-tūh'-i-mi'-i-ōts, tainted meat.

medicine, e-si'-i-hav'-si-wats, red medicine, poison.

tsi-ma-he-yo'-ni-vist, a doctor, or medicine-man.

meet, i-to'-wi-o-wa'-ćis-tōm, to meet, as persons travelling.

melt, i'-ma-tau, to melt or dissolve away, as snow.

his-tas'-i'-ma-tau, the snow melts, or dissolves away.

i'-hōh-pet, to fuse or melt, as metal.

merciful, i-shi'-wats-tai'-yo, merciful, to be merciful.

middle, tai'-si-to.

si-to-wōm', in the middle, midst.

milk, ma-tun'.

ma-tun'-ai-yum, milk grease, butter.

im-i-ta-so'-a-mi, thick milk.

ma-tun'-a-e'-hi-kun, hard milk, cheese.

ma-tun'-i-oh'-i-ōts, hardened or frozen milk.

wi-ho-i'-o-to-a-ma-ta-na'-nist, a cow that gives milk.

e-hi'-wo-i-tan-han', to draw milk, as from a cow.

mirage, i-e'-no-nu-hat, mirage, glimmering of vapors in the sun's heat.

miss, e'-wo-nish, he misses, or to miss the road, to wander and get lost.

na'-wo-nish, I miss the road, &c.

ni'-wo-nish, thou dost miss the road, &c.

mittens, i-to'-a, and to'-a.

na-to'-a, my mittens.

ni-to'-a, thy mittens.

i-to-a'-i-wo (pl.), their mittens.

mix, he-ko'-ma-o-wo'-tsūts, to mix, as mortar.

moccasin, i-mōk'-ći.

i-mōk-ća'-ni-wōts, (pl.)

na-mōk'-ći, my moccasin.

ni-mōk'-ći, thy moccasin.

e-wo-kōn', to put tops on moccasins.

molasses, pa-nu'-i-ha-sa'-i-ōt.

money, mi-ho-ni'-ma-kai'-it.

moon, i'-wo-nit, the moon rising.

i-shi-i'-a-min, the moon passing over the sky.

i-shi-i'-ta-in, the moon passing down into the west.

morning, en-i-wo'-ni-ōts, daylight, dawn of morning.

morose, shu-mi'-i-whai'-i-sin'-ōs (adjective).

mosquito, ho'-o-ma.

mother, ish'-k.

na'-ko-e, my mother.

nih'-ku, your mother.

mourn, i-ah'-ai'-im, to cry or mourn for the loss of a child.

move, im'-o-mo'-ōts, to move about, moving about.

much, e-wo'-ta-ha', very much.

mule, a-ki'-i-wa.

a-ki'-i-wa'-ham, (pl.)

musk, e-ni-si-me'-hast.

muskrat, i-yōh'.

i-yōh'-i-o, pl.

mystery, ma-he'-yo, mysterious, medicine, mystery, spiritual. Anything that the Indians do not understand they consider supernatural, or "medicine."

e-ma-wi'-hu, Great Medicine, Great Spirit.

N.

nail, is-to'-a-no-ni-mo'-i-o-sūn, the nails of the fingers and toes.

e-mi'-si-mi-ōs, the dirt under the finger-nails.

mi-si'-mi-o-sūn, pl. form.

e-ni'-to-i-to'-ni-o, nails of iron, so called because first used in a door.

naked, i'-o-is-tōs, naked, nearly naked, poorly clad.

near, kaksh, near, near by, soon, presently.

neck, ći-hu'-na-ōt, nape or end of the neck.

is-ći'-ōts, back of the neck.

e'-ko-tsi'-na, by the neck.

is-ći-ōts'-to-i-shi, to tie around the neck, as a rope.

needles, e-ko'-wo-is-tōts', and wi-ho-ko'-wōst.

nephew, it-sin'-ōt, his nephew.

na-tsin'-ōt, my nephew.

ni-tsin'-ōt, thy nephew.

na-tsin'-o-ta, my nephews.

ni-tsin'-o-ta, thy nephews.

nest, who'-is, a bird's nest.

never, i-sa-ho-wōh'-po-nit, at no time, never.

new, e-ho-hai'-it.

mo-ni-ma'-nistst, to make new, to renew.

news, ni-ni'-o-tsi-is, to tell the news, to take word to any one.

nih-o'-tsi-is, to arrive with the news.

e-hi-ōh'-ta-o-wa, to bring word or news to any one.

tai-yōh'-ta-o-wa, to have gone to carry the news.

night, ta-e'-wa.

ta-asts', pl.

ōh-ta'-e-shi-to'-iv, beginning of the night, dusk.

nod, i-o-a'-wa-e, to nod or swing the head, as in sleep.

na-wa'-wo-e, I nod.

ni-wa'-wo-e, you nod.

i-a'-wa-i-sto, they all nod.

he-i-e-tai'-yūts, to nod the head, to bow to any one.

noise, i-ha'-i-no-wi'-o, noise, clamor, tumult.

shi-o-ha'-o-no-as, a humming noise, bustle.

hi-ah'-po-ni-ni', to make a grating noise with the teeth.

nose, e'-iv.

e'-iv-o-ni'-wōts, pl.

na'-iv, my nose.

ni'-iv, thy nose.

e'-i-ni-ōts, to wink the nose.

e-he'-e-im, to blow the nose.

he-e-em', the excretion of the nose.

e-si-e'-ma-si-ōts, to sniff or snuff up the nose.

i-ku'-ko-no-me-i-sis'-tūts, the external parts of the nose.

nothing, i'-ho-wa-an.

e-ho-wa'-ni-ni-ho', to become nothing.

O.

obliquely, i-tah-ah', obliquely, from corner to corner.

obstinate, sti-wi'-nis-to, to be obstinate, resolute, to have a mind of one's own.

old, in-o-no'.
i'-tu-si-i-na'-o, to become old.
e-pi'-i-ōts, to become old or rotten, as old clothing.
ma-tum'-ha, an old woman.
im'-ōs, old, worn out.
im'-o-sōts, pl.
ni-ta'-im-ōs, all old, very old.

on, he-am', on or upon.

ooze, ma'-pi-im-i'-ōts, to run or ooze out, as sap or water.

open, i-o-ni'-ain, to open anything, as a bundle; to untie, as a shoe.
si'-to-wo, an open place, a yard.
e-ta'-ōts, to open the mouth, in yawning or gaping.
i-ish-tsin', something that is open, as cloth.
na-ish-tsin'. 1st person sing.

oppose, ev-hav-si'-va, to check, to oppose, put a stop to, forbid.

ornaments, hi-wo', a man's ornaments.
na-wo', my ornaments.
ni-wo', thy ornaments.
ho, brass rings, used as ornaments around the wrist.
ho'-ho-nōts, pl.

orphan, nih-hais', an orphan.
nih-hai'-sōn, pl.

overflow, i-mi'-ish, to overflow, as a flood.

P.

pack, i-sho-po-o'-inst, a pack or bundle of furs.

paint, i-ho'-wo-ni, to paint one's self yellow.

pair, e-no'-ka, a pair.
e-nih-anst', two pairs.
e-na-hanst', three pairs.

pantaloons, wi-shi-su'-nist.

pare, i'-a-tōh, to pare anything with a knife.

pass, i-ta'-a-ain, to pass over, as a hill, in going home.
e'wo-iv, passing off, as clouds.

patient, o-wai-hai'-is-ći-wi'-mi-ist, to count as nothing, to be patient.

paw, e-shi'-ći-tsi-wai'-yōst, to paw up dust, to throw up earth as cattle do.

people, his-tain', a people, tribe, nation, band.
hi-man-hai'-stōts, his people.

pepper, mi'-i-mi-nūts.

perhaps, mu'-i-ni-su'a-ni, hi-ya'-i-nis, } perhaps, probably.

pimple, i-ho'-pi-in', a pimple, a rough place on the skin.

pipe, he'-ōk, a pipe.
he-o'-ko-nōts, pl.
na'-tsi-ōk, my pipe.
ći'-ōk, your pipe.
na-tai'-to-an, I will fill my pipe myself.
he'-pōts, to take the pipe.
si-o'-kis-to-mis, small end of the pipe-stem, which is taken into the mouth.
ha-he-yo', a stick to press the tobacco down in the pipe when smoking.

pitch, o-ho'ma-ni-nih'-a-mo-ćist, to come and pitch one's tent.

pithy, e-wi'-na-ōts, pithy, spongy.

place, tu'-sa, at what place?
tu-sa-ni'-ta-ōts, where, in what place is it?
si-nōts', to place under the girdle, as a hatchet or knife, to wear around the loins.
na-tah'-o-wi-stan, from one place to another.

plain, i-tōh'-tōn, a plain, level.

to pluck, o-ko-wa'-ni, to pluck out, as the hair on the head.

plums, mah'-i-mi'-nōts.
mah'-i-mi-sta'-im, plum pits or stones.
mah'-i-mi-no'-isé, plum bushes.

plunge, i-i'-i-yōts, to plunge or sink down, as in water.

polish, i'-o-wa'-si-to, to rub and make shine, to polish.

poor, usta'-mi-no, poor, miserable, destitute.
usta'-mi-no'-he-hiv.
usta'-mi-no'-hi-o, (pl.)
i-tōh'-o-na, poor, not fat.

pop, e'-ni-sto'-ni-wa, to make pop, as in blowing a leaf.

porcupine, he-ko'-wit.
he-kōst', porcupine quills.

possess, he-ni'-séo, to possess anything, to have for one's own.

pound, e-pin'-hn-nōts, to pound, as corn in a mortar.
pe-nōts', to pound anything fine.
i-si'-o-i'-yats, to ram or pound hard in a hole.

powder, wōh'-i-wusts, a powder-horn.
wōh'-i-wit, (pl.)
e-pa'-im, what remains after powder is exploded.
na-pa'-im, my powder.
ni-pa'-im, your powder.
e-pa'-im-iv, (pl.)

pox, i-wa'-ni-i-ist, small-pox.
i-ōsh'-ki-win', pitted with the small-pox, a pitted face.

prairie, wi-o'-no-tsi'-o-ko-manst, out in the prairie.

preserve, e-ōh'-po-o-ist, to keep or preserve anything with care.

press, o-e'-to-i, to press down on.
e-ko'-no-ho'-e-nōts, to press on, be tight on.
e-nih'-pe-si'-o-wats, to press close together with the mouth.

to prick, e-he'-wōh-so, to prick or dot, as marks on the skin.

proud, e-hi'-is-ta, proud, vain.

pulverize, i-ći'-wa-to'-i-yo, to pulverize, to plough the ground.
i-pin', powdered, pulverized, fine.

pumpkin, ma'-o.
ma'-ōn, (pl.)

punch, i-ōh'-i-wo, to punch a hole, or to make a hole by punching.
mah-o'-yi, to punch to death in a hole.

purpose, e-ōh'-i-mo, to purpose evil against, to desire to take the life of any one.

push, sim-o-ta'-so-ōts, to push, as a boat out from the shore with a paddle.
ai-so-o'-wo, to push against, to push along.
i-i'-e-yōts, to push under and pry up, as a root.
tsi'-i-ne, to push or jog any one with the elbow.
wo-wo-tut'-si-mi-nōts, to push into, as a stick into the sand after turtles' eggs.

put, e-o-tats', to put on and wear, as leggins.
e'-hi-ma'-ma, to put on, as clothes, to wear, to be clothed.
mi-sih'-o-pa'-i-wōh, to put anything (as a child) on one's back under a blanket.

Q.

quarrel, mi'-o-tats, to quarrel or fight with any one.

quarter, niv-sta'-ni-wo-e'-hist, one of the four quarters of anything.

quit, i-ni-sto'-i-no, to quit the lodge, to leave it.

quiver, i-stūs', a quiver.
na-i-stūs', my quiver.
ni-i-stūs', thy quiver.
i-stu-sūn' (pl.), quivers.

R.

rain, i-ho'-ko, to rain.
i-wo'-o-no-ko, a long-continued rain.
no-no-no', rainbow.
e-ōh'-tat, a kind of lizard that is supposed to fall with the rain.

raspberries, ōts-ći-e'-i-hew'h.
i-wi'-po-tsi-wa, raspberry bushes.

rattle, in'-is-to'-ni-wa'-nōts, to rattle the feet when walking.
e-shi'-shi-nōn, nails and hoofs of animals used as rattles.

ravish, i-na'-ko-nan, to ravish, to commit a rape.

ready, no-no'-to-ho-sinst, ready, prepared for anything.

recoil, na-po'-i-shi-ni'-o, to recoil, as a gun.

red, im'-a-o, to become red, reddish.
im-a-o'-nist.
en-i-ma-ho'-i-na, redness of the dawn.

rhubarb, e-si'-i-o-tsi-hōh, yellow medicine.

reject, tsi-wi'-wi-ōm, to reject, to despise, to turn away from.
na-ta-wi'-wi-ōm, I reject.
ni-ta-wi'-wi-ōm, thou dost reject.

remember, mi'-e-ta-nōts, to remember, to recollect.

rest, o-so'-to-mo-ist, rest, to rest.

resemble, i-si-i-shi'-ni-o, to be like, to resemble, to have its father's face.

restore, mi'-tsi, to restore to any one, to give to one what belongs to him.
na-ta'-mil, I restore.

ni-ta'-mit, thou dost restore.
ni-ta'-mi-tats (pl.), they restore.

rice, e'-hi-sŏn.

rich, i-ha'-o-wa, to be rich.
i-ha'-o-wai-yo (pl.), they are rich.
na-ha'-o-wai-yo, we are rich.
na-ha'-o-wa, I am rich.
ni-ha'-o-wa, thou art rich.

ring, ih'-i-wa-ŏts, to ring as a bell, to make ring.
na-a-ni'-a-to-mats, a ringing in the ears.
na-sa-a-ni'-sto-mo-ni, I have a ringing in my ears.

rise, i-o-ha'-a, to rise or get up.
na-o-ha'-a, I rise.
ni-o-ha'-a, thou dost rise.
na-o-hain', we rise.
ni-o-hain', you rise.
i-o-ha'-i-o, they rise.
i-a-ha'-ni-sti'-wa-ha, to rise up again, to recover itself, as grass, that is beat down.
im'-i-an, to rise up in sight, as one in the water.
a-to'-ni-wa-ni, to rise up, to stand up like the hairs on an animal.

river, o'-he.
o-he-ist', (pl.)
o-he-kis', a small river or creek.
o-hik-so'-nŏts, (pl.)
mah-i-yo'-he, a large river.
mah-i-yo'-hist', (pl.)
o-he-i'-ho-hŏm, mouth of a river.
i-ŏh'-o-we, } crossing a river.
e-ŏh'-o-who, }

road, mi'-o.
mi'-o-niv.
oh-o-wi-sta'-mi-o.
o'-ha-mas, by the way, on the road, between one place and another.

roast, mŏh'-ta-wŏh'-po-no-tŏts, to roast or parch, as coffee or corn.
i'-ma-shi'-ni-hu, to be partially or wholly roasted, to be covered with red spots from going too near the fire.
na'-ma-shi'-ni-hu, I roast.
ni'-ma-shi'-ni-hu, thou dost roast.
na'-ma-shi'-ni-hu-i sto, we roast.

robe, ma-tsi'-o-mi-wŏh'-tsit, a summer robe.
tsi-wo'-kŏm-hŏm, a white robe.

rock, o-o-na'.
o-o-na'-i-o, (pl.)
o-o-na'-tsŏn, small water-worn pebbles.
o-o-wai', white, crystalline gypsum, selenite.
wo'-i-sta'-o-na, white rock, or white, smooth rock, quartz.
mŏh-ta'-wo-na, black rock, a primitive rock.
tsi-o'-ho-ist, "the rock that water cuts," cut rock, forming a cañon.
shi'-i-o, sandstone.

roll, e-wo-wo'-ki-tsi-un, to roll anything.
e-a-mo'-in, to roll over and over, as the wheel of a wagon.

room, mi-to-mev', to make room for, as in a tent, to give place to.

rosebud, he-nin'.
he-ni-ni'-o-he, the Rosebud River.

rotten, a-he'-ko-tah, rotten, as wood.

rough, i'-yo-iv, rough, roughened up.
ih-iv'-a-o, rough, as a country.

row, mi-o-na'-nist, a row, as of corn.
mi-o-na'-ni-sto, (pl.)

rub, i-o'-wo, to rub or brush off, as dirt or dust.
ni-o-nis'-to-kan, to rub in the hands.
e-ho-nin', to rub skins with the hand in dressing.
i-ah-e-ish', to rub or scratch the back against anything.
i-o-ŏh'-i-mah'-i-e, to rub a robe or a skin on a rope or cord in dressing.
na-o-ŏh'-i-mah'-i-ist, I rub, &c.
ni-o-ŏh'-i-mah'-i-ist, thou dost rub, &c.
i-o-ŏh'-i-mah'-i-is'-ći-na, they rub, &c.
na-o-ŏh'-i-mah'-i-is'-ći-no, we rub, &c.
ni-o-ŏh'-i-mah'-i-is'-ći-no, you rub, &c.
e-shi-ŏh'-i-mah'-i-e, to be done rubbing a robe on a cord.
e-sho'-ni-o, to rub a robe or skin with the hands.
na-sho'-ni-ŏh, I rub, &c.
ni-sho'-ni-ŏh, thou dost rub, &c.
na-shi-ŏh'-ta-nŏn, we rub, &c.
ni-shi-ŏh'-ta-nŏn, you rub, &c.

run, i-a-mi-mi'-o, to run.

i'-a-mah', to run away, flee, retreat.

rump, aist'-shi-o, the lower part of the back.

nast'-shi-o, my rump.

nist'-shi-o, thy rump.

rush, i-wi'-sto-i-ni-sto, to rush on the buffalo.

o-ha'-i-si-yūs'-ta-i-si-takst', to rise up and rush, as one excited.

rustle, wih'-po-to'-tsi-ih-i-no'-ninst, to make rustle, as leaves.

S.

sacred, i-a-ma'-wi-hōt, to regard as sacred or holy.

sack, ho'-e, an empty bag or sack.

saddle, o-au-kis'-tōts.

o-au-kis'-to-tūts, (pl.)

na-to-au-kis'-to-tōts, my saddle.

ni-to-au-kis'-to-tōts, thy saddle.

o-wa'-ki-stōts, a pack-saddle.

sail, ev'-si-o, to sail round, as an eagle.

scabby, i-yo-iv', scabby, scabbed.

i-yo-iv'-i-o, (pl.)

scales, o-ni'-sta-na-nōts, scales, steelyards.

scampering, e'-wo-so, scampering like colts, unrestrained.

scare, e-a-si-ha'-wo, to scare away by stamping.

i-o-a'-si-ta'-o-wo, to scare all away.

scattered, e'-he-ni-anst, scattered or fallen from, as a rock.

scowl, o-he'-hi-ōh'-tan, to scowl, to make wrinkles on the forehead by raising the eyebrows.

scrape, i-shih'-o-i-ain', to scrape, as a robe.

na-shih'-o-i-ain', I scrape, &c.

ni-shih'-o-i-ain', thou dost scrape, &c.

ni'-ta-i-shih'-o-i-ai'-ni-sto, they all scrape, &c.

i'-ni-to, to scrape the hair from a hide.

na'-ni-to, I scrape, &c.

ni'-ni-to, thou dost scrape, &c.

i'-ni-to-i'-sto, } they scrape, &c.
i-ma'-ni-to-i'-sto, }

e'-shi-ni-to, to be done scraping, as a skin.

na'-shi-ni-to, I am done scraping.

ni'-shi-ni-to, thou art done scraping.

i-shi-ih'-o-i-sto, they are done scraping.

e-shi-ih'-o-ni-o, he was done scraping, &c.

na-shi-ih'-o-ni-ōht, I was done scraping, &c.

ni-shi-ih'-o-ni-ōht, thou wert done scraping, &c.

na-shi-ih'-o-ni-ōh'-ta-nōn, we were done scraping, &c.

ni-shi-ih'-o-ni-ōh'-ta-nōn, you were done scraping, &c.

(Past tense.)

i-si'-si-no, to scrape a skin.

wōht-sit', the scrapings of skins.

o-ni'-o-tōts, to scrape the hairs off a skin.

scratch, ah-e'-i-nats, to scratch, as one itching.

i-ah-e'-i-nats, he scratches.

i-ah-e'-i-stai-im, they scratch.

i-ho'-ta-o, a scratch.

ah-i-a-ta'-o-wats, to scratch with the toes.

screw, ni'-to-yo, gun screw or worm.

scum, i-ta-wo'-ni-wi-siv, to have a scum.

seam, i-a'-mo-to'-i-no, seam in a buffalo robe.

season, i-i-mi'-a-niv, next season, next year.

a-i'-ni-shi'-i-kas, the season when the days are short.

an-sta'-i-ha-as, the season when the nights are short.

see, i-o-ha'-ćist, to see clearly.

na-o-ha'-ćist, I see clearly.

ni-o-ha'-ćist, thou seest clearly.

see-sawing, in-o-no-po'-i-o-a-tsi'-o, see-sawing, an up and down motion.

set, wi-kis-in'-o-o-na, to set, as a bird.

sew, a-po-nōts', to sew or mend.

i'-ha-pi-nōht, to sew on, to patch.

o-im'-sko-nūts, an Indian woman's sewing-bag, which contains all her sewing apparatus.

e'-po-i-nōt, to sew on a round patch.

e-ah'-pi-no, to sew on a long patch, over a rent.

shade, i-ho-wi'-o-o, shade, or shadow.

e-ya-wi'-a-o, a shade, as branches of trees; an umbrella.

shake, ma-ko'-mi-is-i-a'-si-to-to, to shake, to clean by shaking or blowing, as kinnic-kinnic.

i-o-wai'-i-yōts, to shake the head.

i-yo'-ma-ish, to motion with the head.

e-yo'-ma-e'-ūts, to wag the head.

in-is'-to-ni-wa, to be shaken by the wind.

ka-mah'-i-i-ni'-mo-tōt, to shake with the mouth.

sharp, e-o'-kūs.

ći-e'-kūs, } sharp-pointed.
ći-e'-ka-kūs, }

shears, ōh-to-wa'-mo, a pair of shears.

ōh-to-wa'-mo-takst, pl.

shed, wi-ći'-su-i-ni'-si-i-na, to shed quills.

sheep, wo-ka'-i-tsi-wo'-ko-mast, white deer, a sheep; also, kos, a sheep.

shells, ći-mi'-o-na, shells of the genus *Dentalium*, used as ornaments.

ni-mać', a land-shell, *Helix*.

ni-maći'-o, pl.

ma-pi'-ni-mać, water-shells.

shirt, is'-ći, a shirt.

na'-is-ći, my shirt.

ni'-is-ći, thy shirt.

e'-is-ći, his shirt.

is'-ći-in, pl. shirts.

mōh-ta'-wi-is-ći, a black shirt.

wo'-ko-mi-ka-ku'-is-ći, a white shirt.

ka-ku'-is-ći, a yellow calico shirt.

o-i-shi'-nai-wai-o'-tōts, a vest, a shirt with the sleeves cut off.

kah-o'-i-shi-ōn, calico cloth.

shoes, hōh-tsim'-o-ki, round snow-shoes.

shoot, i-ha'-ni-mas, he shoots.

na-ha'-ni-mas, I shoot.

ni-ha'-ni-mas, thou dost shoot.

i-pi'-im-hist, to shoot in pieces.

shore, to-tu-kōm', at the shore, by the shore, at the edge.

ōh-i-en', said of a bluff shore, where the water is deep.

short, ćik-sta'.

i-ćik'-sta-yo, pl.

shot, shi'-shi-ma-hōts.

mah-i-wi'-hu-i-ma, large shot, balls.

shoulder, i-sta'-ta-mo.

i-sta'-tsi-i-ma'-mōh-o-yi, between the shoulders.

i-tsi-o'-is-tak, to shrug up, as the shoulders.

shout, no'-o-nōst, to shout out to any one.

sick, i-ha'-mōh-ta.

i-sa-ha'-mōh-ta, not sick.

side, is-ći'-a-mah'-ist, on one side.

ha-stu', on the other side.

ho-hōm', on this side.

sight, e'-ni-mi-in, to come in sight, as people from over a hill.

ta-si'-a-me-inst', in sight of, afar off.

silently, e-tsi'-a-mi, stilly, silently, as if approaching game.

simmer, i-to-si'-i-so-wōt, to simmer, or make a slight noise just before boiling, as water.

sinew, ho'-tauh, taken from the back of an elk or deer.

he-sis'-tōn, large sinew in the neck of animals.

sing, ni-minst', to sing.

na-ta'-ni-min, I sing.

ni-ta'-ni-min, thou dost sing.

i-ta'-ni-min, he sings.

wa-wa-o'-si-mi, to sing in a low tone, in a whispering, drawling manner, as the Shyenne women do when lulling their children to sleep.

e'-ni-min, to sing in praise of any one.

sink, o-na'-i-hi-ko, to sink down, as a stone.

singe, wi'-he, to singe off, as the down from a fowl.

sister, is-ta-ta-nim', a sister.

is-ta-ta-nim'-i-wo, pl. sisters.

nah'-a-im, my sister.

i-ah'-a-im'-i-wo, pl. my sisters.

sit, en-sta-ni-wa'-e-ni-i, to sit with the knees bent up.

skim, mo-mōlit', to skim off, as grease from a pot.

skin, en-o-iv', all kinds of skins.

o-ev', a green skin, one just taken from the animal.

i-o-ōh'-a-niv, dried skin, parchment.

wo'-ka-e-wōts, all kinds of deerskins.

o-ho'-kuts, a deerskin with the hair taken off.

i-no-ta'-ni-sto, a skin bottle, for holding water.

e-wa-e'-hu-wa, an instrument for scraping skins.

sky, wo-e-i'-a-ta-tan, blue sky.

sleep, i'-o-wish, to sleep.

i-na-au-si'-tan, to sleep or be sleepy.

i-ma'-no-shin, to sleep side by side.
tai-o-wisé', to sleep out, away from home.

slide, i-a-no'-i-o-whit, to slide, as on the ice.

slip, e-sōh'-i-yu-ash, to slip, as on the ice.
e'-bo-ha-in, to let anything drop or slip from the hand.

slippery, e-i-sōh'.
e-ih-o'-a, slippery, ropy, slimy.

slits, o-he-wi'-o-tah, slits cut in a skin when stretched.

slushy, e-mōh'-tsi-e'-no, as snow when soft.

small, e'-ta-ki, anything small.
i-éi-ta'-o, how small? of what size?

smell, i-hav'-si-vi'-no, smelling badly, stinking.
i-hav'-si-vi-mi'-i-ōts, to smell badly, as tainted meat.
in'-a-tōn, to smell.
o-ōh'-i-mi'-yōts, a strong smell.
si'-to-wun, to burn incense, to make a good smell by burning.

smoke, i'-vi-nōt.
im-a'-vi-nōt, smoky, full of smoke.
im'-a-wi-ta'-nist, to smoke.
e-wi'-no-ta-wo-ma'-no, smoky, air filled with smoke.

smooth, i-a'-to-no-wi'-si-nats, to smooth down the hair.

snap, i-a-i-si', to crack or snap, as fire.
i-ōh'-o-ma, to snap or crack as ice in walking over it.

sneeze, e-he-ta-in', to sneeze.

snow, is'-tas.
im-a'-is-ta-siv, all kinds of snow, all the snow.
i'-ho-i-it, falling snow, to fall as snow.
is-ta'-si-ōh'-i-a-no'-iv, a snow-drift.
i-wo'-o-ni-it, to snow in.
i-ho-it', it is snowing.
i-a'-ih-to'-o-in, to snow on anything.
im-a-ya'-to-in, everything covered with snow.

soak, e-shi-ki'-o-wo, to soak a robe for dressing.
na-shi'-ko-wōts, I soak, &c.
ni-shi'-ko-wōts, thou dost soak, &c.
e-shi'-ko-wo'-tsi-no, they soak, &c.
i-su'-a-ni-ōts, to soak through and come out on the other side.

soap, shi-shi'-wo-iv.

soft, e-haié', soft, fine.
em-ah'-e-e, to make soft, as bread.

soldier, no-tah'.
no-tah'-i-yo, (pl.)

something, he-no-wa-e'-tōn, is that something?
he-ni-na'-wo-ni-o-is-éi'-no, to lose something.

sometimes, na-tu'-as, na-tu'-sa, tu-sa-nin'-hiv, na-ni'-shi-ni-na, na-tas'-tsi-nis-tōm, tu'-a-sūs, } sometimes, once in a while, now and then.

sores, in-o-to'-i-yōts, itch sores.
i'-ma-hi-ma'-nit, to be covered with sores.
na-ni-o-i'-wi-uts, to come out on, as sores or pimples, to break out in sores or spots on the skin.

spatter, wi'-si-ōts, to spatter, to fly out, as grease.

speak, i-mah'-i-ha, to speak with a loud voice.
i-wih'-pi-ha, to speak, growl, or sing in a hoarse voice.

spill, e-ni-a'-tsits, to spill, scatter, throw broadcast.
i-hi'-i-yu-ha, to spill over anything.

spit, o-si-a'-nits and o-si-a'-nōts, to spit.

spirit, ma'-hi-o-o-hap'-si-vast, bad spirit.

split, i-ōh'-o, to split, as wood.
i-ōh'-o-nōv', they split.
na-ōh'-o, I split.
ni-ōh'-o, thou dost split.
ka-mah'-i-i-oh'-i-wo, to split wood.
e'-o-kah, to split with a knife.
ōh'-i-yu-stats, to split by shaving.

spoon, a-mi'-ku-a-mik', a horn spoon, made from the horn of the mountain sheep.

spread, o'-i-yatst, to spread out anything to dry.
i-tsi'-o-i-ta, to spread the knees apart.
o-no'-ko-nanst, to make or spread down a bed for one.

spring, wo-tainst', a spring or well.
o-a-me'-wa, a bubbling spring.
o-a-mest', pl.
i-ai'-no, to have spring come to any one.
e-shi-ih'-o-o, coming up, springing up, as grass.

sprinkle, ma-pi-i'-ni-ats, to sprinkle, as with water.
staff, is-tŏh'-to, a staff used in walking.
i-hŏh'-to-yŏts, to use a staff in walking.
stand, ih-a-ma'-yo, he stands bent forward.
nah-a-ma'-yo, I stand bent forward.
nih-a-ma'-yo, you stand bent forward.
ih-a-ma'-yo-i-sto, they stand bent forward.
i-ni-ho'-wi-o, to stand up, to stiffen up, as the hair.
e'-yu-ha, to stand up, rise up, to stand still.
e-ha-tŏs'-tsi-o, to stand up, as the hair on the front portion of the head.
e'-po-po-ŏt, standing apart, separate, as blades of grass.
stars, o-tŏhk'.
o-tŏh'-i-o, pl.
mŏh'-uts, Little Dipper, seven stars.
si-a-me-yu', the Milky Way in the heavens, or the road where the dead walk.
wo-wo'-i-wo, morning star.
start, na-no'-ćist, to start to come, to come.
steal, e'-no-mats, to steal; also, ćŭh'-i-no-mats.
na'-no-mats, I steal.
ni'-no-mats, thou stealest.
na'-no-ma'-tsim, we steal.
ni'-no-ma'-tsim, you steal.
e'-no-ma'-tsi-o, e'-no-ma'-tsi-to, } they steal.
steam, e-i'-shi-o.
step, tau-nist', a step or pace.
tau-ni'-sto, pl.
stern, i-ta'-ko-win, to be stern or cross.
stick, e'-pa-o-i-ŏts, to stick, or make stick, as mud.
e-hi-ku'-ma-o, to mire, to stick in the mud.
i-sa'-ha-to, to stick to, as an opinion, continue to assent.
ha'-nŏm, sticky, clammy.
na-po-pah'-o-i-na'-ots, sticking, like molasses.
stiff, e-hi'-ko-nŏs, to become stiff or hard, as a dead body, or clothes.
i-na-tsi-o-na'-wŏs, to have the hands stiff or numb with cold.
stir, hi-yo'-yo, to stir up the earth, to plough.
stirrups, tŏh-pa-o'-o-nŏts.
tŏh-pa-o'-a-na-sit, stirrup-straps.
stomach, wi-no-ho'-ŏts, the stomach of animals.
e-wŏh-ta'-si-ŏm, the fat around the stomach.
e-to'-nish, the gizzard of fowls.
stone, o-i-sin', a stone for sharpening a knife.
o-a-na'-tsŏn, small stones, gravel.
tsi-ma-ma'-o-ist, red stony hill.
tsi-mŏh-tau'-o-man, black stone that is used for fuel, lignite and coal.
stoop, ha-ma-e'-yŭts, to stoop down.
stop, ta-ha'-yu-hi'-tu-wi, to stop, to obstruct, to hinder one.
i-si-va'-i-ni, to lay hold on, to stop one.
straighten, si'-pi-o-naut, to straighten out, as the arm bent at the elbow.
strange, e-nŏt'-siv, belonging to another tribe.
nŏts, a stranger, an enemy.
no'-tsi-o, (pl.)
strangle, e'-ko-ta-nu, to strangle with a rope, to hang.
e'-ko-tsi-a, to be hung, or strangled with a cord.
stretch, e-si-pa', to stretch, yawn.
i-si'-ho-e-is'-to, to stretch out, as a hide with pins.
strike, ta-si-in'-o-nu'-to-wa, to strike, to make stagger.
no-no-pŏts', to strike a stake or pin, so as to loosen it.
e'-o-mo-no-e', to make cry by striking.
e'-i-ho-ni'-sto, to strike a ball with a club.
string, wu-ka-he'-wuts, a leather string, a thong.
strokes, e-ho'-e-wa, strokes or beats, as the ticking of a watch or clock.
strong, i'-mah-i-ta-niv, a strong man in the prime of life.
na'-mah-i-ta-niv', I am strong, &c.
ni'-mah-i-ta-niv', thou art strong, &c.
to stuff, e'-to-i-a, to stuff in, as hay in moccasins when travelling in cold weather.
succession, i-no-o-wo'-ne-i-shin, in succession, Indian file.
suck, e'-nin, to suck, as a child its mother.
ta'-mi-tsi-a-tsi'-ni-o, to give suck, as a nurse or mother her child.
i-no-ŏh', to suck up, to make a noise with the mouth in eating soup.

ni-ta-nun'-he-po-she, to suck a teat.

ni'-shi-wai'-i-ni, a teat.

sugar, nish'-ki-mai'-i-map, so called from the color that it gives to water, like soup.

summer, i-mi'-a-ni-o.

mi'-a-ni-a-si'-to, midsummer.

sun, i'-shi.

ta-e'-i-shi, night sun, moon.

i-shi-im'-i-e, after the sun is up.

i-shi'-tai-e, sun going to sleep, sun setting, west.

Sunday, i-shi'-ma-yu'-nu, medicine-day, Sunday.

i-shi'-i-ma-he-yu'-niv, a sacred day.

suppurating, i-o-nih'-u-no, suppurating, as a sore.

surfeited, na-in-hu'-i-nu, I am surfeited by eating; to be made sick by eating too much.

suspect, e-ni-ta'-wa, to suspect, to have an inkling of.

swamp, e-he-ko'-ma-o, when the surface of the country is low, wet, or under water.

sweat, i-ho-pi'-öts, to sweat, to pant or give out, including the idea of sweating.

e'-ma-o, to take a sweat.

e'-ma-to, (pl.)

im-a'-am, a sweat-house, sweat bath.

e'-ha-nan, to sweat very profusely.

swell, e'-yu-ha, to swell, as from a wound, inflammation.

e'-yu-ha (noun), a swelling.

i-o'-i-ta, a protuberance or swelling, as a bubo.

e-po'-a-hant, to swell, as corn soaked.

swift, i-ha-ta'-a-o, swift, fast.

swim, it-o-ham', to swim.

swing, i-wa'-wa-a, a swing for lulling a child to sleep.

T.

tadpoles, i-shi'-in-o-töt.

tall, o-ötst'-tsi-sto-o, a tall tree or wood.

take, i-ha'-a-na-i-nöts', to take up and feel the weight, to weigh.

nish-ta-no'-i-ötst, to take home with one.

no-wa' (imp.), take it.

ta-sta'-nöts (imp.), take.

he'-tsit (imp.), take all.

he-töh'-o-nüts-his-ta'-nüts (imp.), take those.

he-to-he'-si-va-nüts (imp.), take these.

o-tai'-is-ta-nüts (imp.), do not take these.

talk, ma-ha-e-yi'-ists'sh, to talk roughly or loudly about anything.

taste, i-tön'-shi-mi'-a-öts, to have a taste or smell.

i-sa-tön'-shi-mi'-a-öts, not to possess taste or smell.

tattooing, e-he'-wi-so, tattooing on the body, blue stained.

tea, wih'-po-töts, all leaves, a great many leaves.

wih-po-tsi'-ho, the tea used as a drink.

tear, öh'-a-öts, to tear, as cloth or leather.

o-ni'-ni-ha'-nüts, to tear in pieces, to destroy.

tears, i-ha-ni-hi'-ho-to.

i-hai'-ni-öh'-i-no-wa'-i-to, the eyes full of tears.

i-mo-ma'-pi-i-ma'-tsin, to make the tears trickle down.

tie, i-to-isé', to tie anything on to something else.

o-pu'-i-si-vist, to tie up and make into bundles and packs.

tired, i-ha-ni'-wa-wo-ish, to be tired or weary, as in walking.

that, nis-i-wo', that one; even that.

thaw, ma'-o-me-i-ma'-töt, to thaw, as ice or snow.

them, en'-shi-no-ka, only them.

there, he'-to.

thick, i-ha'-o-nöt, to be thick, as a skin or board.

thief, shi-no-ma'-tsi-o-nivst, a thief, a stealer.

in-o-ma'-tsi-o, to steal, to be a thief.

think, i-ta'-o-wo, to think, to meditate.

i-hap-si'-vi-sta, to think very badly, to have a bad heart.

ni-i-hap-si'-vi-sta, you think very badly, you have a bad heart.

this, no'-tsi-to.

those, e-to'-is-ta-nüts, and e'-éi-sta-nist.

in-o-ka', those alone.

ta-to-nis'-to-whews, } all those.
no-nis'-to-whews, }

thread, ho'-ta-nun.

throat, he-o-tsik'.

through, so'-i-yatst, through all, through the middle.

throw, i-wo'-ho-o-ist, to throw away.

ho-no-i-wo'-ho-o-ist, to throw anything down.

no-mah'-i-mi, to throw over one, as a blanket.

o'-o-mi, to throw at, to pelt with stones.

ta'-o-mi, a great many throw at one person.

thrust, e'-hi-ku-a, to thrust into with a knife.

thumb, na-ma-a-im'-o-ik.

thunder, no-no'-ma.

tobacco, tsin-im'-o.

tsin-im'-ōn, (pl.)

na-tsi'-ni-mo, my tobacco.

ni-tsi'-ni-mo, your tobacco.

peh'-o-wa-tōts, a cutting-board for tobacco.

peh-o-wa'-to-tōts, (pl.)

tongue, e-wi'-ta-nu.

o-wi-ta-nu'-wi-wōts, (pl.)

na-wi'-ta-nu, my tongue.

ni-wi'-ta-nu, thy tongue.

mi-hi-wi'-ta-nu, a buffalo cow's tongue.

wo-sta'-ni-wi'-ta-na, the tongue of a man.

tongs, ah-pa-ni'-o, tongs, pincers.

tooth, e-wi'-e-sūts.

e-wi'-e-si-wūts, (pl.)

na-wi'-e-sūts, my tooth.

ni-wi'-e-sūts, thy tooth.

e-yo'-tōts, to untie with the teeth.

ih'-o-nōt, to peel off with the teeth, as the rind of a turnip.

i-pa-wi-ōht', to peel or shell off with the teeth.

i-ko'-no-mo, to crack with the teeth.

i'-ni-sta-ni-wa-wōt', to clatter with the teeth or gnash.

touch, mo-mah'-a-ni, to touch, to lay the hand on.

towards, i-ta-si'-o, also e-wi-nōh'.

track, si-a-mōts', a track, footprint, trail.

trade, e-ōh'-to, to trade or barter.

na-ōh'-to, I trade.

ni-ōh'-to, thou dost trade.

e-ōh'-to-wa'-o, } they trade.
e-ōh'-to-wa'-to, }

na-ōh'-to-wam, we trade.

ni-ōh'-to-wam, you trade.

travel, tam-wo-wo'-ist, to travel ahead.

i'-a-me-his'-to, to travel backwards and forwards.

ho-i-na-pi'-ni-i-hōt, I travel on good land.

e-ni-o-who', to travel in the water.

tread, tsi-i'-o-wi, to tread on, to pinch with the toes.

ih-a-wo'-i-yu-ha, to tread or mash down the grass with the foot.

tree, mih-ni-min-ust', hackberry tree, so called because the animals crush the berries.

hi-sta', limbs or branches of a tree.

trinkets, e-nu-wa'-sin, small articles, trinkets.

trot, i-o-ni'-kai-yots, to trot, as a horse.

troubled, ma-pe'-i-ha, to be rough or troubled, as the waves of the sea.

trust, i-ni'-sta-sta-nin, to trust in trade, to give credit.

turn, e-o-si'-nōts, to turn over, as the leaves of a book.

tau'-i-sta-hats, to turn out of doors.

turtle, ma'-in.

ma-i-nōn', pl.

twice, i-o-ni-so-wah'-si-o, twice, in two ways.

twins, hi-sta'-ki, his twins.

na-hi-sta'-ki, my twins.

ni-hi-sta'-ki, thy twins.

ni-hi-sta'-ki-wo-in, your twins.

a-po-na-hi-sta'-ki-ni-wo'-in, I myself have twins.

twist, e-o-ni'-mo-tau'-in, to twist or wring a skin in dressing it.

na-o-ni'-mo-tau'-in, I twist, &c.

ni-o-ni'-mo-tau'-in, thou dost twist, &c.

e-o-ni'-mo-tau'-i-ni-sto, they twist, &c.

o-ni'-mo-ta-o-i'-nuts, to turn or twist around with the mouth.

e'-wi-ōht, to twist anything with the mouth.

twitch, e'-hi-sak, to twitch or jerk involuntarily, as the flesh of animals.

U.

uncovered, i-no-ma'-ha-mi, to be uncovered.

i-no-ma'-ha-mo, (pl.)

under, ah-to'-no.

undertake, sho-me'-a-to-ais-e'-ma-ist, to be willing to do anything, to undertake anything.

unload, e-ho'-ma-nu, to unload, to unharness.

untie, o-ni'-ha-e-nūts, to loose, untie, unharness, release from confinement.

i'-o-ni'-ha-i-ōts, to come untied of itself.

urinate, ih'-a-a, to urinate.

V.

value, im'-i-hŏt, to value very highly, to be very hard with anything.

vermilion, ma-i-tŏm'.

ma-i-to'-mŏn, (pl.)

very, e-sŏs', (last syllable quite emphatic.)

W.

wade, i-huh'-o-wo, to wade, as in the water.

walk, i-ho'-yŏt, to walk or follow after.

in-shi'-wi-ŏts, to walk rapidly.

wandering, e'-wo-nish.

e-wo-ni'-shi-na-o, (pl.)

war, i-wi'-o-ći'-sto, to make war, to lead a war party.

warm, nan-sho', hot, very warm.

nan-sho'-i-o, (pl.)

in-so'-o-mit, lukewarm, tepid as water.

ward, ho-ha', to ward off danger, to defend.

warp, im-o-mi-ka'-nant, to warp.

wash, in'-shi-shi-un, he washes, or to wash, as the hands.

nan'-shi-shi-un, I wash, &c.

nin'-shi-shi-un, thou, &c.

nan'-shi-shi'-o-nam, we, &c.

nin'-shi-shi'-o-nam, you, &c.

in'-shi-shi'-o-na'-o, they, &c.

i-o'-he, to wash, as clothes.

na-i-o'-he, I, &c.

ni-i-o'-he, thou, &c.

na-ho-nin', we, &c.

ni-ho-nin', you, &c.

i-ho-ni'-ni-sto, } they, &c.
i-o-his'-to, }

water, ma'-pi.

ma-pists', (pl.)

ma-pi'-shi-wit, swift-running water.

ma-pi-mŏh'-skin, water mint. *Mentha Canadensis.*

ma-pi-i-wo'-ho-ni-o, water, raised into waves.

i-ha'-o-tum, deep water.

i-ćo'-ki-tum, shallow water.

wŏh-po'-ma-ŏts, salt, sweet-water.

im'-a-ni-tun, to desire water.

in'-a-o, to fall on in drops, like water, to trickle.

watch, ta-wi'-a-o-mi, to watch for, to look out for one's coming.

wave, e'-is-tŏn, to wave the hand.

wear, e-ŏh'-i-ni-a, to wear, as a crown or fillet around the head.

i'-o-ta-o, to wear a hole in the moccasins by walking.

wearied, o-ka'-ni-ŏts, wearied, exhausted, tired and sleepy.

weasel, ha'-a, white weasel.

ha'-i-yo, (pl.)

weave, mo-ći-im'-a-ha-o, to weave, as snow-shoes or a blanket.

web, wi'-ko-no'-no-no, spider's web.

well, i-no-mŏh'-ta (imp. sing.), be thou well.

i-no-mŏh'-tai-yo (imp. pl.), be ye well.

shi'-pan-a, well, done well.

what? he'-nu-wa-it.

hi'-no-wa, what? what is it?

when? to'-nish.

to-nish-niv'-hiv, when was it? when did it occur?

i-to'-ni-is, when, at what time?

im-a-i-to'-ni-is, at what times?

to-as', when, when is it?

where? to-nish-ni'-ta-in, where is it?

whet, i-i'-ha-sin', to whet a knife.

which, tas.

while, i-si-ha'-i-shi-wi'-ha-tsi, for a little while.

whip, o-ha-me'-wo-ŏh.

o-ha-me'-wo-ŏhst, pl.

nish-ka'-ha-me'-wo-ŏh, a large whip, the handle of which is made like a saw.

whiskey, wi'-hu-ma'-pi, the Frenchman's water.

whisper, ni-ni'-a-tsi-o, to whisper.

white, e-wo'-kŏm; also, si-wo-kom'.

e-wo'-ko-mo-nist, pl. si-wo'-ko-mo'-ist.

whistle, e'-ish, to whistle, to call by whistling, as a dog.

na'-ish, I whistle.

ni'-ish, thou dost whistle.

i-i'-shi-o, they whistle.

e'-i-shi-nŏn, to whistle a tune.

i-ni-sto'-ni-wa', the whistling or whizzing sound of a bullet.

wi-ho'-i-ma-i'-ni-sto'-ni-wa, to whizz or whistle, as a bullet through the air.

who, ni-wa'-as.

ni-wa'-si-o, pl.

widow, ŏt-h̄a-e', a widow.

ŏt-h̄a-e'-i-o, pl.

wife, is-tsi'-im, wife, his wife.

na-tsi-im', my wife.

ni-tsi-im', thy wife.

ni-na'-tsi-im', there is my wife.

ta-ma'-ni-tsi-im', that is your wife.

e-is'-tsi-im, to have a wife, to be married.

e-wi'-ŏnst, to have more than one wife.

wind, a-ha', wind, windy.

a-ha'-ish, a windy day.

i-sa-ha'-a-han, no wind.

ma-ta'-in-is-to'-ni-wa'-o, the wind whistles.

e-wo'-wi-tas', whirlwind.

e'-hi-kŏt, calm, still, no wind.

window, i-ko-ŏts', window, port-hole, or any place to look out.

winter, e-yai'-nu, to come winter to one.

wipe, na'-nŏts, to wipe or cleanse, as dishes.

withered, e'-he-kŏnst, withered, dead, dried up, as leaves.

wih̄'-po-to-tse'-a-na, to wilt, or wither, as leaves.

i-ma-ho'-hi-no-it, withered, palsied, numb.

within, ho-to-ma', within an inclosure.

without, a-no-sim', out of doors.

woman, hi.

hi'-i-o, pl.

ksi-e', a young unmarried woman.

ksi-e'-i-he, pl.

wi-o-ai'-wo-i-stŏts, white woman's dress, long gown.

ma-tum-a', old woman.

womb, is-ta-po'-a-nŏt, womb, for a child, or animal.

wood, ka-mah̄'.

ka-mah̄'-i-ŏts, pl.

na-ka-mah̄', my wood.

ni-ka-mah̄', thy wood.

na-ka-mah̄'-i-ham, our wood.

ni-ka-mah̄'-i-ham, your wood.

ka-mah̄'-i-ha'-is, long wood.

e-a'-ma-ta-wi'-sta, wood of all kinds in the sacred language.

ma-ta'-a, a great deal of wood, a forest or grove.

work, i-ho'-tsi-ma-nist, to work at a difficult thing.

i-hi'-ko-na, to work hard or industriously at anything.

worms, i-nŭh̄'-niv, intestinal worms.

worthless, ni-wa-ni'-sta-tu, to be worthless, vile; a term of great reproach.

wound, is-a'-a-na, wounded, a wounded person.

wi-na'-a-mi, to wound without killing.

i'-to-si-i-na'-o, to recover from a wound.

wrap, e'-to-isé, to wrap up anything.

o'-he-i-shi, to wrap up, as a babe in a blanket.

e-ŏh̄'-po-o, wrapped up or around, for safe-keeping.

wrestle, e'-wa-so, to wrestle, or play like two persons wrestling.

wrinkled, e-o'-si-ŏts, wrinkled, not smooth, pitted.

e-he'-hi-no-it, to be wrinkled or shrivelled.

wrist, sin-ih̄-o'-wi-ats.

write, mŏh̄'-i-ŏts, to write, paint, sketch, figure.

mŏh̄-is-to', a book or writing.

mŏh̄-is-to'-o-nŏts, pl.

mŏh̄-is-to'-nis-tŭts, a writing pen.

Y.

yard, i-tai'-i-wun, a measure of a yard used by the traders.

yell, ta-no'-a-nŏst, to yell, to shout as the young men do.

yellow, e'-i-yŏh̄.

e'-i-yo'-wo-nist, pl.

i-ho'-wo-ni, to paint oneself yellow.

yes, he'-hin.

na'-he-hin, same as Dakota, ćin'-to.

he'-i-he, certainly, yes, rather emphatic.

ni'-hi-tŏm, it is good, yes.

na-hi'-na, yes, Dakota, to, tosh.

young, he-na-kis', young of ducks and geese.

ARAPOHO GROUP, B.

CHAPTER IX.

IV. ARAPOHOS.

ETHNOGRAPHICAL HISTORY AND REMARKS ON THE GRAMMATICAL STRUCTURE OF THEIR LANGUAGE.

THE past history of the Arapohos is as little known as that of their relatives, the Atsinas. The former regard themselves as constituting the parent stock, and believe that the latter separated from them. We will now attempt to trace their previous history, as far as it is contained in any of our written records.

I have searched all the works within my reach, and I cannot ascertain with certainty their track of migration. Gallatin speaks of them as a detached tribe from the Rapid Indians, which has wandered as far south as the Platte and the Arkansas, and formed a temporary union with the Kaskaias and some other erratic tribes. At the present time the Arapohos are divided into two portions or bands. The first portion call themselves na-ka-si'-nin, "People of the Sage," and number one hundred and eighty lodges. They wander about the sources of the South Platte and the region of Pike's Peak, also northward to the Red Buttes on the North Platte. Sometimes they extend their journeyings in search of buffalo along the foot of the Big-horn Mountains in the Crow country. They spent a large portion of the winter of 1859 and '60 on the branches of Powder River, near the base of the Big-horn Mountains. The second band call themselves na-wuth'-i-ni-han, the meaning of which is obscure. It implies a mixture of different kinds of people of different bands. They number two hundred lodges, and range along the Arkansas River and its tributaries.

From the fact that Pike in his journals speaks of the Atsinas as the "Minnetarees of the Yellowstone," and does not allude to the Arapohos, we may infer that they did not occupy their present district at the time of his explorations in the Arkansas country. There may be, therefore, some ground for the belief that the Arapohos and Atsinas were at one time all united, and resided together in the region of the Saskatchewan. This point requires still farther investigation. It would seem from "Long's Expedition to the Rocky Mountains," that the Arapohos occupied nearly their present district in 1819 and '20.

Rev. Dr. Morse thus speaks of these Indians in 1820: "Their number is estimated at 10,000.. Their country extends from the headwaters of the Kansas, south to the Rio del Norte. They are a warlike people, and often making predatory and murderous excursions on their eastern and northern neighbors." Since that time very little notice seems to have been taken of them.

During the winter of 1859 and '60, the author, attached to the United States Exploring Expedition, under the command of Capt. William F. Raynolds, T. E., remained several months at the Indian Agency in the valley of Deer Creek, about one hundred miles north-west of Fort Laramie. The Arapohos visited the Agency on their return from the Crow country, for the purpose of receiving a portion of their annuities still due them, and spent some days in that vicinity. Among them was an intelligent Indian, called by the white traders Friday, who had been taken from his people when a small boy, and brought up at one of the trading-posts, where he learned to speak the English language with fluency. When he became a man he returned to his tribe, adopting their habits and costume, and is now the most influential personage among them, acting as a medium between the Arapohos and the whites. From him I obtained the vocabulary given in this work, and all the information I possess of their present condition. A brief account of the early history of this man, as given by himself, cannot be devoid of interest or out of place. He says, that at the time of the separation of the Atsinas from the Arapohos, they were all encamped together on the Cimarron. The Mexicans usually came up from the south to trade with them. At this time thirty of the Mexicans came, and the chief of the Atsina band wished them all to remain at his camp. The chief of the Arapoho band said, "Let half of the traders go to one camp and half to the other." A contest of words grew out of this, and finally the Atsina chief stabbed the Arapoho chief, and killed him. The brothers and sons of the murdered man immediately killed the first chief, and a battle commenced, but the difficulty was settled before a great number were slain. The two bands then agreed to separate, one portion ranging along the South Platte and Arkansas Rivers, the other passed through the North Park to Bridger's Pass, thence along the mountains to the Three Tetons. There they fell in with the mountain trappers, with whom they had a contest, and were driven toward the Yellowstone, where they were again attacked by the Crows, a large number killed, and many taken prisoners. The remainder escaped to the Blackfeet. It will be seen that the above account harmonizes very nearly with that given by the Atsinas.

It was at the time of the separation of the two tribes or bands, that Friday, with several lads, became separated from their people, and lost their way. They had been wandering about for three days, when a Mr. Fitzpatrick, an old mountaineer, and for some years a United States Agent for the Arapohos, as he was taking a train of wagons across the country saw Friday, and thinking him to be an enemy, raised his gun to shoot him. The boy at once rose up, and Mr. Fitzpatrick saw that he was but a child, and took him to his own house. He gave him the name of Friday because he found him on that day of the week.

Friday relates a tradition in regard to the origin of the Red races. The Great Spirit made the Indians all one nation in the beginning. At first He made a woman, then a man. At the beginning the world was covered with water, and then a large mountain was made, on the summit of which the Great Spirit placed the man and the woman. The water continued to rise up toward the top of the mountain, until they were in danger of being drowned, when the woman said to the man, "Let us shut our eyes, and when we open them again there will be no water." They closed their eyes for a large part of a day, and then the woman opened hers, and saw no water; she then said: "We are safe: the water is passing away!" After this, a girl was born to the woman, then a boy. At the proper age the boy and girl were married, and from them sprung the human race. When the Indians became so numerous that they could not live together, the Great Spirit said they must separate. He also said that they should not speak the same language, and so He gave them different tongues. At first He intended to make them white men, but afterwards changed His mind, and made them red. He gave to the red men the game, buffalo, deer, elk, &c., and showed them how to kill the game. He also gave them wood for arrows, and showed them flint for arrow-points and knives. But He says: "I will make a race of white men, who shall be a superior people, who will know everything." The Great Spirit then turned Himself white, and said that the white people He should make, would resemble Him. "I will give you sense enough to get along well in your mode of life, but the superior nation shall be the whites."

When the Arapohos had the cholera, they would take small pieces of rotten wood, and thrust them into the flesh on the painful portion of the stomach, and then set fire to them, and burn them into the wounds. Friday says that many of them recovered by this treatment.

They do not throw away a horse when the children's ears are bored, as the Dakotas do. They cut off one or two joints of the little finger of the left hand in mourning, but do not mutilate themselves after the manner of the Crows.

OBSERVATIONS ON THE GRAMMATICAL STRUCTURE OF THE ARAPOHO LANGUAGE.

1. Arapoho nouns have two numbers, singular and plural, but the terminations of the plural are of varied forms; as (sing.) bet-éa', a leg; (pl.) bet-éa'-wa; (sing.) bet-a', heart; (pl.) bet-a'-ha; (sing.) bĕsh, a nose; (pl.) be'-tha.

2. So far as is yet known the gender of nouns is indicated only by the use of different words to denote the sexes, and the case of a noun is distinguished by its position in a sentence.

3. The pronouns are divided into simple or independent, and inseparable or fragmentary.

4. The simple or independent pronouns are as follows:

non-an'-a, I.
non-an'-in, thou or you.
in'-it, he, she, or it.
na-ne-ni'-na, we or ours.
ne-na'-nin, you.
in-it'-a-na, they.
in'-a, this one, this.
in'-i, that.
in-i-na'-ni, those.
an-i-shin'-a, both.
a-na-a', who? who is it?
to-shi'-hi, how is it?
ta-ti'-na, where is it?
to-u'-hu, when?
to'-is-a, what?

5. The inseparable or fragmentary pronouns are used in connection with nouns, adjectives, and verbs.

1st. In connection with nouns; as,

wah'-a, a knife.
wah'-a-ha, knives.
na-wah'-a, my knife.
a-wah'-a, thy knife.
i-wah'-a, his knife.
na-wah'-a-hin'-a, our knives.
a-wah'-a-hin'-a, your knives.
in-a-wah'-a-hin'-a, their knives.
ka-ko'-i, a gun.
na-ka-ko'-i, my gun.
a-ka-ko'-i, thy gun.
i-ka-ko'-i, his gun.
na-ka'-ko-yun'-a, our guns.
a-ka'-ko-yun'-a, your guns.
i-ka'-ko-yun'-a, their guns.

2d. Pronouns in connection with adjectives; as,

i'-tha-ti, good.
i-tha-ti'-hi (intensive), pretty.
i-thi'-na, I am good.
i-thin', thou art good.
i-thit', he is good.
i-thi-hin'-a, we are good.
i-thi-hith'-in, you are good.
i-thi-hith'-i, they are good.
at-i-hi'-thi-na, it is pretty; looks well.
at-i-hi'-ni-e'-na, he looks gay or pretty.
nah-e-e'-i-thit, I expect he is good.
nah-e-e-i'-thin-a, I will be good.
wa'-sa, bad.
wah'-in, I am bad.
wah'-it, you are bad.

3d. Pronouns in connection with verbs; as,

ta-wi-thi'-na, to eat.
a-tun'-wun-bi-thi'-na, I eat.
wun-bi-thi'-hi, you eat.
a-ta-wun'-bi-thit, he eats.
a-tun'-bi-thi-hin'-a, we eat.
wun-bi'-thi-a-nŭ'-it, you eat, all eat.
a-ta-bi'-thi-hith'-i, they eat.
a-tun'-bi-thi'-hith-i, they are going to eat.
i-si'-wi-thi'-na, I have eaten, or I have done eating.
wa-wa-nis'-wi-thit, he is done eating.
wa-wa-nis'-wi-thi-hin'-a, we are done eating.
i-ni-shi-wi-thi-hin'-a, you are done eating.
ni-shi-wi'-thi-hith-i, they are done eating.

na-sa'-wi-thi'-na, I am going to eat, or I will eat.
a-tun'-bi-thi'-na-a, we are going to eat.
bi-thi'-hi (imp.), eat.
a-nŭ'-it-bi-thi'-hi, all eat.

6. The following miscellaneous phrases may be of service in illustrating the grammatical character of the language.

un-a-hu', warm yourself, you are cold.
a-tun'-ći-ni-bi'-thin, it is going to stop snowing.
na-ka'-ye-na, I am dry or thirsty.
ći-na-ka'-nić, get some water.
ći-na'-ko-he', get a bucket of water.
ni-he-ća-hi'-se, come here, woman.
ba-ya-će'-ta, come straight here.
ni-to-win'-a, call to them.
ći-tan-a'-is-ta, get some fire.
a-tun'-a-nŭḣ'-ti, we are going to run a race.
će-na'-hat-e, he killed himself.
ku-i-na-ha'-wa-wŭḣ-u-ḣa'-ḣa-bi, did you see the horses?
kat-uath'-ab-i-sa, are you going?
bi-ḣa'-tha, I am loved.
bi-ḣa'-thith-in, I love you.
bi-ḣa'-ḣin, you love me.
ath-a'-bi-ḣa-thin, he loves you.
bi-ḣa'-tha-tin-a, I love myself.
bi-ha'-ta-wa, I love.
bi-ḣa'-than-tus'-i-a, I love my wife.
bi-ḣa'-than-e'-ha, I love my child.
bi-ḣa'-that-i'-ha, he loves his children.
bi-ḣa'-that, he loves any object.
na-tun'-i-ni-a-ta'-nan-a, I have sold my horse.
i-tha-i'-tan-u, at the village.
i-tha-bab-i'-ta-wu, in the ground.
ta-shi-ḃi'-ta-wu, on the ground.

7. The Arapoho numerals are as follows:

one, ća-se'.
two, nis.
three, nais.
four, yen.
five, ya-thun'.
six, ni-ta-tŏḣ'.
seven, ni-sa-tŏḣ'.
eight, nai-sa-tŏḣ'.
nine, thi-a-tŏḣ'.
ten, me-tai-tŏḣ'.
eleven, ća-se'-in.
twelve, ni'-sin.
thirteen, nai'-sin.
fourteen, ye'-nin.
fifteen, ya-thun'-in.
sixteen, ni-ta-tŏḣ'-in.
seventeen, ni-sa-tŏḣ'-in.
eighteen, na-sa-tŏḣ'-in.
nineteen, thi-a-tŏḣ'-in.
twenty, ni-sa'.
twenty-one, ni-sa-ća'-sa.
twenty-two, ni-sa'-ni-sin.
thirty, nai'-sa.
forty, ye'-ya.
fifty, ya-tha'-ya.
sixty, ni-ta'-to-so.
seventy, ni-sa'-to-so.
eighty, nai-sa'-to-so.
ninety, thi-a-to'-so.
one hundred, me-ta'-to-so.
one thousand, mai-si'-me-ta'-to-so.

8. NAMES OF DANCES, ETC.

A'-tha-wi, Dog Dance. This is not a common dance, but when a man has a relative sick, and fears his death, he promises to make a feast and a dance if the sick person recovers. Only the young men join in this dance. They are marked with the sign of the dog. Among the Indians, a feast always accompanies a dance.

Ni-na-taḣ'-wan, War Dance. All the braves join in this dance. The Arapohos dance and sing less than any Indians I have yet seen.

Ben-a-ti'-sin, Buffalo Woman Dance (ben'-a, a buffalo, and is'-in, a woman). Only the women join in this dance. They have a peculiar costume or dress, the head-dress of which is a buffalo's head.

ća'-ha-wi', Little Dog's Dance. The men form a circle, and the women dance in the ring.

Bi-tai'-hi-nin, People that scrape robes (hi-tai'-bi, an instrument for scraping robes). Only the men join in this dance.

A-tha-hu'-ha, Foolish Dog's Dance. This dance is performed by a band of young men, about the same age, called the Foolish Dogs.

A-ha'-kai-nin, Foolish People, is a band of young men, about the same age. At one time they numbered fifty persons, but the small-pox reduced them to about thirty. They have a dance peculiar to themselves.

9. NAMES OF INDIAN TRIBES, RIVERS, ETC.

nat-o-ne'-bin-a, Dakotas, people that cut their enemies heads off, cut throats.

a-i-nun', Crow people, Crows; a-i-na', a Crow, Corvus.

ka-wi'-na-han, Blackfeet, black people.

it-us-shi'-na, Shyennes, the scarred people, from their having so many scars on their arms and breasts.

wa-tan'-a-hith-i, black people (ith'-i, people, wa-ta'-ya, black).

ni-ći'-he-nen-a, water men or people, Kiowas (ni-ći'-a, water, nen'-a, a man.

ća'-tha, Comanches. The Arapohos formerly called them the Snake people, but they now call them a name derived from the fact that they have plenty of horses.

e-wu-ha'-wu-si, Snakes; Sho'-sho-ni, people that use grass and bark for their lodges or huts.

ah-i'-hi-nin, Wolf people, Pawnees; ah-i', a wolf.

ka'-nan-in, people whose jaws break in pieces, Arickaras.

ka-ka'-i-thi, Flathead people.

thah-a-i-nin', Apaches, people who play on bone instruments. Buffalo ribs are used; notches being cut in one of the bones, the other is rubbed continually backwards and forwards over it.

to-i-nin'-a, people that beg, Gros Ventres of the prairie, Atsinas.

wa-nuk'-e-ye'-na, Minnetarees, lodges planted together.

be-in-i-ći'-a, Shell River, pearl shells used in trade, Platte.

bas-ni-ći'-a, Large River, Yellowstone.

a-hai'-ni-ni-ći'-a, Flint River, Arkansas.

ni-nun'-i-ni-ći'-a, Fat River, South Platte.

a-a-ha'-i-te, "River with a lone house on it," Cache la Poudre.

i-shit'-ćun-ni-ći'-a, Deer Creek, Antelope Creek.

ha-hu'-i-sin-i-ći'-a, Box-elder Creek.

i-nah'-in-i-ći'-a, "River with many crossings," Sweetwater.

thah-a'-ih-ut-un'-i, Hammer Mountains, Medicine Bow Mountains.

o-i-nin-i-ni'-ni-a'-ha, Crow Mountains, Big-horn Mountains.

će-than'-i-ći-a (će'-tha, powder), Powder River.

10. NAMES OF ANIMALS, PLANTS, ETC.

na-kah', a white bear.

wa-tai'-nah, a black bear.

wah'-a, a badger.

is-i'-ća, an antelope.

bi'-hi, a deer.

a-ta', a big-horn, mountain sheep.

ah'-i, a-wa'-ta-tas, } large wolf.

ka-a', ka-a-wo'-ŭ, } prairie or medicine wolf.

ai-wa-ta'-ka, large hare. *Lepus campestris.*

na-wa-ta'-ka, small rabbit. *Lepus artemisia.*

a-bas', a beaver.

i'-ha-ha, a muskrat.

si'-a, a weasel.

ba-hŭ', a large fox. *Vulpes macrourus.*

no'-a-ha, kit fox. *Vulpes velox.*

bah-un-i', large squirrel, ground hog. *Arctomys flaviventer.*

ho-hoi'-yun-i, spotted-backed squirrel. *Spermophilus tridecem lineatus.*

na-ŭ', striped squirrel. *Tamias quadrivittatus.*

ća-thun'-i, prairie dog. *Cynomys ludovicianus.*

ća-thun'-i-si-a, ground weasel. *C. Gunnisoni.*

hu, na-ku'-ha, } spotted-backed polecat.

o'-hu, porcupine.

yeh, otter.

ba-ha-ku', "large rat." *Neotoma cinerea.*

ka-ka'-sa-ni, "scar bird," so called from the spots on the head, which look like scars. *Charadrius montana.*

sas-ku'-it-o, a ground sparrow, a bird that frequents the edge of a stream or bank.

tuth'-e-i-the'-ka-na, "a bird that the heron carries on its back;" from tuth'-e, a heron, and i-the'-ka-na, to carry on the back.

a-wuth'-na-ku'-we-e, white-nosed duck. *Mergus Americanus.*

ba-bi-thin'-a-he, "little red-winged bird." *Leucosticte tephrocotis.*

bas-nak-than', a bush growing near Fort Bridger, and used by the Arapohos as kinnic-kinnic.

ni-ha-na'-i-na, "yellow flower." *Ranunculus glaberrimus.*

ća-nat'-an-a-i'-na, "blue flower," blue bell. *Mertensia Virginica.*

ća-e'-i-hi, "wild potatoes." *Dicentra.*

i-tuh-ŭ'-ŭ, "sharp leaves;" a small species of *Phlox.*

i-ćun'-i, pomme blanche. *Psoralea esculenta.*

ka-i-ya'-i-no, "yellow flowers, with gum on them." *Grindelia squarrosa.*

sath-i'-win, "little pine berries," a species of trailing *Juniperus.*

bis-ći'-hin, a species of *Eriogonum*, growing on the gravelly hills; word derived from bi, a cow, and ći'-hin, smoke, buffalo smoke, a weed used for smoking meat.

ni-ća'-ćut-e, a chenopodiaceous shrub, salty weed or shrub.

ni-ća'-in-a, a plant growing on rocks in the mountains.

thi-kun-bi'-tun, a kind of moss, "dead man's porcupine work."

bi-te-ba'-yak, a kind of ground lichen.

ći-wan-i'-na-ka'-si, "half sage." *Artemisia Canadense.*

si-si'-yi-wish, "snake-bush." *Sarcobatus vermicularis.* Word derived from si-si'-ye, a snake, and bish, a bush.

wŏh-a-ha'-bi-thi-it, "bush that horses eat." *Obione canescens.*

ba-će-wi'-she, red willow. *Cornus sericea.*

it-a-he'-win-a, "hot berries." *Arctostaphylos uva-ursi.* The leaves of this shrub form the real kinnic-kinnic of the Western Indians, which they mix with their tobacco in preference to the leaves or bark of any other plant. The bark of *Cornus sericea* is used as a substitute only in the absence of the *A. uva-ursi.*

sath, common pine. *Pinus ponderosa.*

tha-ki'-sath, spruce pine. *Abies Douglassi.*

a-hat', sweet cottonwood. *Populus.*

a-ha'-tin-wi'-tin, bitter cottonwood. *Populus.*

bi-tin'-a, quaking asp. *Populus.*

ha-hu'-is, box elder, "the hollow wood." *Negundo aceroides.*

CHAPTER X.

VOCABULARY OF THE ARAPOHO LANGUAGE.

A.

above, nan-ah-u'-it-e, above, up the river.
afraid, i-ni'-ah-a, to be afraid.
afterwards, tah-u'-ŭ.
again, ći'-a, again, once more.
ago, wa-ni'-hi, not long ago.
agreeable, ya-ni-sat', pleasant, agreeable.
ahead, a-tha'-i-nin'-a, before, ahead.
alive, i-nin-ek'-ti-na, to be alive.
all, a-nŭ'-it, all, the whole.
always, ć-nai'-yi-wu'-hu, always, forever.
angry, a-na-wiȟt', to be angry.
another, a-na-thiȟt', different, another.
antelope, is-i'-ća.
apples, ka-hu'-win-a, red thorn apples.
arm, in-usȟ', his arm.
nen-usȟ', my arm.
un-usȟ', thy arm.
be-nuȟ'-a, the whole arm.
bath'-a-in'-a, the armpit.
around, ka'-i-na, around the lodge.
arrow, ath.
ath-i' (pl.), arrows.
ne-nić', my arrow.
e-nić', thy arrow.
in-ić', his arrow.
ashamed, a-tut-iȟt', modest, ashamed.
a-ti-ti'-na, to be ashamed, bashful.
ashes, će'-tha, ashes, the same name as powder.
asp, bi-tin'-a, quaking asp.
assemblage, a-e'-sa, a council, an assemblage of chiefs.
assemble, ći-wa'-a-nis'-a, to assemble together.
asunder, na-ye'-si-he, far apart, asunder.
autumn, ta-yu'-ni.
away, a-si'-sa, to go away.
axe, a-ha-naȟ', an axe.
na-ta'-ha-naȟ', my axe.
a-ta'-ha-naȟ', thy axe.
it-a'-ha-naȟ', his axe.
ći-ȟo'-a-na, hatchet, axe.
ka-ȟo'-i-te'-na-naȟ, a ground-axe, a hoe.

B.

back, na-ku'-ȟa, spotted back.
tut-a', back-bone of an animal.
i-thi-ka'-na, to carry on the back.
bad, wa'-sa.
badger, waȟ'-a.
bag, ća-a-tha', a bag or sack.
banks, a-ȟut-a'-na, banks of a stream.
bark, ben-a'-bat, to bark as a dog.
beads, ća-nat'-ai-yu.
bear, waȟ.
na-kaȟ', a white bear.
wa-tai'-naȟ, a black bear.
beard, bi-si-tin'-a-na.
beat, wat-e-ha'-yo, to beat on a drum.
ta-ta-win'-a, to beat, as to beat a person.
bottle, ćen-ith'-ća, a glass bottle, vial.
bottom, i-tha'-be, bottom upwards.
bow, bat'-a, a bow.
bat'-e (pl.), bows.
na-bat'-a, my bow.
e-bat'-a, thy bow.
i-bat'-a, his bow.
bowels, wa-nut'.
box elder, ȟa-ȟu'-is, the hollow wood.
boy, ni-a-tho'-i-sa, a white boy.
brains, i-taé, brains of an animal.
brave, ni-ha'-ha-niȟt', to be brave, courageous.
break, ka-i-na', to break open.
ta-wi-ku'-ti, to break in pieces.
bridle, ći-wi-te'-wi.
bright, i-ya'-a-na-kus'-a, bright, shining, glistening.
breast, aȟ'-a-bĕ.
breathe, a-wuth'-ŭn, to breathe.
brother, ni-thi-sa', my brother.
ni-thi-sa'-wa (pl.), my brothers.
in-a'-ha-wa, his elder brother.
na'-ha-va, younger brother.
ko-hu'-ni'-sa, half brother.
i-ni'-thi-san, father's brother.
ya, brother-in-law.

na-ya', my brother-in-law.

beaver, a-bas'.

a-bes'-na-yat', a beaver trap.

bed, a'-a, a bed.

beg, ni-ta-win'-a, to beg.

behind, ka'-ba.

belly, in-ut'-a, a belly.

na-nut', my belly.

bend, na-ho'-i-si'-na, to bend.

na-nu'-i-sa, to bend forward, stooping.

a-ba-ho'-a-ta, a bend in a river or stream.

berries, it-a-he'-win-a, hot berries. *Arctostaphylos uva-ursi.*

bind, ći-ta-ya'-kut-i, to bind up, bandage.

bite, tai-yo-win'-a, to bite.

bladder, na-nis'.

black, wa-tai'-yo, black.

wa-ta'-nit, it is black.

blind, nan-i'-na-kut, to be blind, blind.

blood, ba.

ba-e'-ni, bloody.

ba-e'-nit, to bleed.

na-nat'-i-o-it, to be besmeared with blood.

blow, ći-ta'-thi, to blow, as the wind.

blue, ća-net'-ai-yo, ća-net'-oi-nit, it is blue.

board, kun'-i-uh'-u-na, a board for cutting tobacco.

boat, thi'-wa.

body, bet-un'-e-ya', body.

net-un'-e-ya', my body.

et-un'-e-ya', thy body.

it-un'-e-ya', his body.

boggy, ćith-si-wa', boggy, marshy.

boil, a-na'-na-wak'-thi-nat, to boil over, as water.

bone, ih.

both, an-i-shin'-a.

to brush, ku-c-tith'-e-ha, to brush away, as with the hand.

burn, ka-ha'-ho, to burn or blaze, as fire.

ba-tuh'-a-ha', to burn anything.

burst, ka-na'-in-a, to burst open.

bury, ka-tai'-yat, to bury, as the dead.

bush, bish, a bush.

buy, a-ta'-na-ta, to buy, purchase anything.

C.

calf, wa, a calf turning black, or six months old.

wa'-ū, a red calf, just after birth.

candle, ai'-se-ya, a light, a candle.

care, wa-ta', take care.

careful, ni-ya'-ho-in, careful, to be careful.

cat, beh-a'-ka, a wild cat, small panther.

cherries, bi'-na.

chew, ses-i-ya'-ta, to chew fine with the teeth.

child, te-ya-na', a child.

te-ya-na'-ha, pl. children.

na-ni'-sa, my child.

a-ni'-sa, thy child.

i-ni'-sa, his child.

a-te'-ya-ne-win'-a, your children.

na-te'-ya-ne-win'-a, our children.

it-e'-ya-ne-win'-a, their children.

a-ći-hi'-sa, a child just born.

a-si-nat', to give birth to a child.

ni'-na, sister's child.

a-tun-ćin'-i-sit, a young child, soon after birth.

chin, wa-tah'-a.

wa-tah-an'-a, pl. chins.

na-tah'-a, my chin.

a-tah'-a, thy chin.

i-tah'-a, his chin.

choke, a-thit', to choke, to be choked in eating.

cholera, a-sit'-at, sickness in the belly.

climb, ou'-ha, to climb a tree.

close, i'-će-wa, close, near by.

cloth, wat-an'-i-hath-a'-yu, black cloth.

wu'-it, breechcloth.

clouds, a'-na.

i-ni'-na-nai'-tu, cloudy.

i-na-nait', moving clouds.

cluster, ban-i'-ni, a bunch, cluster, as of beads or grapes.

coals, wa-as', burning or live coals.

coil, a-hi-'-a, to curl or coil about.

coffee, wa-tai'-yo.

wa-tai'-na-wo, coffee for drinking.

comb, ća-ta-e'-hi, to comb the hair.

come, na-he'-ća, come here.

ci'-te, to come in.
confusion, na-tun'-a-he'-na, trouble, confusion.
cook, bi-thi-ba', to cook food.
cool, ta'-a-ta, to cool anything that is hot, by blowing.
cord, san'-ak, cord, twine, thread.
cottonwood, a-hat', sweet cottonwood.
a-ha'-tin-wi'-tin, bitter cottonwood.
cough, i-shi-si'-ve.
count, na-ye'-thi, to count.
countenance, tah'-a-wi'-an-e, face, countenance.
court, ne-wi'-a, to court a girl, courting.
cousin, na'-si, male cousin.
na-tha'-the, female cousin.
cow, bi, a cow.
bi'-hi, pl. cows.
cowardly, kun-a-nit'-ut, cowardly, easily scared.
crack, ta-ta-nat'-a, to crack, as the ground.
ko-huth'-an, to crack or snap as wood burning.
ha-ya-win'-a-a-te, to crack with the teeth, as lice.
cramp, i-nié-thin'-a-a-at, the cramp.
crazy, na-ni-sin'-o-at, to be crazy.
creep, ée-wa-ki'-sa, to creep up to, or approach, as game.
crooked, na-ho'-is-a.
crupper, éi-thi'-hi-na'-ya.
cry, ben-i-wa'-it.
cup, bas-na'-i-ni'-i-ben'-a, a drinking vessel, cup.
currants, ne-e'-win-a.
cut, na-ho-éi'-ah-a, to cut up fine.
éi-ah-a', to cut slices.
na-hi-ha', to cut notches, notched.
ba-ya-ka'-ah-a, to cut in two in the middle.

D.

dance, bet-at', to dance.
éa-a-tit', a scalp dance.
daughter, na-ta'-na, my daughter.
i-si'-ni-shi-a, my granddaughter.
at-a-net'-a-ni-ha, an adopted daughter.
na-siv', my daughter-in-law.
day, i'-shi.
éin-a-a'-kak, daybreak.
na-kus-eé, daylight.
thun'-a-tha-ni'-so, about the middle of the day.
debility, i-a-nat'-i-hu'-in, weary with heat, debility on a hot day.
deaf, a-ye'-éi-ta, hard of hearing, deaf.
decayed, tha-nu'-sa, rotten, decayed.
deceive, nan-ta'-yi, to tell a lie, to deceive.
deep, ta'-wi, deep, as water.
deer, bi'-hi, a deer.
wa-tan-bi'-hi, black-tailed deer.
a'-tha-wa-ni'-hi, white-tailed deer.
die, na-éa', to die.
a-tun'-i-éin-a, we will die.
dig, koh-o-ha', to dig in the ground.
dirty, ée-hath'-a, to be dirty, as a gun.
disappointed, éi-ni-ith'-éa-na, sorry, disappointed.
discouraged, how-wu'-it-a, to be discouraged, disheartened.
distance, éi-ni-ha'-i-te, a long distance.
ditch, ben'-i-tha-ka'-ne, a ditch, hollow, ravine.
dive, i-i-ka'-hu, to dive as a duck under the water.
divide, ée'-a-na, to divide.
dizzy, ne-in-e'-na, to be dizzy, lightheaded.
do, éin-in-in'-i, I cannot do it.
dog, eth, a dog.
eth'-e-wi (pl.), dogs.
na-ha-ta'-ni, my dog.
ka-ha-ta'-ni, thy dog.
double, a-wai'-e-na, to double up.
dream, ka-nat', a dream.
ka-na'-na, to dream.
drink, na-a-ben', to drink, as water.
drive, a-ta-ha', to drive in, as tent-pins.
drop, éa-ni-a', a drop, as of water.
drown, na-ta-ka'-nat, to drown, to be drowned.
drunk, nan-si'-he-wi, to get drunk.
dry, ni-ha-na'-ta.
duck, si'-sié, a duck.
dull, i-ha'-o-éa'-ya-nis, dull, blunt, not sharp.
dusk, ta-wa'-be-ni'-hi-ya.
dust, ka-na-a'-i-ta-si.
dye, bah-o-hai'-yi, to dye or color red or scarlet.

E.

eagle, nat-sa'-i, bald eagle.

in-a-kuth'-un-it, the war eagle.
ear, wun-a-tun'-a, the ear.
bi-hi'-hah, a mule, big ears.
earth, bi-ta'-wa, earth, dirt.
a-mŭ'-it-bi'-ta-wa, all the earth, all the prairie.
eat, a-ta'-wi-thi'-na, to eat.
echo, bat-ath-u'-ni-tu'-hi-nith, an echo.
elk, wuh'-a, a female elk.
wuh'-a-he, a male elk.
elbow, i-ći-a'-na.
empty, ou-it-ćni'-es, to be empty.
end, na-nah'-ŭ, the end of anything.
enemy, et-sha-the'-win, an enemy, of a hostile nation.
envious, i-ni-a-ya-thin'-a, to be jealous or envious.
equal, ta-se-na', to be equal, equal to.
esteem, na-tan-at'-a-wa, to esteem highly, to think well of any one.
evening, ith-o-ak', in the evening.
expect, ais-tha-ća'-na, I expect so.
explain, na-tith'-i-ća-win, to explain anything.
eye, besh-i'-se, an eye.
nesh-i'-se, my eye.
esh-i'-se, thy eye.
ish-i'-se, his eye.
ći-ni'-wak-at, squint-eyed, cross-eyed.
na-kak', white-eyed.
na-u'-i-sa, to shut the eyes.
ka'-na-ki, to open the eyes.

F.

fan, na-nas-i'-ha-wa, a fan.
na-nas'-i-ha, to fan oneself.
fall, ća-ni'-sa, to fall down, as any object.
fasten, a-ta'-ha, to fasten, as a door.
father, ni-ha', father.
ni-sun'-a, my father.
e-sun'-a, thy father.
i-sun'-a, his father.
na-shith'-a, my father-in-law.
feast, na-o'-het-e, to call to a feast.
fence, ni-tha-hai'-ya, to make a fence.
fill, i-ha'-ka-ha, to fill the pipe.
find, ben-i-in'-a, to find.
fingers, ba-ćit'-in.
wah'-a, finger nails.
fire, sta.
i-shit'-a, a fire-place, fire-bed.
ai'-ćis, a fire-steel.
fish, neb, a fish.
na'-wa, pl. fishes.
flat, sa'-a.
flavor, ni-ya-ni'-ćit-a, taste, flavor.
float, na-wo'-a, to float, as upon water.
flock, nath-i-tuk'-a, a flock, a herd.
flower, na'-i-na.
fly, ća-wi'-at, to fly, as a bird.
fold, ni-si'-ta-na, to fold, as cloth.
follow, tha-ku'-i-na, to follow after one.
foolish, a-ha-kai'-nit, to be foolish.
foot, na-he'-tan, my foot.
ford, ni-i'-ta-ka'-ni, a ford, crossing.
a-kai'-e, to cross, as a stream, to ford.
forehead, ni-tah'-a-wi.
forget, na-ni'-hi-na, to forget.
forked, ni-su'-ni, forked, as a stick or stream.
fountain, ah-ub', a spring or fountain.
fox, ba-hŭ', a large fox.
no'-a-ha, kit fox, animals that come out of holes.
to freeze, ni-a'-ta, to freeze, as ice.
friend, ni-tai-he', my friend.
ni-ni-tai'-eth-e'-ćat, to be friendly.
frog, ći-nat'-an-a'-ka-be, a green frog.
full, a-na-tha'-a-he, to be full.

G.

gallop, na-ha'-kut-e, to gallop, as a horse.
gashes, i-tas', to cut gashes, to make marks in the flesh.
gather, a-no'-i-tan-ći-ni'-na, to collect or gather together.
get, ko-hai'-e, to get up.
girdle, ka-ya'-ta, girdle or belt.
girl, is-i'-he.
is-i'-hi-ha, pl. girls.
give, a-ta-wi'-ni-thin, to give.
a-tun-be'-no, to give, to bestow for nothing.
glad, bab-i-in'-a, to be glad.
a-tha-wa'-wi-in-a, I am glad.
gnaw, ha-ha-yu'-it, to gnaw.
go, na'-e, to go out.

a-si'-sa, go away.

a-tha'-na-na-wi'-a-ta-si, to go against the wind.

gonorrhœa, ba-ha'-kai-ya.

good, i'-tha-ti.

i-tha-ti-hi', pretty (intensive form).

goose, na.

tuh-u-wi'-na, gooseberries.

gopher, ći-tat'-si-hi.

grapes, ta-ta'-ći-win'-a, grapes, berries that grow on vines.

grass, woh-u'-i-na.

ni-ah'-u, sweet-smelling grass.

ni-a-će'-he, a grasshopper.

se-na-se-yat'-a, to graze, to eat grass, like cattle.

gravel, ći-hi-na'-kai-na, gravel, earth.

grease, ni-nun'-i.

grind, mo-ku'-i-ti, to grind, as coffee.

ground, i-tha'-ba-bi'-ta-wu, in the ground.

ta-shi-bi'-ta-wu, on the ground.

grow, bi-shi'-a-ha, to grow, as grass.

growl, ses-iht', to growl like a dog, or a cross person.

gum, ku'-i-ya, a gum or resin.

gun, ka-kih', a short gun.

ni-si-ti'-ne-na, a double-barrelled gun.

ha-ha-it'-in-an, a rifle-gun, one with creases in the inside of the barrel.

na-sa', a gun-flint.

H.

hackberry, na-tai'-ye-ći-wish.

hair, bi-tha-a'.

bi-tha-a'-na, (pl.)

ne-tha-a', my hair.

e-tha-a', thy hair.

in-i'-tha-a, his hair.

ći'-nan, all kinds of hair.

half, ka-u'-he, half of anything.

hammer, thah-a', a stone hammer, to drive pins.

hand, ba-ćet', the hand.

na-ćet', my hand.

a-ćet', thy hand.

i-ćet', his hand.

ba-ćet'-in-a (pl.), hands.

ba-wa-tha-ta-wi'-na, to wave the hand.

ka-hu-it-o'-i-no-wat, a handful.

hard, bath'-a.

hasten, na-ha-ni', to hasten, to be in a hurry.

he or it, in'-it.

head, i-ni'-thi-a.

i-ni'-thi-a'-na (pl.), heads.

health, nat-un-a-ya'.

hear, ni-tun'-a, to hear.

heart, bet'-a.

bet'-a-ha (pl.), hearts.

net'-a, my heart.

at'-a, thy heart.

it'-a, his heart.

hiccough, i-tha-nat', to hiccough.

hide, ya-ti', to hide from, to conceal anything.

high, ća-o'-it-a, high, anything high.

hill, ća-ut'-e-yu, a hill.

na-ha-hu'-he, up hill.

ćen-a-hu'-he, down hill.

ah'-a-bi, a side hill.

hiss, si-win'-a, to hiss.

holes, ći-nat-un'-a-ti, full of holes.

horn, ni'-nis.

a-ta', big-horn.

horse, woh'-a-hah, a horse.

woh'-a-hah'-a-wi (pl.), horses.

na-ta'-ni, my horse.

a-ta'-ni, thy horse.

i-ta'-ni, his horse.

na-ta-ni'-ha, my horses.

a-ta-ni'-ha, thy horses.

i-ta-ni'-ha, his horses.

na-kit', a white horse.

house, a-a'-wi.

ya-huth'-it-ni'-na, a good house.

ći-ta-wu', in the house.

how is it? to-shi'-hi.

hungry, ash-i-nan'-a, to be hungry.

hunt, i-na'-e, to hunt, as for game.

husband, ih.

nas, my husband.

hush, te-ta-nuk'-ŭ, hush! be still!

I.

I, neo-an'-a.
ice, wa'-o.
implements, ći'-na-te, tools, implements.
inquire, ta-ti'-na, to inquire, to ask a question.
iron, be-ćith'-a.
na-ku'-wi-ćith'-a, white iron, silver.
ni-ha-ni-be-ćith'-a, yellow iron, brass.
ba-aȟ'-a, red iron, copper.
itch, yun-ćis'-it-sha, to itch.

J.

jump, ćen'-a-a, to jump.

K.

kick, taȟ'-un-a, to kick, as dust.
kidney, ti'-thith.
kill, ne-hin'-a, to kill.
kindred, in-i-ni'-tun-a, family, kindred.
knee, ba-ća-e'-tai-yi.
ba-ća-e'-tai-yi-iȟ'-o-na, kneepan, patella.
knife, waȟ'-a.
waȟ'-a-ha, (pl.)
knock, tat-a'-ta, to knock, as on a door.

L.

lake, ni-aé', a little lake or pond.
lame, ći-ni-iȟt'.
large, ben-a'-sa, great, large.
ben-a-si'-tha, very large.
na-ath-i'-a, so large.
lariat, a-ni-tha'-tan.
last, taȟ'-sa, last, youngest.
lately, wa-ni'-hi, lately, a little while ago.
laugh, a-ȟo'-an, to laugh.
laziness, tha-nu'-it, lazy.
lead, ka-ku'-ya-na'-thi, balls, lead.
leaf, bi-ćish', a leaf of a tree.
leak, thi-ni-i'-kut-e, to leak, as a vessel of water.
lean, ni-ha'-shi, to lean against anything.
leg, be-ća', the leg.
be-ća'-wa (pl.), legs.
ne-ća', my leg.
e-ća', thy leg.
it-ća', his leg.
wa-a'-ta, the whole leg.
leggins, wa-ta'.
lend, ni-ća'-ta-nan-an, to lend anything.
lengthwise, ba-ya-tha'-tha-ni-hi.
less, ni-ta-ći'-i-ni.
lick, ni-sa-ta', to lick, as with the tongue.
light, wut-un'-e, to make or light a fire.
lightning, ći-ba'-ko-hu'-it, to lighten, lightning.
like, bi-ȟa'-tha, to be like to, like anything.
lip, is'-is.
listen, ći-hath'-te, to listen.
little, a-ka-ći'-hu.
lizard, san-i'-wa, a rock lizard.
load, bi-na-tha', to load up, as horses.
lodge, ne-i-nun', a lodge or tent.
ne-i-nun'-a (pl.), lodges.
na-ye'-i-hi, my lodge.
a-ye'-i-hi, thy lodge.
i-yo'-i-hi, his lodge.
na-ye-hin'-a, our lodges.
a-ye-hin'-a, your lodges.
i-ye-hin'-a, their lodges.
ne-i-nun'-a-ben-e'-ni-se', only two lodges.
shi'-sin-a, to take down the lodge.
i'-tan, a cluster of lodges, a village.
i-sa'-a-ta, the door or entrance to the lodge.
a-kaȟ'-in, lodge-poles.
nith-nu'-it-a-ćith'-it-a, the hole in the top of the lodge for the smoke to pass out.
look, na-ni', look here!
lose, a-nuth-i'-na, to lose anything.
an-i-ti'-na, lost.
loud, a-nun'-a-un-et'-i, to speak loud.
loved, bi-ȟa'-tha, I am loved.
low, ta-ko'-it-a, low, low down.
lungs, i-kun'-a, lungs, lights.

M.

magpie, wo-u'-he.
make, nish'-ti, to make anything, to form.
man, in-en', a man.
in-en'-a (pl.), men.
ni-a'-tha, a white man.

married, ni-wi'-na, to be married, to take a wife.
meat, wa-na-se'-na, fresh meat.
a'-wa-na, dried meat.
medicine, woh'-in, medicine or mystery.
bat'-at, a medicine-man.
melt, taé'-hu-ha, to melt, as lead.
middle, na-i-thi', in the middle.
midnight, na-hi-thi'-tut-éi.
mine, ni-nis'-tat (pronoun).
mire, ka'-thi-éa, miry, muddy.
kath-éi'-si, to mire, to get stuck in the mud.
mist, éin-i-a-sa', mist, fine rain.
mix, nah'-ut-i, to mix, mingle together.
moccasins, wa'-na.
more, ni-bas'-i-ni, more, over, more than.
morning, na-ku'-seé, this morning.
mother, na'-a.
ne'-na, my mother.
e'-na, thy mother.
i'-na, his mother.
na-he'-ha, my wife's mother.
na-tus'-i-ha'-ni-wa, my wife's grandmother.
mould, ni-na-ku'-si, mould, mouldy.
mountain, a'-he.
a'-he-ni (pl.), mountains.
mourn, as-e'-shit, to mourn for the dead.
mouse, a-ku', a rat or mouse.
mouth, bet'-i.
bet'-i-na (pl.), mouths.
net'-i, my mouth.
et'-i, thy mouth.
i'-ti, his mouth.
ni-thi-a'-ta-wa-ni, a mouthful.
mud, ah-ush'.
muskrat, i-ha-ha, named from the melt in cattle.

N.

name, a-si'-hit, a name, names of persons.
navel, ith, beth.
neck, bes-un'-a, the neck.
nes-un'-a, my neck.
es-un'-a, thy neck.
is-un'-a, his neck.
wai-e'-nun-a, a necklace of beads, &c.
never, a-ti-na'-a-sin', never, ever.
night, bi-ka'.
no, éi-ni'-ni.
ka-ko'-yun, nowhere.
nodding, ni-si'-nun-ai'-a-ha'-na, nodding as in sleep.
nose, bŭsh, the nose.
be'-tha (pl.), noses.
nŭsh, my nose.
ŭsh, thy nose.
ish, his nose.
na-ho-ish'-i-va, crooked nose.
ni-i'-wa, to blow the nose.
nothing, i-ka-ku'-a.
now, i-wan'-ha.
numb, ben'-i-sa-nu'-kut-i, numb, stiff with cold.

O.

obey, i-tha-wat'-a-ni, to be obedient, to obey.
oftentimes, ni-hou'.
old, ba-a-ye'.
one, na-na-ye'-shi-ni, each one.
ta-na'-ni-si-thet'-éat, neither one.
in-i-éa'-sa, the other one.
only, ben-e'.
ooze, ta-sa-éi', to ooze out, as sap from trees.
open, ta-tin'-a, to open, as the mouth.
ka-nin'-a, to open, to make an opening in anything.
ka-nit'-a-na, open the door yourself.
ornaments, ée'-ta-na, ear-rings, or ornaments.
orphan, e-nuh-u'-i-sa, an orphan, fatherless and motherless.
overhead, i-éi'-wa-ni'-than, overhead, above.
overtake, wa-ni-ta'-wa, to overtake one in travelling.
owl, bath-i', an owl.

P.

pace, ba-he'-kut-e, to pace, as a horse.
pack, i-ni'-nuh-it, a pack, a load.
paddle, i-thu-ha', to paddle a canoe.
paint, ha-ha', to paint.
parch, ka-ye-na', to parch, as corn or coffee.
parfleche, o-wa'-na.
pass, ni-the-na', to pass the pipe.

passionate, ći-ni-no'-wu-it, to be passionate, to get angry quickly.

peace, i-ni'-tai-wa'-na, a peace.

na-ti-ni'-tai-wa'-na, to make a peace.

peel, ka-ku'-i-na, to peel, as bark.

ćin-aȟ'-a, to pare, to peel off, as the rind.

perhaps, naȟ-u'-i-he, perhaps, maybe.

pheasant, na-na'-be-ćen'-a, drumming pheasant.

bas-ćen-an', wild turkey, spotted-wing.

pick, ka'-i-ye, to pick, as berries.

ku-i-tan-a', to pick off, as a scab.

ba-ȟa-ku'-na, to pick off, as ears of corn from a stalk.

pinch, a-ȟo'-as-i-na, to pinch.

pine, sath, a pine. *Pinus.*

tha-ki'-sath, spruce pine.

ba-thi'-na, and to-sath', *Juniperus.*

pipe, e-ća, a pipe.

e-ća'-ha-na (pl.), pipes.

na-ti-ca', my pipe.

a-ti-ća', thy pipe.

i-ti-ća', his pipe.

a-ti-ća'-a'-nin, your pipe.

i-ti-ća'-en'-a, their pipe.

pity, a-we'-nun-i, to take pity on one.

plain, i-tha-be', a level plain.

plan, tas-ći'-ni-na, to plan anything.

plenty, wa-na'-the, a plenty.

wa-na-the'-thi (intensive form of the above), a great number or quantity.

plough, bi-ta-wu-ni'-tha-ku, a plough, a ground-breaker

plums, ba-si'-win-a.

point, ni-thi-so'-hai-a, to point with the finger or hand.

poor, a-ći'-ni-na-ni'-ni, poor in flesh.

pounce, ith-ku'-te, to seize or pounce on anything.

pound, is-tha'-ba, to pound fine.

ȟa-ya'-ȟe, to pound or crush, as bones.

pour, e-ta-na', to pour out, as water.

powder, će'-tha.

praise, bi-with-tun'-a, praise, compliments.

prairie, i-tha-wu'.

to prick, kut-a-ha', to prick with a pin.

tha-wut'-a-ta-ka'-it, to prick up the ears, as a horse.

pride, i-sit', pride, to be proud.

prisoner, wa-wa-e-na', a prisoner, captive.

pull, ka-nan'-a, to pull out the hair from the skin.

ka-ku'-na, to pull in pieces.

push, un-ku'-i-ti, to push down.

ka-ȟa-e'-na, to push aside, to separate, as high grass.

put, ći'-tha-wi, to put on, as clothes.

ka'-wo, to put anything in the mouth.

na-će', to put up the lodge.

Q.

quick, na-ȟu'-hu, to be quick, in a hurry.

quiver, ći-tuth'-a, a quiver for arrows.

baȟ-a'-ka-ći-tuth'-a, a panther-skin quiver.

baȟ-a'-ka, a panther.

R.

rabbit, ai-wa-ta'-ka, a large rabbit.

na-wa-ta'-ka, small rabbit, left, or not pure breed.

rain, a-na'-sa.

a-sa'-ti-nit, it rains.

na-yat', a rainbow, the Great Spirit's fishing-line.

ramrod, ći-ta-hai'.

rattle, kōȟ'-un-a-ku'-i-te, to ring or rattle anything.

ravine, ka-ha'-wo-e, a ravine or hollow among the hills.

reach, će-ti', to reach out the hand, to take anything.

red, ba-a'.

ba-iȟt', it is red.

relationship, i-ni'-ta-in.

rest, tai-yu-nu'-shi, to rest, to take rest.

revenge, wa-wa-ni'-shi-ni'-tai-wa, to get revenge.

rib, i-ća'-na, ribs of any animal.

rich, ni-thai'-ye-ti, to be rich.

ride, ta-hu'-ki, to ride, as a horse.

ring, ni-ȟa-nath'-a-tha, finger-ring.

rip, ta-tin'-a, to rip.

river, ni-ći'-a, a river.

ni-ći'-a-ȟe, a little river.

road, na-na'-ća-ba', milky way, white road.

roast, a-ku'-ha, to roast.

robe, na'-ća, a buffalo robe.

rock, a-bet'-a-na'-ka, a large rock.
ni-ha'-na-na'-ka, yellow rock, rock with thick moss on it.
roll, ta-tuó-ku'-i-te, to roll, as a ball or stone.
root, the'-ći, roots of a tree or a bush.
rough, tha'-thi-a, rough, uneven.
e-tus-shi'-ne-et, pimpled, rough.
round, ća-a', round, as a ball.
rub, i-tha-ha', to rub anything.
run, ćeth'-ko-ha, to run.
ći-wa'-a, to rush on, to make an attack.

S.

sacrifice, bi-ta'-tha, to make a sacrifice to the Great Spirit.
saddle, a-ka-aħ'.
saliva, ku-i-thai'-yat, spittle, saliva.
ku-i-thai'-ye, to spit.
salt, ni-ća'-o.
same, na-a-thu', the same.
ni-sti-ath-i'-a, of the same size.
sand, na'-ba.
satisfied, ni-ith-i-ća'-na, to be satisfied, to have enough.
scalp, bi-thes'.
scattered, ni-e-i-ni'-hi, scattered about.
scorch, a-ku'-he, to scorch, as meat held over a fire.
scrape, a-na-ħŭ'-ħa-ha, to scrape.
bi-tai'-hi, an instrument for scraping robes.
wuth-ta'-the-a, to scrape off with the foot.
scratch, ćes-ća'-a, a scratch on any part.
kōt'-ćin, to scratch.
na-ħu'-a, to scratch with the foot.
secretly, nes-ta-ni'-hi, secretly, slyly, covertly.
sell, at-ni-a-tan'-a-na, to sell anything.
sensible, a-ćħt', to be sensible, to have good sense.
sew, ko-i-ya-ta', to sew on a patch.
shake, ka-kun'-ku-i-ti, to shake, to clean by shaking.
shell, a-hi', a mussel-shell. *Unio.*
a-hi'-ha, small shells.
shelter, tu-ka-ha', a shelter, covering, booth.
shield, a-ći'-hi, a shield.
a-ći'-hi-na (pl.), shields.
ni-ta'-ći-hi, my shield.
a-ta'-ći-hi, thy shield.
i-ta'-ći-hi, his shield.
shine, na'-ha-e, to glisten, to shine.
shirt, bi-ħu'-it.
shoe, na-a'-na, a shoe.
ne-ni-na-a'-na, a man's shoe.
is-i-na-a'-na, a woman's shoe.
bih-a'-na, snow-shoe.
shoot, će-ba', to shoot.
shore, sus-hith', on or along the shore.
shoulder, te'-ya.
shut, a-wet-in'-a, to shut, as the mouth.
sick, na'-ko-wi, to be sick.
side, na-sit'-ath-an'-i-ni, on one side.
aħ'-a-na, on the other side.
ća'-thi, on the outside.
ći-taħ'-a-na, on this side.
i-tun-i'-hi, on both sides.
signs, bath-sa'-win, to make signs to any one.
bath-sa'-hai-e, to make signs.
ben-ath-sa'-hai-e, to make signs at a distance.
sing, ni-be', to sing.
ni-ba'-ti-na, a song.
sink, e-nu'-wo-a, to sink, as in water.
sister, na-tus'-i, my sister.
na-tus-i'-wa (pl.), my sisters.
na-tus'-i-wa, younger sister.
ka-hŭ'-e-na-tus-i, half sister.
ni-thub'-i, sister-in-law.
sit, će-nuk'-a, to sit down.
skilful, ni-tha'-wa-te, skilful, smart.
skim, ći-na'-ka-ha, to skim off, as grease on a pot.
skin, ya-ćes'-ći-ħu'-in, irritation of the skin when heated by the fire.
sleep, na-ka'-it, to sleep.
na-wun'-in, sleepy, drowsy.
slip, i-ħa-ħu'-ći-hi-shi, to slip.
small, na-ath'-i-u, so small.
a-ka-ći'-u-hu-hu, very small.
smell, a-ben-a'-to-wa, to smell.
smoke, će'-i-ta.
ka-na'-ta, smoky.
i-shi-a'-ħa-ha, to smoke a skin.
smooth, a-shi'-thi-ya, to make smooth.
i-ħa'-ha-nau-a, to smooth down, as the hair.

snake, si-si'-ye.

snarled, ći-ni'-na-ći'-ya, tangled up, snarled as thread.

sneeze, i-thi'-vi, to sneeze.

snow, i, snow.

ben-a'-ći, it snows.

soak, ni-o-i-thi'-ti, to soak a skin, preparatory to dressing it.

ni-a-ka'-nat-i, to soak, or make soft.

soft, sa-si-na', soft, tender, as meat.

something, a-i-thu'.

somewhere, a-e-to-hin'-i.

son, ne'-ha, my son.

e'-ha, thy son.

i'-ha, his son.

ne-shi'-a, my grandson.

e-shi'-a, thy grandson.

in-i-shi'-a, his grandson.

na-thaħ', my son-in-law.

a-tun'-i-he-wa, an adopted son.

soon, na-ha-ni'-hi, soon, after a while.

sore, wa-ħa'-ħa-nat, sores on the body, small-pox.

soup, a-kuk', broth, soup.

sour, ya-sis'-i-nak-ćat.

source, ath-ai'-sin, at the head or source of a stream.

speak, ka-an-a'-i-net'-i, to speak slow.

spear, ħa-wa'.

spill, a-kŭsh'-ku-te, to spill, as water.

spirit, iħ-ći'-wa-ni-a'-tha, the Great Spirit, half white man.

splinters, an-an'-as-iħt-a-sin'-en-a, stuck full of splinters or briers.

split, ta-ti'-ħa, to split.

spoon, a-wi'-ya, a spoon.

sport, ak-se-si'-hin-a, to play, or sport.

spotted, ka-kut-an'-i, spotted, speckled.

spring, ban-i-o-nŭ'-in.

sprinkle, e-ći'-i-ku'-te, to sprinkle, as water.

squat, thi-yuk'-a, to squat down on the ground.

squeeze, ni-ći'-na, to squeeze.

tat-a-e'-na, to press or squeeze the hand.

squirrel, baħ-un-i', large squirrel, ground hog.

stab, kŏħ-o-hum', to stab one with a knife.

stamp, ta-ħa', to stamp in pieces with the foot.

star, a'-tha.

starve, as-na'-tin, to be starving, to starve.

steal, a-wi'-ta, to steal.

step, a-ku'-hu, to put the foot on, to step on anything.

stick, thi-a'-ku-te, to stick or thrust, as in the ground.

still, na-ni-tha'-ni, still, quiet, to be silent.

stingy, ći-ni-ka'-a-tiħ, stingy, covetous.

stink, wŏħ'-a-ba, to stink, to become putrid.

stirrups, ći-thi-uk'-in.

stomach, be-ćat', stomach.

ne-ćat', my stomach.

e-ćat', thy stomach.

i-ćat', his stomach.

stone, a-na'-ka.

straight, ba'-ya.

ħu-ben-a', to straighten, make straight, as a stick.

strangle, ni-ća'-na-wa-tha'-wa, to strangle, to suffocate.

streaked, ħa-ħa'-ye, striped, streaked.

stretch, thiħ-o-ha', to stretch, as a skin.

strike, ta-win'-a, to strike.

kai-ye'-thi-ha, to strike and knock loose, as a stake or pin.

strong, ti-ni-iħt'.

a-tha'-na-tin'-i-in-a, I am strong.

stumble, ta-ush'-i, to stumble.

suck, ni'-na, to suck, as a child.

sugar, ni-sis'-ća.

summer, bić.

sun, is-is'.

bi-ku-sis', night sun, the moon.

i-shish'-bi-set, sunrise.

na-is-et', sunset.

surround, aħ-o-in'-a, to make a surround, as of buffalo.

suspend, o'-i-ti, to hang up, suspend anything.

swallow, a-ta-wa-ku'-i-te, to swallow anything.

bi-te-bi'-ħo-hu'-ħu, mud swallows, birds that build their nests of mud, like the muskrat.

sweat, ći-ba', to take a sweat.

ći-bat', a sweat-house.

ko-no'-wa-na, to perspire freely on a hot day.

sweet, ya-ni-sis-ćat.

swell, ka-na'-a-na, to puff out, swell like inflammation.

swift, ni-nan'-a, swift, swiftly.
swim, tu-i-si'-vi, to swim.
swing, ća-ća-i'-hi, swinging backwards and forwards.

T.

take, na'-tha-wi, to take off, as clothes.
a-thi'-wi-hut'-un-e, to take it over.
talk, a-na'-ti, to talk with any one.
tear, tut-e-ku'-i-ti, to tear or rend.
tho-wu'-thi-a, to tear anything with the foot.
tent, na-tun'-i, flaps of a tent.
thi-ha-an'-a, tent pins.
thankful, a-hŏu', to be glad, thankful.
that, in'-i.
thaw, a-na'-ku-a, to thaw, as ice.
they, in-it'-a-na, they or them.
thick, na'-kai-ya, thick, thickly.
thigh, it-sa'-wi.
think, i-wi-na'-ais-tha-ća'-na, to think, consider.
thirsty, na-ka'-ye-na, thirsty, to be thirsty.
this, in'-a, this one, this.
those, in-i-na'-ne.
thou, na-ne'-nit.
thunder, be-ha'-ni-tŭ-it, to thunder.
threaten, a-tun-a'-ha, to threaten one.
throw, to'-o, to throw.
tickle, a-na-ha-hai'-in-a, to tickle.
tie, to'-kte, to tie.
tight, ne'-a-na, to hold tight.
toad, ka-na-na'-ka-we, a large toad.
tobacco, si-sa'-wa, tobacco.
si-sa'-wan, pl.
na-si'-sa-wa, my tobacco.
na-si'-sa-wan, our tobacco.
i-si'-sa-wan, their tobacco.
to-day, i-wan'-hat-i-shi'-na.
together, i-uh'-a-ti'-ni-hi, close together.
to-morrow, na-kak'.
tongue, wi-thun', the tongue.
ni-sa-ta', to lick, as with the tongue.
tooth, bi'-ćit-a, a tooth.
ne'-ćit-a, my tooth.
e'-ćit-a, thy tooth.
in-i'-ćit-a, his tooth.
te-ći'-na-na'-ta, to make a grating noise with the teeth.
kak-si-nan'-at-a-hoć'-ta, to rattle with the teeth, to chatter.
top, ta-shi'-he, on the top.
touch, bes-in-a', to touch with anything.
ti-en'-a, to touch one, to call his attention to anything.
track, nah-a-hit', the track of any animal.
trade, a-ta'-ne, to trade anything.
a-ta'-ni-hi, a trader, a merchant.
trail, ba, path, road, trail.
ba'-na, pl.
trample, a-na-hin'-i, to trample down, as grass.
transparent, wa-hu'-i-na-a, clear, transparent.
travelling, nōh'-a-na, to meet any one travelling.
a-ta-bi'-hi, to pass by any one travelling.
tree, a-hat', a tree.
a-ha'-tin-a, pl.
tremble, a-hi'-na-e, to tremble.
trot, sas-es'-kut-e, to trot, as a horse.
trouble, na-tun'-a-he'-yat, to trouble, vex, annoy.
turn, thet-ći-na', to turn over anything.
ith-et-ći-na', turn him over.
na-a-ku'-i-ti, to turn around, as a wheel, or spin a top.
turtle, ba-en'-a.
twins, ka-ka-u'.
twist, ći-thi'-wi-na, to twist.

U.

uncle, na-tha'-i-tha, my mother's brother, uncle.
understand, ka-in'-a, to understand, to know what is meant.
unload, a-wa-ća'-in-a, to take off, unload.
untie, a-kun'-a, to untie anything.

V.

village, i-tha-i'-tan-u, at the village.
vomit, bath-an'-a, to vomit.
bath-an'-o-wa-te'-nu, to nauseate, so as to wish to vomit.

W.

wadding, a-ko-ha', wadding for a gun.
wade, si'-a-ho, to wade out after anything.
wag, nan-ak'-a-ni, to wag the tail, as a dog.
walk, ći-wi'-sa, to walk.
warm, ash-ta', to be warm.
un-a-hu'-a-toi, warm yourself, you are cold.
wander, an'-a-ha, to wander, to lose one's way.
war-party, nut-i-kun'-it.
ta-wa'-he, a war-club.
wash, a-he'-si-ta, to wash, as the hands.
watch, a-na'-yi-ha'-ta, to watch, to look out.
a-na-ye', watching, waking.
water, nić, water.
ni'-ći, (pl.)
kah-a'-ya-wi-kut'-e, shallow water.
ben-a-ha'-wi-te, wide water.
way, i-tha-ba'-ya, in that direction, in that way.
we, na-ne-ni'-na, we or ours.
weak, na-tiht', weak, feeble.
wear, a-hu'-be, to wear on the shoulders, as a blanket.
weasel, si'-a.
weather, wa-hu-sa'-ti-hi-ni, to be bad, stormy weather.
weave, ni-tha-tan'-a, to weave or braid.
well, i-nin-tan', to be well.
wet, sa-ya-ka'-na.
what, to'-is-a, what is it? what?
to-shi'-hi, what is the matter?
to-u'-hu, how long? at what time?
a-ha', what? is it possible? is it so?
to-huć'-ha-ta, how far? to what place?
when, to-u'-hu.
where, ta-ti'-na, where is it?
whetstone, i-ta'-ha-ha.
which, an-a'-a-huk.
while, ku-thi'-hi, a long while.
whip, is-ko-ha', a whip.
is-ko-ha'-na, (pl.)
nis-ko-hin'-a, to whip or flog any one.
whirlpool, ka-ka-ai'-na-wa, an eddy, whirlpool.
whisper, i-wi-na-ye'-ti, to whisper.
whistle, ni'-si-hi, to whistle.
white, nun-a'-ća.
why, tat.
who, an-a-a', who is it?
widow, i-ni-wi'-si.
wife, i-nain', a wife, or married woman.
na-tus'-i-ha, my wife.
a-tus'-i-ha, thy wife.
it-us'-i-ha, his wife.
willow, ba-će-wi'-shi, red willow. *Cornus sericea.*
nōh-than', bark of red willow.
ba-ći-ya'-ka, a large willow, growing near the foot of the mountains.
wind, a-se'-si.
na-kai'-si-si, with the wind.
window, na-e-ha'.
wink, na-o-si'-ći, to wink with the eyes.
winter, ćeć.
wish, at-i-na-e'-na, wish, disposition.
with, na-ku'-in, with, together with.
ći-ta'-wo, inside, within.
ća'-i-thi, out of doors, without.
wolf, ka-a', prairie wolf.
ka-a-wo'-u, same as last.
ah'-i, large wolf.
a-wa'-ta-tas, same as last.
woman, is'-i.
is-i'-na, (pl.)
a-na'-e-ha-wu'-is, an unmarried woman.
wood, beh'-a.
ah-u'-in-i, green wood.
wa-thi'-ni, dry wood.
it-ush', pith of wood.
wrinkles, wa-tha-pa'-hain.
write, ća-thun-a-he', picture-writing on a robe.
ẘa-thun-a-he', to write with a pen.

Y.

yawn, na-ka'-ni, to gape, to yawn.
yellow, ni-ha'-ya.
ath'-i-na-ni-ha'-ya, very yellow.
yes, a.
yesterday, un-hu'-bat-i-i'-shi-in-a.
yonder, in'-a, yonder, there.
you, ne-na'-nin.
young, wa-na-niht'.
yours, ni-nis-tat'.

CHAPTER XI.

V. ATSINAS.

ETHNOGRAPHICAL HISTORY.

THE Atsinas are undoubtedly a branch of the Arapoho nation, as the great similarity in the two languages would indicate. The cause of their separation from the Arapohos probably originated in some feud, so common among savage tribes. They then crossed the Rocky Mountains (the nearest route to the Blackfoot country from the Platte is to cross the mountains near the sources of Snake River, and recross at the sources of the Missouri), and associated themselves with the Blackfeet. When this division took place is not now correctly known, though we think it must have occurred some time within the last century. Their former hunting grounds, as indeed were those of the whole of the Blackfoot nation, were on the tributaries of the Saskatchewan, in which region buffalo and other game was abundant. Previously to the opening of the trade with these Indians on the Upper Missouri, they sold all their skins to the Hudson's Bay Company, seldom visiting the country about the sources of the Missouri except for hostile purposes.

It is said that the Atsinas captured one of the English forts, murdered the people, and were, on that account, obliged to change their location for the one they now occupy. This is very probable, as they are a subtle, revengeful people, social and united in their undertakings, and easily influenced and guided by their chiefs. At the present time, and for many years past, their range has been along Milk River, on the east side of the Missouri, extending nearly as far as Cypress Mountains. From this line to the Marias River stretches a beautiful, level country, well covered with grass, and adapted to the pasturage of buffalo. Here the Indians under consideration may be found at all seasons,—in the winter, along the banks of Milk River, where wood can be obtained, and on the plains in summer, where fuel is not so necessary.

As we have before stated, the Atsinas were originally a portion of the Arapoho tribe, now occupying the country about the sources of the Platte River. We may here say, in giving an account of their past wanderings, that the precise time of their separation from the Arapohos is not known. For the last hundred years or more they have lived on the Saskatchewan and near the sources of the Missouri. With the Blackfeet they have always been on terms of peace and amity, having intermarried with them and learned to speak their language. It is worthy of remark, that while nearly all of them speak the Blackfoot language fluently, very few, if any, of the Blackfeet have ever acquired that of the Atsinas. They usually converse in a low, quiet tone, and there is apparently such a similarity and monotony in the words, as well as sounds, that their language is regarded by the traders and Indians as the most difficult to learn of any on the Upper Missouri.

No trader has ever acquired it sufficiently to carry on even an ordinary conversation, much less to make a speech, though some of the old residents can pronounce the names of different articles of trade with tolerable accuracy. All dealings or intercourse with them by whites or Blackfeet are conducted through the language of the latter nation, which abounds with interpreters.

In the year 1818, the Atsinas, having surprised and robbed one of the forts of the Hudson's Bay Company, on a tributary of the Saskatchewan, fled to the sources of the Missouri, where they passed the winter; but, finding no traders there to furnish them with supplies or purchase their peltries, they continued their route across the mountains, and joined once more their old relations the Arapohos. Here they resided and hunted in common with the latter tribe for the space of five years, during which time the small-pox passed among them, having been communicated through other tribes with whom they were at peace or carried on a traffic. This disease, at that time, destroyed about half their number, but secured the remainder from the next attack, which occurred in 1838. At this latter period the small-pox only acted upon the young, and destroyed numbers of them, but the chiefs and elderly men escaped, so that the tribe was not reduced to the disorderly and helpless condition of the Blackfeet and other surrounding nations.

In the summer of 1823, the Atsinas became dissatisfied with the country of the Arapohos, and longed for their old district, or at least, for some place where the buffalo were to be found in greater abundance than among the valleys of the mountains. The Crow nation had been on terms of peace with the Arapohos for several years, but not being acquainted with the Atsinas, regarded them as enemies, from their previous union with the Blackfeet. This fact the Atsinas well knew, and to avoid meeting with the Crows on their journey to the Missouri, they made a circuit of many miles west of the Crow district, passing near the Columbia. During this trip across the mountains, they came in contact with a few white men trapping for beaver, some of whom they killed and robbed of their property, while others escaped, and carried the intelligence of the murder of their comrades to the main body of trappers. This was a company of sixty to eighty men, all well armed, and versed in the different modes of Indian warfare. They were brave men, headed by renowned leaders, Sublette and Fontinelle. Most of these trappers were assembled at their rendezvous, on a tributary of Big Snake River, not far from the place where the murders were committed.

Always ready to avenge the death of any of their party, and to drive hostile Indians from the mountains, they at once started to attack the advancing camp of the Atsinas. The latter discovered their approach in time to erect several small forts and other breastworks, with such materials, hastily thrown together, as the country afforded. The trappers arrived, and one of the most severe engagements took place ever known in the Rocky

Mountains. The Indians had the advantage of position and defensive barricades, the trappers that of arms, ammunition, and skill. For two days a sharp firing was kept up on both sides, the whites from behind trees and rocks, aiming at the openings in the forts, and the Indians shooting any trapper that exposed his person to view. A number of exhibitions of individual daring occurred on the part of the trappers; some of them leaped into the middle of one of the defences, which contained about twenty Indians, whom they killed and scalped, losing a few of their own party at the same time. Mr. Sublette, the leader, received a severe, though not mortal wound, from a ball passing through his body, after breaking his arm. At the end of forty-eight hours, the trappers left the place, being unable to dislodge the Indians from their barricades. In this conflict, fifty-six of the Atsinas were killed, and about double that number wounded. The trappers had nine men killed, and several wounded, some of whom subsequently died from their wounds.

As soon as possible after this battle, the Atsinas decamped, and pursued their journey by long and rapid marches. Considering themselves out of the reach of their white enemies, and beyond the limits of the range of the Crows, they travelled more leisurely, and inclined more northward, with a view of reaching a portion of the Blackfeet, near St. Mary's Valley. Even when they considered themselves most secure, still greater misfortunes were impending over them. It so happened that the whole Crow nation had been on a visit to the Flatheads to obtain horses by barter, as was their usual custom. Having concluded their traffic, the Crows returned home in two camps, about the same time that the Atsinas were travelling through that region. Neither tribe was aware of the proximity of the other, this portion of the mountains being unoccupied by Indians, and seldom visited by war-parties. The Crows, also, were travelling from west to east, whilst the others marched from the southwest in a northern direction. One of the Crow camps was about two days' journey in advance of the other, when four young men started from the hindmost camp to join the one in front. In the meantime, the Atsinas had advanced nearly to the trail when the Crows had passed, and these young men, seeing the lodges, supposed them to be their own people, and went directly to their village. They soon discovered their mistake, for the Atsinas at once killed three of them. The fourth, escaping among the rocks and bushes, fled back to his people, and informed them of the fate of his friends. To secure a signal revenge without farther loss, the Crows waylaid the Atsinas in a certain pass which they knew their enemy would be obliged to travel through. This spot they surrounded, and lay in ambuscade until their enemies entered and filled it without suspicion. The Crows then fired upon them from behind rocks and trees with safety. The Atsinas were panic-stricken, and fled, leaving behind them their wounded, and some of their women and children. They scarcely attempted a defence: only a few shots were fired at the Crows, but without effect. Sixty-seven Atsinas were killed, and double that number of women and children taken prisoners, many of whom can be seen among the Crows at this time. The remainder of the Atsinas reached their people, the Blackfeet, without farther loss, with whom they have continued to reside to this day, and are classed as Blackfeet when that nation are spoken of as a body.

We have now given as correct an account of this nation as can be obtained from the most intelligent Indians and traders of the country at the present time. We have searched in vain among all the old books of travel for any definite account of the Atsinas or Arapohos, and consequently, any accurate information in regard to them must be important.

Umfreville, as far back as 1790, seems to have known of the Atsinas, and to have obtained a vocabulary of forty-four words of their language. According to his account, the Hudson's Bay Company and the Nehethewas or Crees, called them Fall Indians, from the fact of their inhabiting a district on the southern branch of the Saskatchewan, where the rapids are frequent. He says: "As they are not very numerous, and have a harsh, guttural language peculiar to themselves, I am induced to think they are a tribe that has detached itself from some distant nation, with which we are not yet acquainted." He also alludes to the impropriety of calling them Big-bellies, inasmuch as they are as comely and as well made as any of the surrounding tribes. "They seem not to be acquainted with the hunting of beaver, dressing skins, and killing small peltries, for they bring us nothing but wolves, which they take by a variety of contrivances. Though we have interpreters for all other Indian languages, none as yet have been able to attain a fluency sufficient to be understood, and the general method of conversing is by speaking the Blackfoot tongue, which is agreeable and soon acquired."

Mackenzie, in 1801, merely alludes to the Fall or Big-bellied Indians living on the Saskatchewan.

Brackenridge* says: "The Gros Ventres of the Prairie speak the Crow language, and wander on the South Fork of the Saskatchewan."

Morse† speaks of them as Rapid Indians, and remarks that they call themselves Paw-is-tuck'-i-e-ne-wuck. From what source he obtained his information, he does not say.

Gallatin‡ also seems to have procured very little accurate information in regard to these Indians, and in his comparisons, he used the small vocabulary of Umfreville.

The brief list of Atsina words given in these pages seems to be the only one, so far as I can learn, that has ever been secured, except that of Umfreville, in 1790. It is a matter of great surprise, that so little is known of this tribe, though it may be due to the fact, that the Atsinas have always been classed with the Blackfeet.

These Indians have received a great variety of names, as Paunch, Fall, Rapid Indians,

* 1819. † 1822. ‡ 1836.

Gros Ventres of the Prairie, Minnetarees of the Prairie, &c. They have also been confounded with the Minnetarees of the Missouri, and one author says they speak the Crow language. I will now endeavor to correct some of the errors which authors have fallen into, in regard to these Indians.

The tribe under consideration call themselves Atsina, the meaning of which I could not ascertain. They now live in and about the valley of Milk River, in latitude 48°, longitude 108°, while the Minnetarees, or Gros Ventres de Missouri, as they are called by the Canadians, reside in a permanent village on the left bank of the Missouri River, near latitude 47°, longitude 102°. The latter speak a dialect of the Crow language, and know very little, if anything, in regard to the former, for they have never met, either in war or peace.

Their numbers have been variously estimated by different authors. The Prince Neuwied, in 1832 and '3, made their number about 200 lodges, and 400 to 500 warriors. Gov. Stevens, in 1853, estimated them at 360 lodges, 900 warriors, and a total population of 2520. The last estimate is probably correct for the present time. In 1855, I took a careful census of 60 lodges of Atsinas, and found that there was an average of a fraction over five persons to a lodge.

VOCABULARY OF THE ATSI'NA DIALECT OF THE ARA'POHO LANGUAGE.

alive, life, na-tha'-ni-ta.
all, ba'-hi.
arm, nin'-is.
arrow, uts.
axe, a-nas'.

bad, wun'-a-tha.
bark, na'-si.
beard, bi-a-thut'-i.
bear, wa'-si.
beaver, a'-bit.
belly, wa-nut'-a.
bird, ni-i'-ha.
blood, ba-uts'.
boat, tse'-e-wa.
body, ni-tun'-i-ya.
bone, mun-i'-ya.
bow, ma-ta'.
boy, a-na'-be.
bread, kat'-san.
brother (elder), ni-ti'-wa.
younger, na-tha'-wa.
buffalo, it-a'-nun.
bull, a-ni'-ke-a.

chief, ni-ke'-a.
child, te'-a-na.
corn, mis-ka'-ta.
cow, bi.

day, ba-a'-a.
darkness, bi'-hi-ka.
daughter, ni-ta'-na (my).
dead, death, na-kik'.
deer, ut-i-vi'-a-nin'-a.
dog, a'-te.
duck, ni-hi'-a.

ear, ke'-ta, mo-no-tun'-i.
earth, pi'-tŏn.
egg, nau'-na.
evening, i-to'-a.
eye, ba-si'-the.

face, it-a'-thi-wi'-a.
father, ne'-ha.
feet, i-thet'-tŏn.
finger, ba-kit'.
fire, sit'-a.
fish, na-qua'-a.
fox (red), ba'-thew.
(gray), no.
forehead, wa-thaut'.
friend, ba'-ni.

girl, i-the'-e.
go, ke-tats'.
good, i'-ta.
goose, ne'-i.
grass, wa-se'-na.
great, be-na-thi'-a.

hair, mi'-ta.
hand, ma-kit'-in.
handsome, sin-i-sa'-ti,
hare, nat'-sa.
head, bi'-ta.

heart, nut'-a.
hen (prairie), kin'-a.
hill, ka-te'-ni.
house, hut, ni'-nun.
husband, na'-si.

I, ni-na'-ni.
ice, wa'-ku.
Indian, ni-thit'.
iron, bet'-ste.
island, ka-a'-pn.

kettle, bet'-ste-na.
kill, nan-a'-a.
knife, wa-tha'.

leaf, bi-ćish'-e.
leg, na-ats'.
light, ni-sin'.
lightning, e-sa'-an.
love, pi-tha'-ta.

man, ni-thun'-a.
many, much, wun-a-tauts'.
meat, a'-than.
moccasins, wa'-a.
moon, bi-ko'-is-is.
morning, na-na'-ka.
mother, e-naun'.
mountain, a-ha'-ni.
mouth, it'-i.

nails, wa'-us.
near, ek-i'-ba.
neck, wa'-thun.
night, tu'-ki.
no, tsc.
nose, ba'-is.

old, bi-e-a'-wa.

pail, pi'-nats.
pipe, e'-tsa.

rain, na'-tha.

sea, ti-yo-ni'-ća.
see, na-na'-ha-qua-ki.
sing, ma'-ki-ha'-ke.
sister, te'-ya.
sleep, na-kasé'.
sky, un'-u.
small, a-ksi'-o.
snake, si'-sa-a.
snow, hi.
son (my), ni'-kun.
speak, na-ne'-kik.
spring, bi-ni'-ka.
squirrel, ba-thaut'-si.
star, ou-to-ba'.
stone, a-na'-ken.
strong, tin-a'-ik.
sun, is'-is.

this, i'-na.
thou, na'-na.
thunder, pa'-a.
tobacco, se-tha'-wa.
to-day, wa-ni'-i-hu-sin.
toe, wa-tha'-a.
to-morrow, na-kast'.
tongue, ni'-tun.
tooth, bi-it'-a.
town, ni'-i-nun.
tree (pine), tha'-a-ta.

ugly (bad heart), na-ta-wun'-a-tha.

walk, be-ni-ta'-pe-ki.
warm, a-sit'-e.
warrior, ne-ta'-tit.
water, nets.
white, nun'-au-ćo.
who, hai'-yo.
wife, na'-ti-tha.
wind, a-tha'-tha.
winter (cold), na-ka'-ta.
wolf, kai-i-ki'-tha.
woman, ith'-a.
wood, bes'-a.

yes, a'-e.
yesterday, a-ta'-ni.
young, wun-a-he'-ka.

one, nin-i-thi'-ki.
two, nin'-i-sits.
three, ni'-nić.
four, kin'-a-nits.
five, kin-a-ta'-nits.
six, ni-ka-ta'-sits.
seven, nin'-i-ta-ta'-sits.
eight, nin'-a-tha-ta'-sits.
nine, e-na'-na-pe-ta'-sits.
ten, ma-ta-ta'-sits.

PAWNEE GROUP, C.

CHAPTER XII.

VI. PAWNEES.

ETHNOGRAPHICAL HISTORY.

It is somewhat remarkable that so little information of a definite character should have been placed on record in regard to a nation which has been so long known as the Pawnees.

I have searched with much care all the works within my reach, and can find no detailed account of their history, only incidental allusions to them in the writings of various travellers. Gallatin remarks that they were visited by Bourgmont as early as 1724, and observes that they occupied very nearly the same district of country over which they range at the present time. I can find no reliable account of their migration from any distant point to their present location. It is the opinion of Mr. Shea that Cavilier alludes to them under the name of Panismahans, in his account of "La Salle's Voyage to the Mouth of the Mississippi, in 1688," where he notes the information given him by three Shawnee Indians, "that there were other nations to the northwest, who had kings and chiefs, and observed some forms of government, honoring and respecting their kings as Europeans do theirs." Again, in the narrative of Father Doway, who, it seems, was a member of La Salle's party, in his attempt to ascend the Mississippi, in 1687, we find the following paragraph, which throws much light upon the location of numerous other tribes now inhabiting the Missouri Valley: "We crossed the Ouabache (Wabash) there on the 26th of August (1687), and found it full sixty leagues to the mouth of the River Illinois, still ascending the Colbert. About six leagues above this mouth there is on the northwest the famous river of the Massourites, or Osages, at least as large as the river into which it empties; it is formed by a number of other known rivers, everywhere navigable, and inhabited by many populous tribes, as the Panimaha, who had but one chief and twenty-two villages, the least of which has two hundred cabins; the Pancassa, the Pana, the Panelozа, the Matotantes, each of which, separately, is not inferior to the Panimaha. They include also the Osages, who have seventeen villages on a river of their name, which empties into that of the Massourites, to which the maps have also extended the name of Osages. The Arkansas were formerly stationed on the upper part of one of these rivers, but the Iroquois drove them out by cruel wars some years ago, so that they, with some Osage villages, were obliged to drop down and settle on the river which now bears their name, and of which I have spoken." The above account seems to me to be somewhat confused, according to our present ideas of the geography of the Mississippi Valley; but I am inclined to think that the various tribes of Indians alluded to were located in the Missouri Valley. In the narrative of the "Travels of Lewis and Clarke," may be found the most reliable account of the location and condition of the Pawnees at the time when these enterprising explorers ascended the Missouri. At that time, 1803, their principal village was situated on the south side of the Platte, about forty-five miles above its mouth, and contained about five hundred warriors. Not many years previously were added the Republican Pawnees, so called from their having lived on a branch of the Kansas of that name. This band numbered two hundred and fifty warriors. The third band was called the Pawnee Loups, or Wolf Pawnees, who resided on the Wolf or Loup Fork of the

Platte, and numbered about two hundred and eighty men. There was also a fourth band, who originally ranged over the country bordering on the Kansas and Arkansas, but were so often defeated in their wars with the Osages that they removed to Red River, forming a tribe of four hundred men. "All these tribes live in villages and raise corn; but during the intervals of culture rove in the plains in quest of buffalo." The band last mentioned undoubtedly includes the Huecos and Witchitas, whose villages are now located near each other, between the Washita and Red Rivers. According to Gregg, these two tribes have been called Pawnee Picts, from their habit of profuse tattooing.

At the time of Major Long's Expedition to the Rocky Mountains, in 1820, three bands, Grand Pawnees, Pawnee Republics, and Pawnee Loups, all resided on the Platte and its branches, and numbered about ten thousand souls. They seem to have been at that time in a prosperous condition, and much devoted to agricultural pursuits.

The Pawnees at this time reside on the Loup Fork, a tributary of the Platte, having been assigned a reservation on that river by the United States Government.

Very little attention has been given to the language of the Pawnees, as well as to their history. So far as I can learn, the first vocabulary of their language was taken by Mr. Say in 1820, and published in the report of Long's Expedition to the Rocky Mountains. The Prince Neuwied also obtained a few words, and Gallatin, in his "Synopsis" (Archæologia Americana, Vol. II, pp. 305–367), simply repeats Say's list of words. Rev. Mr. Dunbar, for a long time a missionary among the Pawnees, prepared a small elementary work in their language for the use of the mission, but as yet I have been unable to secure a copy. No attempt has ever been made to work out the grammatical structure of the language. The following vocabulary was obtained for me by the Rev. William Hamilton, of Bellevue, Nebraska, and, from his great experience in such matters, it is entitled to much confidence. I have simply made some changes in the letters employed, to render the orthography uniform throughout the entire memoir, and arranged the words in alphabetical order.

VOCABULARY OF THE PAWNEE LANGUAGE.

A.

alive, ki'-si-kit.

all, kit'-o.

ant, pit'-a-ru.

antelope, a-pi'-ka-tōs, flat horns.

arm, pe'-ru.

arrow, li'-ksu.

autumn, lits'-ko-ki.

axe, ka-ta'-ra-ki.

ka-ta'-ra-ta'-īt, a battle-axe.

B.

back, līk-sta' ku, lĕk-sta'-ku.

bad, kau-ku'-ra-hi.

bag, ka-dōs'.

ćat-ka-tōs', a woman's bag or satchel.

bark, laks-kūs'.

beak, ćūs, beak, or nose.

bean, at-it'.

at-it'-di-wi'-ru, round bean, or pea.

bear, ko-rōks'.

beast, i'-ta, and i'-to.
beard, a-ka'-da-rūs, and a-ku'-da-rūs.
beaver, ki-tūk'.
bird, li-kūts'-ki, a bird.
kit-o-ka'-ru, all kinds of birds.
black, ti'-ka-tit.
bladder, ka-sīt'-ki-ra'-ku.
blood, pa'-tu.
blue, ta-ri-ūs'.
boat, la-ku'-hu-ru.
tu-wau'-rūks-ti, a ship, sacred, medicine.
la-ku-ha-wau'-sīks-ti, steamboat, medicine-boat.
body, ki-si-kīt'-ri, a living body.
bone, ki'-su.
bow, ti-ra'-kish.
boy, pi'-ras-ki, and pi'-rūs-ki.
bread, i'-ćo-ta.
breechcloth, kau'-di-o-kau'-i-o.
brother, i-da'-di-ko-ta'-ti, my brother.
buffalo, ta'-ra-ha.
ta'-ra-ha-ta'-ka, domestic cow, white buffalo.
to burn, ti-ta'-ra-ri.

C.

call, ti-wa'-ko-la'-ru, he calls.
cat, pak-sits'-ha-wi'-ru, wild cat.
pak-sits-ka'-ki-ats, panther.
chief, ni-sha'-ru.
chicken, pūks, prairie chicken. *Tetrao cupido.*
coat, na-ha'-si.
cold, ti-pit'-si.
corn, li-kis', } corn in the ear.
lēks, }
le-ki-sha'-kūts, coarse grass, corn.
copper, pa-pi'-ći-spa.
cry, ti-ki'-kat, he cries.
me-ti'-ki-kat, crying.
crow, ka'-ka. *Corvus.*

D.

darkness, ta-ti'-sta-ha.
death, we-si'-kit.
we'-ti-kōt, dead.
ti-ko'-kōt, he is dead.
he-tō'k, he dies.
daughter, ćo-ra-ki'-ko-ta-ti, my daughter.
deer, a-ri'-ki-ra'-ru, a male deer.
tōh, a female deer, a doe.
dog, as-ak'-i.
door, le-ka'-wi-u.
drink, ti-ki'-ha, he drinks.
we-ti'-ki-ka, drinking.
duck, ki'-waks, and ki'-sat.

E.

eagle, līh'-ta-kats.
earth, a-ra'-au.
eat, ti-wa'-wa, he eats.
we-le-wa'-wa, he is eating.
ear, ūt-ka-ha'-ru.
a-do-ru'-sa-ka'-ha, long ears, a horse.
egg, li-pi'-ku.
elbow, pa-ro-ćūć'-kīs.
elk, nah.
enemy, ća-hiks-o'-pi'-in.
evening, wa-ti-sak'-u, dark, evening.

F.

face, ska'-u.
far off, kīts-ti-kūts'.
fat, a-bit'-ki.
father, a-ti'-as-ko-ta'-ti, my father.
a-ti'-as-ko-ta'-se, your father.
a-ti'-as-ko'-ta, his father.
feather, hi'-tu.
finger nail, īks-pi'-to, and iks-pi'-to.
fire, lak-tit'.
fish, kat-se'-ik.
flesh, ki-sats'-ki.
flint, ta-hi-u'-ru.
flour, a'-rīh-i-tu.
flower, ki-dōk'-ta-rah'-a-ta.
fly, pi-ra-ras'-a-līt, horse-fly.
foot, as'-u.
forest, o-kat'-u-ha'-ri.
forever, lo-ho'-ri-rēt.
forenoon, ki-ka'-rūs.
friend, i-ra'-ri, } friend or brother.
i-da'-ri, }

G.

girl, o-da'-o, sha-lo', a boy, any of the Loup Pawnees.
ćo-wat', a little girl.
ti'-ki, a little boy.
ćo'-ras-ki-ta-lūs'-ki, a little girl.
pi'-ras-ki-ta-lūs'-ki, a little boy.
god, ti-ra'-wa-kau-ku'-rau-hi, bad gods.
good, tu-ra'-hi.
gone, ne-tēt', he has gone.
goose, kat-o'-rūt. Loup Pawnees say ko-hat'.
kat-o-rūt'-a-ka, white goose.
grass, ka'-ta-ru.
ha-rut'-ki-i-di, cut grass, hay.
great, ti'-ri-hu.
green, tit-a-ri-ūs'.
gun, ti-ra'-ku.

H.

hail, nih'-ōts.
hair, o'-sa.
a-kau-da'-rūs, hair of the mouth.
half, hūks.
hand, ek-su.
handsome, tah'-ni.
hare, pa'-rūs.
hawk, pi'-a-ki.
he, ti-ra'-ku.
head, paks, pūks.
hear, tat-kōk', he hears.
heart, pi'-tsu.
heel, as'-kau-ki'-tu.
hill, pa-o-ti'-di-ho, a large hill.
hog, koh'-o, ko-shan', a word derived from the French traders.
hot, ta'-wi-rits-to.
house, we'-ti-kau, in the house.
ak-a'-ra, a house.
husband, ta-wa'-ri-ko'-ta-ti, my husband, my married one.

I.

I, lat.
ice, ta-si'-tu, hu-ra'-o.
in, ti-hak'.
Indian, ća'-hiks-i-ća'-hiks, literally, men of men, or the last of men.
island, a'-wa-u.

K.

killed, we-tih'-o-tit', he killed it.
knife, lēt'-sik.

L.

laugh, ti-was'-ko, he laughs.
wo'-ti-was'-ku, laughing.
lead, ti-ra-ka'-wi-u, lead balls.
leaf, sh'ki'-ka-la.
leg, kau-su'.
leggin, a-ka'-o-ku.
life, ki'-si-kīt.
light, ūks-e-kut'.
lightning, te-wau-wau'-pits.
liver, ka-di'-ku.
lodge, ak-a'-ska-rīt'-ki, a skin lodge.
looked, to-ti-ri-ku', he looked on.
long, kau-ki-ra'-ki, not long.
love, ti-ra-pi'-ri-hu, ti-ki'-si-kīt', } he loves.

M.

man, pet'-a.
ti-pa'-hat, red man.
ća-hiks-ta-ka', white man.
ta-wa'-re-pīt, pi-to-ko'-ta-ti, } my man.
meat, ki-sūts'-ki, fresh meat.
midday, sak-u-i-ka-ri'-kat.
midnight, i'-das-i-ka'-u-kat.
moon, ko'-ru.
ki'-waks, Duck moon, November.
lūt, Snake moon, October.
kat-i-ha'-ru, six months, six moons.
morning, wet-a-he'-sha.
mother, a-ti-ra'-ko-ta-ti, my mother.
mouth, a'-ka-u.
muskrat, kit'-a-ka.

N.

navel, kau-su', and la-wats'.

near, té-ks'-ku-rat.
neck, pa-hiks'-kis.
no, kau'-hi.
nose, ćūs.
nothing, kau-hōt'.

O.

oar, kits-ka'-wi-tsa'-ku.
oats, li-ki'-sha-kūts, } food for horses.
a-ru'-sa-ko'-ta, }
old, ku'-ra-būsh.
on, ti-hū'-ki-ta-sa.
otter, kīt-a'-pat.
outside, o-ki-ta-ha'-hi-ri.
owl, pa-ho'-ru.

P.

part, kau'-ki.
partridge, ōt-kis'-is.
perhaps, ki'-ri-ku.
ki'-ri-ku-i'-rit, perhaps so.
pepper, kats-kau-pit', black pepper.
pipe, nōt'-a-wi-ska'-ru.
ka'-ta-ra-pīk'-skīt, tomahawk pipe.
plover, ūt.
potato, īts, ēts.
powderhorn, a-di'-i-ki.
pumpkin, pa-haks'.
pa-hak'-sa-las, ripe pumpkins.

R.

rain, ta-tsōn'.
red, ti'-pa-hat'.
river, kits-wa'-rūk-sti, Medicine River.
kits-ka-tūs', Shallow River, Platte.
road, hat-o'-ru, a trail or road.
rose, pa'-hat.

S.

salt, kau'-it.
scalp, pūks-sīt'-skūs.
sea, ki-ra-rik'-shis.
seat, ki-di'-ru, seat or rump.
see, si-sit', he sees.
September, ki-shōt'.
sheep, a'-ri-ka-rits'.
shoe, as-o'-ru, shoe or moccasin.
shoulder, kīt-ska'-su.
silver, wa-pi'-ći-sta-pi'-ri-hu, best metal.
sinew, as-kats'-ki.
sing, ti'-ra-rūh.
sister, i-la-he', used by the men, my sister.
i-da-di', women use this form.
skin, ska-rīt'-ki.
sky, ska'-u, sky, heaven.
slough, ki'-wa-ha'-ru, lake, slough.
ki-wa'-ha-kūts, big slough.
small, ki-ta-lūs'-ki.
smooth, ki-ri-bats'-ki.
snake, lūt'-ki.
snipe, paks-ki-ra'-rūts.
snow, we-tōh'-sha, it snows.
tōh'-sa, snow.
son, pi-ras'-ko-ta'-ti, my son, or my boy.
speak, ti-wa'-ku, he speaks.
spear, u-rūk'-sis.
spirit, te-ra'-wa, Great Spirit.
le-kat-sa'-ro, a ghost, wandering spirit.
spring, a-ra'-ri-ka.
kits-taks', spring or fountain.
squirrel, ski'-pis.
stomach, la-ća'-kīts.
stone, ka-rit'-ki.
ka-rit'-ki-ti-di-hu', large stone, rock.
strike, ti-ta'-hi, he strikes.
strong, tit-a'-rah-ish'.
sugar, la-ki'-tsu.
summer, li'-at.
sun, sak'-o-ru.

T.

thigh, pa'-ki-su.
thistle, pi-ra-ha'-tūs.
thou, las.
thumb, skits'-kūts, big finger.
ske'-tsi, finger.
thunder, tōh-i'-ri-ru.
tie, sta-dīt', he ties.

toad, sko-rōh'-iks.
tobacco, na-wis'-ka-ru.
toe nail, as-pi'-tu.
to-morrow, la-hi'-sa.
tooth, a-do', a-du'.
tree, la-kīsh'.
la-hi'-di-buts'-ki, a shrub, or small tree.
ti-hu'-ki-ta-hu, on the tree.
turtle, i-ćaus', i-ćūs'.

U.

ugly, kau-bōh'-ni.

V.

valley, kat-ōs', kat-ūs'.
vein, pa-tu-hu'-ru.
village, a'-hi-ta-ra, a town or village.

W.

walk, ti-wa'-ri, he walks.
wampum, ki-dīks-ūć'-ka-u-da'-wis.
war-club, a-da-ke'-du-ću'-ku.
warrior, a-ri-pu'-kūs.
water, ki-tsu'.
wasp, pats'-hu, wasp, bee.
we, a'-hats.
weak, kau-ki-ta'-rah-ish.
weed, i'-du.
what? ka? (asking a question.)
ta-ki'-ru-ća'-hiks, what person?
white, ti-ta'-ka, ta'-ka.
who, ta-ki'-ru.
wife, ća'-nat-ko-ta'-te.
wind, o-to'-ru.
winter, pi'-ći-kat.
wish, ti-wits'-ke, he wishes.
within, kau'-wi-hi-ri.
without, o-ki'-ta-ha'-hi-ri.
woman, ća'-pat.
ćo'-ras, ćo'-ra-ke, } a young, unmarried woman.
worm, pi'-ras.
woodcock, kau'-pat.

Y.

year, ti-ra'-ku-i-kat'-i-ha'-ru.
yellow, ti-rah'-at-a.
yes, i'-rit.
yesterday, ti-rūks'-a-ha'-ta-ki.
young, pi'-ras-ki.

CHAPTER XIII.

VII. Ari'karas.

ETHNOGRAPHICAL HISTORY.

The Arikaras, or Rees, as they are called by the French traders, were originally the same people as the Pawnees of the Platte River, their language being nearly the same. That they migrated upward, along the Missouri, from their friends below, is established by the remains of their dirt villages, which are yet seen along that river, though at this time mostly overgrown with grass. At what time they separated from the parent stock is not now correctly known, though some of their locations appear to have been of very ancient date, at least previous to the commencement of the fur trade on the Upper Missouri. At the time when the old French and Spanish traders began their dealings with the Indians of the Upper Missouri, the Arikara village was situated a little above the mouth of Grand

River, since which time they have made several removals, and are now located at Fort Clark, the former village of the Mandans.

The Arikaras have never manifested a very friendly disposition toward white men; indeed, it is said, that feelings of bitter animosity and hatred toward them are taught to their children, as soon as they are able to understand. This appears to have been a traditionary custom handed down from their ancestors, originating, no doubt, in some difficulties with the first settlers of the Western borders, which also were the probable cause of their emigration. Whatever the cause may have been, this system of education has been persisted in with the young even to the present time, and the consequences have been severely felt through successive generations. It was with great difficulty that a trade could be opened with them, when they inhabited their old village near Grand River, and individual enterprise had established trading-posts for the Dakotas and other tribes lower down. Their thieving and murderous propensities were so great, that but few men would run the risk of living among them, and repeated attempts resulted in the deaths of those who tried the experiment. Still others ventured, and in the course of time a trade in their village was begun, though not established on a very secure basis. At the time the trade commenced on the Upper Missouri, the Arikaras numbered from one hundred and eighty to two hundred cabins, and eight hundred warriors.

The cabins or huts of the Arikaras and other stationary tribes are built by planting four posts in the ground in the form of a square, the posts being forked at the top to receive transverse beams. To the beams other timbers are attached, the lower extremities of which describe a circle, or nearly so, the interstices being filled with small twigs, the whole thickly overlaid with willows, rushes, and grass, and plastered over with mud, laid on very thick. A hole is left in the top for the smoke to pass out, and another in the side for the door. This is the position of the building above ground, but within the circle an excavation is made two to four feet deep, and thus persons can stand upright or walk about with ease in the interior, except at the portion of the circle where the beds of the inmates are made. The door opens a few steps distant from the main building, on the surface of the ground, from which by a gradual descent through a covered passage of about ten feet, the interior of the hut is reached. The door is of wood, and the aperture large enough to admit a favorite horse to the family circle, which is often done. Around the house on the outside a small trench is dug, to carry away the rain.

These buildings are located within fifteen or twenty feet of each other, without any regard to regularity; nothing like streets are formed, and the houses are so much alike that a stranger is liable to lose his way in the village.

These Indians cultivate small patches of land on the Missouri bottom, each family tilling from a half to one and a half acres, which are separated from each other by rude brush and pole fences. The land is wrought entirely with hoes by the women, and the vegetables raised are Indian corn, pumpkins, and squashes of several kinds. The corn is said to be the original kind discovered with the continent, and is quite different in appearance from that raised in the States. The stalk is from three to six feet in height, seldom more than four or four and a half feet, and the ears grow in clusters near the surface of the ground. One or two ears sometimes grow higher upon the stalk, which appears too slender to support any more. The grain is small, hard, and covered with a thicker shell than that raised in warmer climates. It does not possess the same nutritive qualities as food for animals as the larger kind, but is more agreeable to the taste of the Indians. It is raised with so little labor that it seems well calculated for them. An acre usually produces about twenty bushels. When green, a portion is gathered and partially boiled, after which it is dried, shelled, and laid aside. This is called sweet corn, and is preserved any length of time, and when well boiled it differs little from green corn fresh from the stalk. The Indians plant about the middle of April or the beginning of May, according to the mildness or severity of the spring, and the ears are gathered about the beginning of August. The crops are not uniformly good, being subject to inundations from the Missouri, or to long periods of drouth. A moderately wet season is always favorable, and from two thousand to four thousand bushels of corn are raised by this nation. Cellars are dug within the houses, in which the various kinds of produce are stored.

Many superstitious rites and ceremonies are performed at the time of planting corn, and also at different periods during the growth of the crops; some or perhaps all of which take their rise in ancient tradition, and are very singular, and exhibit the original modes of thought and worship practised by their forefathers. Some of them are very indelicate in their character, and indicate the lowest state of animal degradation.

After corn, squashes next claim their attention in agriculture. They grow on large and very strong vines, and are of various sizes and shapes. They are either boiled and eaten when green, or cut up and dried for winter use. In the latter case they become very hard, and are scarcely edible when cooked, except by the natives, who seem to devour them with a gusto and a preference not shown for any other vegetable except sweet corn.

The crops being gathered in, are stored away in the cellars before alluded to, or buried on the field in different places, in what are called by the Canadian traders *cachés*, so constructed as to be impervious to rain, and so well covered that no one could discover them without a knowledge of their locality. Whatever is concealed in this way is intended to remain in the ground until the succeeding spring, at which time buffalo usually being far distant, it is their only resource for food. Besides the great advantages accruing to themselves over other wandering tribes, by tilling the soil, they have two markets for their surplus produce. The first is the fort of the American Fur Company, located near their village, at which they trade from five hundred to eight hundred bushels in a season. This trade on the part of the Indians is carried on by the women, who bring the corn by panfuls or the squashes in strings, and receive in exchange knives, hoes, combs, beads, paints, &c., also ammunition, tobacco, and other useful articles for their husbands. In this way each family is supplied with all the smaller articles needed for a comfortable existence; and though the women perform all the labor, they are compensated by having their full share of the profits.

The second market for their grain is with several bands of the Dakotas, who are at peace with them. These Indians make their annual visits to the Arikaras, bringing buffalo-robes, skins, meat, &c., which they exchange for corn; and the robes and skins thus obtained enable the Arikaras to buy at the trading-post the various cloths and cooking utensils needed by the women, and the guns, horses, &c., required by the men.

At the commencement of the winter the Arikaras leave their village in quest of buffalo, which seldom approach near enough to be killed in the vicinity of their cabins. They then encamp in skin tents, in various directions from the Missouri or along its banks, wherever the buffalo may chance to range. They pass the winter in hunting, and return to their permanent village early in the spring, bringing with them their skins in an unprepared state, with a great supply of meat. The buffalo skins are then dressed into robes before the season for planting arrives, and the meat with their reserves of corn enables them to live well. The Arikaras are also good fishermen, and take the fish by placing pens made of willows in the eddies of the Missouri. The fish entering the door of the pen or basket, it is closed, and often large numbers are thus secured. The Arikaras are also good swimmers, venturing out on floating cakes of ice when the Missouri breaks in the spring, and bringing ashore the bodies of drowned buffalo that are drifting by. Multitudes of these animals, in attempting to cross the river in the fall before the ice is strong enough to support them, break through, and often whole herds are thus drowned, their bodies remaining in the mud until the ice moves in the spring, when they are carried down by the current. They are often piled up along the shore, impregnating the air with their decomposing flesh. Even in this condition the Arikaras seem to prefer the meat, which is eaten raw, and though one would suppose that disease in its worst forms would be engendered, no injurious results follow.

The gathering of drift-wood in the spring is also a very hazardous employment, and is performed almost entirely by the women. There being but little timber for fuel in the vicinity of their village, it becomes necessary for them to secure the drift-wood in the time of high water in the spring, and then the women sail out on the masses of ice, attach cords to the floating trees, and haul them to land. Whenever there is an unusual quantity of wood floating down the current, all the village, men, women, and children, turn out, and the river is alive with them from shore to shore, leaping from one cake of ice to another, sometimes falling in and whirling by in the rapid current. It is very dangerous employment, yet they are so nimble, so expert swimmers, and such good judges of the solidity of the ice-cakes, that comparatively few accidents occur. Such are some of their resources for living, and poor as they are they are better than those of the Dakotas and other wandering tribes.

The Arikaras, though stupid in many respects, show considerable ingenuity in making tolerably good and well-shaped vessels for cooking purposes. They are wrought by hand out of clay, and baked in the fire, though not glazed. They consist of pots, pans, porringers, and mortars for pounding corn. They are of a gray color, stand well the action of fire, and are nearly as strong as ordinary potter's ware. For pounding corn and other hard substances, they make also mortars of stone, working the material into shape with great labor and perseverance. These utensils, though clumsy, seem to be preferred by them to metallic ones, for though the latter can now be had at a trifling cost, they continue their manufacture, and will scarcely exchange them for others, to us, more convenient and durable. They also possess the art of melting beads of different colors, and casting them in moulds of clay for ornaments, some of which are very handsome. In common with the Mandans and Minnetarees, they make skin canoes, which are of great service to them. The body of the boat is made of willows, bent round like a basket, and tied to a hoop at the top, which forms a circle about three or four feet in diameter. The hide of a buffalo, either fresh from the animal, or if dry, well soaked in water, is stretched over the frame, the hair side within. It is then turned upside down, dried, and sometimes smeared with tallow. The whole is made of a single skin, can be carried easily by a woman from place to place, and will convey three men across the Missouri with tolerable safety.

The domestic character and habits of the Arikaras are decidedly more filthy than those of any other tribe on the Upper Missouri. In their dress, they are greasy and slovenly, both men and women, and their hair is seldom untangled by a comb, though frequently amongst the men stuck together in tufts with gum, and then plastered over with clay, grease, and paint, affording excellent pasture-ground for vermin, which grow to a great size, multiply and spread over the cranium and clothes, and even into every nook and corner of their cabins. There are neither handsome men nor women among them; the former have sharp, sneaking, thieving looks, shabby in their dress, and ungraceful in their general deportment, and the latter coarse features, thick lips, short and thick-set persons, and both young and old are often more or less tainted with syphilitic diseases.

Many of the Arikara families are said to sleep indiscriminately together, the father beside the daughter, the brother with the sister, and this is the only nation in which incest is not regarded as disgraceful and criminal.

The literature of the Arikara language is quite brief. They call themselves Sa-nish′ or Ta-nish′, which means "the people," a common form of expression among the Indian tribes, indicating their supposed superiority in their own estimation. Rees, Ricaras, Aricaras, Arickaras, &c., are names which have been given them by the early traders, but their origin is obscure. The first vocabulary of their language, which is quite an extensive and excellent one, was obtained by the Prince Neuwied, in the winter of 1833 and '4. At that time, the Arikaras did not occupy their village on the Missouri, but had removed the year before, far into the prairie country toward the southwest, and were said to live somewhere near the sources of the Platte River. The exact time of their return is not known to me, but it must have been soon after, or rather their absence could not have been more than three or four years. At the time when Catlin visited the Upper Missouri, the Arikaras lived in their dirt village near the mouth of Grand River. In the appendix to his important work on the North American Indians, he has given an excellent though brief vocabulary. No others of importance have been published, so far as I can learn. The following vocabulary, which is more extensive than any ever before obtained, was taken by me from the lips of an Arikara chief, aided by Mr. Andrew Dawson, an intelligent Scotchman, who was superintendent of Fort Clark for many years, and spoke the Arikara language with a good degree of fluency. From the Indian chief I obtained the correct pronunciation, and from Mr. Dawson the true meaning of the words. I therefore publish it in this memoir, with a good degree of confidence in its accuracy.

PHRASES, NUMERALS, ETC.

ti-he-pe′-nu-he, on the tree yonder.
a-ka′-nu-tik-a′-ku, inside the house.
wet-heu′-kut-a, go across the water.
shish-hau′-kut-a, come across the water.
ka-weu′-tre-ha-na′-ni-ku, are you married?
će-kŭn-hau-whit′, where are you going?
sku′-hu-ne-sić-ah-u, give me a knife.
koh-ti-kut′-ćish, I will be glad.
tut-i-tik′-ŭsh, I am strong.
tre-tik′-ŭsh, you are strong.
aps-ko′-tik-ŏt, he will die.
kōh-he′-kōt, you will die.
kōh-tik-ōt′, I will die.
we-te-ko′-te-hem′, I am dying.
we-tŭh-nu′-ba-ik, he speaks bad of me.
na-tu-tēsh′-ha, I am wise.
tash-ha′, you are wise.
ka-kēsh′-ka, you are not wise.
kōh-tēsh′-ka, I will be wise.
koh-ēsh′-ka, you will be wise.
će-kŭn′-hau-kre, where have you been?
we-tut-swin′-heu, it rains hard.
wi-ta′-su, it is raining.
wi-ta′-ha, it is snowing.
shŭh-kre′-nit, put some wood on the fire.
tir-aub′-sha, it is smoking.
ta-we′-ris-ta, it is a warm day.
tir-i-wi′-it, it is hot.
tip′-si, it is cold.
wet-ik′-ōt, it is dead.
wet-ster′-it, it is tied.
kak-ster′-it, it is not tied.
shŭh-he-re′-pi, } tie it, (imp.)
shŭh-ster′-it, }

shŭh-o'-tit, kill him.
shŭh-tait', strike him.
ta'-ku-to-tit, I killed him.
we-ta-tŭh'-o-tit, I have killed him.
kŏh-tik-o'-tit, I will kill him.
wet-a-tuh'-ster-it, I have tied it.
kŏh-ster'-it, I will tie it.
ta-tu-te'-rit-ku-nŭh, I saw a bear.
ta-tu-te'-ri-ku, I see it.
we'-ta-tu-ter'-it, I have just observed it.
ka-ka-ku'-ter-it, I do not see it.
će-ku-na'-rit, where does it stand?
ti-it'-ne-sić, this is a knife.
sa-nish'-ta-ka-a-ka'-nu-tish-ku'-nit, the white man's house is near.
we-ta'-ti-kut'-ćish, I am glad.
we-tre-kut'-ćish, you are glad.
kŏh-e-kut'-ćish, you will be glad.
ni-ku'-ta-wi-ku'-su-na'-ka-wa, where the sparrowhawk builds its nest, Square Butte Creek.
wi-sa'-sa-nin'-i, Heart River.
wi-tets-han-sa-nin'-i, Gros Ventres Creek.
wa-hu-tu'-nu, Wind Butte.
sa-ka-nin'-i, our village, the Ree Village.
ka-nu-na-e'-wat, the stone that reveals the news. This rock is seen about two days' journey from the Ree Village, and is considered sacred by the Indians.
ka-nit', Mandans.
wi-tets'-han, Minnetarees, well-dressed people.
sun-nun'-at, the Dakotas, meaning of the word unknown.
sa-nish', "the people."

NAMES OF BANDS.

1. sŭh-ut'-it, Black Mouths.
2. ho-sŭk'-hau-nu, Foolish Dogs.
3. ha-će'-pi-ri-i-nu', Young Dogs.
4. hi'-a, Band of Crees.
5. o-kŏs', Band of Bulls.
6. ka-ka', Band of Crows.
7. ho-sŭk'-hau-nu-ka-ke'-ri-hu, Little Foolish Dogs.
8. pau-shŭk', Band of Cut-throats.

NAMES OF PRINCIPAL MEN OF EACH BAND.

1. su-ta'-ka, The White Shield.
2. sit-hau'-će, The one who first rushes on the enemy.
3. ći-na'-ni-tu, The Brother.
4. će-re-na'-kut-a, Yellow Wolf.
5. ku-nu-te'-shan, Chief Bear.
6. tŭh'-ni-na-ka-ta'-au-u-kut, He who strikes the foe between two fires.
7. ti-ga-ra-nish', He who strikes many.

NUMERALS.

one, ah'-o.
two, pit'-i-ku.
three, ta-whit'.
four, će'-tish.
five, she'-hu.
six, sha'-pis.
seven, tup-sha'-pis-wan.
eight, tup-sha'-pis.
nine, nuh-i-ni'-wan.
ten, nuh-i-ni'.
eleven, pit'-i-ku-nŭh-i-ni'-wan.
twelve, pit'-ik-ŏh'-in-i.
thirteen, na'-ku-git'-a-wan.
fourteen, na-ku'-git.
fifteen, ah'-ko-git'-u.
sixteen, wi-tŭć'.
seventeen, wi-tŭć'-is-ku'-git.
eighteen, wi-tau'-an.
nineteen, wi-tau'-ah-ko-ka'-ki.
twenty, wi-tau'.
twenty-one, wi-tau'-ah-o.
twenty-two, wi-tau-pit'-i-ku.
twenty-three, wi-tau'-ta-whit'.
twenty-four, wi-tau'-na-će'-tish.
twenty-five, wi-tau'-na-she'-hu.
twenty-six, wi-tau'-na-sha'-pis.

twenty-seven, wi-tau'-na-tup-sha'-pis-wan.
twenty-eight, wi-tau'-na-tup-sha'-pis.
twenty-nine, wi-tau'-na-nŭh-i-ni'-wan.
thirty, sa-wi'-u.
thirty-one, wi-tau-pit'-i-ku-nŭh'-i-ni'-wan.
thirty-two, wi-tau-pit'-ik-ŏh'-in-i.
thirty-eight, pit'-i-ku-na-nu-wan'.
thirty-nine, pit'-i-ku-na-nu'-ah-o-ka'-ki.
forty, pit'-i-ku-na-nu'.
forty-one, pit'-i-ku-na-nu'-na-ah'-o.
fifty, pit'-i-ku-na-nu'-na-nŭh'-i-na.
fifty-one, pit'-i-ku-na-nu-pit'-i-ku-nŭh-i-ni'-wan.
fifty-eight, ta-whit'-ku-na-nu'-wan.
fifty-nine, ta-whit'-ku-na-nu'-ah-o-ka'-ki.
sixty, ta-whit'-ku-na-nu'.
sixty-one, ta-whit'-ku-na-nu'-na-ah'-o.
seventy, ta-whit'-ku-na-nu'-na-nŭh'-i-ni.
seventy-eight, ćc'-tish-ta-nu-wan'.
seventy-nine, ćc'-tish-ta-nu-ah'-o-ka-ki.
eighty, ćc'-tish-ta-nu'.
eighty-one, ćc'-tish-ta-nu'-na-ah'-o.
ninety, ćc'-tish-ta-nu'-na-nŭh'-i-ni.
ninety-eight, she'-hu-ta-nu-wan'.
ninety-nine, she'-hu-ta-nu-na-ah'-o-ka-ki.
one hundred, she'-hu-ta-nu.
one hundred and one, she-hu'-ta-nu'-na-ah'-o.
one hundred and eighteen, sha'-pis-ta-nu-wan'.
one hundred and nineteen, sha'-pis-ta-nu-ah'-o-ka-ki.
one hundred and twenty, sha'-pis-ta-nu.
one hundred and thirty, sha'-pis-ta-nu-nŭh'-i-ni.
one hundred and thirty-eight, tup-sha'-pis-wan-a-nu'-wan.
one hundred and thirty-nine, tup-sha'-pis-wan-sa nish'-ah'-o-ka'-ki.
one hundred and forty, tup-sha'-pis-wan-sa-nish'.
one hundred and fifty, tup-sha'-pis-wan-sa-nish'-nŭh'-i-ni.
one hundred and fifty-eight, tup-sha'-pis-ta-nu-wan'.
one hundred and fifty-nine, tup-sha'-pis-ta-nu'-ah-o-ka'-ki.
one hundred and sixty, tup-sha'-pis-sa-nish', or, ta-nu'.
one hundred and seventy, tup-sha'-pis-ta-nu'-na-nŭh'-i-ni.
one hundred and seventy-eight, nŭh'-i-ni-wan'-na-nu-wan'.
one hundred and seventy-nine, nŭh'-i-ni-wan'-sa-nish'-na-ah-o-ka'-ki.
one hundred and eighty, nŭh'-i-ni-wan'-sa-nish'.
one hundred and ninety, nŭh'-i-ni-wan'-sa-nish'-na-nŭh'-i-ni.
one hundred and ninety-eight, nŭh'-i-ni-na-nu-wan'.
one hundred and ninety-nine, nŭh'-i-ni-na-nu'-ah-o-ka'-ki.
two hundred, nŭh'-i-ni-na-nu', or, sa-nish'.
three hundred, ah-o-git'-u-sa-nish'.
four hundred, wi-tau'-sa-nish'.
five hundred, wi-tau'-na-she'-hu-sa-nish'.
six hundred, sa-wi'-u-sa-nish'.
seven hundred, wi-tau'-ah-o-git'-u-sa-nish'.
eight hundred, pit'-i-ku-na-nu'-sa-nish'.
nine hundred, pit'-i-ku-na-nu'-na-she'-hu-sa-nish'.
one thousand, pit'-i-ku-na-nu-na-nŭh'-i-ni-sa-nish'.

VOCABULARY OF THE ARI'KARA DIALECT OF THE PAWNEE LANGUAGE.

A.

above, as'-kut.
as-kut'-nu-he, far above, in the sky.
afar, ći'-stit, afar off, away.
alive, tit-ćit-ćit'.
all, git'-u, all, the whole.
we-ku-tu'-ut, all the time, always.
ankle, in-e-sa-wi'-o.
antelope, na-nu-naé'.
ant, pit'-a-ru.
arm, wi'-nu.
arrow, ni-shu'.
ash, ćin-i-na'-ku.
autumn, nis-kŭh'.
awl, tŭh'-ni, an awl.
axe, ka-ta-rŭć.

B.

back, sta'-ku.
bad, ka-ku'-na-he'.
bark, na-sku'-hu.
bead, ći'-nish.
ći'-nish-ai-re-push', small beads.
ći'-nish-ta-ka'-ta, yellow beads.
ći'-nish-ka-tik', black beads.
bean, at'-it.
at'-it-hu-na'-nūn.
bear, ku-nūh'.
ku-nūh'-ta-ka, white bear.
ku-nūh'-a-tik, black bear.
beard, a-ra'-nu-hu'.
beaver, git-ūh'.
belt, sah-se'-ish, a leathern belt.
bird, niks.
he-rūs', a snow-bird. *Junco hyemalis.*
black, ti-ka-tik'.
bladder, kah-ći'-ra-nu.
blanket, nau-wi'-nu.
nauh-ta'-ka, gray or white blanket.
nauh-ta'-ka-re-hu', blue blanket.
nauh-ta'-ka-ka-tik', black blanket.
nauh-ta'-ka-pa, a red blanket.
blood, pa'-tu.
blue, tit-e-re'-ūh.
boat, na-ko-hōn'.
na-ko-hōn'-ska-rué, a skin boat.
na-kūh-wa'-na-kūh, steamboat, roaring boat.
ku'-su, a large boat.
naé, a wooden boat.
éer'-i-pasé, a small boat.
body, tan-ith'-tan.
bone, ći'-shu.
bow, na'é.
box, ha'-ku.
boy, mi-nūh'é'.
bread, iz-et'-ta-ta-ish'-u, hard bread.
breast, wa'-ku-ka'-u.
bridle, a-ka'-ra-ka'-ra-ku.
brother, a-ti'-tat, a brother.
i-na'-ni, big brother.
shi-na'-ta-ni, my brother.
na-ra-nit'-ish-u, elder brother.
ka-wi'-ta, younger brother.
brush, wa-pe'-i-sūs, a brush for clothes.
buffalo, ta'-na-ha.
ći-wi'-e-ku, a male buffalo.
wa-tash', a female or cow.
burning, wet-wheu'*-ni-wit.
burn, t'wheu'-it, to burn.

C.

calf, ha-nit'.
ha-ni'-pat, a red calf.
cap, su-na-we'-wa.
chief, ne-sha'-nu.
child, pi'-ra-o.
pi-re-ha'-re, a young child, a year old, or more.
pi-re-ćip'-e-ri, a new-born child.
cloth, na-wi'-nu.
na-wi-na'-wish, strouding, or blue cloth.
ka-ni'-u-ka-bi'-u, a breechcloth.
club, na-kuh'-sin-it-i-wa'-ru, a war-club.
coal, a-ni'-tu-a, a coal of fire.
coat, u-ka'-wié.
u-ka'-wié-ti-pas'é', a shirt, thin coat.
coffee, ska-tit'.
cold, tip'-si.
cord, hat-se'-i-shu, a string or cord.
corn, ne-ći'-i-shu.
cow, wa-tash'.
ta-na-ha'-ta-ka, white man's cow.
crow, ka'-ka. *Corvus.*
crying, ti-ći'-kut.

D.

darkness, tik-a-tis'-tit.
daughter, su-naé'-ku-ta'-ti, my daughter, or the girl belonging to me.
su-naé'-kut'h-ra, your daughter, or the girl belonging to you.
su-naé', a girl.
day, sha-ker'-i-ćish'-kut.
sha-u'-nu-ker'-i-kut, midday.
wait-hi'-i-sha, daydawn.
shak'-u-git'-u, all the day.

* Pronounced like whew.

dead, tik'-aut.
deer, nu-naé'.
ta'-pat, red deer.
a-rik'-a-ra'-nu, a male deer.
ta-ka-tit', black-tailed deer.
did, ta-tŭh'-na, I did it.
dish, tŭh-ći'-ka, a cup or dish.
disposition, wi-su-tŭh'-ni, a good heart, a good disposition.
dog, hané.
ha-ta'-ka, a white dog.
ha-kŭn'-hauf, an old dog.
ha-sŭh'-tit, an old, female dog.
door, ne-kub'-i, and ne-ka-wi'-o.
dove, waé. *Zenaidura Carolinensis.*
dress, ah-ka'-ku, head-dress.
drink, wi-tut'-ska-ni'-is, ći-ka'-hu, } to drink.

E.

eagle, pi-aé', gray eagle.
ne-tuk'-as, war eagle.
ar-ĕt', bald eagle.
ear, at-ći'-ish-u, and a-tik-a'-nu.
earth, hu-na'-nu, ground, earth.
eat, ti-wa'-wa-a, to eat.
egg, ni-pi'-ku.
elk, na.
'wa-o-kōs', a male elk.
wa-wa'-tash, a female elk.
wa-ha'-nié, a calf elk.
enemy, pa'-tu, and hish.
eye, ći-ri'-ku, and her-i-i'-ku.
her-i-nu-nau', sore eyes.

F.

face, ka'-u.
fat, hié.
father, at-i-uh', my father.
ha-uh', your father.
i-uh'-tik, his father.
at-i-uh-wa-ruh-te, my medicine father, the Great Spirit.
feather, he'-tu.
few, sah'sh, a few.
finger, sći'-shu.
shu-wi'-tu, finger-nails.
fire, ti-kai'-it, and ha-ni'-tu.
fish, gi-waé'.
han-we-ru'-kut-ŏh, flatfish.
gi-wa-nau'-shish-a, catfish.
hish, a pike.
flint, ne-sit'-a-nu.
flower, pa-kish'.
fly, sup-i-na'-nu.
foolish, ti-sa'-ko, foolish, crazy, a lewd woman.
foot, ah'-u.
forest, tu'-hu-na'-će.
forever, ti-ra'-naué.
fort, na-wi'-u, a fort.
fowl, nuks-ći'-re-kūc'.
fox, gi-wa-ku', a gray fox.
gi-wa-ku'-ku-su, a large fox.
friend, si-nau'.

G.

girl, su-nuh'é'.
good, tŭh'-ne.
nŭn-hi-nan-tŭh'-ni, beyond good, better.
tŭh-ni-nŭn'-hi-nan-git'-u, good beyond all, best.
tŭh'-ni-su-shu'-bin-i, good among inferior objects, used only in comparison.
ka-kŭh'-ne, not good, bad.
goose, ko'-ut, so named from its cry.
grass, kut-a'-nu.
grease, ćiz'-hié, marrow grease.
great, ti'-er-wheu.
green, ti-ta-re-hu', green or blue.
ground, tŭh-na-nin'-e, plain or smooth ground.
hu-na-nin'-e, in the ground.
gun, na'-ku.
na-ku'-ti-pa'-kŭt, an old gun.
e-na'-ta-ra', a double-barrelled gun.
ka-wi'-u, a gun-flint.

H.

hail, kat.
hair, o-hu', and pah'-tis-kŭn.

pah'-ta-ka-ta, yellow hair.
hand, ish'-u, and sha-na'-ku.
ska-tus'-u, inside the hand.
hare, wa-rūh'. *Lepus campestris.*
nis. *Lepus artemisia.*
hawk, ćin'-it, a small hawk.
hay, ha-ta'-nu, dried grass.
head, pa-hu'.
ći-ni'-tu, back of the head.
ti-ku-pah'-tau, headache.
heart, wi'-su.
heel, ah-a-ći'-no-tu.
hen, ūt, prairie hen. *Pedioccetes phasianellus.*
ūt-ka-wit', sage hen. *Centrocercus urophasianus.*
hill, wa-u', a mountain.
wa-hin'-i, a hill.
wa-kut'-e-buh, a place called Cut Butte.
kut'-e-buh, cut off.
hog, ku-kūh', pork, hog.
horse, ha-wa-rūht'.
ha-ći-za-wet'-a, a white horse.
ha'-wa-rūh-te, medicine dog, horse.
hot, ta-ba-ris'-ta.
house, a-ka'-nu, and a-ka-nūh'-ner.
husband, nah-tuk-u'.
ni-kōh-tuk'-u, my husband.
te-na-ta'-ku, your husband.

I.

I, na'-tu, I, me.
ice, nah'-e-tu.
insect, pi-rūh'.
iron, waps'-ish-u.
waps'-ips-wat, red iron, copper.
island, a-wa'-u.

K.

kettle, ko-shap-shi'-shu.
knee, pa-ći'-shu, and na-hu'-na-ći'-shu.
knife, no-sić'.

L.

lake, ib-wha'-nu.
land, tūh-na-nin'-i, fine land, fine country.
git-u'-hu-na-nin'-i, the whole land.
lariat, ha-wi'-shi.
laugh, te-bah'-u.
lead, nish-ći-su.
leaf, na'-ga-ru'-ku.
leg, ka-hu'.
leggins, no-ko'-kić.
nauh-ta'-ka-pa-o-ko'-kić, red blanket leggins.
light, tits-er'-i-ćish.
lightning, ti-wa-waps'.
limb, nut-ći'-ta-wi-u, a limb or branch.
little, ka-ki-ra'-ni-hu, not much, little.
liver, ka-ri'-ku.
lizard, st'ćer'-ut.
lodge, te-ka'-ni-hu.
a-ka-pa'-tu, skin lodge, or an enemy's lodge.
love, te-sish'-ta, to love.

M.

man, ter'-i, and wi'-ta.
sa-nish', a man, a people.
sa-nish-ta'-ka, a white man.
ti-ger'-ish, a weak man.
te-tir'-a-ćish, a strong man or animal.
ne-sha'-nu-nau-ćish'-u, a great man.
wi-te-shūć, a young unmarried man.
kūn'-hauf, an old man.
many, ter-heu'.
ta-ra-ni-hu', a great many, a heap.
marsh, tūh'-nu-nan'-ai-i-wun'-u, a bog or marsh.
me, na'-tu.
meat, sus'ć, ćash'ć, } fresh meat.
ta-kah'ć', dried meat.
mine, ku'-ta-te.
mirror, na-nu'-ka-te'-ris-ku.
mist, spen.
mink, e-rūh'.
moccasin, hanć.
moon, pah.
morning, hin-uh'-tit.
mother, at-na', my mother.
hah, your mother.

shŭh′-te, his mother.
mouth, ka-ka′-u.
a-ka′-ra-nŭh, hairy mouth.
mud, ho-rŭh′-tu.
t′wheu′-rŭt, muddy.
muskrat, git-uk-a.

N.

nail, shi-ni′-tu, also the claws of an animal.
navel, nis-ka-ku′-hu.
near, tish-ku′-nit, near by, not far off.
nan-shu′-tish-ku′-nit, very near.
tish-ku′-nit-nuh′-in-i, near ten, or about ten.
neck, na-ti′-nu, and sen-a′-nu.
night, hi-nŭh′, and nut-ik′-a-nu.
no, ka-ki′.
nose, si-ni′-tu.

O.

oak, ska-nŭh′.
off, ćis-tit′, far off.
old, ti-pa′-kŭt.
one, o-pi-nu′-te, the other one.
a-re-isht′, either one you like.
ti-će-nu′-tu, which one is it?
otter, get-a′-put.
owl, p′hau′-ru.

P.

paddle, wi-er-ha′-ku.
part, heuć.
penknife, ći-rak′.
people, sa′-nish, people.
san-ish-ta-ka, white people.
git-u-san′-sta-ka, the whole people.
pepper, a-kat′-i-tić.
perhaps, ći-ra′-to.
pine, na-hi′-shu, pine, pine wood.
nuć-e-ish′-u, a pine tree.
pipe, na-wis′-kŏć.
polecat, ni-bit′.
potato, is-ku′-su.
powder, hit-i-ka′-nu.

R.

rain, ta-su′.
we-ta′-tu, it rains.
ramrod, nuć.
red, ti-pa′-at, and pa′-at.
river, u-sa′-nu, and hu-ka-ha-nu′.
ka-to-hu′-ni, a small river, a branch.
road, a-ta-nu′, a road or trail.
robe, sa-ŭć, a buffalo-robe.
rock, kan′-i-ta-wi′-ut.
rotten, tih′-o-ut.
run, shu-nŭh′ (imp.), run.

S.

saddle, na-ni′-ći-tan-i.
salt, ka′-it.
scalp, pah′-sku-hu.
ha-wah′-ka-wi, scalp-lock.
seat, ka-tuks′, and shŭh′-wi-ta.
see, ti-re-wat′, to see.
net-i-re′-wat, seeing.
sheep, a-rić′-in-is.
shirt, o-kau-ić′.
shoe, hauh′-e-shu, a leather shoe.
shot-pouch, par-e-tak′-u-hu.
shoulder, ska′-nish.
ha-ha′-re-shu, shoulder-blade, or hoe, so called because the shoulder-blade of a buffalo was formerly used as a hoe.
silver, waps-ips-tap′-er-wheu.
sinew, ah′-a-su.
sister, i-ta′-ni, his sister.
a-ti′-tat, my sister.
skin, ska-ŭć′.
wa-rŭh′-tu, a dressed skin.
sky, ska-a-kat′-ha-wu.
sleep, to-kris-ći′-pi, to sleep.
small, ka-ker′-wheu.
small-pox, sći-ri-ći′-shi-wa-ta.
smoke, ni-wi′-shu.
snake, nŭt.
snow, hu-na′-u.
wo-ta′-ha, it snows.
son, na-ti-na′-hu, my son.

na-hi-na'-hu, your son.
ni-ha'-o, his son.
sour, ka-kŏh'-ta-ne, not sweet.
spear, hu-nŭh'.
spirit, ći-ci'-tu.
spring, ish-cip'-it.
ne-ka', spring, fountain.
squash, wa-hauh'.
star, sa'-ka.
o-per'-i-ku-su, a collection of stars, constellation.
stirrup, ha-ka-ta-tau'.
stomach, wa-ku'-kre-ni, and ni-ku'-ci-shu.
stone, kas-nie', a stone, rock.
stream, sa-nin'-i, a stream or creek.
strong, tik-hash'.
ka-ke-hash', weak, not strong.
sugar, ka-c'-na-ka-ta.
summer, ha-wi-rit'-i-kut.
sun, sha-ku'-nu.
sunset, nit-suk'-o-nish.
swan, sha'-tu.
sweet, tŭh'-ta-ne.

T.

thigh, ka-taks'.
thin, ti-pas'é'.
thou, na-hu'.
thunder, wa-rŭh'-te.
toad, sku-na'-ka-ku.
tobacco, na-kush'-ka-nu.
to-day, ti-wen-sa'-ker-ić.
toe, ah-ći'-shu.
tongue, ha-tu'.
tooth, a-nu'.
true, t'ha'-pe.
ti-wać', it is true, it is so.
turkey, nu.
turtle, sah.

U.

ugly, pir-a-nin'-o-ći.

V.

valley, ta-wat-e-ru'-hu-nu.
vein, pa-te'-hu, a road for the blood.
village, i-tu'-nu.

W.

warrior, nu-ti-wun'-u-hu, one who goes to war.
water, sto'-hu.
t'ćin-wheu, big water, sea.
ka-kŭh'-p'si, bad water.
weather, ta-wi'-ris-tu, a fine day, fine weather.
what? ti-će'-nu, what is it?
ti-će'-nu-wi'-ta, what man or person?
ta-će'-nu, who, or which one?
where? ću-hu-ni-he', where is it?
whip, pin-hu', a small riding whip.
whiskey, ći-sin'-ah.
white, ta'-ka, and ći-sha'-wa-ta.
whole, ći-tu', the whole of anything.
wife, na-ti-na'-ta-ku, and ta-wi'-ni.
wind, t'wheut, and hu-tu'-nu.
t'wheut'-a-her'-heu, a strong wind.
windpipe, pah-nj'-shu, and o-ka-kŭh'.
winter, p'si-kut'.
within, o-ki'-i-kut.
without, o-wat'-ik-ut.
wolf, sti-ćer'-ić.
ći-wa'-ku, a small wolf.
pa-kać', medicine wolf.
pa-kać'-ti, it is a prairie wolf.
woman, sa-put'.
ta-će'-nu-sa-put', what woman?
sŭh'-tit, an old woman.
su-nah', a young, unmarried woman.
wood, nuć.
na'-kŭn, logs or drift-wood.

Y.

year, ti'-kut-i'-a-nu, the whole year.
yellow, ti-ra-kut'-a.
yes, an, and ni-ku'-ti.
yesterday, ti-su'-sa-ker-ić.
you, na'-hu.
young, tit-ćip'-er-i.

DAKOTA GROUP, D.

CHAPTER XIV.

VIII. Dakotas.

ETHNOGRAPHICAL HISTORY.

The country claimed by the Great Sioux or Dakota nation, prior to the organization of the Territories of Nebraska, Dakota, and Minnesota, was very extensive. Commencing on the northeastern limit at Lac qui Parle, an imaginary line would run in a northwest direction, taking in Lac du Diable, thence inclining south by west, including Turtle Mountain and the head of Pembina River, would strike the Missouri River at the mouth of Apple River, below the Gros Ventres village. Crossing the Missouri, it would proceed up the Grand River of the Arikaras (or even some distance west of this river), bearing west by south until reaching near the head of Powder River. From this point it would continue along the range of mountains called the Black Hills in a southern direction, until reaching Fort Laramie on the Platte, thence down that river for some distance, afterwards extending east to the junction of the Niobrara with the Missouri River, thence down that stream to the mouth of Big Sioux River, this being the boundary line to which their claims had been extinguished by the United States. Proceeding along the Big Sioux River inclining northeast, taking in the Vermilion and James Rivers, their lands would terminate by a junction with the starting-point at Lac qui Parle. Within a few years, the United States Government has purchased of the Indians much of the territory comprised within the above limits.

That portion of their lands east and north of the Missouri is quite sterile, and with the exception of some coulées and hills, formed by the rivers and creeks, presents a most monotonous prairie, many hundred miles in length and breadth, very level, and devoid of trees, or even shrubs. The soil is loose and sandy, grass rather thin, and in no great variety, that known as the short, curly, buffalo grass being the most abundant. In former times, this was the great range for the buffalo, but of late years, they are found in greater numbers west of the Missouri. The soil is generally too dry for agricultural purposes, except along the borders of streams, where it is for the most part quite fertile. In some parts where the vegetation is luxuriant, the grass is very nutritious, and would, in common with most of the Northwest Territory, afford good grazing for horses, horned cattle, and sheep. Small lakes are to be met with in this region, from which the Indians get their supply of water when travelling across the prairies, which they do not attempt to do except in the summer and autumn, when the "buffalo chips" answer the purpose of fuel. The terrible snow-storms that sweep over these plains in the winter, compel them to place their camps along the rivers where timber is to be found. Along the Coteau de Prairie, or dividing ridge between the waters of Iowa and Missouri, near the source of James River, is found the celebrated Red Pipestone Quarry, to which the Indians pay yearly visits, to procure materials from which to make their pipes. This material is found in no other portion of their country, and is considered by them of great value.

The surface of the country west and south of the Missouri River, is more rolling and diversified, on account of the large streams that course their way through it. The principal rivers on that side of the Missouri are Niobrara, White, Medicine, Teton, Big Shyenne, Moreau, Cannon-ball, Heart, and Grand Rivers. Most of these streams have been navigated by the traders with skin boats during the spring thaws. They are well timbered along their banks, the trees growing in large groves or points, frequently reaching from one bluff to the other, the whole width of the valley. The largest and most common trees are the cottonwood, elm, and ash, though others of smaller growth are found. Though there are many tributaries to the rivers named, running through the interior, most of them are short, and only convey the water produced by rain or snow to the parent stream. These are termed by the traders and voyageurs coulées, seldom extending more than from one to three miles in length, and usually covered with various bushes, small trees, grass, and weeds. Between rivers, and beyond the heads of the coulées or dry valleys, are large tracts of table land, from ten to fifty miles in breadth, on which no timber is seen, but where the spontaneous grasses are very thick, and of excellent quality. It is in such spots as these that the buffalo delight to remain undisturbed, quietly cropping the choice blades in happy ignorance of the hordes of hunters roving through the country. Springs impregnated with saline substances are often met with, and the water is drank with eagerness by these animals. The most fertile region, however, and the one approaching nearest to a habitable district, is on the head waters of the Shyenne and Moreau Rivers, commencing at the eastern base of the Black Hills, and running northeast for the distance of sixty or eighty miles. The prairies here are undulating, well wooded, well watered, and present much varied, beautiful, and enlivening scenery to the eye of the traveller. Indeed, with but the exception of that portion of the Dakota lands situated west of the "Mauvaises Terres" or "Bad Lands," on the source of White River, the rest cannot be regarded as an entirely barren district, though to what extent grain could be produced has not been determined.

Many fabulous stories in regard to the Black Hills are related by the Indians, and are believed by them even to this day. They say that rumbling noises, like the sound of distant thunder, are not infrequent, and one of the principal peaks is called by them the Hill of Thunder. In 1833 they supposed it to be on fire, and on almost any clear day they say large volumes of smoke could be seen, which they regarded as the breathing of the great white man buried beneath. Unnatural noises are said to be heard, which, whether originating in their fancy, or caused by wild beasts, are thought to be the moans of the great white giant when pressed upon by rocks, as a punishment for being the first aggressor on their territory. They say that he issues forth occasionally, and his tracks seen in the snow are twenty feet in length. He is condemned to perpetual incarceration under the mountain as an example to all white men to leave the Indians in quiet possession of their hunting grounds. This story, though fabulous, shows their ancient and intense repugnance to the encroachments of other and distinct races.

Southeast of the Black Hills is a large area of country known as the "Mauvaises Terres," or "Bad Lands," which is very remarkable for its unique scenery and the organic remains entombed in its strata. The portion of country to which this name has been especially applied is about one hundred and fifty miles in length, and sixty miles in width. There are many other portions of the Northwest to which this term is applicable, but no other area so large possesses this uniform character. It is hardly possible to describe this singular country. Along White River, for sixty miles in length and fifteen to twenty in breadth, the country presents the appearance in the distance of one vast city, and but little imagination is required to see immense public edifices, towers, churches, &c., with people on their summits. What tends to make the illusion more perfect, is that the mountain sheep (*Ovis montana*), sometimes alone and sometimes in small bands, are seen on the tops of these towers, several hundred feet high, and entirely inaccessible to the approach of man. Here they remain in security, rolling their large horns from side to side, and casting suspicious glances at the traveller below. It is somewhat strange that this animal should prefer the most rugged and inaccessible places where scarcely a spear of grass is seen, and no shrubs but here and there a solitary bunch of stinted sage. A few small grassy spots, like oases, are found in this region low down at the base of these lofty ridges and towers, to which the mountain sheep descend early in the morning to feed. Although the absence of vegetation in their favorite places of resort would induce the belief that they fared badly, yet when killed they are invariably fat, and the meat is superior even to that of our domestic sheep. The Indians prize it next to the meat of the buffalo. The road from Fort Pierre across the country to Fort Laramie runs directly through this region, and is the only road that can be travelled with safety with carts or wagons. In the spring of 1855, the writer passed up the valley of White River with carts, but scarcely a day passed that they were not upset, and their contents more or less injured. Water is very scarce, though a few springs and small streams occur, and these are of great importance to the Indian as he winds his devious way through this region. But the objects of the greatest interest to the scientific man, and curiosity to the Indian and voyageur, are the organic remains which abound here. They consist for the most part of the remains of vertebrata, which have been described by Prof. Joseph Leidy in the Proceedings of the Academy of Natural Sciences, Philadelphia. They all belong to extinct species, representing with a good degree of completeness the mammalian Fauna of a district. All the remains of Turtles appear to belong to a single species, but the individuals are very numerous and of large size, some of which were estimated to weigh from five hundred to one thousand pounds. The materials of which the rocks are composed are light-colored clay, grits, and marls, more or less indurated, and worn into these fantastic shapes by atmospheric agencies. The presence of land and fresh-water shells, and the absence of all indications of marine origin, show this region to have been a vast inland lake some time during the Miocene Tertiary period. For some distance up the White River Valley from its mouth, the country is very fine, and clothed with an excellent growth of vegetation, but towards its source for two or three days' march the sandy desert prevails, and travelling is very difficult. Passing across the country to the Niobrara, toward the Platte, the prairie assumes its usual character, and travelling is much better; and though much of that region is occupied by patches of bad lands and denuded places, still the greater portion is clothed with good grass, and has a cheerful appearance. Along the Platte, Loup Fork, and portions of the Niobrara, are the Sand Hills, a large area of not less than twenty thousand square miles, composed of loose sand, which has been thrown up into hills and ridges fifty to two hundred feet in height by the wind. The material is derived from the eroded portions of the more recent Tertiary beds in this region, and as the winds are mostly from the west and northwest, this loose sand is slowly moving onward toward the east and southeast. Though totally unfit for agricultural purposes, this tract of country cannot be said to be destitute of vegetation. In the valleys and depressions among the hills are many fine spots of grass, and sometimes the hills are covered with varieties of grass adapted to so meagre a soil. The soap plant, *Yucca angustifolia*, grows here very abundantly, and sending its roots deep into these sandy hills, protects them from being diminished by the winds. The sand plum, *Prunus pumila*, grows very abundantly all through the Sand Hills, and supplies an astringent but not unpalatable fruit. On the head of Loup Fork, and between that stream and the Niobrara at various localities, are numerous saline and fresh-water lakes. The fresh-water lakes contain a great profusion of various species of water-plants and their peculiar animal life, while those that are impregnated with saline matter present the appearance of desolation, no vegetation growing in their vicinity except a few weeds adapted to a saline soil. In former years these Sand Hills were a famous resort for the buffalo, and even at this time a few may be found, but they have been for the most part driven away by the Indians to other and less frequented parts.

Among the many objects which come under the observation of the traveller in the Dakota country, none are of more interest than the numerous villages of the prairie dog, scattered all over the dry and gravelly plains. Sometimes they are situated upon the high terraces along the rivers, but generally they are upon the high, arid plains, many miles from water. A good deal of a fabulous character has been written in regard to the habits and habitations of this little animal. Some have even observed a council-house in the centre of the village, which is supposed to be laid out in regular streets, reserving a public square for meetings and discussions for the general good of the community. Others have imagined a particular large sleek dog to be the chief, and contend that they have seen him receive visits and apparently give directions to many of the citizens, who, after receiving the same, departed to give others an opportunity to state their requests. With a zeal for knowledge, and a perseverance in labor, truly creditable in many respects, attempts have been made to dig to the bottom of their subterranean abodes, as well as to drown them out, but most of these experiments have resulted in failure. It does not occur to the laborious hunters that the dog can dig as well as they, and that if their holes are so constructed as not to be affected by the heavy rains that fall on the level places, where their villages are always situated, they would not be likely to be disturbed by a few pails of water. The truth is, the animal does not dig deep, seldom more than four or five feet, but penetrates the earth in a horizontal direction. It lays up no stock of provisions for the winter, but lives on the roots of grass, which it reaches by digging up toward the surface when the ground is covered with snow. This explains their extensive burrowing in different directions, seeking support, and crossing each other's routes in many places, leading persons to suppose their different chambers are thus connected for convenience, to associate and talk over their national and domestic affairs during the long winter evenings. The uncertainty of success in digging them out is thus seen, and a man might continue his excavations for miles without securing the inhabitant. The dog must have food, and having but little hair upon his body cannot endure the cold on the surface, therefore he finds his food below it in winter, and in his subterranean travels comes across others of his village friends engaged in the same pursuit. In this manner they destroy in the course of time all the vegetation in their immediate vicinity, and are obliged to remove to some other locality, and abandon their holes to the owls and rattlesnakes.

Crossing the Dakota country through the middle portion south and west of the Missouri, from the Niobrara to Grand River, the prairies, though occasionally twenty to fifty miles in breadth, cannot come under the head of level plains like the district on the opposite side. The distance is not great between the rivers on the west side. Although their junctions with the Missouri are widely separated, yet their sources all occur near each other, as they take their rise in and near the Black Hills. In travelling across this portion of the country in a transverse direction, a man on foot is seldom obliged to camp without wood or water, the heads of the valleys or ravines of one watercourse extending to within a distance from five to forty miles of the tributaries of another.

Springs and small groves of trees frequently occur in the intervening prairie, and good encampments can usually be found by any one familiar with the geography of the country throughout the length and breadth of the interior. In the winter, however, it happens that persons are frozen to death in crossing these prairies; for when storms occur it is often impossible to travel, the sun is invisible, and all objects are hidden at the distance of from fifty to one hundred paces by the particles of snow that are whirled through the air by the wind. This is called by the Canadian voyageurs *poudrie*, and when occurring in extreme cold weather, leaves but two alternatives to the traveller,—to ramble on at hazard, in the hope of keeping himself warm by walking and stumbling on timber, or to lie down and let the snow blow over him, remaining in this temporary grave until the atmosphere becomes clear, and his course can be determined by the sun or stars. Both of these methods are often resorted to by the Indians and traders when caught in snow-storms, where timber is not at hand, and sometimes success and sometimes failure attends their efforts.

The three streams, Shyenne, Moreau, and Grand Rivers, approach so near each other that there is no broad stretch of level prairie between them. As we proceed west, the surface becomes more broken and intersected by valleys, which are clothed with excellent grass. In all the small streams beaver are very abundant. Grand River has the largest valley, is best wooded, and best stocked with game. Buffalo are found along this river when there are none in the country around. Elk rove in large bands through the wooded bottoms, and antelope are abundant upon the grass-covered hills. Many deer, both white- and black-tailed, are found in the valleys of the little tributaries.

The fruits and succulent roots indigenous to this region are few but quite palatable, and form no small item in the bill of fare of the Indian in times of scarcity. The prairie turnip, *Psoralea esculenta*, ti'-psi-na of the Dakotas, *Pomme blanche* of the voyageurs, is found everywhere on the high prairies. It may be eaten raw or boiled, and is collected in large quantities and dried by the Indians for winter use. It is quite farinaceous, and when dried and pulverized makes a very good substitute for flour, and in any form it will sustain life for several months without the assistance of animal food. This root is also the favorite food of the grizzly bear.

The wild artichoke, *Helianthus tuberosus*, pan'-ći, grows in great abundance along the marshy banks of the rivers. It is roasted or boiled, but often eaten uncooked.

Dakota peas, *Apios tuberosa*, ōm-a-ni'-ća, grow very abundantly in the rich valleys of the streams. This plant has a vinelike top, and the tuberous roots form the edible portion. In the fall of the year large quantities of these tubers are collected by a species of field-mouse for its winter store, which is in turn robbed by the Indian squaws, who often secure half a bushel from a single nest. They are boiled with dried buffalo-meat, and the writer can testify from personal experience that they make a most palatable dish to the hungry traveller.

The plum, *Prunus Americana*, kun′-ta of the Dakotas, grows very abundantly along the Niobrara and White Rivers. The fruit is ripened usually in October, and is much sought after by the Indians.

The choke-cherry, *Prunus Virginiana*, čaŋ′-pa, and the bullberry, *grain de bœuf* of the voyageurs, mash-tin′-pu-ta of the Dakotas, grow in the greatest quantities all over the country. These fruits, with the plums, form, in their season, the principal food of the bears and wolves. Both of these fruits are dried, the former pounded with the seed and cooked in various ways, sometimes made into soup, but more often mixed with dried buffalo-meat and marrow-grease. This is called pemican among the voyageurs, and is very convenient in travelling, on account of its nutritious and concentrated character. The *grain de bœuf* is a small red berry, with an acid taste, and when dried is often made into soup, or takes the place of cherries in the composition of pemican.

A few service-berries, *Amelanchier Canadensis*, and here and there a patch of wild strawberries, are found, but not in sufficient quantity to be relied upon as a means of support. The Indians are very fond of fruit of any kind, and seem to prefer that grown and preserved in their own country to the dried fruits introduced from the States by the traders. It is impossible, except from actual observation, to form an idea of the immense quantities of cherries and other kinds of fruit eaten by them in their season, and these, with certain edible roots, constitute a most important resource to a people dependent upon the chase for their subsistence. They can be easily preserved, packed, and conveyed from point to point, and they are of special service to their children when meat is not to be obtained. The fruits of the wild rose, which are very plenty and remain on the bush during the winter, are eaten both raw and boiled, but are quite indigestible, as are also the red thorn-apples, called tas′-pan by the Dakotas.

Some of the dishes prepared by the Indians in the yet undeveloped condition of their culinary science are not enticing even to the eye of the hungry traveller, and are by no means adapted to delicate stomachs or fastidious palates. In this class may be placed a favorite dish of theirs, made of blood boiled with brains, rosebuds,* and the scrapings of rawhide, until the whole assumes the consistency of warm glue. Pounded cherries boiled with meat, sugar, and grease, are esteemed a rare dainty, and are eaten with great relish. The prairie turnip boiled with the dried stomach of the buffalo, or the Dakota peas abstracted from a mouse's nest and cooked with dried beaver's tail or a fat dog, are dishes much admired and regarded fit to set before soldiers, chiefs, and distinguished visitors.

A great variety of roots, leaves, barks, and plants are used by these Indians, in common

* The seed-vessels of the Rose, which remain on the bushes during the winter, and often supply a scanty nourishment to the famishing voyageur, are called by the Indians and traders "rose-buds."

with other nations on the Upper Missouri, for medical purposes, the principal of which, together with their manner of application, will be alluded to elsewhere.

The animals inhabiting the Dakota country, and hunted more or less by them for clothing, food, or for the purposes of barter, are buffalo, elk, black- and white-tailed deer, bighorn, antelope, wolves of several kinds, red and gray foxes, a few beaver and otter, grizzly bear, badger, skunk, porcupine, rabbits, muskrats, and a few panthers in the mountainous parts. Of all those just mentioned the buffalo is most numerous and most necessary to their support. Every part of this animal is eaten by the Indians except the horns, hoofs, and hair, even the skin being made to sustain life in times of great scarcity. The skin is used to make their lodges and clothes, the sinews for bowstrings, the horns to contain powder, and the bones are wrought into various domestic implements, or pounded up and boiled to extract the fatty matter. In the proper season, from the beginning of October until the 1st of March, the skins are dressed with the hair remaining on them, and are either worn by themselves or exchanged with the traders.

In the year 1833, that part of the Dakota nation residing on the Missouri and its tributaries, and trading there, was divided as follows:

Titoŋwaŋ-Dakotas.	Se-ćang'-ćos, Brulees, Burnt-Thighs,	500 lodges.
	O-ga-la'-las,	300 "
	Min-ne-kaŋ'-zu, those who plant by the water,	260 "
	Si-ha-sa'-pas, Blackfeet-Dakotas,	220 "
	Wo-he-nōm'-pa, Two-Kettle-Dakotas,	100 "
	Hunk'-pa-pas,	150 "
	I-ta'-zip-ćo, *Sansarcs*, Without-Bows,	100 "
Yancton-Dakotas	Lower-Yanctons,	300 "
	Pa-bak'-sa, Tête-Coupées, Cut-Heads,	250 "
	Wa-ge'-ku-te, Gens des Pin, the Pine-Band,	100 "
	Band, name not obtained.	50 "
	I-saŋ'-tis,	30 "

These 2360 lodges, averaging five souls to a lodge, would make a total of 11,800 souls. The above estimate may be relied upon as correct at that time. The nomadic Dakotas have slowly but steadily increased in numbers since that time, and in 1857, Lieut. Warren estimated that the same bands mentioned above numbered 3000 lodges and 24,000 souls. From various causes, as the introduction of contagious diseases, and other calamities, some of the bands have diminished in numbers, while others have greatly increased, and it is believed that at the present time the Missouri Dakotas are in the aggregate more numerous than at any former period.

These bands at that time (1833), occupied separate districts, though they could if they chose, hunt unmolested by each other, in any portion of the common territory. But being generally intermarried, and connected by societies of dances and clans, they usually preferred locating at a distance from each other, that their hunts might be better carried on, and their domestic arrangements and tribal government conducted by the chiefs and soldiers appointed to these positions by the general consent of each band. When two camps are joined, each having its own head, opinions and interests clash, quarrels follow, and separation, with angry feelings toward each other is the result, often extending to the stealing of each other's horses. But by each band confining its hunting operations as nearly as practicable to a certain tract of country, accustomed to the rule of its own chief, and its own domestic associations, differences that arise when several bands who are comparative strangers are thrown together, are prevented. Partly with this view, and partly to occupy their entire country where game is found, but mainly on account of the hunting advantages, the following sections were agreed upon as the residence of the different bands mentioned, which arrangement has been continued, with little deviation, up to the present time.

The portion of the country inhabited by the Si-ćaŋ'-ćos, or Burnt Thighs, is on the head waters of the White and Niobrara Rivers, extending down these rivers about half their length. The Teton River formed the northern limit. For many years, this band was headed by a chief named Ma-ka'-to-ẗa'-ẗa, or the Clear Blue Earth, who governed them wisely and well. He was very friendly to the white man, and few Indians have had the power, dignity, and influence which he held over this band. Though some have been more feared, others more brave, yet by his constant and uniformly good management and just government, he kept his people in order, regulated their hunts, and usually avoided placing them in the starving situations incident to other bands, led by less judicious rulers. They were good hunters, usually well clothed and supplied with meat, had comfortable lodges, and a large number of horses. They varied their occupations by hunting buffalo, catching wild horses, and making war expeditions against the Arikaras, then stationed on the Platte, or the Pawnees, lower down on that river. Every summer, excursions were made by the young men into the Platte and Arkansas country, in quest of wild horses, which abounded there at that time in large numbers. Their mode of catching them was by surrounding them, and running them down on their own horses. Taking their positions at different points, they pursued them from one to the other, until they became so fatigued as to be lassoed, after which they were thrown down, bridled, and packed or rode by these fearless cavaliers. Often forty to sixty of these wild horses were brought home as the results of a single expedition.

In their wars with the Pawnees and Arikaras, the Brulees were usually victorious, and seldom a summer passed that they did not secure many of the scalps of their enemies. Indeed, the periods of time at all seasons were short that the scalp-dance was not going on, and the monotonous war-song heard through the village, accompanied by the lamentations of the friends of those who had fallen in battle. Their foes did not remain idle.

Every now and then some of the Brulees' horses would be stolen, or some lone wanderer outside the camp killed. In 1835, some Pawnees and Arikaras stole forty or fifty of the Brulees' horses from their camp on the Niobrara, when the latter pursued and defeated them within a short distance of the village. Twenty-two of their enemies were killed, their horses recovered, and the successful warriors returned bringing the heads, hands, feet, and other parts of the enemies' bodies into camp. The hands and feet were thrust on sticks and paraded through the village by old women, and the scalpless heads were dragged about with cords, followed by small boys shooting them with arrows and powder, and pelting them with stones, encouraged by the old women, who followed after heaping abuse upon the helpless and mangled remains of their once dreaded enemies.

One of the amusements of this band is the driving of antelope over precipices into pens made for the purpose, thus inclosing and destroying several hundred at a time. The broken country about the source of White River is very favorable for this object. The animals being surrounded by several hundred people are driven through some gap in the hill, beyond which is a perpendicular descent of many feet, inclosed around the base with logs and brush, raised to a sufficient height to prevent them from jumping over. The antelope once through the gap or pass, cannot recede, and the pressure of those from behind forces those in front over the descent, the rear being followed up quickly by the pursuers.

Since the emigrants to California and Oregon have passed through the Dakota country, the Brulees have suffered more from diseases thus introduced than any other division of these Indians, being located nearest to the trail. Small-pox, cholera, measles, &c., have year after year thinned their ranks, so that comparatively few of this once numerous band remain, and these are hostile towards the whites, to whom the cause of their destruction is attributed. Their ties of relationship have been severed by the deaths of their friends, their head men have fallen victims, their former good order and flourishing condition have been deranged; and thus they have acquired a sullen and permanent hatred towards the white man. They now comprise about one hundred and fifty lodges, scattered through this district in small divisions, the inmates poorly clothed, with very little game and but few horses. They have paid some attention to the cultivation of the soil, and with proper encouragement might be made an agricultural people. The game has left their country, and with it the means of obtaining supplies from the traders, and now they are mainly dependent upon the small amount of annuities or presents given them by the United States Government.

The Ogala'las occupy that portion of the Dakota country from Fort Laramie on the Platte, extending northeast, including the Black Hills, the sources of the Teton River, and reaching as low down as the fork of the Shyenne. They sometimes range as far west as the head of Grand River. This region, until a recent period, was well stocked with buffalo, and even at this time elk, antelope, deer, and mountain sheep are found in sufficient numbers to afford the Indians a moderate support. A portion of this band have obtained rifles, and are expert in their use, and the consequence is that they are better clothed and less subject to extremes of want than some of their neighbors. They are remarkable for having the most handsome women in the nation, who are neat and tidy in their dress and modest in their deportment.

The Mi-ne-kaŋ'-źūs are usually found from Cherry Creek on the Shyenne to Slender Butte on Grand River, in which section the buffalo, until within a few years, were very abundant. This band, though peaceable when ruled by good chiefs, has always been very wild and independent, seldom visiting the trading-posts either on the Platte or on the Missouri, and having no intercourse with white men, except with a few traders during the winter season.

The Hūnk'-pa-pas, Si'-ha-sa'-pas, I-ta'-zip-ćos, occupy nearly the same district, and are so often encamped near each other, and otherwise so connected in their operations, as scarcely to admit of being treated of separately. That part of the country under their control lies along the Moreau, Cannon-ball, Heart, and Grand Rivers, seldom extending very high up on Grand River, but of later years reaching to the Little Missouri. Although the bands just mentioned are often stationed near each other, they are sometimes found several days' journey apart, and each is headed by its own chief. Of the leading men, the Little Bear Chief is the most prominent. He wields great influence over all the bands, and from his youth up he has manifested an intense hatred toward the white man.

The Two-Kettle band, Wo-he-nōm'-pa, confine themselves to the Shyenne and Moreau Rivers, seldom going higher on the former river than the mouth of Cherry Creek, but passing up and down the Shyenne, Moreau, and Grand Rivers, but not uniting with the bands just described. The principal chief of this small band is Ma'-to-to'-pa, or Four Bears, a man of moderate capacity, but exercising a good influence on his people. They live entirely in the plain country, seldom go to war in any direction, are good hunters and shrewd in their dealings with the traders. Very few complaints have ever been made against them. They have observed faithfully the stipulations of their treaty with the United States, and have always treated white men who came among them, either as traders or visitors, with respect, but they are too few in numbers to give direction to the actions of large and more powerful bands. Neither contagious disease nor war seems to have reduced their numbers, and it is believed that they have remained nearly stationary in that respect for the last twenty-five years. Many portions of their country could be cultivated with success, and with their tractable disposition they could be made an agricultural people.

The Cut-Heads and Pine Indians, all come under the head of Yanctonais. In 1833 the whole of this division of the Dakota nation was governed by the great chief Wa'nata, but after his death in 1840 it became separated into three distinct bands, each having its own rulers. All of them, however, range and hunt on the east side of the Missouri, and very rarely are found beyond its western shores. They range in their hunting excursions from Apple River down to the mouth of the Little Shyenne, north to the neighborhood of the Lac du Diable, and east along the Coteau de Prairie, but never going as low down as the source of James River. Most of this district, though formerly the favorite range of the buffalo, is now nearly abandoned by them, and at the present time these animals are found only near the northern and western boundaries. In 1830, the Yanctonais, and a few Indians from other bands, being encamped opposite Fort Pierre, on the east side of the Missouri, killed fifteen hundred buffalo at a single surround. This is the largest number that was ever known by the traders to be destroyed at any one time. The fact was ascertained by the trader securing the tongues as the Indians returned from the hunt. Since this period the buffalo have gradually retired from the eastern districts, moving westward and northwest, and thus compelling the Indians to follow. From 1833 to 1844 they were found in considerable numbers on the head branches of the Little Shyenne, and east in the direction of the Coteau de Prairie, but since that time few are seen so low down, which accounts for these Indians occupying their western limits, and hunting north as far as Pembina River. In their travels during the fall they not unfrequently come into collision with the half-breeds from the Red River of the North, who sometimes hunt buffalo in this country in parties of from three to six hundred men, bringing with them a thousand carts or more to transport the meat and skins to their settlement. Several skirmishes have occurred, in most of which the half-breeds have been the victors, and they are known to be better warriors than the Indians. The latter, not gaining much in actual contests, retaliate by stealing the horses of the former at their village near Pembina in the absence of the men on their hunts. Of late years their visits in that direction have been more frequent and bold, several residents have been killed in the village, and many horses stolen. This predatory warfare becoming very serious and annoying, the half-breeds applied a few years ago to the United States Government for permission to make war on the Indians on a large scale. They claimed that they would be compelled to make war or remove to their original homes in the English possessions.

NAMES OF DAKOTA BANDS, WITH THEIR PRINCIPAL CHIEFS.

DAKOTA BANDS.	PRINCIPAL CHIEFS.
min-i-sha',* Red water band,	ćāŋ-te-ni'-tku, Foolish Heart.
ta-shunk-'e-o-ta,† Plenty of horses,	kāŋ-ge-ni-a'-ke, Crow Feather.
wak-po'-ki-an, Flying river band,	he-wa-zin'-ća, One Horn.

* This band numbers eighty lodges.

† Seventy-five lodges.

DAKOTA BANDS.	PRINCIPAL CHIEFS.
i-na-ha'-o-wīn, Stone ear-ring band,	wi-a-ka'-o-win, Feather Ear-ring.
wa-ḣa-le'-zo-wen, Striped snake ear-ring band,	ma-ka-ći'-ka, Little Ground.
shunk'-a-yu-tēsh'-ni, Band that eat no dogs,	caŋ-te'-wa-ni'-će, No Heart.
min-i-kaŋ'-źu, Band that plants near the river,	o-pa'-no-to-no'-ma-ni', The Elk that whistles running.
wak-to-ni'-la, The band that kill no people,	ta-taŋ'-ka-ći-ka'-la, Little Bull.
o-ho-nōm'-pa, Two kettle band,	mi-wa-ta'-ne-haŋ'-ska, Long Mandan.
pa-ha-hi'-a, Those who camp at the end,	wa-min'-i-mi-du'-za, Whirlwind.
min-i-sha', Red water (an Oglala band),	wam'-bi-li-shi'-a-na, The Eagle that sails.
pe-ḣi'-pte-ći-la, Short hair band,	ho-po'-ma-za, Iron Arm.
ōg-la'-la (meaning not known),	ta-shunk'-a-wit'-ku, Foolish Horse.
si-ćaŋ'-gu, Brulees, Burnt thighs,	wa-ki'-a-ći-la, Little Thunder.
wam-bi-li'-ne-ća, Orphan band,	ću'-wi-wam'-bi-li-shi, Eagle's Body.
wa-ći'-ōm-pa, The band that roasts meat,	wi-sa'-pa, Black Moon.
si-ća'-wi-pi, Band with poor guns or bows,	ki-a-kam'-pi, He who gives praise.
a-a'-ko-za, Big ankle band,	a-ḣa'-ka-haŋ-ska, Long Elk.
wa-źa'-za, Band rubbed out,	wak-pe'-sha, Red Leaf.
hunk'-pa-pa (meaning unknown),	ma-to'-ći-ūk-sa, Bear Rib.
ta-lo'-na-pi, Fresh meat necklace band,	shi'-o-taŋ'-ka, Large Pheasant.
će'-ḣa-na-ka',* Half-centre cloth band,	shi'-o-ći-ka'-la, Little Pheasant.
ći-o-ho'-pa, Sleeping kettle band,	ma-to'-ći-ka'-la, Little Bear.
ćaŋ-ho-ham'-pa, Band with bad backs,	ma-to'-wa-na'-ḣe, Bear's Spirit.
si-ha'-sa-pa, Blackfeet,	wa-wa-ćaŋ'-ka-to, The Blue Shield.
ći-hu'-pa, Jawbone band,	si-ćo'-la, Bear's Foot.
pa-a'-bi-a, Those who camp at the end,	ma-to-wa-ku'-a, The man who runs the bear.

NAMES OF MONTHS OR MOONS, RIVERS, ANIMALS, ETC.

1st moon, ma-ga-ga'-li-wi, when the geese come up from the south, March.

2d moon, pe-źi'-to-i-wam'-pi-wik, when the grass springs up, April.

3d moon, shunk-a-ma-ni-tu-ćin'-ća-tōn-wik, when the wolves have their young, May.

4th moon, pte-ki-u'-ḣa-wik, the rutting time of the buffalo, June.

5th moon, ćam'-pa-sha-wik, when the cherries are red, July.

6th moon, ćam'-pa-sa'-pa-wik, black cherry moon, when the cherries are ripe, August.

7th moon, ćāŋ-wak'-pe-hi'-wik, when the leaves become yellow, September.

8th moon, ćāŋ-wak-pe-inḣ'-pa, when the leaves fall, October.

9th moon, wik-to-ka-i-ća'-mi-na, when the first snow falls, November.

10th moon, pte-yu'-kta-ha-shi'-na-wash'-te, when the robes are good, December.

11th moon, pte-i-ću-la-wash-te-yu-ta-wik, the time when the young buffalo (in utero) are good to eat, January.

12th moon, shunk-a-ma'-ni-tu-ga-nash'-ki-wik, when the wolves go mad, February.

we'-tu, spring, three moons, coming in of spring.

bel-o-ke'-tu, fair weather, coming of summer.

ptaŋ'-e-tu, coming in of autumn, three fall months.

wa-ni'-i-tu, coming in of winter, three winter months.

* Cloth cut from corner to corner,—tri-cornered clothing.

ma-ka-si'-ća, Mauvaises Terres, or Bad Lands of White River.

wi-wi'-la-wak'-pa-la, Spring Creek or Bear Creek, in the Bad Lands.

pe-zi-ho'-ta, Sage Creek, or Gray Grass Creek.

ćaŋ'-wi-ta, Wood Island Creek.

wak-pa-si-ća-o-inh-pa', Pinaus Spring, source of Teton River.

ho-ki-ha'-lo-ka, hole through the hill, or Opening Creek, a branch of the Shyenne.

i-ruh'-a-pa-ha', Whetstone Hills, where the Indians procure sandstone for whetstones.

pa-ha'-sa-pa, Black Hills.

wag-a-ćaŋ'-haŋ-ska, Long Cottonwood Creek.

pi-spi-za-o-ti-taŋ'-ka, Big Prairie Dog Village Creek.

wi-ća-ag-e-wa-ka'-pi, where they place the dead on scaffolds, Shepoi Creek.

shunk'-a-kaŋ-pa'-o-ta, where the Indians lost many horses, the Great Hole.

ćoh-waŋ'-zi-ća, Willow Creek.

wak-pa-wash'-te, Good River, Great Shyenne.

kaŋ-ta-o'-ta, a plenty of plums, Plum Creek.

ćam'-pa, the cherry, Cherry Creek.

o-ki'-źa-te, forks of any river.

hi-haŋ-wak'-pa, Owl River, Moreau River.

wak-pa-shi'-ća, Teton, Little Missouri, Bad River.

ma-ka-i-zi'-ta, Smoking Earth River.

ta-to'-ka-la'-o-ti, where there are plenty of antelopes, Antelope Creek.

ćān-te-sha', Cedar Creek.

pa-ha'-wa-kan, Medicine Hill Creek.

mi-la-haŋ-ska', Long Knife, or American Creek.

pa-la-ni-ta'-wa, where the Rees had their village, Ree River, Grand River.

i-aŋ'-wa-ka-ha'-pi, the river that makes rocks, Cannonball River.

sha-he'-e-la-wo'-źu, the river where the Shyennes planted corn, Little Shyenne.

min-e'-taŋ-ka, Big River, L'eau qui Court, running water.

o-pa-wo'-źu, where the Indians make cornfields, Ponka River.

ma'-to-pa'-ha, Bear Butte.

mash-tin'-ska, white rabbit, in winter pilage. *Lepus campestris.*

he-tōŋk'-taŋ-ka, a wood rat. *Neotoma.*

wam-bi-li', the bird that sails, golden or war-eagle.

pa-ća-shi'-wa-ta, short bill. *Junco hyemalis.*

wa-zi-zit'-ka-la, yellowstone bird. *Leucosticte tephrocotis.* A bird that lives among the yellow ferruginous sandstones.

mash-tin'-ća-la, sage rabbit. *Lepus artemisia.*

shi'-o, birds that eat rose-buds.

shi-o'-ći-ka'-la, sharp-tailed grouse.

wa-zi'-shi-o, yellow wood bird, pine pheasant.

ūnk-ći'-ki-ća, a magpie.

i-ha'-mi-ko-ti-la, the owl that lives with the prairie dogs.

źo'-a-to-pi, poor-will, so named from its note.

ćān'-ska-sa-pa, blackbird.

hi-hu', the hooting owl, named from its note.

pa'-pe-sto-la, "sharp-nose," fish-duck.

zit-ka'-to, bluebird, Maximilian's jay.

ho-pa-wa'-to-to, blue wings, blue-winged teal.

ćāŋ-o-hu'-ya, "wood-color," cheewink.

pi-spi'-za, the animal that calls to people "come here," prairie dog.

pa-hiŋ', derives its name from its quills, porcupine.

psi-psi-ćai'-la, jumping mouse. *Hesperomys.*

het-ka'-la. *Spermophilus quadrivittatus.*

sink-pe'-la, flat-foot, muskrat.

zi-ća', "yellow-wood," a pine squirrel.

VOCABULARY OF THE DAKOTA LANGUAGE.

alive, ni.
all, si-to'-mi-ni.
arm, ish'-to.
arrow, wa-hink'-pi.
autumn, pta'-e-tu.
axe, ma-zōn'-spe.
bad, shi'-ća, si'-ća.
bear, ma'-to.
beard, pu-te'-hi.
beaver, ća'-pa.
belly, te'-zi.
bird, zit-ka'-la.
black, sa'-pa.
blue, to.
body, taŋ'-ćaŋ.
bone, hu'-hu.
bow, i-ta'-zi-pa.
bread, a-hu'-e-a-pa, flour.

brother, ći′-c.
buffalo, ptc.

canoe, wa′-ta.
chief, i-taŋ′-ća.
cold, us′-ni.
copper, ma-za′-sha, red iron.

dance, wa-ći′, to dance.
daughter (my), mi-ćunk′-shc.
dead, ta.
deer, taȟ′-ća.
dog, shunk′-a.
drink, at′-ȟa, to drink.
duck, ma-ga-si′-ća.

earth, ma′-ka.
eat, yu′-ta.
eye, is′-tc.

face, i′-tc.
father, at′-c.
finger, shash′-tc.
fire, pe′-ta.
foot, i′-ha.
forehead, na-su′-na.
fox (red), shunk-u′-la.
friend, ko′-la.

good, wash′-tc.
grass, pe′-źi.
great, taŋ′-ka.
grouse, shi′-o.

hail, wa′-su.
hair, pe′-hi.
hand, na′-pc.
he, i′-yc.
head, pa.
heart, ćaŋ′-tc.
hill, pa-ha′.
husband (my), mi-hing′-a-na.

I, mi′-yc.
ice, ća′-ra.

infant, ŏk-shi′-ća-la.
iron, ma′-za.
island, wi′-ta.

kettle, će′ra.
kill, ktc′-pi, to kill.
knife, mi′-na.

lake, bi-lc′.
leaf, wak′-pc.
leg, hu.
lightning, wa-ki′-an.
lodge, ti′-pi.
love, te-wa′-ka, to love.

maize, wa-ka-me′-za.
man (red), wi-ća′-sha.
many, mi-će′-ta, much.
meat, cĕk′-pi.
morning, am′-pa.
mother, in′-a.
mountain, ha.
mouth, i.

nail, sha′-kc.
near, ki′-c-la.
neck, ta′-hu.
night, aŋ-hi′-pi.
no, hi′-ya.
nose, pa′-su.

old, c-ha′-na.

pipe, ća-nŏm′-pa.

rain, ma-ra′-zu.
red, lu′-ta.
river, waȟ′-pa.

sea, min-i-wa′-ća.
see, wai-a′-ka, to see.
shoe, nam′-pa.
sister, tank′-c.
sky, maȟ-pe′-a-to.

sleep, is-ti′-ma, to sleep.
small, ćis′-ći-la.
snow, wa.
soldier, a-ki′-ći-ta.
son (my), mi-ćink′-shi.
speak, wo-ga la′-ka, to speak.
strong, wa-źa′-ka.
summer, bi-lo-ki′-tu.

this, lc.
thou, ni′-yc.
thunder, wa-ki′-an-o-tŏmp.
tobacco, ćaŋ′-li.
to-day, lc-am-pe′-tu.
toe, si-hu-ka′-za.
to-morrow, am-pa′-kc.
tongue, će′-shi.
tooth, hi.
turtle, ke′-a.

water, min′-i.
white, ska.
who, tu′-a.
wife (my), mi-ta′-wi.
wind, ta′-tc.
winter, wa-wi′-c-tu.
wolf, shunk-to′-kc-ća.
woman, wi′-a.
wood, ćaŋ.

yellow, zi.
yes, tŏsh.
yesterday, uk-ta′-lc-ha.

one, wunć.
two, nŏm′-pa.
three, ya′-mi-ni.
four, to′-pa.
five, za′-pta.
six, sha′-ko-pi.
seven, sha′-ko-wi.
eight, sha′-gc-lo′-ga.
nine, na-pći′-ŏn-ka.
ten, wik-ćim′-i-ni.

CHAPTER XV.

V. Assiniboins.

ETHNOGRAPHICAL HISTORY.

In regard to the origin of the Assiniboin tribe, but little authentic information can be obtained from their traditions, though many singular and fabulous tales are related concerning it. As a portion of a people, however, once inhabiting another district, and being incorporated with another nation, their history presents a connected and credible chain during the last century.

The Assiniboins were once a part of the great Dakota nation, residing on the tributary streams of the Mississippi, as the head of the Des Moines, St. Peter's, and other rivers. This is evident from the similarity and almost identity of the language spoken by the two tribes or nations. Moreover, there lived a few years since, on the Missouri, a very old chief, known to the traders as "Le Gros Français," though his Indian name was Wah-e'-muz-a, or the "Iron arrow-point," who recollected perfectly well the time of their separation from the Dakotas, which, according to his data, must have been about the year 1760. He stated that when Lewis and Clarke came up the Missouri in 1805, his band, about sixty lodges, called *Les Gens des Roches*, had, after a long conflict, made peace with those bands of the Dakotas who resided on the Missouri, and that he saw the expedition referred to near the mouth of White Earth River. This was the first party of white men ever seen by them at their camps, though they had been accustomed to deal with the fur traders of the Mississippi, who visited the interior of their country in the winter. After their first separation from the Dakotas, they moved northward, made a peace with the Crees and Chippeways, and occupied a portion of the country on or near the Saskatchewan and Assiniboin Rivers, in which district some two hundred and fifty or three hundred lodges still reside.

Some time after the expedition of Lewis and Clarke, or at least after the year 1777, the rest of the nation, at that time numbering about twelve hundred lodges, migrated towards the Missouri, where superior advantages for game and trade presenting themselves, they located permanently, and continue to reside there to the present time.

The principal incident, and one which forms an era in their history, which they have every reason to remember, is a visitation of the small-pox in 1776 or 1777, when they occupied the British territory. Even yet there are two or three Indians living (1855) who are marked by the disease of that period, which greatly thinned their numbers, though owing to their being distributed over a large district, some bands escaped entirely. However, the small-pox does not appear to have been as destructive to them at this period as it was on the Upper Missouri in 1838, which will be noticed hereafter.

Before proceeding further with their history as obtained from the old men of the tribe, let us present a summary of the notices of different travellers as far back as we have the means of ascertaining. Inasmuch as an extended history of the Indian tribes of the Missouri Valley is in process of preparation, only the more important and standard works of travel will be referred to in this memoir.

Umfreville calls these Indians Assinnee-Poetuc, and says that they obtained their name from the Crees, which signifies in their language Stone Indians. He also states that they are a "detached tribe from the Naudawissees of the Mississippi, who anciently separated from the general stock on account of some intestine commotion." He gives a vocabulary of forty-four words of the Assiniboin language, and, so far as I can ascertain, the first ever published. Henry speaks of them as Osinipoilles or Assiniboins, who at that time lived in the vicinity of and traded at Fort de Prairie. He says that they are the "Issati of older travellers, and have sometimes been called Weepers." He gives much interesting information in regard to this tribe, and suggests that their language connects them with the Nadouwesis. La Hontan merely alludes to them as "Nadouessis or Scioux." Gallatin, who seems to have had access to works beyond my reach at this time, thus sums up their ancient history: "The Assiniboins (Stone Indians) are a Dakota tribe, separated from the rest of the nation, and on that account called *Ho-ha*, or Rebels, by the other Sioux. They are said originally to have formed a part of the Yanktons, but we are not acquainted with their real name. Their separation must have taken place at an earlier date than has been presumed by late writers. Father Marquette, writing in the year 1669, from the Chagouadmigong Mission, after having mentioned the Nadouessies as a formidable nation, speaking a language altogether different from the Algonkin and the Huron, adds, that the Assiniponiels have almost the same language as the Nadouessies, and live about fifteen days' journey from the Mission on a lake, which, from a map annexed to that volume of the Relations, must have been Lake Winnipek."

Carver (1796) alludes to the "Assinepoils" as having revolted from the "Naudowessie nation," and formed a league with the "Killistinoes," keeping up a continual warfare, however, with other neighboring tribes. Mackenzie (1801) also alludes to the Assiniboins as a detached tribe of the "Nadowasis," and residing upon the river which bears their name.

A number of vocabularies of the Assiniboin language have been published from time to time. So far as I am able to learn, the first one given to the public was published by Umfreville (1790), consisting of forty-four words.

The Prince of Neuwied, in his excellent work, "Travels in North America," 1839–41, gives quite an extended vocabulary, with some interesting remarks in regard to their manners and customs. Prior to this time, however (1817), Major S. H. Long obtained a small but accurate list of words of their language, which was published in the appendix to his "Account of an Expedition from Pittsburg to the Rocky Mountains, in 1819 and 1820."

The most important vocabulary of the language of this tribe ever published may be found in the fourth volume of Schoolcraft's great work, which consists of over four hundred words, prepared by Mr. E. T. Denig, an intelligent trader, who resided for many years at the junction of the Yellowstone and Missouri Rivers, as superintendent of Fort Union, the trading-post for the Assiniboins. I know of no others that are of sufficient importance to mention here.

We will now continue the history of the Assiniboins as given by the most intelligent men of the tribe. The name of this tribe among themselves is Dakota, the same as that of the numerous tribes along the Missouri and the sources of the Mississippi, and with them it signifies "our people." By the Dakotas they are called "Ho'-he," or Fish-eaters, perhaps from the fact that they lived on fish while residing in the British possessions, as most of the Indians do in the absence of other food. By the Crees and Chippeways they are called A-si-ni-poi'-tuk or Stone Indians,—thence the name of Assiniboins is derived. As has been stated, at the earliest date known they roved about the sources of the St. Peter's and Des Moines Rivers, Lac du Diable, Lac qui Parle, &c., and were then joined with the Dakotas proper, who inhabited and claimed all the land between the Mississippi and Missouri as low down as Big Sioux River, reaching to the source of James River, and stretching thence northward as far as Lac du Diable. There were also other bands of Dakotas (Tetons), occupying the country west of the Missouri. The number of the Assiniboins when they separated could not have been much less than fifteen hundred lodges, averaging six souls to a lodge. Their migration has already been alluded to, and the extent of territory which they traversed in search of game, in the Hudson's Bay country, along the Saskatchewan, was very great, but at the present time their location is entirely different, which we may as well define at this time.

The northern Assiniboins roam over the country from the west banks of the Saskatchewan and Assiniboin Rivers, in a western direction, to the Woody Mountains, north and west amongst some of the small outliers of the Rocky Mountains east of the Missouri, and on the banks of the small lakes frequently met with on the plains in that district. They consist of about two hundred and fifty or three hundred lodges, and they occasionally make peace with some of the most northern bands of Blackfeet, which enables them to extend a little farther west, and deal with those Indians, but these peace arrangements are usually of short duration, and thus they are, for the most part, limited in their hunting operations, and confined to the prairies east and north of the Blackfoot range. The remainder of the tribe, now reduced to two hundred and fifty lodges, occupy the district defined as follows. Commencing at the mouth of White Earth River on the east, extending up that river to and as far beyond its source as the Grand Coulée and the head of La Riviere aux Souris, thence northwest along the Coteau de Prairie, or divide, as far as the beginning of the Cypress Mountains, on the north fork of Milk River, down that river to its junction with the Missouri, thence down the Missouri to White Earth River, the starting-point. Formerly they inhabited a portion of the country on the south side of the Missouri, along the Yellowstone, but of late years, having met with great losses in that direction, from war-parties of the Blackfeet, Dakotas, and Crows, they have been obliged to abandon it, and now never go there.

Until the year 1838 the tribe still numbered from a thousand to twelve hundred lodges, trading on the Missouri, when the small-pox reduced them to less than four hundred lodges. They were also surrounded by large and hostile tribes, who continually made war upon them, and in this way their number was diminished, though at the present time they are slowly on the increase.

The chief rivers running through the Assiniboin country are, first, the Missouri, which is so well known that it needs no description here. The next is Milk River, on the northwest boundary, a very long and narrow stream, rising in some of the small mountains east of the Missouri, and lakes on the plains, runs a southwest course, and empties into the Missouri about a hundred miles above the mouth of the Yellowstone. Its bed is about two hundred yards wide, though the water seldom occupies more than one-third of that space, except during the spring thaws, when for a week or two it fills the entire bed, and even overflows the valley. It is fordable on horseback the year round, except at the time above mentioned, or when swollen by continued rains, and it might even be navigated with Mackinaw boats, when full, though the undertaking would be attended with some risk, owing to the large quantity of drift-wood, snags, and other obstructions. The water in a high stage has a white and milky appearance, caused by its flowing through beds of white clay, which are found along nearly the entire length of it, but more especially near the sources of most of its tributaries.

The Riviere aux Tremble, or Quaking Asp River, empties into the Missouri about fifty miles below Milk River, is about half the length and breadth of the other, and takes its rise in the range of hills constituting the divide called the Woody Mountains. It is fordable at all times, except during spring freshets, or when filled by heavy rains, at which times it could be navigated with small Mackinaw or flatboats, if floating ice and drift-wood would permit.

Several creeks or small streams, of comparatively little importance, flow into the Missouri lower down on the east side, called Porcupine, Big Muddy, Little Muddy, Knife River, &c., none of which contain much water. These, with several small coulées, serve to drain the plains of the waters caused by snow and rains, and are for the most part miry, and only fordable on horseback in certain places where gravel bottoms are found.

After these comes White Earth River, on the eastern boundary of the district now under consideration, which is about one hundred miles in length, and at the mouth over one hundred yards wide. This like the others becomes very full from the melting of snow in the spring, but falls low enough in course of the summer to be fordable in most places, either on foot or on horseback. This stream could be navigated with small canoes during the months of April and May. It takes its name from a kind of white pipe-clay, which occurs about half way to its source, and is supplied with water from springs in the Coteau de Prairie.

The entire country occupied by the Assiniboins, or hunted in exclusively by them, the outline of which has been given, embraces an area of about 20,000 square miles, and presents the same general features as the rest of the Upper Missouri territory, on the east side of the Missouri River. From James River up, it may be said to be one great plain, hills and timber only occurring where rivers run, and even the small streams are wooded only a short distance above their mouths, so that the traveller may pass for days over large tracts without meeting with a tree or shrub. In the valleys of the rivers, there is some good land for agricultural purposes, but the level plains present a sterile aspect, and can only be adapted to the grazing of cattle. The soil for the most part is not deep, but light and sandy, absorbs rain readily, and the hills, which are usually composed of indurated sands and clays, are often washed by atmospheric agencies into most grotesque and singular forms, called by the Indians ma-ka-si'-ća, or "Bad Lands."

The indigenous grasses are quite numerous in species, and very nutritious, affording most excellent pasturage for horses, horned cattle, and sheep. The dry season of autumn gradually desiccates the vegetation, so that all the nutritious substances remain, and it is not until the melting of the snows of spring that their nutritious character is lost. At this period, all the herbivorous animals of the plains become quite weak and thin in flesh, but quickly recover in the months of May and June. This monotonous and barren surface of the country only terminates after crossing the Coteau de Prairie, which divides the waters of the Missouri from those of the Red River of the North, where both the nature of the soil and the general appearance present an entirely different character, to which allusion has already been made in our description of the Crees.

Though wood cannot be found to any extent in the Assiniboin plains, and dried buffalo-dung, usually called "buffalo chips," is used by the natives for fuel during the summer season, or any portion of the year when the ground is not covered with snow, yet water can be had at all times from small lakes, or rather large ponds. These are met with in many places on the prairie, are formed by rain or melted snow, and have no visible outlet, but diminish by evaporation and saturation. They differ in size from one hundred yards to two or three miles in circumference, usually contain tolerably good water, are surrounded by a border of tall flags and rushes, and in the autumn covered with myriads of wild fowl. A few small springs are seen occasionally, but most of them have a mineral taste, and possess active cathartic properties.

Notwithstanding the dull and dreary appearance always presented by naked and extensive plains, there are no places that could properly be termed deserts, though there are some marshes, pools, and swamps, which, however, are not very near together, or of a nature to present any formidable obstruction to travel, neither do they seem to affect the health of the natives, any farther than being the breeding-place of hosts of mosquitoes, which are very annoying to man and beast.

The principal hindrance to foot travellers in this district, is the great abundance of a few species of Cacti, or as they are usually called, "prickly pears," some of which are armed with long, sharp, barbed spines, and readily pierce the moccasined feet of the Indian or voyageur. The dogs, also, used by the Indians for carrying burdens on the plains, suffer severely from these spines, though the older and more experienced have the faculty of perceiving and avoiding them even while running. The principal varieties known in this region are *Opuntia Missouriensis* and *O. fragilis*, both species of which cover thousands of acres over the West. The smaller and most annoying form is the *O. fragilis*, the joints of which separate very readily, and adhere by the spines to the legs of horses or the clothes of travellers, and owing to the barbed character of the thorns, produce often quite serious and painful results.

The climate in this latitude is pure and dry, and perhaps the healthiest in the world. In the months of April, May, and to the middle of June, when east winds prevail, much rain falls, but during the rest of the summer and autumn, the weather is dry and moderately warm, there being only a short period in July and August of intense heat. There are not unfrequently severe thunderstorms during the hot season, accompanied by rain or hail, which in a few hours swell the small streams so that they overflow their banks, but with the cessation of the rain, they fall as suddenly as they rise. The Missouri and most of its tributaries inundate the neighboring valleys, when rain falls for ten or fifteen days in succession. This usually happens in the month of June, when they are already nearly full of water from the snow melting near their heads. This is not, however, of very frequent occurrence. Strong gales of wind also come from the west and southwest in form of sudden gusts, prostrating numbers of trees along the banks of the Missouri, but these storms only last for a few moments, and are not common. The summer season, being short, leaves vegetation but little time to decay, and the firing of the prairies, which happens more or less every year in different parts, burns up all the old grass, fallen timber, and underbrush along the river bottoms. Owing partly to these facts, partly to the very equable temperature, and the absence of excessive moisture, the air is pure and invigorating, and few epidemics rage among the migratory Indians. Fevers are almost unknown, and nervous diseases seldom met with.

The transition from summer to winter is very sudden; no long period of time intervenes equivalent to the Indian summer of the States. A few days are often sufficient to deprive the trees of leaves, freeze up the running streams, and clothe the yet partially green plains with a garment of snow. The winters are variable, mostly very cold, with deep snow. During the period of greatest cold, the mercury freezes. It often remains frozen for several days, and for weeks together the temperature ranges from thirty to forty degrees below zero. The snow-storms at this period are terrible, and almost certain death befalls those who are so unfortunate as to be caught on the plains. During every extremely cold winter Indians are frozen to death, many instances of which might be recorded here. Other winters are mild, but little snow falls, though there is always a short spell of intense cold, mostly in the month of January. When the winter proves mild and open, a disagreeable spring follows, snow falls in May, and March and April produce cold winds, rain, snow, and sleet. Occasionally, however, the spring opens finely, and the change from winter to summer is as sudden as from warm to winter weather. The constant exposure to cold, inseparable from the lives and occupation of the Indians, sleeping on damp ground, wet feet, and insufficient clothing, bring on bronchitis, pulmonary affections, rheumatism, and sometimes quinsy. These diseases do not often prove immediately fatal, but usually enfeeble the constitution. By reference to some tables of temperature kept at Fort Union, we find the longest winter on record to be that of 1844, when the Missouri closed on the 9th of November, and opened on the 21st of April.

The Assiniboins do not raise any cattle or sheep, but judging from the stock reared at Fort Union, near the mouth of the Yellowstone, the country is well adapted to grazing purposes. The grasses of spontaneous growth are very nutritious, and their supply inexhaustible. The only obstruction seems to be the severe cold of winter and the deep snow, though if animals are housed and provided for during a month or two in midwinter, it has been proven that no hardier or better stock can be raised in any country than in this. Sheep especially would thrive well if properly cared for, as far as grazing is concerned, though the great number of wolves with which the country abounds would present a formidable objection. Large quantities of good hay can be cut either on the Missouri bottoms or in the valleys of other streams, and, by experiments made near Fort Union, it has been ascertained that oats, corn, potatoes, and all garden vegetables grow well in favorable seasons. The soil, being light and sandy, requires frequent rains to produce a good crop, which happens about one year in three, the others failing from drouth and destruction by grasshoppers and other insects. The natural productions of the soil which are useful for food to man are not very numerous, but are held in high esteem by the

Indians. Wild turnips (*Psoralea esculenta*), artichokes (*Helianthus tuberosus*), bullberries (*Shepherdia argentea*), choke-cherries (*Prunus Virginiana*), red plums (*P. Americana*), service-berries (*Amelanchier Canadensis*), rose-buds, gooseberries, currants, sour grapes, and a plant resembling the garden rhubarb, are the principal fruits, and are eagerly sought for at their proper season. When dried or cooked in various ways, they are considered great luxuries. Wild hops (*Humulus lupulus* var. *Americanus*), are found in abundance, possessing all the properties of the cultivated plant.

When the Assiniboins migrated to the Missouri and the contiguous territory now occupied by them, they numbered, as has been observed, from ten to twelve hundred lodges. They did not all come at the same time, but by bands, at different periods, from 1800 to 1837, when the whole tribe may be said to have established themselves on their present lands, except that portion which still remains in the British territory. Their first interview with white people was at the time when the traders of the Mississippi pushed their traffic as far as their camps, when joined with the Dakotas proper, at which time they were the poorest of all Indians. They used knives made of the hump-rib of a buffalo, hatchets of flint, cooking utensils of clay or skin, awls and other tools made of bone, and arrow-points and spear-heads of stone, some of which articles can still be found among them, though most of them have been replaced by more durable metallic instruments obtained from the traders. As soon as enough had arrived on the Missouri to afford a trading establishment, the American Fur Company built a fort on White Earth River for their trade, which post was removed in a year or two and a large substantial fort built three miles above the mouth of the Yellowstone, on the east side of the Missouri. It required some years to bring these savages to anything like an appreciation of order or system, and ammunition, guns, knives, &c., had to be furnished them gratis; horses were sold to them very cheaply, and every inducement held out to them to improve their condition by labor. Though wretchedly supplied with arms, clothing, and other necessary articles, and subject to extreme want at all times, yet they were so lazy and improvident, their wants were so few, that many years passed before the proceeds of their hunts more than paid the expenses of their trading establishment. They were also of a thievish and malicious disposition, seldom bloodthirsty, but perpetually annoying the traders by stealing their horses, robbing and insulting the men in their employ when found on the prairie, killing their domestic cattle, and obstructing them in their operations in every way. They were the most impudent beggars, and having been supplied with many things to induce them to work, they at once came to the conclusion that this state of things must continue, and any refusal to supply their demands was resented in some of the ways just mentioned. This condition of affairs continued to grow worse and worse, until the gates of the fort were closed upon them, and they were compelled to trade within range of a loaded cannon.

The first calamity which cast a gloom over this nation occurred when the small-pox visited them in 1838. This disease made its appearance at Fort Union when the steamboat arrived in the month of June with the annual supplies for the post. No Indians were then in the vicinity, except the wives of the employés of the Fur Company in the fort, every one of whom caught the infection, and in a short time thirty persons were attacked. When the first band of Assiniboins came, they were met a mile or more from the fort by good interpreters, who represented to them the danger of going near, and goods were taken out to them with the intention of trading with them at a distance; but all efforts of that kind were disregarded, and they passed on to the fort, and two hundred and fifty lodges, or upwards of one thousand persons, contracted the disease at the same time, and in a short period they were reduced to about thirty lodges, or one hundred and fifty persons, old and young. Other bands coming in from time to time caught the disease, some of which remained at the fort, where the dead bodies were daily thrown into the river by scores. Others attempted to escape by running away, and the different roads leading from the fort were dotted with dead bodies, and occasionally lodges were standing in which whole families lay dead. The Indians in vain tried their own remedies, and the disease continued until midwinter, when it seemed to have spent its power and ceased. Out of one thousand lodges of Assiniboins only four hundred remained, and of these two hundred were saved by having been vaccinated in former years by the Hudson's Bay Company.

At the present time the Assiniboin tribe is separated into the following bands:

1. wah-to'-pah-an-da-to, Gens du Gauché,	100	lodges,	averaging four persons.
2. min'-i-shi-nak'-a-to, Gens du Lac,	60	"	"
3. i'-aŋ-to'-an, Gens des Roches,	50	"	"
4. wi-ić'-ap-i-nah, Gens des Filles,	60	"	"
5. wah-to'-pap-i-nah, Gens des Canots,	220	"	"
6. wah-zi-ah, or to-kum'-pi, Gens du Nord,	30 to 50	"	"

Several smaller bands are also found near the Montagne du Bois, but these, for the most part, belong to and reside in the English territory. The Gens du Gauché, above named, inhabit that part of the district described, along the Woody Mountains on the west side in summer, often moving westward to the sources of the Quaking Asp River, and toward autumn locate their camp at or above Big Muddy River, or along the first-named stream. In this direction, along the east shore of the Missouri, wintering-houses are built by the Fur Company for the convenience of the Indians, and also for collecting the buffalo-robes and other skins they obtain by hunting.

The Gens des Canots are commonly found along White Earth River, and extend their travels, in the summer season, as far north as the sources of La Riviere aux Souris, Grand

Couleé, and Pembina River. Indeed, the entire extent of country east of Fort Union as far down as the Great Bend is hunted in by them at different times; but owing to the absence of fuel on this broad plain, they are obliged to place their camp on or near the Missouri during the winter season. They are, therefore, usually found at that time either on White Earth River or above that point, where trading-houses are established for their benefit. Some fifteen or twenty lodges of this band trade at the posts of the Hudson's Bay Company, or with the half-breeds of Red River, who visit their camp during the winter with dog-sledges loaded with merchandise. The remaining bands mentioned, are scattered over the intervening region between those of the two bands just mentioned, moving from point to point near the Coteau de Prairie in summer, approaching the Missouri in the autumn, and stationing themselves on its banks or low down on some of its tributaries. These bands commonly make their winter hunt near the Quaking Asp River, and along that stream, but when the weather permits them to travel over the unwooded plains, proceed as far north as the Cypress Mountains. Some of them, especially the Gens du Nord, go still farther, and trade either at some of the Hudson's Bay Company's posts on the Assiniboin River, or with the Red River half-breeds.

The Assiniboins subsist almost entirely on the proceeds of their hunts. The buffalo is the principal animal killed, which is found in greater numbers through this territory than in other districts. The meat of this animal, either fresh or cured by drying, is their principal food. Smaller game, such as elk, deer, and antelope, are not killed to any extent. Some indigenous fruits and roots aid considerably in their support, at times when buffalo are too far from camp. The skins of the animals killed by them serve for their clothing, and lodges, or are exchanged with the Fur Company for articles of use and comfort, assorted to suit their wants. Owing to their nomadic life, they seldom have a supply of meat laid up for the future, and consequently often live on a short allowance for a time; but when buffalo are near at hand, there is continual feasting throughout the camp. It also sometimes happens that from an entire disappearance of these animals, they are distressed by actual want, which was the case in 1846, when they ate their dogs and horses, and, in some instances, even their own children. They have but few horses, and these are required to transport their tents and children when travelling. Dogs are used to a great extent for carrying burdens, but they cannot carry heavy packs, and when killed for food, their means for migrating from point to point is taken away, especially in the winter, when the snow is so deep that horses cannot travel. This inability to transport provisions prevents the desire to lay up for the future, and militates against any economy. They are compelled to follow the buffalo at all times when one day's travel from their camp. In this respect they are not as comfortable as those tribes who live in stationary villages, as the Mandans, Minnetarees, &c., who take care to lay up a good store of provisions for the future. Their roving habits prevent the accumulation of much baggage. All useless articles must be thrown away to make room for those that are necessary, and thus personal property cannot be acquired to any amount. Even their horses, the main stay of their existence, are very precarious stock, being subject at any moment to be taken away by the hostile tribes in the neighboring territories. These things united produce a carelessness of character and an apathy of disposition which runs through most of their actions.

In their personal appearance, they are not remarkable for either beauty or homeliness. The men average about the middle height, and usually have a determined, dogged look, especially when in a strange place. In their homes, however, they are more sociable. Each master of a lodge preserves a degree of dignity in his family circle, and exhibits a determination to be respected. They do not play or joke much with their women or children, nor do they enter into useless quarrels or recriminations. Trifling differences are settled by decision of the master in a tone of authority, and more serious quarrels are ended by the sudden application of the tomahawk. They are affectionate to their children, kind to strangers, distant in their manners to each other unless to kindred, and very revengeful when roused into passion.

There are but few handsome women amongst them, and virtue is somewhat rare except in very young females. In these matters, however, they are very sly and modest, exhibiting none of the bold and barefaced vulgarity of the Arikaras and Crows. They do not seem to be an amorous people, and marriages are often contracted for the first time at twenty-five or thirty years of age.

VOCABULARY OF THE ASSINIBOIN DIALECT OF THE DAKOTA LANGUAGE.

above, a-kan'.
alive, ni.
all, o-was'.
ankle, si-kun'-paz-o.
arm, ish-to'.
arrow, wa-hink'-a-pa.
autumn, pi-ti'-i-tu.
axe, ŏns'-pe.

back, ta-pe'-ta.
bark, ćuŋ-ha'.
bear, ma-to'.
beard, pu-te'-hi.
beaver, ća'-pa.
belt, i-pi'-ya-ka.
bird, tit-ka'-na.
black, sa'-pa.
bladder, ta-ne'-ha.
blood, o-we'.
blue, to.
boat, wa'-ta.
body, ta-ćun'.
bone, hu-hu'.
bow, i-tas'-i-pa.
boy, oh-shi'-na.
breast, maŋ-ka'.
breechcloth, će-gi-min'-ka.
brother, ćin-ću', elder brother.
sŭn-ka'-ku, younger brother.
buffalo, wo'-ta-ća, buffalo in a herd.
ta-tun'-ga, a bull.
burn, spaun, to burn.

call, ki-paun', to call.
cap, wa-pa'-ha, hat or cap.
certainly, tŏk.
chicken, ŏm-pau'-ho-to.
chief, hŭn-ga'.
coat, ća-i-gi-nunk'-a.
cold, sni.
copper, muz'-a-zi, gold or brass.
cow, pte.
crow, a'-a-na.
cry, će'-a, to cry.

dance, wa-ći′.
darkness, i-oh′-paz-a.
daughter, ći-wint′-ku.
day, aum′-pa.
dead, ta, to die.
deer, tah′-ća, red deer.
sin-te′-sa-pa, black-tailed deer.
dog, shunk′-a.
door, ti-o′-pa.
drink, yat-ka′, to drink.

eagle, wa-min-di′.
ear, noh′-a.
earth, man′-ka.
eat, wo′-ta.
wo′-tap-i, eating.
egg, wit′-ka.
enemy, to′-ka.
evening, h′ti′-i-tu.
eye, ish-ta′.

face, i-te′.
far off, to′-hund.
fat, wa-shi′.
father, at′-e.
feather, wi′-ya-ka.
finger, nap-e′-wash-i.
fire, pe′-ta.
fisher, ske′-ća.
flesh, ćo-ni′-ća.
flint, ćaŋ-ki′-a-pa.
flour, ah-u′-a-pi.
flower, wah-ća′.
foot, si-ya′.
forest, ćaŋ-no′-ha.
fox, to-ka′-na, gray fox.
shunk-a-sha′-na, red fox.
friend, ko-da′.

give, wi-ćin′-ćin-na.
go, i′-a, to go.
good, wash′-te.
wi-wash′-te, a handsome woman.

goose, ma-ha′.
grass, pe-źi′.
gray, ho′-ta.
grease, wa′-su-na.
great, tun′-ga.
green, wi′-to.
grouse, shi-o′.
gun, ćo-tun′-ga.

hail, wa-su′.
hair, pa-ha′.
hand, nap-e′.
hawk, će-tun′.
he, i′-a.
head, pa.
hear, na-ho′.
heart, ćaŋ′-te.
heel, si-e′-te.
hill, pa-ha′.
horse, shūn′-ga-tun′-ga.
hot, ka′-ta.
mash′-ta, hot weather.
house, ti′-pi, house or lodge.
ti-ma′-hēn, in the house.
husband, hi-ku′-nun-ku.

I, mi′-a.
ice, ćah′-a.
Indian, īks-će′-wi-ćas′-ta.
infant, ta-ku-ski′-na.
iron, muz′-a.
island, wi′-ta.

kettle, će′-ha.
kill, kit′-e, to kill.
knee, ta-hun′-ke.
knife, mi′-na.

lake, min-de′.
laugh, i-ha′-ha, to laugh.
lead, muz-a-su′.
leaf, wah-pe′.
leg, hu.
leggin, hōn′-ska.

lightning, o-wa-ni-hiok′-an-da-ka.
little, to′-nun-a.
live, ni-wa′, I live.
liver, pi.
love, ćān-te′-do-za.

maize, wa-ko-mo′-hi-za.
man, wi-ćas′-ta.
wa-si′-ću, a white man.
meat, ta-do′, raw meat.
wa-ćo′-ni-ća, dried meat.
midday, wi-ćo′-kun.
midnight, hi′-i-tu-ćo′-kun.
mink, i′-ku-sa.
mole, wi-ash′-pu-na.
moon, ha-wi′.
moose, tah′.
morning, hi-a′-ki-ni.
mother, i-na′.
mountain, he.
mouth, i.
much, o′-ta.
muskrat, sink′-pe.

nail, shak-e′.
navel, ćēk-pa′.
near, ash-ka′-na.
neck, ta-hu′.
night, hi′-i-tu.
no, hi-ya′.
nose, po-ha′.
nothing, ta-ko-nish′.

oar, wa-ti′-ća-ga-bo′-ga.
old, we-ća′-ća.
otter, pi-tun′.
owl, hi-hun′-a.

part, a-pa′.
perhaps, ća.
pipe, ćān-du′-pa.
plain, o-min-da′.
polecat, ma-ha′.
potato, pa-he′.

rabbit, mus-tin′-ća-na.

red, sha.
rock, i-ya-tun′-ga.
run, du-za′-ha, to run.
scalp, wi-ća′-pa-ha′.
sea, min-i-wa′-zi-ća.
seat, ŏn′-za.
see, wa-ya′-ka, to see.
shirt, ma-hĕn′-ta-ŭm-pi.
shoe, caŋ-ham′-pa.
shot-pouch, tah-c-ik-un′.
shoulder, a′-min-do.
sinew, ik-un′, sinew of a man.
ta-kun′, sinew of an animal.
sing, do-wan′, to sing.
sister, tunk-shi′.
skin, ha.
sky, moh-pi′-a-to.
small, ći-ka′-na.
snow, wa.
soldier, a-ki′-ći-ta, warrior.
son, ći-hint′-ku.
speak, i-a′, to speak.
spear, wa-hu′-ka-za.
spirit, nah-e′.
wa-kaŋ-tun′-ga, Great Spirit.
spring (of water), wi′-wi.
spring, wo′-tu, a season.
star, wi-ća′-pi.
stomach, ah-ća′.
stone, i′-yaŋ.
stream, wah-pa′-na.
strike, a-pa′, to strike.
strong, su-ta′.
summer, min-do-ko′-tu.
sun, wi.
swan, ma-ha′-ska.
sweet, sku′-ya.
thigh, će-ća′.
think, i-uk′-a-ćăn.
this, do.
thou, ni′-a.
thunder, o-te′.
thy, i-um′-pi.
tobacco, ćăn-di′.
to-day, am-pe′-ha.
toe, si-ya′-ink-pa.
to-morrow, hi-ak′-a-ća.
tongue, će-źe′.
tooth, i.
town, wi-ćo′-te.
turtle, pat-ka′-sha.
ugly, shi′-ća, bad.
wi-ća-si′-ća, an ugly man.
under, o-kŭn′.
valley, kŏh′-a.
vein, kun.
walk, ma′-ni, to walk.
war-club, ćun′-pi.
water, min′-i.
min-i-o′-han, through the water.
we, ŭn-ki′.
weak, wăn′-ka-na.
what, ta′-ko.
which, tŭk-te′-wash-i, which one?
white, ska.
who, tu′-a.
wife, tau-i′-ću.
wind, ta-te′.
windpipe, lo-te′.
wing, hu-pa′.
winter, wa-ni′-i-tu.
wish, wa-ćink′-a.
within, ma-hĕn′.
without, tun-kăd′.
wolf, shunk-to′-ka-ća.
woman, we′-ya.
wood, caŋ.
yellow, zi.
yes, ho.
young, kŏsh′-ka.

CHAPTER XVI.

X. Aub-sa′-ro-ke, or Crow Indians.

ETHNOGRAPHICAL HISTORY.

The Crows were once united with the Minnitarees or Gros Ventres, who now occupy a stationary village on the Missouri. They resided with them, they say, at different places along the banks of the Missouri, where the remains of dirt villages are still to be found. About eighty years since, a quarrel arose which divided them. The nation was governed by two factions, each headed by a separate chief, both of whom were desperate men, and nearly equal in the number of their followers. Jealous of each other, and striving after supreme command, many difficulties and differences arose from time to time, though they had never proceeded to extremes on these occasions, there being always a sufficient number of wise, cool heads to check or quell such disturbances. At one time, when both the chiefs with their followers were on a hunt together, and a large number of buffalo had been killed, the wives of the leaders quarrelled about some portion of one of the animals. From words they came to blows, and from blows to knives, and finally one of the women killed the other. The relatives on both sides then took part, and each faction headed by its chief joined in the affray, and a sharp contest ensued, in which several were killed on both sides. The result was that about one half left the other portion on the Missouri, and migrated to the Rocky Mountains, through which wild extensive region they still continue to rove. Why they are called Crows we cannot tell; the word Aub-sa'-ro-ke, the name they give themselves in their own language, does not mean a crow in particular, but anything that flies. Since leaving the Missouri, their language has changed to some extent, but still they can converse with ease with the Minnitarees.

The country usually inhabited by the Crows, is in and near the Rocky Mountains, along the sources of Powder, Wind, and Big-horn Rivers, on the south side of the Yellowstone, as far as Laramie Fork on the River Platte. They are also often found on the west and north side of that river, as far as the source of the Mussel-shell, and as low down as the mouth of the Yellowstone. That portion of their country lying east of the mountains, is perhaps the best game country in the world. From the base of the mountains to the mouth of the Yellowstone, buffalo are always to be found in immense herds. Along that river, elk may be seen in droves of several hundreds at a time; also large herds of deer of both species, *Cervus leucurus* and *C. macrotis*. Antelope cover the prairies, and in the "Bad Lands" near the mountains, the mountain sheep (*Ovis montana*), and the grizzly bear are found in the greatest abundance. Every creek and river teem with beaver, and almost every stream furnishes a great supply of fish and fowl in the proper season.

The once almost fabulous country of the Rocky Mountains is now so well known as scarcely to need description here. The scenery of the district now under consideration does not differ materially from other portions of the mountain region. The same high stony peaks and eternal snows are seen, interspersed with fertile valleys of rich land. Most of the rivers whose sources are in these mountains are clear, rapid streams, formed from springs, which widen into lakes of different sizes, according to the nature of the obstruction the water meets with in its descent. In their course through the prairie country, these rivers usually assume a muddy character, from the alluvial nature of their banks. The valleys between the different ranges of mountains are clothed with thick grasses, many flowers, shrubs, and trees, presenting numerous beautiful landscapes. The higher ranges of mountains may be divided into three different zones. The first third, from the base up, is well covered with tall pines, poplars, and other trees of large growth. The second portion is composed of gigantic masses of rock, overhanging in such a manner as to present a frightful appearance to the traveller below. Among these, a few stinted cedars and pines, with some other shrubs struggle for an existence, sometimes taking root where there is apparently no earth. In the last zone, the vegetation has ceased, and the snow commences, which continues to the summit. This snow is perpetual, though a portion of it melts annually, which loss is supplied the ensuing winter, yet it is presumed that no thaw takes place on the summit, but on the sides some distance down. When the snow accumulates on the projections so as to lose its balance, it is precipitated below in the form of avalanches, something like those of the Alps. Taking in their way large rocks, and increasing in size as they descend, trees give way before them, until they find rest in some portion of the lower zone, where they melt away, and aid in forming the sources of rivers. Snow-slides are also common, by which piles of snow miles in extent are detached, and force their way into the valleys, or at least as far as the thickly timbered section. Some of the springs near the sources of the Yellowstone are bituminous, sending forth an inflammable substance like tar; others are sulphurous, and a few are hot, or boiling. The water of the last is hot enough to cook meat readily. Most of the tributaries of the Yellowstone are well fringed with timber, though the river itself is wooded only about half the way from its mouth to the base of the mountains, that is, many portions of it for considerable distances are destitute of trees. The lower portion of the valley contains wide belts of cottonwood, and the soil is moderately good for agricultural purposes. Considering the Crow district as a whole, it can never become thickly settled, and all the land that can ever be rendered useful for cultivation, is found only in the valleys of the streams, and along the base of the mountains.

The Yellowstone, like the Missouri, rises to the top of its banks every spring, owing to the melting of the snow along the sides of the mountains. This rise usually commences about the middle of May and continues until the middle of June, when it begins to fall, unless kept up by heavy rains. During this high stage of water steamers of light draught might navigate it to the first rapids, which are about one hundred and fifty miles from its mouth. The ice commonly yields about the first of April, and when broken up suddenly, by pressure of water from the mountains, it forms dams quite across the valley, raising the water fifty or sixty feet, and inundating the neighboring country. The Crow Indians are greatly in fear of the water on these occasions, and suffer severely when taken unawares. One of these breakings up occurred a few years ago, early in the month of February. About one hundred and thirty lodges of the Crows were encamped in the valley of the Yellowstone, where the distance from bluff to bluff is more than three miles. The water came down upon them in the night so suddenly, that they had barely time to escape with their lives by running to the hills. But the land near the bluffs is often lower than that near the bank of the stream, and consequently in running that way they encountered water, wading and swimming through it and carrying their children. They lost the products of their whole winter's hunt, besides nearly all their arms, ammunition, and other property. When the water fell it left immense quantities of ice piled up around their lodges, causing great difficulty in securing them again. Their entire loss on this occasion could not have been less than ten or twelve thousand dollars worth of robes and merchandise. At another time the American Fur Company's fort at the mouth of the Big-horn was inundated in the same way, and a large amount of property destroyed. This river is, when high, very rapid and dangerous to navigate, on account of the rocks, snags, and other obstructions. Mackinaw boats descend it every year, but they are often lost and the men are drowned.

The Crow Indians live in skin huts like the other migratory tribes. They formerly numbered about eight hundred lodges or families, but from the usual causes of diminution, disease and war, are now reduced to four hundred and sixty lodges. These are separated into different bands, each governed by a chief, and occupying different parts of their territory. Those belonging to the band headed by the "Big Robber," usually make their hunt on the head of Powder River, and of late years take their robes to the trading-houses along the Platte River in the spring. Here they obtain supplies to continue their operations, and move back to winter quarters early in the fall. The largest band is led by a chief named "Two-face," and numbers about two hundred lodges. These range through the Wind River mountain region, and deal with the traders of the American Fur Company located on the Yellowstone. A third portion, under their chief, "Bear's Head," wander along the valley of the Yellowstone, from mouth to source, sometimes passing the winter with the Assiniboins near Fort Union. The whole nation have a rendezvous every summer, when, after performing several national solemnities, they move across the mountains to exchange the greater part of the merchandise for horses. This traffic is carried on with the Flat-heads in St. Mary's Valley, or with the Snake and Nez Percé Indians on the head waters of the Yellowstone. With the nations just named the Crows have been at peace for many years, and also with the Assiniboins since 1850. But their natural and perpetual enemies are the Blackfeet on the west and the Dakotas on the east, with both of which nations they have kept up a continual warfare from time immemorial.

I have before me the materials for an extended sketch of the manners and customs, together with biographical sketches of the principal chiefs of this tribe, but, as they will doubtless appear in a future work now in course of preparation, I will close with a brief notice of the different vocabularies of the Crow language which have been published from time to time.

The first one ever taken, so far as I can learn, was published in "Long's Expedition to the Rocky Mountains," and consists of about thirty words. In the "Reise in das Innere Nord Amerikas, in 1832–1834," Vol. II, Prince Neuwied gives us twenty words. Mr. Gallatin also obtained brief but excellent vocabularies from Mr. Kenneth Mackenzie, who was for many years superintendent of Fort Union, near the mouth of the Yellowstone. In Vol. III of Schoolcraft, twenty-two words are compared with the Minnitaree. No idea, however, has ever been given in regard to the grammatical structure of the Aub-sa′-ro-ke or Crow language. The following vocabulary and grammatical sketch I obtained from the Crows, with the aid of an intelligent Scotch trader, Mr. Robert Meldrum, who has lived thirty-three years with that tribe and speaks the language with the fluency of a native. I was also very much aided by a MS. vocabulary of over a thousand words, obtained by Rev. Mr. Brauninger, a Lutheran missionary among the Crows during the years 1859 and 1860, who was killed by a wandering war-party of Dakotas in the valley of Powder River during the summer of 1860.

REMARKS ON THE GRAMMATICAL STRUCTURE OF THE AUB-SA′-RO-KE OR CROW LANGUAGE.

I. NOUNS.

1. As a general rule, no change occurs in the termination of nouns to indicate number or case. There are a few exceptions to this rule, however, as, it-si′-ri, a horse, it-si′-ru, horses; da-ka′-ka, a bird, da-ka′-ku, birds.

2. No change is made in the termination of nouns to indicate gender, but different words are used for male and female; as, ći′-ro-pe, a bull; bi-shi′-e, a cow; bat′-si, a man; mi′-a, or, mi-a-kat′-e, a woman.

II. ADJECTIVES.

3. Adjectives follow the nouns which they qualify; as, it-si′-ri-ma-ni-tum′-a-kat, a gentle horse; mi′-a-ha-bu′-ro-ka, a virtuous woman.

4. Sometimes the adjective assumes the plural termination; as, it-si′-ri-ship-it′-uk, black horses; mi-ship-it′-uk, black rocks.

5. The idea of comparison is expressed in the following graduated form; as, it′-si, good; it-se′-e-shĕk, better; it-se′-bat-saé′, very good, or powerful good; ka-wi′, bad; ka-wi-ka′-te, a little bad; ka-wi′-e-shĕk, quite bad, or worse; ka-wi′-a-bat-saé′, worst, or exceedingly bad; bat-saé′, strong, or powerful; a-baé′-kat, a little; i-a′-kat, very small; i-san-ié′-kat, a little larger; i-sa′-e-shĕk, larger than the last; i-sa′-bat-saé′, very large.

6. Wherever adjectives or nouns are used as verbs, they are conjugated like verbs; as, hin-i-et′-dĕk, healthy, or well; mi′-hin-i-et-dĕk, I am well, &c.

7. The cardinal numerals are as follows:

one, ha-mat.'
two, nŏp.
three, nam.
four, shŏp.
five, tsiḣ'-ŏp.
six, a-ka'-mak.
seven, ḣa'-pu-a.
eight, no'-pa-pe.
nine, a-ma'-ta-pe.
ten, pi-ra-ka'.
eleven, pi-ra-ka'-ma-ta.
twelve, pi-rak'-nŏp.
thirteen, pi-rak'-nam.
fourteen, pi-rak'-shŏp.
fifteen, pi-rak'-tsiḣ-ŏp.
sixteen, pi-rak-a'-mak.
seventeen, pi-rak'-saḣ-pu'-ak.
eighteen, pi-rak-no'-pa-piḣ'-te.
nineteen, pi-rak'-a-ma'-ta-piḣ'-te.
twenty, no-pa-pi'-ra-ka.
twenty-one, no'-pa-pi'-ra-ka'-aḣ'-pa-mat-kat.
twenty-two, no'-pa-pi-ra-ka'-aḣ-pi-no'-pa.
twenty-three, no'-pa-pi-ra-ka'-aḣ'-pi-na'-mo.
twenty-four, no'-pa-pi-ra-ka'-aḣ'-pi-shŏp.
twenty-five, no'-pa-pi-ra-ka-aḣ'-pi-tsiḣ'-ŏp.
twenty-six, no'-pa-pi-ra-ka'-aḣ-pa-ka'-mak.
twenty-seven, no'-pa-pi-ra-ka'-aḣ-pi-sa-pu'-a.
twenty-eight, no'-pa-pi-ra-ka'-aḣ-pi-no-pa'-pi.
twenty-nine, no'-pa-pi-ra-ka'-aḣ-pi-ma-ta'-pe.
thirty, na'-ma-pi-ra-ka'.
forty, sho'-pa-pi-ra-ka'.
fifty, tsiḣ'-a-pi-ra-ka'.
sixty, a-ka'-ma-pi-ra-ka'.
seventy, ḣa'-pu-pi-ra-ka'.
eighty, no'-pa-pe-a-pi-ra-ka'.
ninety, a-ma'-ta-pe-pi-ra-ka'.
one hundred, pi-ra-ka-sa'.
two hundred, no'-pa-pi-ra-ka-sa'.
three hundred, na'-ma-pi-ra-ka-sa'.
four hundred, sho'-pa-pi-ra-ka-sa'.
five hundred, tsiḣ'-o-pi-ra-ka-sa'.
six hundred, a-ka'-ma-pi-ra-ka-sa'.
seven hundred, ḣa'-pu-pi-ra-ka-sa'.
eight hundred, no'-pa-pe-a-pi-ra-ka-sa'.
nine hundred, a-ma'-ta-pe-pi-ra-ka-sa'.
one thousand, pi-ra-ka-sa'-pi-ra-ka'.

The Aub-sa'-ro-ke, or Crows, like all the Indians with whom I am acquainted, use their fingers in counting, bending them down temporarily against the inside of the hand as they proceed, until they reach ten, when one finger is allowed to remain down. They do not usually count higher than a thousand, as they say honest people have no use for larger numerals; aḣ'-pi, means added to, as $20 + 1 = 21$.

8. There are also, though rarely in use, numerals of the adverbial form; as, a-ma-tak', once; en-e-nŏm'-pe, twice, a second time.

III. Adverbs.

9. Adverbs precede the words which they qualify; as, a-ma-ta'-aḣ'-pik, I shot it only once; i-uk-ŭs'-na-ra, go there.

IV. Prepositions.

10. Prepositions follow the nouns which they govern; as, mo-na-ke'-da, up a tree; min-mo-in'-a, in the water; shi-ća'-ke-da, up a hill; shić-bu-uk'-i-sa, down a hill; min-a-sa', by the shore; a-she'-a-ke'-da, on the top of the house; a-she-mo'-na, inside of a lodge.

V. Conjunctions.

11. Conjunctions usually follow the nouns which they connect; as, a-pe', and; ći'-ro-pe-bi-

shi'-a-pe', bulls and cows; da-ka'-ka-na-ka-a'-pa, the bird and its young. Sometimes the conjunction is repeated after both nouns; as, ći'-ro-pe-ho-it-si'-ri-ho, a bull or a horse; uh-ho', it is either the one or the other.

VI. Interjections.

12. There are but few interjections; as, ha-hi'-a! halloo there! to call to one at a distance; di-du'-ka-źa! hurrah! to one only; di-du-ka-źa'-ra! hurrah, my boys! a common word used in the act of fighting; ho! come! nēs-ha'-ra! get out! nah'-a-ra! go away!

VII. Pronouns.

13. Pronouns are of two kinds, the simple and the fragment pronoun. The simple pronouns are complete in themselves; the fragment-pronoun is found only in connection with other words. The simple personal pronouns are,

bi, I.	bi'-rūd, we.	bi'-ru, us.
di, thou.	di'-rūd, you.	di'-ru, you.
i, he.	i'-rūd, they.	i'-ru, them.

14. The possessive personal pronouns are declined in the following manner:

AFFIRMATIVELY.

bi-bēk', it is mine.
di-dēk', it is thine.
i-dēk', it is his.
bi-ru'-dak, it is ours.
di-ru'-dak, it is yours.
i-ru'-dak, it is theirs.

bi-di'-duk, it was mine.
di-di'-duk, it was thine.
i-di'-duk, it was his.
bi-ru'-duk, it was ours.
di-du'-duk, it was yours.
i-du'-duk, it was theirs.

NEGATIVELY.

bi-be'-sa, it is not mine.
di-de'-sa, it is not thine.
i-de'-sak, it is not his.
bi-ru-be'-sa, it is ours.
di-ru-de'-sa, it is yours.
ko-de'-sak, it is theirs.

15. The fragment-pronouns are used in conjugating verbs and declining nouns, and are placed at the beginning, in the middle, and sometimes at the end of the word, as the form of the noun or verb may seem to require. Those pronouns denoting possession are attached to all nouns which represent objects of ownership. The following illustrations will explain themselves without further remark. Changes of vowels occur according to the form of the word or particular vowel with which they stand connected.

mi-nup'-he, my father.	ba-ćin'-a, my husband.
ni-nup'-he, thy father.	da-ćin'-a, thy husband.
i-nup'-he, his father.	is-ćin'-a, her husband.

ma-nak'-mi-a, my daughter.
na-nak'-mi-a, thy daughter.
ko-nak'-mi-a, his daughter.

ba-ku'-pe, my brother.
da-ku'-pe, thy brother.
ko-a-ku'-pe, his brother.

ma-shu'-a, my head.
na-shu'-a, thy head.
i-shu'-a, his head.

bi-sas'-ku, my horses.
di-sas'-ku, thy horses.
i-sas'-ku, his horses.
bi-ru-ba-sas'-kŭk, our horses.
di-ru-di-sas'-kŭk, your horses.
i-ru-i-sas'-kŭk, their horses.

ba-sah'-e, my mother.
da-sah'-e, thy mother.
i-sah'-e, his mother.

mu'-a, my wife.
nu'-a, thy wife.
u'-a, his wife.

ma-nak'-ba-tse, my son.
na-nak'-ba-tse, thy son.
ko-nak'-ba-tse, his son.

ba-smi'-a, my sister.
da-smi'-a, thy sister.
ko-i-smi'-a, his sister.

bas-ba'-źe, my boat.
das-da'-źe, thy boat.
is-ba'-źe, his boat.

mi-ba-rut'-shik, I have got good sense.
a-mu'-kak, I saw or have seen.
i-rŭd'-mi-ié'-ish-ŭk, they love me.
bet-dis-ió'-a-da, you love each other.

16. The adjective-pronouns are quite numerous:

First, distributive, as, ko'-ta, each, every, or all; bi-rup'-tse-pi'-ra-ka-ko'-ta, each one ten charges of powder; ma-e-ha', neither, or something else.

Second, demonstrative, as, hin-e', this or that; hin-e-ma-nu'-a, this object or thing; hi-dĕd, these; hi-dĕd-bi-ruh'-pa-ke, these persons.

Third, interrogatives, as, sap, or sa'-pa, what? sa-pe', who, or who is it? sap'-te, why, or why is it? sho or sho'-rak, where, or where is it?

VIII. Verbs.

17. (1.) In Aub-sa'-ro-ke verbs, there are three moods, indicative, imperative, and infinitive.

(2.) Three tenses, past, present, and future.

(3.) Two numbers, singular and plural. No dual form has as yet been observed.

The following list of forms, imperfect as it is, will convey some idea of the character of the conjugation of the verbs in this language.

ba-shik', I am dead.
sa-hik', thou art dead.
ka-rish'-e, he is dead.
ba-sŭk', we are dead.

ka-re-sŭk', they are dead.
sa-ha'-kek, to die, or it is dead.
sa-match'-e (imp.), die.

ma-ne'-shik, I am hungry.
na-ne'-shik, thou art hungry.
a-ne'-shik, he is hungry.
ma-ne-shis'-a, I am not hungry.
na-ne-shis'-a, thou art not hungry.
a-ne-shis'-a, he is not hungry.
ma-ne-shi'-ink, I will be hungry.
na-ne-shi'-ink, thou wilt be hungry.
a-ne-shi'-ink, he will be hungry.

bi-ba-kuć'-ik, I am thirsty.
di-da-kuć'-ik, thou art thirsty.
a-kuć'-ik, he is thirsty.
bi-ba-kuć'-is-a, I am not thirsty.
di-da-kuć'-is-a, thou art not thirsty.
a-kuć'-is-a, he is not thirsty.

mi-a-pak', I am cold.
ni-a-pak', thou art cold.
i-a-pak', he is cold.
bud-e-a-pak', we are cold.
i-ru'-da-pak', they are cold.
mi-a-pa-sak', I am not cold.
ni-a-pa-sak', thou art not cold.
i-a-pa-sak', he is not cold.
bud-e-a-pa-sak', we are not cold.
i-ru'-da-pa-sak', they are not cold.

ba-bu'-she, I eat, or am eating.
ba-du'-she, thou eatest, or art eating.
ba-būsh'-mīk, I will eat.
ba-dūsh'-mīk, thou wilt eat.
ba-de-dūsh'-nīk, wilt thou eat?
ba-būsh-is-a'-nīk, I will not eat.
kun-ba-bu'-she, I am done eating.
kun-ba-du'-she, thou art done eating.
ba-de-dūsh'-kōm-nak, art thou done eating?
kun-ba-būsh'-ko-mak, I am done eating.
nam-ba-būsh'-mōk (imp.), let us eat.
du'-she (imp. sing.), eat.
ba-ru-sa'-ra (imp. pl.), eat.

ba-dić'-ik, I strike.
da-dić'-ik, thou dost strike.
i-dić'-ik, he strikes.
bi-dēd'-ba-dić'-ik, I myself strike.
di-dēd'-da-dić'-ik, thou thyself dost strike.
i-de-dić'-ik, he himself strikes.
bi-rić'-ik, I will strike.
di-rić'-ik, thou wilt strike.
i-rić'-ik, he will strike.
bi-dēd'-ba-rić'-ik, I myself will strike.
di-dēd'-da-rić'-ik, thou thyself wilt strike.
i-dēd'-a-rić'-ik, he himself will strike.
it-a-ba-dit'-nak, I am going to strike.

bi-ōź'-ik, I am burnt.
di-ōź'-ik, thou art burnt.
i-ōź'-ik, he is burnt.
bi-dēd-ash'-tak, I myself burnt them.
di-dēd-ash'-tak, thou thyself didst burn them.

mi-hum-ish'-ik, I am sleepy.
ni-hum-ish'-ik, thou art sleepy.
hin-um-ish'-ik, he is sleepy.

ba-rēk', I go.
ba-re-mi'-a-mak', I would like to go.
ba-re-mi'-ink, I shall go, or shall I go.
ba-re-sa'-mīk, I will not go.
ba-re'-mīk, I will go.
da-de'-nīk, thou wilt go.
de-sa' (imp.), do not go.
na-ma'-ra (imp.), go, all of you.
di-tut'-da (imp.), you go alone.
da (imp.), go.
mi-ne-ki'-a (imp.), let me go.

ba-she'-ćik, I mashed it.
de-she'-ćik, thou didst mash it.
i-she'-ćik, he mashed it.
bi-rūd'-ba-she'-ćik, we mashed it.
i-rūd'-a-she'-ćik, they mashed it.

ma-ma'-nik, I did shoot.
bi-ma'-nik, he shot me.
di-ma'-nik, he shot you.
bi-ru-ma'-nik, he shot us.

bi-pu-a'-mĭk, I will shoot.
ma-di-pu-a'-mĭk, I will shoot you.
di-pu'-a-ka'-ni, thou mayst shoot.

ba-de-dŭsh'-ni-shik, dost thou want to eat?
ba-bŭsh'-mi-shik, I want to eat.
mi-uh-pŭsh'-ik, I am full, *i. e.*, I have eaten enough.

mi-ić'-ish-ĕk, I am loved.
ni-ić'-ish-ĕk, thou art loved.
ko-ić'-ish-ĕk, he is loved.
mi-ćc'-mućish'-c, I love myself.
nić-c'-nuc-ish'-c, thou dost love thyself.
a-muć-ish'-ĕk, I did love.
a-muć-ish'-e-sak, I do not love.
it-a-a-muć-ish'-e-nak, I am about to love.
a-muć-is'-a-mĕk, I will not love.
bud-e-its'-ish-ĕk, thou lovest us.
ni-e-muć-ish'-ĕk, I love you.
mi-its-ish'-e-ki-a (imp.), let me love.
ić-is-sa'-ra (imp.), love.
mi-ić-ish'-e (imp.), love me.

bu-ru-pi'-uk, I hate.
du-ru-pi'-uk, thou hatest.
i-ru-pi'-uk, he hates.
bat-bu'-ru-pi'-uk, we hate each other.
bu-ru-pi'-a-mink, I will hate.
du-ru-pi'-a-mink, thou wilt hate.
i-ru-pi'-a-mink, he will hate.
ni-bu'-ru-pi'-uk, I hate you.

mi-hin'-i-ct'-dĕk, I am well.
di-hin'-i-et'-dĕk, thou art well.
hin'-i-et'-dĕk, he is well.
bud-e-hin'-i-et'-dĕk, we are well.

a-ma'-ka, I see.
a-da'-ka, thou seest.
i'-ka, he sees.
a-ma'-ku, we see.
a-da'-ku, you see.
i'-ku, they see.

a-mak-is'-ak, I do not see.
a-dak-is'-ak, thou dost not see.
i-kis'-ak, he does not see.
a-na'-ka, do you see.

i-ki'-a (imp.), look at.

mi-hu'-shik, I run.
di-hu'-shik, thou dost run.
hu'-shik, he or it runs.
mi-ho'-sŭk, we run.
di-ho'-sŭk, you run.
ho'-sŭk, they run.
ka'-na (imp.), run away.

aub-sa'-ro-ke-mi-ić'-ish-ĕk, I am loved by the Crows.
ish'-mĭk (participle), drinking.
bi-min-ish'-mi-mik, I am drinking water
ba-hi-ri'-pa-sa, there is no scarcity.
bi-dup-ish'-e, or bi-dup'-det, there are no beaver.
a-ma-su-a-di-c'-ba-mik, I am going to build a fort.
bat-se'-da-de, have you been out hunting?
sap'-du? what did you kill?
mi'-dak-po-sak, if you do not kill me.
di-bak'-pe-mik, I will kill you.
bi-ruh-pa'-ke-ba-sić'-e-bak, } I love the people.
bi-ruh-pa'-ke-a-muć-ish'-ĕk, }
i-o-ke'-be, to wear.
i-a'-ra (imp.), wear that as a blanket.
da-hin'-e-et-a'-ra (imp.), go and do it.
ba-a-ta'-na, I steal.
a-ta'-na, it steals.
ba-a-tan'-mi-uk, I would like to steal.
do-tuć'-ik, you bite it.
bi-ru-tuć'-ik, he bites us.
bo-ro-ta'-hĕk, I break it in two.
do-ta'-hĕk, you break it in two.
hu-a'-mać, to come and sit down.
bi-dĕd-ba-da'-mać, we come and sit down.
a-muć-ish-im-ink'-pak, I think I love.
a-uć-ish'-e-tats, you think you love.
min-e-ska'-pik, he fell into the water.
ship-i-a-sić', he threw it into the mud.
ship-i'-a-ko-sić, it was thrown into the mud.

bi-de'-sić, I threw it in the fire.
a-she-ku'-kak, he is in the village.
bat-sah'-puk-na-ra (imp.), go all together.
bat-sa-buh'-me-mŭk (imp.), let us all go together.
i-ćo-ken'-i-ćĕk, he has whitened himself with clay.
ba-ret-in-e'-pać, I think not.
ba-re-ta'-ra (imp.), let it not be.
ba-ra-ta'-rik, it shall not be.
bi-nŏp'-ka-ti'-a-ma-ku, we all see two of them.

18. There are certain words used only by the women and children; as, i'-ka, attention, used when a woman calls to her friend; hi'-na, comrade or companion; ba-sa'-ka, mother; a little girl addresses her mother as ba-sa'-ka, and a little boy his father as, ah'-e; ba-sa'-na, older brother; ba-sa'-kat, older sister; ba-so'-ka, younger sister.

19. PHRASES AND SENTENCES.

ba'-źe is-a-kat'-a ći'-a-ka-ta min'-a-ta da-ka'-puk
canoe beautiful white on water floats
bu'-uk i-sa'-dĕk.
goes down.
A beautiful canoe floats on the water, or goes down the stream.

ba-hu'-ra bat-sa'-ća e'-kus na-na'-mĕk.
blackbird great the other side flies.
A great blackbird flies to the other side.

ah-pa-nah'-e a-she' a-ho' wat-saé'.
in the sky house a great many very large.
In my Father's house are many mansions.

ba-sa-pe' ah-i-ta' ka-wi'.
moccasins wet bad.
Wet moccasins are bad.

ah-pa-nah'-e a-she' ka-wi' ka-wi-ka-wi-ti'-a-sa.
in the heavens house bad bad bad very.
In the heavens are houses, bad, bad, very bad.

i-sa'-ka-wat'-e ah-pa-nah'-e he'-re-re.
Great Spirit heavens among.
The Great Spirit is among the heavens.

bi-ruh-pa'-ke ta-pi'-ŭk pat-pa-tsi'-ŭk.
a person has been killed in the war.
A person has been killed in the war.

ah-pa-nah'-e a-she' a-mah'-e ak-tsi'-se.
in the heavens lodge sky on the other side.
In the heavens, in the lodges on the other side of the sky.

it-si'-re a-hŭk' bi-she' a-ho' wat-saé'.
horses plenty buffalo a heap very great.
A plenty of horses, and a very great abundance of buffalo.

A Prayer to the Great Spirit.

Mi wa-tsĕsh'-yat ka-wi' mi mba-tse'-tse-rik it-si'-re
I am poor; that is bad; make me a chief; give me
a-ho' be'-mi ba-sap'-ka-te it-sih-at'-te-be i-mi-a'-wa. It-si'-
a plenty of horses, give me fine clothing. I ask for good
re it-si-ka'-ta ma-ka'-ku shi'-a-kat a-she'-i-sa' be-i-mi'-a-
spotted horses; give me a large tent, give me a great
wa it-si'-re a-ho' be-i-mi'-a-me it-si'-re it-sih-a' a-ta'-nu-a
many horses; let me steal fine horses; grant it to me.
be-i-mi'-ma. O-mat-ma-nah'-e gu-ru-tats be-mih' mi-a it-
Give me guns by cheating; give me a beautiful woman;
si-ka'-ta a-pah'-pa-mih bi-shi'-a-te-kat. Pi'-a na-mo' ba'-
bring the buffalo close by. No deep snow; a little
ret pi'-a hep'-kat it-si'-ka ish-te-pit'-e a-te-kat'-ham ba-
snow is good. Give me Blackfeet to kill or to die, close
ba'-mih ha-hu'-a. Pa-pe-mih' bi-ruh'-pa-ke su'-a ka-ra-
by, all together. Stop the people from dying, it is
ko'-me-o it-sih'; ma-nah'-u-a sap'-ka-te-e-i-ru'-ke it-si-
good; instruments for amusement, blankets too; fine
ka'-ta tu'-shi bi-ruh'-pa-ke ba'-ka ba-kak-shi'-at bi-she'
meat to eat; give the people altogether a plenty of fine
it-si-ka'-ta a-hŭk' tu'-shi a-hŭk'.
buffalo, and plenty to eat.

Mi-nup'-he ak-ma-ku'-ko a-ma'-ća; do-ha'-ra da-źa-
My Father above resides; let thy name be

ćik'; is-a-me-bu-ka'-ra; a-na-mis'-ćo ko-mik'-a-ra ma-
good; let thy country come; thy will let be done above

ku'-ko a-hin'-e a-me-ko-mik'; hin'-e ma'-pe e-bud'-e
on high as here on earth is done; this day food

ku'-a ku-re-shīt' bud-e-ku'-a-ra e-rup-a'-re bi'-rūd aup-
give

a'-she a-mis'-će ba-ka'-wi a-ku'-sa-ni ku-ru'-tu a-me' it-

ći'-uk a-sīk' ba-ko-ći'-ta ba-ko-ći'-ta ka-ra-ko-mi'-sa.
forever, forever, let it be done.

Ka-ra-ko'-mik. May it be so.

NAMES OF TRIBES, CHIEFS, ETC.

aub-sa'-ro-ke, the Crows, the original people.
da-ko'-ta or ma-ko'-ta, the Sioux, or Dakotas of the Missouri.
i-sōnsh'-pu-she, the Shyennes: meaning undetermined.
ba-ra-shūp'-gi-o, Dakotas or Sioux: meaning undetermined.
bik-ta'-śa-to-tu'-se, a-shi-ap'-ka-wi, } very bad lodges.
bik-ta'-she, and sho'-sho-ni, Grass lodges or Snakes.
a-ra'-po-ho or -hose, the Arapohos.
tse'-twa-tse, tuft of hair.
u-ka'-she (ūk, earth, a'-she, a house), earth houses.
a-shu'-e-ka-pe, the Flat-heads.
a-pū-pe', to paddle, paddles.
ak-min'-e-shu'-me, the tribe that use canoes.
a-pi'-mi-she, people having beards.
ish-te-pit'-e, the Blackfeet.
kam'-ne, Blood Indians.
i-e-wat-se' (i'-e, mouth, wat-se', men), mouth men.
a-ma'-te-wat-se', iron men.
a-me-she' (a'-me, earth, a-she', a house), people who live in earth houses, Gros Ventres of Missouri, Minnitarees.
a-pan-to'-pse, Arickaras.
as-a-ka-shi, the Mandans.
bat-se'-e-a-kaé, Gray chief.
bi-rūh'-us, the Ice.
a-ra-éu'-ra-sash, the Big Robber.
au-ma-ha'-be-éi'-se, Mountain Tail.

CHAPTER XVII.

VOCABULARY OF THE AUB-SA'-RO-KE, OR CROW LANGUAGE.

A.

abdomen, be'-re-a-rēh', sickness in the abdomen.
abominable, ban-di-shi'-i-nit, horrible, abominable.
above, ma-ku'-ku-re.
ma-ko'-ko, above, upward, in the sky.
a'-ga-tsi-sa'-re, ma'-gu-gu-re, } above, over, uppermost.
absent, a-tsi'-sak, away.
i-ha', i-ha'-kūk, } away, not here.
abuse, ban'-dać, to abuse, to misuse.
accompany, bat-sah'-pak, to accompany, to go together.
ache, a-rēk', mi-ah'-u, } to feel pain.
active, in-i-she'-tuk.
added to, ah-pe'-ta, and ah-pe', or ah-pi'.
advanced, i'-se-ko, a long time, advanced in age.
afar off, a-ma-te'.
a-ma-te'-me'-mōk, to go afar off together.
affable, ba-e-de'-te, affable, courteous.
afraid, ta'-sash, ta'-sa-si-o, } to be afraid.
tsi'-tik, to be afraid, as of enemies.
after, in-sa-ku'-sa, after a while.

ago, ba-ku'-sko, long ago.

i-sko'-ka-e-shi'-e-ka-she, a long ago.

agriculture, a-ra'-ćik, tilling the ground.

aid, at-bak', to aid, to assist.

aim, mish-ćush'-mih, to take aim at anything, to take sight with a gun.

ma-is-ću'-se, to aim at anything.

alder, ma-nis'-će, white alder.

alike, ba-tsi-ćĕk', two things alike, it is alike.

all, ko'-ta, the whole.

a-a-tsi'-e-ćĕk, all around, about.

alone, tats'-yat.

ba-ma'-ta-tats-kat, to be alone, or anything standing alone.

altogether, ha-hu'-e-ka-se, and ba-kak'-she.

amorous, to'-ka-sak.

and, a-pe'.

ankle, at-sa'-ra-bi-she.

annoy, is-is-dis-će-shi'-e, to annoy one.

annually, a-me-shi'-i-she, yearly.

a-me-tsu'-se, semi-annually.

arm, ba-ro-pa'-ko-ba-re, the right arm.

ba-rah-tsi'-sko-ba-re, the left arm.

da-ća-mu'-a, hollow of the armpit.

arrow, a-nu'-e-te.

ba-sa'-e,
ma-sa'-e, } an arrow-point.

ba-sa'-e-wa-pah'-mih, to cut off an arrow-point.

ba-rak'-she, arrow-stick, wood part of an arrow.

a-no-mut'-a-i'-sha,
ma-re-wa-is'-ko, } a quiver for arrows.

ash, min-e'-pit-e, the white ash.

ask, ma-ku',
ba-ma-ku'-e, } to ask, to beg.

mi'-e-baé-u'-e-ma-ku', to ask a woman for an awl.

assist, a-rah-di'-a-hu, to assist.

autumn, ba-se'.

avoid, ti'-a-su, to avoid, to cease from doing.

awl, ba-tsu'-e, a sewing awl.

ba-tsu'-e-ta-re, an awl blade.

axe, ma-ći'-pe.

B.

back, shu'-a.

shu'-a-pu'-a, a sore on the back of a horse.

backbone, a-rŭh'-a-ro.

bad, ka-wi'.

ap-ka-wi',
ti'-a-sa, } very bad.

a-ni-ka'-wi, Bad Pass in the Rocky Mountains.

badger, tsi-pa'-mu-ne.

band, tsih-ba-wa'-ik-tse, a band of Crows.

bank, ma-pe', a bluff, bank.

bark, wa'-ak-she, the inner juicy bark of the sweet cottonwood, of which the Indians are very fond.

bead, ba-ro.

ba-ro-pu'-she, a bunch of beads.

teh'-at,
ban-teh'-at, } ash-colored beads.

ba-sah'-ba-ro, beads on moccasins.

ba-sa'-tse-ba-ro, beads on leggins.

a'-shi-she, yellow beads.

bear, dah-pit-se', a grizzly bear.

dah-pit-sŏh'-e, a hog, swine.

dah-pit-seh'-ne-she, a kind of berry, of which bears are fond.

beard, mi'-e-tsi-e.

mi'-e-tsi-e-wa-tse'-re-shu'-i-tse, to shave the beard.

mi'-e-tsi-e-wa-ku-rŭsh'-tse, to pluck out the beard.

beat, wat-wa-ru'-ŏk, to beat another.

ba-rit'-mih, to beat or strike any one.

bed, o-ma'-će, a coverlet for a bed.

before, ishb-tsi'-sa-re.

beggarly, ba-ka'-ni-tuk.

beginning, hu-ku'-se, at the beginning, formerly.

behind, bish-tsi'-sa-re, behind, in the rear.

hau'-ga-she, to be behind.

bell, ba-te-bu'-e, and ba-te-wi'-e.

ba-te-wi'-e-a-mu'-e, a bell-tongue.

bellowing, sah'-ik, the bellowing of bulls.

belt, mi-be'-ru-pde,
mi-pe-tah'-e, } my belt.

bend, a'-ra-bat'-sak, to bend.

ta-ka'-ke-we, to bend the bow.

bird, da-ka'-ka, birds in general.

da-ka'-ki-sko-ći, wild turkey, or the birds' enemy.

da-kak-shu'-ak, bluebird.

da-ka-kĭm'-po-ka-te, the bird whose tail rattles.

da-kak-ći'-a, red-headed woodpecker.

da-kak'-ba-de'-de-pe, a bat, winged mouse, lips of the vagina.

da-kak-is-ći'-tse, a bird's nest.

tsi'-naħ-da-ka'-ke, a feather.

a-ma-sha'-is-da-ka'-ko-sha, hay-bird. *Icterus.*

is-ka'-će, a yellow singing bird.

ba-hi'-ri, blackbird.

bitter, ba-e-saħ'-a-ba, a bitter root.

blanket, bi-ka-sa'-pi, and ba-sa'-she.

ba-sa'-she-hu'-a-ka-we, give me the blanket.

bi-she-pit'-e, a dark blue blanket.

bi-sho'-shi, a red blanket.

bi-shu'-e-ka-te, a light blue blanket.

blister, ba-tsiħ', blisters from friction.

blood, i'-de.

i-dĭn'-de, vein.

i'-de-e-taħ'-e, } to bleed.
i'-riħ, }

a-hu'-a-nŏm'-pe, mixed blood, a half-breed.

blue, sho'-shu-kat.

boat, ba'-źe.

ba'-źe-bi'-de, a fireboat, steamboat.

ba-źe'-aks-mŏk, the boats are crossing the river.

boil, a-tak'-e, boils on any part of the body.

bone, tu'-shi-to-ćo'-se, the white bones lying on the prairie.

hu-a-rĕk', pains in the bones.

min-ŏk'-se, large mammoth bones in the West.

du'-pe, marrow-bones.

book, ba'-re-ma-ma-na-tse-i'-she, a writing or painting.

boot, rŭsh'-te.

rŭsh'-te-a-wu'-e-mĭħ, to pull off the boots.

borrow, ba-ka'-nik, I borrow.

bowel, i-smu'-a, the internal parts of an animal.

i-smu'-a-re, any bowel disease.

bowstring, ma-naħ'-e-ka-she-aħ-e'.

box-elder, mish-pe'.

boy, ba-ko'-te, and shi-ki'-a.

ba-i-e-ka'-te, a small boy.

brave, bi-ruħ-pa'-ka-ri'-će, a warrior, a brave.

bread, baħ'-a-wa, and baħ'-a-ba, bread or flour.

baħ-a-bu'-e-ri'-e-wa-miħ, kneading dough.

baħ'-a-wa-ta-reħ', to bake bread.

break, dŭħ-shi'-she, } to break.
ta-huk', }

bu-ru-ta'-i, to break off.

breast, buħ-u'-e, and du-shu'-a.

breath, ku-ći-ri'-ak, to breathe.

breech-cloth, ba-da-in'-ća-sa-će, and ba-sa-shi'-aħ-tsi.

bridle, ba-sa-shi'-aħ-tsu'-me-te, } a bridle for a horse.
i-aħ-tse'-o-ma'-te, }

bring, o-ka'-be, to bring.

o (imp.), bring.

a-na'-ku, to bring, as a message.

broad, shŭħ'-ak, large, broad.

broken, bu-rŭħ'-shishʹ, broken, it is broken.

hu-daħ'-shi-she, a bone broken in any other way than by a bullet.

brother, mi-ke', an elder brother.

ma-na-sha', my brother-in-law.

brush, bik-ta-sa-pi-a-ku-ru-ka'-tu-a, a clothes-brush.

bud, a-si'-rik, a bud of a tree or flower.

buffalo, bi-she'.

bi-she'-a, a cow or female buffalo.

bi-sheħ'-tse, a white buffalo.

bi-she'-i'-će, buffalo tracks.

bug, pa-re-a-pu'-she, a coleopterous insect about the excrement of animals.

bullet, a-ro-pa-pa'-she'-a-hŭk, a great quantity of bullets.

burn, a-ra'-pĕħ, it burns.

hu'-pa-miħ, to burn a hole in wood with a hot iron.

burr, ba'-ke, a sticking burr, of the *Glycyrrhiza lepidota*, very annoying to travellers, by clinging to the clothes.

bush, bish-yaħ-tsi'-e.

ak-bud-e-tsi'-she, a hawthorn bush.

button, be-ro-sho'-ma-te, and o-mué'-e-ćuħ'-e.

buy, ma-e'-śće-be, to buy anything.

C.

cactus, i-ći-ri'-e-hi-e, *Opuntia.*

ba-saé', the pricking of the spines of the cactus.

calf, naħ-up-ka'-te.

call, ta'-sash, to call.

care, ba-bu-sih'-i-se, I care nothing about them.

carry, tsi'-ŏk, to carry.
ba-ći'-ak, I carry anything.

carve, i-dank'.
wa'-tats, to carve or cut.
wa-tats'-e-mih, I carve or cut.

cat, i-spi'-o-ha-she, a wild cat.
i-spi-i'-sa, a panther.

cattle, bi-she'-i-tsi'-re, domestic cattle.

cedar, ĭp-tse-tsi'-ha-he, *Juniperus*, running cedar.
min-ah'-pe, the upright cedar.
min-ah'-pe-bat-su'-e, the fruit of the cedar.
o-ma-ko'-ći-ru-e, the ground cedar.
o-ma-ko-ma'-na-ke, kinnic-kinnic.
min-ah'-pe-aź-ka'-te, Little Cedar River.

chain, i-tsi-ti'-e, a chain.

challenge, bat-si-eksh'-mi, to challenge to conflict.

charge, to-ka-ki'-shi-ke, to charge a gun.

chase, ko-mak', to give up the chase.

cheat, tsu-se-a-tu'-se, to cheat.

cheek, i-se-rūh'-e.

child, na'-ke, a child, any young animal.
ma-na'-ke, my child.
ma-na'-ke-ha-hu'-a, all my children.
i-san'-det, a step-child.

chilliness, a-pah'-te.

chop, de-puh'-e, to chop.

clap, ti'-shi, to clap the hands.

claw, i-tah'-pu-a, the claws of a bear.

clay, o'-ke.
o-ke-ći'-e, white clay.

clean, o-kin'-i-tuk, to clean.
bah-u-ru-shi'-tsh, to clean a gun.

clear, sa'-shik, and ta'-shik.
min-e-ta'-shik, clear water.
min-e-pih'-tak, clearly.

clench, bash-tih-nu-he', to clench the hand.

close, ah'-ta-kat, near at hand, close.

cloth, ba-sap'-ka-te, any kind of clothing.

cloud, a-pah'-e.

coat, mi'-ta-shi-ne.
mi'-ta-shi-ne-a-mu'-ke, a vest or undercoat.
ba-da-sho'-i-shi'-ste, chief's coat.
ba-da-i-tash'-ne-hap-ka'-te, an Indian shirt.

cold, ho-te-shi'-re, and tsi-ni'-ak.

comb, ma-ne-shu'-ge-ru-ga'-tse, a coarse comb.
mbe-ta-ni'-o, a fine comb.
ba-de-a-shu'-e-ku-ro-ha'-tse, a comb made of porcupine's tail.

come, ho, (imp.)
hu'-be, come here, in speaking to a child.
hu-ka'-be, come here, in speaking to a grown person.
hu'-e (imp.), bring it.
hu-a-ma'-ka-mih, come, let me see.
hu-a-maé', to come and sit down.
bo'-mek, come back.

comrade, min-e-pah'-e, a male comrade.

cook, ti-o'-ka-wi, ti-e'-ka-wi, } to cook.
bu-rūk', to cook or roast meat.

cord, bi-shih'-pe, a rope or cord.

corn, ho-pa'-ste, corn, or maize.
nikt-ya'-pa-pa-she', the ear of corn or wheat.
a-mu'-e, a grain or kernel of wheat or corn.

count, ma-ne-mik', to count.

courageous, ba-e'-tse-ret, spirited, brave.

crack, i-nu'-a, a crack or split.

crippled, man-dĕk'.

crooked, shi-shu'-pih, not straight.

cross, man-tu'-pah-e, used in the Catholic worship.

cruel, ba-tah'-te.

cup, be-dah'-de-a.

cure, di-a-ma-kūh'-e, to cure the sick, to make medicine for the sick.

curlew, o-haé'-ke, long-bill.

cut, wa-pash'-tsu-mih, to cut off.
bash'-ki-o, to cut off the neck.
a-sa'-tu, a-sa'-tsi, } cutting through with a knife.
a-sat-mih', I cut through with a knife.
a-me-ko'-wah-e, to cut with a knife.
a-pa-hu'-a, de-ći'-pe, } to cut with an axe.

cry, i'-bĕk, to cry.

D.

dance, bas-wat-si'-pe, a stick with numerous figures on it, used in dancing.
daughter, ma-nak-mi'-a, my daughter.
day, ma'-pe.
dead, she-ĕk'.
she-i-ŭk', dying.
ba-daħ'-te, to be in the agonies of death.
a-mu-sa-ma'-miħ, to bury or inter, as the dead.
deafness, a-kŭħ'-de-tuk.
deep, na'-mo, deep, as water or snow.
deer, ŏħ'-bish-ke.
oħ'-bish-kat, a young deer.
oħ'-a-te, an antelope.
dependent, mi-um'-i.
die, sa-ha'-kĕk, ka-ra'-she, } to die.
bash-mĕk', I will die.
difficult, ma-ma-ni'-stĕk, it is difficult, with difficulty.
dig, a-ma-eć'-ka, to dig.
dip, ab-e-stĕk', to dip, as water with a cup.
wa-shik', o-źĕk', } to dip up.
direct, min-e-shi'-o, to direct.
disease, ba-di-sa'-de, any kind of contagious disease.
ba-du-pu'-pe, cholera, spasms.
na-se-ta-a'-re, disease of the chest.
a-sha'-re, any disease of the heart.
be'-re-a-rĕħ', sickness in the abdomen.
a-raħ'-a-he-ra-be-pu'-a, disease in the neck of a horse, poll evil.
dish, ba-te'.
dismount, ba-tsi-naħ'-pi-miħ, tsi-naħ-pe', } to get off from a horse.
disposition, ma-na-sić'-ik, a good disposition.
distribute, ba-wu-mat'-miħ, to spend.
do, di-e-ba'-mik, I will do it, or I am willing to do it.
dog, bis'-ka.
bis-ka-bu'-ra, a male dog.
bis'-ke-mi'-e, a female dog.
bis'-ke-na'-ke, young dog, puppy.
bis'-ka-me-na'-paħ-u-e, dogs biting each other.
bis-ke-a'-ma-ma, a dog song.
tsiħ-pe', a prairie dog. *Arctomys.*
door, bi-di'-a, a door of a lodge.
double-tongued, mi'-shik, a hypocrite.
doubtful, ba-re-na'-se-nop, two hearts, deceitful.
dove, ma-i'-paé-ka'-she, a turtle dove.
down, bak'-se, bu-a-ka-re', } below, as down the river.
draw, tŭħ'-pŭk, to draw down anything.
drink, is-mi'-mik, to drink.
ish-i' (imp.), drink.
ma'-ku-si-a, to drink out.
ku-ta-ki-shi' (imp.), take and drink.
ka'-ku-tse, to be drunk.
drop, he, to drop anything.
drum, bi-raħ'-e.
duck, mi-haħ'-e.
dung, na-tse'-re, the fresh excrement of a buffalo.
dusty, u'-ke-shik, to be dusty.
dry, ka-ru'-tsiħ.
ta-shi'-tsiħ, to dry anything.

E.

each, shi'-she, each one, every.
eagle, da-a-ka'-ħa, war-eagle.
ear-ring, maħ-pa-ma'-na, miħ-pa'-e-te, } ornaments.
early, tsi-na'-ki-sa, early in the morning.
earth, a-me-ko'-ta, the whole earth, the world.
a-ma-pi'-ni-e, rich earth, a fertile soil.
a-me'-ħa-tsi-e, earthquakes, explosions in the mountains.
a'-ma-she, earth houses, like those of the Minnitarees.
easily, ba-i-tu'-ka.
eat, tu'-shik, ti-ru'-shik, } to eat.
ba-bu'-she, I eat.
egg, i-ke-ka'-te.
elbow, mish-baħ-e', and is-pa'-ba.
eloquent, ba-i-di'-tuk.
embroider, bam-pash'-tsik, to garnish or embroider.
empty, ham-nets'.
enemy, bas-ko-ći', an enemy at home, in camp.
enjoy, ba-si'-tse-wak, to be glad, to enjoy, to take pleasure.

enough, ka-ra-ha'-mik, ka-ra-ko'-mik, ka-ra-ko'-mi-o, } enough; I am done,—usually said when a speech is finished.

exchange, bat-ba'-ke-re, in exchange.

exist, ma-ka'-ku, to live, to exist.

eye, is'-te.

is-te-i'-e, mish-ti'-e, } eyebrows.

is-tah'-pe, eyelids.

is-te'-a-re, sore eyes.

is'-te-wa'-tsi-bah-u'-e-mih, to rub the eyes.

is-te'-pi-ŏk, to have the smoke come into the eyes.

is'-te-o'-ma-te, iron for the eyes, spectacles.

is-te-re'-de, to be blind.

is-ta'-re-tuk, blindness.

F.

face, i'-se, ni'-se, ni-shi'-se.

ni'-se-bi'-shi-kat, a red face.

ni'-se-hi-ri-shi'-tse, to wash the face.

fall, ta-ni'-o, to fall down.

farther, na'-ue.

fat, shi-me'.

ta-ra', the fatty portions of an animal.

father, ah-e'.

mi-nup'-he, my father.

feather, ma-ĕp'-ha-ha, a quill or feather.

ma-ĕp'-ha-ha-ĭpsh, the tail feather.

feel, bu-ru-shi'-ćik, to feel, feeling.

find, a-mo-nup'-ik, to find anything.

fire, bi'-de.

bi'-de-ka'-te, a small fire, a candle.

a-rah'-i-a, to light, as a candle or a fire.

bi'-de-go'-hi-a, the fire blazes up.

bi'-de-a-ra'-peh, the fire burns.

bi-ra'-de, the fireplace.

bi'-di-tu'-a, fire-wood.

bi'-di-tak, matches, friction.

a'-će-bi-de, a fire-horse, locomotive, furnace.

fish, bu'-a.

bu-a-na'-ka, all kinds of small fishes.

bu-a-hah'-a, spotted fish, trout.

bu-e-du'-sha, the blue heron, fish-eater. *Ardea herodias.*

bu-e-ku-ku'-e, fish-hook.

i-min-deh'-o-me, the fins of a fish.

float, da-ka-pe', to float.

flower, ba-ha-bu'-e, and ŏm'-pe.

fly, ma-na-me', to fly.

i-nu'-shu-shik, to fly in pieces.

ma-pu'-e-te, a fly, insect.

ma-pu'-e-ćo'-se, the common house-fly.

min'-e-te-i'-she, a butterfly.

foam, po'-he.

foe, is-ma-hi'-he, all foes.

foolish, ma-ma-nah'-e, a foolish man, one with no sense.

foot, ba-tse', and ić-e-ta'-re.

ba-tsi-ni'-će, foot-racing.

it-mu'-a, sole of the foot.

forehead, mi-e-hi'-e.

forever, ko-će-te'.

fork, a-ra-sah'-ta, and ba-ću'-e.

ba-ću'-e-sa-te-ka'-te, a small fork.

forwards, i-se'-ko.

freeze, a-ka-pe', it is freezing.

a-ka-pak', it is frozen.

mi-a-pak', to be cold, to freeze.

friend, a-mats'-ćik, and min-e-ba'-a-tse.

ma-na'-ke, my friend.

hin-a-ke', my friend,—used in addressing a person.

ma-na-se', my heart, my friend,—a term of endearment in social life.

frighten, ah-pa-ret', to terrify.

frog, sa'-ke.

sa-ka'-re-ću-ka'-re, a large toad.

fruit, ma'-na-pa-pa, berries.

ma-nit-nauk', to bring berries or fruit.

ma-nit-na'-kŭk, to gather fruit.

o-źik', ripe fruit.

o-źi'-se, green fruit.

ma-ne-shi'-she, bullberries.

ma-ne-shi'-she-ba'-ra-da-ru'-a, to beat the bullberries off the bush.

ma-na-ka'-she, service-berry bush.

bi-tse'-tih-te, a black edible berry growing on the high mountains.

bish-kat-mu'-e, a red berry, species not known.
bi-tash-tse', white berries.
ba-e-saḣ'-pit-e, black fruit, a kind of service-berry.
ba-e-saḣ'-ĕs-tse, a small, edible fruit, growing in clusters.
ba-dup'-i, a palatable dish formed of cherries and meat mixed.
ba'-tsu-a, small cherries. *Cerasus Virginianus.*
ba'-tsu-a-ra-tsi-tu'-e, to beat the cherries off of the bushes.
ba'-tsu-a-mu'-ni-te, black haws.
i-sko'-shi-ke, a kind of red berry.
iḣt-ye-pi'-ti-eḣt, red berries growing on the Rocky Mountains.
hŭm'-ba-ta-te, a species of blackberry.
ka-pud'-i-i-ste, the whortle-berry.
i'-aḣ-she-di-a-wa'-me-nak'-miḣ, to make a soup or stew of meat and berries.

G.

gall, a-pi-tsu'-a.
gallop, a-pash'-kuḣ-gi-a-hu'-i-tse, galloping, as a horse.
ba-ge-rŭsh'-i-mĕḣ, galloping on horseback.
gamble, ba-de'-aḣ'-pe-dik, to gamble.
game, ma-no'-pe-de, a favorite game with the women, in which plum-pits are used.
aḣ-o'-a-da, to hide the dish,—a favorite game with all.
a-ba-tsink'-i-sha, a game somewhat like billiards.
gather, baé-ki-o'-kik, to gather, to collect.
get, bin-e-éi'-nĕk, to get up, as from a bed.
nĕs-ha'-ra (imp.), get out.
ba-tsi-nĕk', I got up.
girl, ma-naé-ka'-te, a little girl.
give, be'-miḣ, to give, as a present.
ba-ru'-sa-ŭk, a present, a gift.
ha-ho'-ka-shi'-na, to give thanks to the sun for any favor.
tu'-sauk, to give up anything.
glass, ba-de'-e-tsi-éi'-ke, a looking-glass, mirror.
glue, ba-i-éo'-sa.
go, a-sa'-nup, } to go.
na'-ma-niḣ, }
dĕk (imp.), go.
mi'-ma-miḣ, to go in.
bin'-a-be-wa'-miḣ, to go across the river.
ka-me'-mŏk, to go together.
kan-tu'-i-tse-nŏk-tsi-na'-ne, to pack up and go on a journey.
na'-ne-kan-tĕk', to go farther.
tu'-ḣi-nan, to go to the war.
bu-re-shik', I let it go.
hi-ris-pa'-riḣ, I am going outside, or out of doors, in answer to the question: "Where are you going?"
naḣ'-a-ra (imp.), go away.
ko-tu-éeḣ'-pa-da (imp.), go with one only.
aḣ'-pa-da (imp.), go with them.
a-ma'-su, to descend, to go down.
goitre, ap-hi'-she.
good, it'-sik, it'-siḣ.
ko-tué'-it-sik, he alone is good.
goose, mi'-ne, and mi'-na.
grass, bik-te', grass of any kind, generic term.
bik-ta'-kat, short, low grass.
bik-ti-a'-shu-a, the grass growing.
bik-ti-a'-sa-ti, edible roots of plant like a carrot.
bat-su'-a-te, sweet-smelling grass.
aḣ-pa-naḣ'-e-sip-siḣ-she', horsetail grass. *Equisetum.*
pu-pa'-e, dry grass, hay.
naḣ-pit'-e, black grasshopper, a cricket.
mi-shu'-ke, common grasshopper.
great, bat-saé', strong, powerful.
i-se', } great, large.
i-sa', }
green, shu'-e-kat.
ground, a-mi'-a-mo-na, in the ground.
grow, ba-a-pi'-ni, anything that is growing.
a-pa'-na, to grow.
gum, i-u'-she, gums of the teeth.
gun, be-rup'-tse-ma-naḣ'-e.
ma-naḣ'-i-she, a gun-cover.
ma-i'-a, a gun-flint.
bash-taḣ'-e-ma'-e, percussion caps.

H.

habit, is-e-ta'-be, custom, habit.
is-e-ta'-be-it'-sik, good habits.

is-e-ta'-be-ka-wi', bad habits.

hail, ma-ka-pe'.

hair, mi'-shi-e, my hair.

mit-su'-a-nu'-mi-ne, a tuft of hair, scalp-lock on the back of the head.

nu'-mi-ne, a tuft or lock.

mih-e'-a-nu-mi'-ne, tuft or lock of hair on the forehead.

hallo, u-ka-he'! an exclamation.

ha-hi'-a! hallo there! to call to one at a distance.

hand, ba-sku'-re, and bash'-tse.

bash'-tse-a'-ko, the upper part of the hand.

bash'-tse-mu'-e, the hollow or inside of the hand.

mash'-tse, my hand.

tēsh'-tse, thy hand.

tēsh'-tse-pah-u-ru-shi'-mih, to wipe the hands on anything.

bas-mi-tsu'-a, a wart on the hand.

hang, i'-shi-e-wa'-mih, to hang up.

hard, ba-ra-hip'-sat, indurated.

hat, ba-da-e'-am-pe', a hat or bonnet.

mit-yūh-pe', a cap.

hate, mi-du'-pi-uk, they hate me.

mi-du'-shi-ći'-se, they care nothing for me.

hawk, a-pi-te', seems to be a generic term of that class of birds.

be'-rets, a kind of hawk.

be-rets-ge-na-hi'-o, a branch of Wind River.

is-a-ći'-sa, a small hawk.

is-e-ke-ki'-she, a mosquito-hawk.

head, a'-shu.

a-shu'-a-ćo-se, white skull, as of a buffalo, long exposed on the ground.

a-skep'-ka-wi, a bad head, a Dutchman.

hear, mi'-ka-kūk, to hear.

heart, na'-se.

na'-se-it'-si-ka, a good heart.

nas-ka-wi', a bad heart.

na'-se-kōsh'-te-kat, little heart, despondent, faint-hearted.

na-se-hi-ni'-a, undoubted, firm, to be depended upon.

na'-se-nōp, uncertain, deceitful, two hearts.

heavy, tash-ta-tsip'.

herd, man-ći-ćūh'-e, a herd or drove.

hexagon, a-ka'-mak-a-tak, six-cornered.

hill, shi-ća'.

shi-ća'-kē-da, up a hill.

shić-bu-uk'-is-a, down a hill.

i-she', the height of a hill.

hin'-e-sha-ke'-ma-kūk, at the foot of a hill.

hold, ta'-hash, to hold anything, as a book.

bu-ru-ba'-shik (imp.), hold on.

hole, ha-hi'-e-pak, to make a hole in the ground.

a-wat'-sit-mi, to look through a hole.

horn, aź-ka-ru'-će.

aź-i'-si-a-de, a horn spoon.

horse, it-si'-re.

it-si'-re-tsi-ri'-tu-a, to drive the horses.

it-si'-re-i-ne-ka'-su-a, picket stakes for horses.

it-si'-re-tsi'-sho, horsehair.

tse'-shi-shi-a, a horse-blanket, or other cover.

i-shu'-e, the mane of a horse.

it-si'-ri-ka-she, elk, or real horse.

it-si'-ri-ka-she-ru'-pa, male elk.

it-si'-ri-kash-bi-shi'-a, female elk.

it-si'-ri-ka-nak', to become frightened and run away, as a horse.

it-si'-ri-na'-ka, a colt.

it-si'-ri-ak-se'-re-te, a free or wild horse.

it-si'-ri-ma-ni-tum'-a-kat, a gentle horse.

it-si'-ri-i-ni'-she-tuk, an active horse.

it-si'-ri-i-tah-pu'-e, the hoof of a horse.

it-si'-ri-mi-ne-shi'-te, to water the horse.

it-si'-ri-man-dēk', a crippled horse.

it-si'-ri-ha-tsi-ni'-će, horse-racing.

hospitable, ba-ke-tuk'.

ba-tse-ba-ke'-tuk, a hospitable man.

hot, ta-meh'.

house, a-she'.

a-she'-a-ke'-da, on the top of the house.

how do you do, ba-tsa'-bah-a'-pe, "how do you do?" literally, "we find each other."

hungry, na-ni'-she, to be hungry.

hunt, ba-će-tsi'-mik, I hunt for anything.

hurt, i-ah'-ōk, to hurt or injure.

I.

ice, bi-rūh'-e.

ignorance, ma-nah'-e, ignorance, simplicity.

ma-nah'-at, ignorant, simple.

ma-nah'-tuk, I do not know.

ill-natured, in-i-shi'-pĭk, badly disposed.

imitate, ka-re-kŏt', to imitate.

increasing, ah-pa-tak'.

independent, ba-du'-she-tsi'-a.

Indian, bi-ruh-pa'-ka-ra.

indigo, mi-shu-ah'-shu-pit'-e.

mi-shu-ah', bluestone, sulphate of copper.

industrious, i-sam'-bat-sa, an industrious man.

influential, i-sa'-ke-ka-te, large, influential, a great man.

innocent, ma-ni-tum'-e-ka-te, good-natured.

inside, ko'-rak-mo, the inside of anything.

intelligent, bat-si'-tah.

iron, o'-ma-te, any kind of iron or metal, &c.

o'-ma-te-a-pi'-a, a medal, literally, iron on the neck.

o'-mat-shi-re, yellow iron, brass.

o'-ma-ći-di'-e, the iron that rattles.

i-mah'-o-pi'-a, a kind of iron wire.

island, min-e-pi'-źe.

J.

jawbone, du-de-pe'.

jump, a-na-push'-a-ma-ta, where the buffalo jump a great distance.

K.

kettle, bi-rah'-e, a kettle, or kettle drum.

bi-rah'-a-te, a small kettle.

bi-rah'-te-tu'-e, to beat the drum or kettle.

bi-rah'-tsi-e, a white kettle.

bi-rah'-i-tsi-ti'-e, the chain on the kettle.

bi-rah'-e-ci'-nu, a tripod, from which a kettle is suspended.

bi-rah'-e-i-ćū'-sa-tse, a kettle cover.

bi-rah'-e-i'-de, the bail or handle of a kettle or pail.

bi-rah'-e-ra'-tsi-ka-tse, the seam on the side of a kettle.

bi-rah'-e-a-pe', the ears to which the handle of a kettle is attached.

bi-rah'-e-i-tsi'-she, the bottom of a pail.

kill, ha'-mi-o, to kill.

kiss, mis-bash'-tse, a kiss.

mis-bash-tse'-mih, to kiss any one.

knee, i-shu'-de, and i-shu'-she.

ba-shu'-she, my knee.

di-shu'-she, thy knee.

knife, mit-si'-e.

mit-si'-e-nŏp'-kat, a pair of scissors, two knives.

mit-si'-e-bat-si-shik', to sharpen a knife.

mit-si'-e-it-she', to sharpen any edged tool.

mit-si'-e-tsi-re-tsi'-she, a pocket-knife, one that opens and shuts.

mit-si'-she, knife-scabbard.

mit-si-hin'-ŏk, here is a knife.

mits-ka-hat'-ska, long knife, an American.

knock, mi-ta-me'-a-mit-nak, to knock, or strike.

wa-pah'-mih, to knock anything loose.

L.

lame, a-nah'-uk.

land, a-me', a-re', } both words used.

large, i-sa'.

i-sa-nić'-kat, rather large.

i-sa-e-shĕk', still larger.

i-sa-bat-saé', very large.

lariat, i-ah-će', and i-nah-tu'-e.

last, a-ha'-ka, at last, last.

laughing, ba-rūk', we are laughing.

lay, ha-pik', to lay down anything.

lazy, i'-shi-tuk, indolent, lazy, careless.

i'-shi-tŭk, a lazy fellow.

ba-am-be'-ret, to do nothing, to be lazy.

lead, is-ba-se', to lead or conduct.

lead, i-e'-re-pe-pu'-she, a mineral.

leaf, a'-pe.

a-pe'-ta-ni'-o, leaves falling from the trees, autumn.

lean, mi-wah-pūk'-mih, to lean on another.

mi-sak'-spah-e, to lean on any one, used in social intercourse.

leg, mi-hu'-re.

mi-hu'-re-a-ka'-ta-wa-mih', to put the legs into another's lap.

leggins, i'-shi-she, } leggins or pants.
ho-će', }

ho-će'-e-a-she', garnishing for leggins.

lengthwise, baé'-ku-ko-ni'-a.

lie, bash-tsit'-mih, to lie on anything, as a bed.

ho-pik', to lie down.

hu-pa'-re (imp.), lie down.

da-ka'-pik, lying down on any place.

ba-hŏp'-nik, I will lie down.

lift, du-e', to raise or lift up.

ba-ru-e', I lift up.

light, tah-pih'-at, light, not heavy.

lightning, shi-re-sho'-re.

ka-ni'-tsi-e, to lighten, as just before a storm.

lignite, ŏm-bi-dah'-i-tah-pu'-a, "stone coal."

lips, i-e-ah'-pe.

listen, hin-e', look here! say! listen!—used to call attention.

little, i-e-ka'-shi-at, little, applied to any child.

live, in-ĕk', to live.

in-e', alive.

in-e-shi'-uk, long life.

hi-ri-tsi'-sa-re, to be or to live close by or near.

lizard, ma-ka'-pe (species unknown).

mi-shu-ka'-re, a ground lizard.

lodge, a-she', a tent or lodge.

a-she'-mo-na, inside of a lodge.

ash-kum'-u-a, inside of a house.

a-she'-ih-i-mo'-a, the tent is full of persons.

a-she'-kan-tuk'-puk, to break down the lodge.

ash-it-sik', a good house.

bi'-ro-pe-ash'-u-a, a beaver lodge.

a-she'-e-kat'-kat, a red tent or lodge.

ash-ah'-tsik, a white tent or lodge.

a-she'-ap'-ka-wi, a very bad lodge.

bik-ta'-she, grass lodge, a house built of grass.

is-ki-she'-pu-a, rotten medicine lodge (Clarke's Fork).

bish-kish'-e, to place buffalo-meat in a lodge.

ba'-tsi-e, } lodge-poles.
i-e'-ni-e, }

ba'-tsi-e-a-nŭk', to bring the lodge-poles.

ba'-tsi-a'-źe, } Pine Wood Creek, or Pole Creek.
i-e'-ni-e-a'-źe, }

ma-su'-a, } to live in a tent or lodge.
ih-a-mo'-a-re, }

is-miź'-pe-re, a lodge-skin that has been used.

look, a! look here!

ba-te-ek'-yak, he is looking at us.

aé-kah'-a-ka-ba, go and look out.

lose, ko'-re-sak, to lose anything.

louse, mbe.

love, a-ma-tsi'-she, } to love.
in-ći'-sa-kits, }

lungs, da-ho', lungs or lights.

M.

magpie, ĭm-pi'-a-kat.

make, wah-sa'-ko, } to make anything.
ti'-a-wak, }

ié-ĕk', to make up.

male, ba-a-sa'-ne, the male of any animal.

mallet, mi-paé'-ke, a stone mallet, used for driving down lodge-pins.

man, bat-se', and wat-si'.

bat-se'-tse, a chief or warrior.

bat-se'-it-sik, a good man.

is-ah'-a-she, a young man.

wah-pĕk', medicine-men.

ma-ste-shi'-re, yellow eyes, a white man.

ma-ste-shi'-re-ship-it'-e, a black man, a negro.

ma-ste-shi'-re-is-de-ka'-ke, white man's birds, domestic fowls.

bi-ruh'-pa-ke, a human being, person, a man, the people.

ak-ba-di'-o, a doctor or medicine-man.

manœuvre, wa-tsi'-ek-tsŭk, to drill.

marrow, tu'-pe.

marsh, ma-ha'-shi-pi-e'.

meat, i-ru'-ke, any kind of meat.

i-rŭh'-pu-a, stinking meat.

i-ru'-ka-ha-pih, the meat falls down.

i-ru'-ke-bu-e-bŭsh'-mik, to bring meat and eat.
is-du'-she-she, fresh meat.
ma'-ni-she, dried meat.
hŭk'-pi-e, *bouillon*, the liquor after boiling meat.
meet, a-ni-ch'-teh, to meet another.
melt, ba'-kats, to melt.
ba-ka'-ćik, to melt, as ice.
memory, a-wats'-kap-ma, to commit to memory.
mend, ić-e-ha-kŭk, to mend.
middle, ku'-a-de, in the middle.
milk, at-si-mi'-na.
mine, bas, (possessive pronoun.)
bas-mit-si'-e, my knife.
bas-mit-si'-e-hu'-e, give me my knife.
bi-be', it is mine.
mint, shu-shu'-e, a kind of mint, *Mentha*.
shu-shu'-e-re-ću'-ku-re, horse-mint, balm.
miss, ba-ru-sak', to miss the mark in shooting.
mistake, ka-bi'-ŭk, to make a mistake.
mix, wa-re-ba'-o, to mix.
moccasin, ba-sa-pe', and ba-sah-pe'.
ba-sa-pe'-bu-retk, moccasins torn or broken.
ba-sah'-pa-ke, moccasin strings.
hŏmp-ta'-re, shoes or moccasins.
hŏm-pi-she-dah'-pe, white man's shoes.
moose, o-pis'-pi, seen by the Crows in the North.
mortification, a-no-mut-si'-rus-tse, mortification in disease.
mosquito, a-pa'-ka.
mother, ba-sah'-u-e.
ba-sah-'e, my mother.
bu-sha', my mother in law.
mountain, a-ma-ha'-be.
a-ma-ba'-ba-i-a-ka'-te, little mountain.
mourn, mi-ma'-tse-shi-a'-te, to mourn, to be in mourning.
ba-ta'-ŏk, mourning.
mouse, i-su'-e-ka-te, a kind of field-mouse.
mouth, a-ma-tsi'-e, the mouth of a stream.
move, ah-a', to move away, from one place to another.
dŏs-ha' (imp.), move up close.
much, a-hŭk, a "heap," a great deal.
a-ho'-i-shŏk, more, very much.
na'-nih, how much?
mud, shi-pi'-e.
shi-pi'-e-de-sa'-ćik, to stick in the mud.
mule, ah-pi-se'.
mystery, bah-pa, medicine or mystery.

N.

nail, is-mah'-pe, the finger nail.
bas-mah'-pe, my finger nail.
it-ah'-pu-a, toe and finger nails, the claws of any animal.
it-ah'-pu-a-shi'-tik, a claw or nail when broken off.
neck, ma'-a-pe.
ma-a'-pi-e, a necklace of beads.
ba-de'-e-ah-pu'-a-te, a necklace of bears' claws.
needle, mit-se'-wat-su'-a, a sewing needle.
neither, ma-i-he', neither, something else.
nest, ish-tsi'-se, a nest of any kind.
news, ko-te'-ba-re-ta'-re, ill news, bad news.
a-ni-tsi'-me-bi'-she, I have received the news.
night, o'-tsi-ek.
nipple, a'-at-se, teat or nipple.
no, ba-ret'.
a-ra-di'-a-wa-sa, same as ba-ret'.
ba-re-ta'-re, not at all.
ba-re-ta'-re-ba-re-ta'-re, no, never can be.
a-rĭn-det', for no purpose.
nose, ba-pe'.
nothing, ham-net', nothing, there is none.
now, hin-e-ka', hin-ak'-ek, } at this time.
hin-a-ka'-će, not long ago.

O.

object, ka-ni-ni'-a-tek, a thing, anything, an object.
often, a-hŏn'-ha, many times.
old, ba-ha-di'-a.
ka-ra-shi'-e, a long time, advanced age.
shi'-a-kat, old, of great age.
is-a'-ka-kat, an old man.
ornament, o'-ma-te-pa-pash'-ka-te, small, round, brass ornaments.
map-ma'-she, a ring hanging from the neck, as an ornament.

otter, ba-huh'-te.

out, a-ma-ne'-na, out of doors.

oval, tsi-tsih'-ih-ats'-hi-kat, oval, like an egg.

over, i-tsu'-sa.

owl, po-pa'-te, owls in general.

own, bin'-bauk, to own anything.

P.

paint, ma-ma-ma-na'-tūk, to paint.
ma-ma-na'-će, to write.
ma-ma-ne'-će, painting or picture writing.
mish-tsi-she-wa'-mih, to paint oneself.

pan, i-ma-mi-ni'-su-a, a frying-pan.

paper, ma-na'-ma-na'-tse.

part, ha-ka-kat', any part.

pass, bak'-mih, to pass the pipe.

patella, a-ho'-ha, kneepan.

paw, tsi-ki-ak', tsi-ki-e', } to paw the earth, as horses.

peace, mash-tse'-she.
mash-tse'-she-tsi'-wa-mih, to make peace.
mi-a-ah'-pe, a peace with nations.

pelvis, is-i-shu'-re.

pencil, i'-ma-ma-na-tse.

people, aub-sa'-ro-ke, "the people," the Crow nation.

peppermint, tsu'-shu-a.

perspire, mi-ta'-meh, i'-ūs, } to sweat or perspire.
i-ah-pi'-se, perspiration.

pheasant, sīts'-ke-se, the cock of the plains.
sits'-ke-ta-re, prairie chicken.
sits'-ke-īm-po-hah-e, mountain pheasant.

pick, du'-ća, to pick up anything.
bi-wah-tse'-ba-wūsh-yu'-mih, to pick the teeth.
bu-ru'-će, I picked it up.

pinch, bu-ru-tsi'-ap-mih, to pinch.

pine, ha-rūh'-a-ne-mik, to pine away.
bat'-si, a pine tree.
bat'-si-ūh-pe, pine cones.

pipe, īmp-tse'-ush, se-īp'-tse, īp'-tse.
īp'-tse-ri-su'-a, the pipe dance.
a-wa'-ko, to take hold of the pipe near the bowl.
a-wa'-ko-pa'-ko, to take the pipe near the stem.
ba-kash'-mih, to place the pipe in another's hands with some force when done smoking.
bat'-si-ba-shi'-tsih, to stir up the contents of the pipe with a stick.
a-mu'-e, the oil which accumulates in a pipe when smoking.

pistol, ma-nah'-e-po'-me-ka-te.

plant, a-mu'-o-bu-ru-shi'-mih, ma'-e-me-mu'-se, } to put anything in the earth, to plant.
ba-ka'-i-sa-tse, thistle plants.
ma-ōm'-pe-hi'-she, a large thistle.
ma-o-pe'-shi-re, a gummy plant, with yellow flowers.
i-ha', pomme blanche, prairie turnip. *Psoralea esculenta.* Abundant throughout the Western country, and most useful to the Indian as an article of food.
i'-re, a sweet-smelling root like parsnip.
īmp-će'-ća-ha'-he, a species of *Chenopodium.*

play, ma-nah'-shik, to play.

pleased, me'-ka-matsh, I am pleased.

plum, ma-nūh-pe'. *Prunus Virginiana.*
ma-na-pi'-e, plum bush.
ma-na-pu'-a. *Cerasus.*

pocket, ba-ro'-she, and ba-re'-she.

point, a-wa'-mi-e-mōk, to point out, to direct attention.
a-me'-tsi-re-tsi'-she, a point of land between two streams.

polecat, ho-a-će'.

poor, wa-tsūsh'-yat.

porcupine, a-pa'-ni.
a-pa'-ni-ći'-se, the tail of a porcupine.
a-pa'-ni-aź-i'-sa, Great Porcupine Creek.
a-pa'-ni-aź'-i-e-ka'-te, Little Porcupine Creek.

powder, bi-rup'-tse.
bi-rup-tsaź'-e, Powder River.

pretty, it'-se-kat, pretty, handsome.
it-se'-i-shōk, quite pretty, more handsome.
its-kat'-saé, very pretty, or prettiest.

prime, a-kōh-bi-rup'-tse, to prime a gun with powder.

probable, ko-te'-ba-sak, probably it is so; there is no reason to dispute it.
ko-ta-re-tse', it is probable.

sho′-tuk-ko′-tuk, it may or may not be.

pull, bu-ru-tsi′-miħ, to pull out.

to′-sha, to pull on anything.

push, ba-tsi′-ne-miħ, to push away.

put, a-waħ′-ska-miħ, to put on, as moccasins.

tas′-ke, to put in, as in a vessel.

do′-sha, to put on.

Q.

quantity, a-ho′-bat-saé′, an enormous quantity.

a-haé′-ka-te, considerable, a moderate supply.

kash′-te, ko′-ste-kat, } a little or small quantity.

tso-na′-ne, a little.

quick, sus-kat′, soon, quick.

R.

rain, ha-rak′.

ha-rĕk′, it rains.

raise, wa-paħ-shi′-miħ, to raise up.

ramrod, bash-taħ-e-wa-ku′-te, the ramrod of a gun.

raven, pa-re-éi′.

read, ma-ma-ma-nat′-miħ, to read, as a book.

rectum, u-shi′-a, the rectum of any animal.

red, bi′-shi-kat, red, scarlet, as a red blanket.

hi-it′-si-ka-te, light red, rose color.

i-a-pe′-pa-ne-a′-she, the cochineal insect, used for coloring the quills of the porcupine scarlet, an important article of trade among the Western Indians.

remain, a-ma′-tuk, to stay, to remain.

bat-ba-ba-tsi′-mŭk, to remain in one place against an enemy, as Crows against Black-feet.

report, saħ′-e-wa-tsi′, the report of a gun.

reserved, be-te-di′-se, shy.

revengeful, ba-tuħ′-te.

rib, du′-sa.

rice, bi-she′-tsiħ.

rich, ba-i′-ée.

ride, a-ki′-na, to ride.

ka-ru′-she-i-ru′-kash, to ride a horse on a gallop.

a-ra′-ki-ni, a-wa′-ki-ni, } to ride on horseback.

i-na-mi′-pet-bi-she′-ri-ŭk, three persons riding out together to hunt buffalo.

ba-se′, to ride ahead of another on horseback.

ha′-kak, to ride behind another person.

bu-she-pa′-tsiħ, bu-she-ba′-miħ, } to be made sore from riding on horseback.

bat-saħ′-pi-ro, riding side by side together.

ring, bas-tsa′-sa-shi, a ring, circle.

ta-bu′-e, to ring, as a bell.

rip, a-su′-tuk, to rip.

rise, tsi-na′-ke, to rise up.

tsi-na′-ke-ma′-tsiħ (imp.), rise up and sit down.

tsi-ne′ (imp.), rise up, get up.

a-sik′, rising, as the sun.

river, aź-e′.

aź-ka′-te, a creek, or small river.

aź-kat′-it-se, Good Creek.

aź-e-ni′-tsi-a, Stinking River, a branch of the Big-horn.

aź-kat′-bak-aħ′-pa, two parallel creeks.

aź-i′-sa, Great River, Missouri.

kan-tu′-se, the source of a river.

robe, ba-sa′-she, buffalo-skin with the hair on, a robe.

rock, ma-shi′-pit-e, a black rock.

ma-pu′-e, Rocky River.

ma-pu′-e-ma-nat-bi′-she, painted rock.

roll, iħ-tsa′-miħ-tsiħ, to roll, as horses.

bi-ra′-miħ-tsa-miħ, to roll on the ground.

a-me-gipé′, rolling land, wave-lines.

rope, i′-eħ-i-e, a rope made of buffalo-skin.

ma′-she-i-aħ′-tse, the rope used for cordelling or towing a boat.

rose-bud, bits-ki-pe′.

round, ba-pa′-she, round, circular.

run, bat-si′-ri-tuk, to run a race.

ho-shik′, it runs, or anything runs.

a-mo-a′-te, running water.

S.

saddle, a-na-gu-ruħ-tse′, to saddle, as a horse.

a-na′-gu-ru-shi′-be, to take the saddle off, as from a horse.

a-na-me′-ma-ga′-tsi-e, to cover over the saddle.

a-na′-gu-ruh′-pi-wah′-sa-ko, to make a saddle-cover.

wa-tsa′-ne-shi′-she, saddle stirrups.

sage, i′-sats-ho-me, a species of *Artemisia*.

i′-sats-ho-me-ha′-kūk. *Artemisia trifida*.

i′-sats-ho-me-i-ni′-tsi-tse, a kind of sage, used as a tea.

saliva, i-mi-ne′.

sash, ba-da-e′-pa-ta′-će, a belt or sash.

satisfied, mih-pa-shik′, to be satisfied.

saw, i-ma′-ne-pus′-ku, a hand-saw.

i-ma′-ne-sa′-će, a large saw.

scalp, mi-ne′.

a-ću′-ru-tu′-e, to take a scalp.

scatter, a-e-ća′-a-da′-ća, to scatter.

scrape, a-ka-ki′-ra, to file, to scrape.

bi-sa′-tse, steel edge, or scraper.

scratch, tap′-hi-e, bats-ha′-mih, } to scratch.

pa-ha′-će, a scratch.

scream, i-mi′-shŏk, to scream.

screw, mu′-me-mih.

see, a-ma′-ke, to see.

a-ma-ka′-muk, he will see.

send, de-bat′-sĕk, to send anything.

a-nu′-ak, to send, as a message.

sensible, ba-ra′-tsi, good sense.

separate, wa-tsip′-mih, to separate the flesh from a skin.

set, o-mać′, to set anything down.

i′-mah-pik, the setting sun.

sew, inh′-ać, to sew.

ba-inh′-ać, I sew, as on cloth.

bat′-si-ka-tsih, to sew buttons or beads on anything.

shade, a-rat′-si-e, a shade or umbrella.

shake, ta-wu′-e, to shake or ring the bells.

bat-si′-u-bi-ri′-u-mih, to shake the dust from a blanket.

shame, min-o-shi′-ćik.

shave, ba-sak′-she-ti′-a-wak, to cut or shave an arrow.

shell, bi-sho′-će, ma-ka′-ki-e, } mussel-shells. *Unio.*

ba′-she-ri′-e-ka-te, small shells.

ba-hah′-e, "the shell that glistens," a shell obtained in California, and sold to the Indians by the traders for ornaments, a *Chama.*

ba-tu-wu′-e-pa-pa′-she, small shells, used as ornaments. *Dentalium.*

sheep, i-sah-pu′-e-ta-tse, mountain sheep. *Ovis montana.*

i-sah-pu′-e-ta-tse-a′-źe, the Big-horn River.

shield, mi-na′-tse.

shoot, sah′-e, to shoot one another.

ba-pe′-mih, to shoot down.

bi-bah′-pik, I shot it.

a-me′-to-ah′-pik, to shoot an object at a great distance.

bat-bat′-si-uk, to shoot at a man in battle.

bi-rup-si′-she, a shot-pouch.

shore, am-ni′-e.

short, bu′-meh-at.

shoulder, ba-rash′-pe, and ish-u′-re.

ah′-tse, suspenders, shoulder-straps.

a-pe-i-sūh′-e, a shirt-collar.

shout, te′-wa-tsi-mih′, to shout.

shut, bi-ri′-e-ći (imp.), shut the door.

sick, ba-ku′-pak, sickly.

wa-kūh′-pa, to be sick.

mi-ba-ku′-pak, I am sick.

side, ak-tus′-ko, on this side.

a′-ka-ko, ak-tsi′-se, a′-kūs, } on the other side.

a-ka′-re, on the opposite side.

ak′-tus-ko-ūm-pa′-se, on this side of the river.

sight, a-sŏk′, in sight.

a-si′-sa, out of sight.

i-ma′-mih-tsu′-ste, the sights on a gun.

sinew, ba-tsu′-a, and a-ra-tsi′-se.

sing, ma-nah′-u-a, to sing.

a-kik′, to sing, as a bird.

ma-nah′-ik, singing.

sink, a-muh′-ak, to sink.

sister, a-ku′-pe, brothers and sisters.

mu-o′-i-sap, my sister-in-law.

sit, a-mat′-sih, to sit down.

wat′-sa-wah-a-mat′-mo-uk, sitting together.

skin, ba-hu′-a, the cuticle or skin of a person.

ba-ra-ku'-a, } a buffalo-skin stretched on the ground to dry.
ba-ra-ka'-su-a, }

ba-a-ta'-tse, any kind of a skin, as beaver, &c.

ash-ti'-shi-re, a grained skin.

sky, a-mah'-e, sky, or heaven.

a-mah'-a-ra-da, in the sky.

sleep, a-gi'-tse-mih, to sleep.

hin'-a-me-ka-ra-kōt', to feign sleep, like sleeping.

sleeve, a-ri-she'.

slowly, na-ni'-ka-se.

small, i-e-ka'-te.

small-pox, a-pa'-ke, ba-ka'-ke, ma-pa'-de.

smell, wa-push'-ik, } to smell.
ma-nōp'-mih, }

ma-ōm'-pe-shi'-re-i-ni-ći'-će, sweet-smelling, yellow blossom.

pu-e', it smells badly, to have a bad odor.

smile, bah'-ak, to laugh or smile.

smoke, pu'-e.

snake, i-ah'-i-se, any kind of a snake.

ma-kaé'-ke, common striped snake.

i-ah'-i-se-a-ri'-shi-di'-e, a rattlesnake.

snore, sah'-e, to snore.

snout, a-pish', snout or muzzle.

snow, bi'-pe, and bi'-a.

ba-ah'-pe, snowing.

du-pu'-re, a snow-storm.

bi-pa'-e, it snows.

bi-bi'-she, there is snow.

softly, ho'-kat, } softly, low, not loud; also slowly.
ha'-ho-kat, }

soldier, a-ki-sat'-ni, a body of men who constitute a sort of police about camp in time of peace.

some, hum-bi'-she, some, a part.

au-hu'-sak, there are some.

ba-bi'-she, something.

son, ma-nak-bat'-se, my son.

sore, pu'-a, a wound or sore.

soul, ba-de-nah'-e, the living spirit, the soul.

ah-pa-nah'-e, a spirit or ghost.

sound, po-ka'.

shi'-ri-ko'-ri-kat, to sound well, it sounds well.

Spaniard, o-ku'-she.

speak, ba-dōk', I speak.

spear, ka'-e-ke, } a spear or lance.
ba-a-ke', }

i-sa'-me, a wooden spear.

i-sa'-me-sho-shu'-ru-e, to hurl the spear or javelin.

spider, a-ma'-go-he.

spirit, ah-pa'-nah-ke, spirits of the dead.

is-ah'-e-hu'-e-te, the Great Spirit.

is-ah'-e-ka'-wi, the bad spirit.

splinter, a-sash'-ta-e.

split, i-nu'-shish, } to split.
a-sa'-ća, }

spring, mi-e-mah'-i-se, (season.)

sprinkle, ba-rah'-a-ra'-he, it sprinkles.

spyglass, i-ma-tsi'-nu.

square, sho-pa-tak', four-cornered, square.

squirrel, sta-rehé'.

stalk, wa-tsēh'-e-shi, the stalks of *Glycyrrhiza lepidota*.

star, ih-e'.

ih'-e-sa'-sat-nash, the stars twinkle.

start, kan-tu'-e-tūk, to start, to break up a camp.

steal, wa-ta'-nu-a, } to rob or steal.
a-ta'-nu-a, }

steel, bish-ke'-rah-u-a, a steel for striking fire.

stick, de-sa'-ćik, to stick.

still, ko-tak', keep still! quiet! stop!

ko-tak'-mi-ne-ki'-shi (imp.), stop drinking water.

tsis, keep still!

ka-tsi'-se, still! be quiet!

stir, pa'-pa, to stir up, as in a kettle.

stirrup, ma-nu'-źe, and ba-de'-i-ćaŋ-a-sa'-she.

stomach, i-ah'-e.

stone, mīk, and mi'-a.

mi-a'-ra-ka-tse, a gravel-bank, gravel-stones.

mi-e-hi'-a, a war-club made of stone.

mi-de-ah'-e, a flint-stone.

i-mah-ah'-i-u, a whetstone.

stop, i-ma-shi'-e, to stop.

a-tsi'-sa, to delay a little, to stop.

tsi-tsi'-pe, to stop, obstruct, to put in the way.

storm, hu-pu'-me.

straighten, ba-tsih-yūh'-at, to straighten, as an arrow or ramrod.

ta-će', } straight, not crooked.
ka-ra-tats'-yat, }

bah-a-na'-mih, to make anything straight.

strap, ku-si'-re, any kind of leather strap.

strawberry, ko-shi'-te.

stream, ŭm'-pa-se, up the stream.

bu-ru'-a-ka-se, down the stream.

strike, ma'-nesh-tash'-tu-e, to strike or whip, as to whip the dust off of cloth.

strip, is-ba-dŭsh'-te, to strip one naked.

bas-be'-bo-rĕsh'-tik, I stripped something.

strong, i-ći'-uk, strength.

i-ru'-kash, strong, hard, as to strike hard.

suck, a-tsi'-a, to suck.

suffer, ma-i-ni'-shĕk, to suffer.

sugar, bat-sih-u'-a.

summer, mi-e-mah'-e.

sun, a-ka'-she.

a-ra-ka'-she, sunlight.

superfine, ba-rŭh'-pe-rĕt, superior, there is nothing like it.

surprised, i'-sa-si-u, to wonder, to be surprised.

suspender, ba-shi'-she-kai, suspenders to hold up the leggins.

swallow, ĭm-pi'-e-sa-te.

a-ma-ko'-mish-tsish-e-a'-su-a, nests of bank swallows.

swan, mi-ne-ći'-e.

sweet, tsih-u'-a.

swell, ta-pu'-she, to swell up, from inflammation.

swim, mi'-me, to swim.

sword, nun-i-she'.

T.

take, ru'-shi-bi, to take off, as a saddle from a horse.

ru'-te (imp.), take it.

dis-mit-si'-e-ru'-te (imp.), take thy knife.

bi-te' (imp.), take it.

ku-ra-ta' (imp.), take from.

taste, ko-pik', to taste, tasting.

tattoo, ih-i-e'-ra-pe', to prick colored images into the skin.

tear, i-nŭh'-etsh, } to tear or rend.
tŭh'-e-tsu, }

tears, is-tum'-ne, water from the eyes.

that, i-aé-bi-ruh'-pa-ka, that person, those persons.

i-aé-ma-no'-a, those things.

thaw, shi-shu'-shik, to thaw.

thick, i-rŏp'-kat, large, thick.

think, ba-ći'-će-wat'-sik, I think.

ko-tin-paé', I think so.

thirsty, a-kué'-ik, to be thirsty.

this, hin-i'-a-te, this, this one.

hin-i'-at-kat, is this what you are looking for? in answer to a question.

hi-de'-dĕk, this person, or a person here.

hi-dĕd'-bi-ruh'-pa-ka, these persons.

thread, ba-tsu-pu'-a.

through, tsu-ka-sik', through any object.

tsi-ru'-shĕk, gone through and through.

throw, a-muh'-i-a, to throw away.

thumb, is-mu'-se.

thunder, su'-a.

su'-ni-ćĕk, the thunder-bird, that roars in the distance.

tie, bah-tsi'-mih, a knot, a noose, a tie.

bah-tsi'-ma-si-tsi-mik, to tie, to bind, to join anything.

dĕh'-ći, } to tie anything.
tu'-sa, }

tinder, mi-ni'-te, tinder, spunk.

tired, a-push'-a-he, to be tired.

tobacco, o'-pe, the common tobacco of commerce. *Nicotiana.*

o'-pi-she, Indian tobacco. *Lobelia.*

o'-pi-she-ba'-tsu-a, the leaves of Indian tobacco-plant.

ŏp'-mi-o, to smoke tobacco.

ŏp'-te-wits, to mix tobacco with bark or leaves, as kinnic-kinnic.

o'-pe-di-nih-shu'-me, to bring tobacco.

ŏp'-ti-a-wa, to put tobacco in a pipe.

o'-pi-she-ŏt-wa'-mih, to dry tobacco by the fire.

to-day, ka-na'-shik.

hin-e-ma'-pe, this day, to-day.

toe, ić-a-re'-te-be.

together, bat-sah'-pŭk, } together, in company.
bat'-sa-wah, }

bat'-sa-wah-ma'-ni-mo-uk, walking together.

bat'-sa-wah-pe'-mo-uk, sleeping all together.

bat'-sa-wah-pa'-wa-ku-re'-mo-uk, to run together.

bat'-sa-wah-pa'-wa-pa'-mo-uk, to slay or slaughter together.

bat'-sa-wah-pe'-mu-shi'-uk-a-shi, to throw the lodges together in one place.

bat'-sa-wah-pe'-shi-uk-aub-sa'-ro-ke, to have the Crows altogether in one place.

to-morrow, tsi-nak-ći'-uk.

tongue, de'-źe, the tongue.

de-źish'-ka, the palate.

de-źa'-źe, Tongue River, a branch of the Yellowstone.

tooth, hi'-e, and i'-e.

toothache, i-e-rŭk'.

top, ak'-a-da, on the top of anything.

tough, tsi-tsu'-tse, tsi-tsu'-tsih, } tough, tenacious.

trade, ma-esh-tsi-we'-mih, to trade.

truthful, mi'-shi-sak, to speak straight.

turn, ta-bah-u', to turn over.

turtle, na'-ko, a soft-shelled turtle.

two, nu'-pe-re, both.

ni-nŏmp'-ta, you two, both of you.

U.

under, bik-sa'-tsi-sa-re, under, underneath.

understand, hu-a-ka'-re-e'-wa-tsih, I understand it all.

untie, bu-ru-ship'-mik, to untie a knot or noose.

V.

valley, o-ma'-re-ću'-ke.

au-bat-su'-a, Wounded-man Valley.

vapor, a-ma-shi'-e, fog.

vein, a-pi-de', the jugular vein.

vermilion, a-mah'-o-me, red coloring material.

o'-me, a red earth, used by the Crows for painting.

virtuous, ba-bu'-ro-ke.

W.

wagon, wa'-pa-ta-tsi.

waist, ba-da-e'-haŋ-sup'-te.

wait, o-tsi-ek-me-o'-ne, a-mo'-nik, } to wait, to delay.

o-tći'-e (imp.), stop.

wake, ka-ni'-ta, to wake up.

it-sĕk', to wake up, as from a sleep.

wampum, ba-da-ah'-e-da-ha'-ro-ka'-te.

warm, it-si-tum'-ĕk, to warm.

a-rĕk', the weather is warm.

a'-re, hot.

war-party, dŏh'-a.

ŏm-pa-te', a war-club, pogamoggin.

wash, i-shu'-me, to wash.

bih'-ta-sa-pi-a'-a-ni-shu'-mi, to wash clothes.

wasp, is-će'-de-ka'-she, yellow-jacket, the insect that bites with its tail.

water, min'-e.

min'-e-ka'-wi, bad water, whiskey.

min'-e-shi-pit'-e, black water, coffee.

min'-a-nah'-e, the noise of water rolling over stones, a waterfall.

min'-e-pah'-u, to spill water.

min-e'-is-nu'-mik, to drink water.

min-ĕh'-pi-ra', to sprinkle, as water.

min'-e-ma'-a-mŭk, deep water.

min'-e-hep'-kat, shallow water.

min'-e-a'-źe, river water.

min-e'-bu-he', foam on water.

min-e'-ma-ku'-me, pike-poles, to push a boat in the river.

min'-e-tum'-e, Hot-spring Valley.

min'-e-ni-net'-e, the water that does not run, Big Rose-bud.

min'-e-ro-ći'-pe, the water that drives, Cross Creek.

min'-e-tum'-e-aź-ka'-te, Warm Water Creek. The ice never freezes over this creek. A branch of the Yellowstone.

min-e-pu'-e-bi-she, smoky water.

min'-ić-ke-aź-ka'-te, Lake Fork of Bird River.

min-e'-nits, rapids in the river.

min-its-ke'-i-se, the sea, big water.

min-it'-si-ćŭh'-e, a little lake.

min'-e-tsi-e', a lake.

min-e'-tsi-ka'-ta, willow-bushes.
min-it-shi'-re, yellow willow.
min-e'-i-ta'-ri, the common willow.
ma-ha', ma-he', } a spring of water.
ma-he', to boil up, as water from a spring.
ma-ha'-e-ho, a multitude of springs.
ma-mi'-miħ, to walk in the water.
i'-e-pu'-ħe, to weep, to make water come from the eyes; the name of a hill or butte on Crazy Woman's Fork, a branch of Powder River.

weak, ba-ba'-ćūk, feeble.
wealthy, ba-e'-tsiħ, rich.
weapon, bat'-sa-rek, ba-ba-ku'-ra, } any kind of defensive weapon used as arms.
ma-e-tsi'-pe, a battle-axe.
wear, i-e-ke'-be, to wear, as clothes.
weasel, u'-te.
weed, ba-de-i-ćap'-do-ke, a nettle weed.
ba-a-pa'-ne, any kind of weed.
well, hin'-e-et-de'-te, healthy, well.
lai-tho-ko', it is well.
wet, a-gi'-tsiħ.
what, sap.
sa'-pa, what is it?
sa-pe', who is it?
sa-paħ'-pi-ra, what are you looking after?
sap-ti'-re, what are you doing?
sap'-te, why is it?
sa'-me, how much? how many?
ma-no'-e-sa'-pa, what thing is it?
hin'-e-sa'-pa, what is that?
i'-mi-she, what is it? tell me.
where, sho.
sho'-rak, where is it?
sho'-tats, how do you do?
sho-te'-ra, where? in what place?
sho-ta'-će, how? in what way?
sho'-ka, where is that?
shōsh'-te-re, where are you going?
sho'-i-ni-ći'-re, when? when is it? at what time?
whip, is'-a-sin'-it-se, and it-si'-rit-se, a riding whip.
whistling, ki'-e-shik, the whistling of the male elk.
white, tsi'-e-kat.
sho'-rŭsh, a white root.
wife, u'-a.
wild, ak-se'-re-te.
wind, be'-će.
saħ-ik', wind from the stomach.
ap-će', windpipe.
no-mi'-na, to wind up anything.
window, ba-sa-she'.
winter, ma-se', and ma'-na.
wipe, ku-ru-siħ', to wipe.
wish, ma-o-ne'-ćik, to wish.
within, o-ma'-e-ke.
without, o-me'-na-ku.
wolf, tse'-e-te, a large wolf. *Canis occidentalis.*
tse'-e-će, a mad wolf.
tse'-e-te-a-pish', a wolf's nose.
bu'-a-ta, prairie wolf. *Canis latrans.*
woman, mi'-e.
mi'-e-ka-te, a girl.
mi'-e-de-ki'-se, a bashful woman.
mi'-e-e'-pe, a jealous woman.
mi'-e-ba-bu'-re-ke, a virtuous woman.
mi'-e-ka'-te-ba-bu'-re-ke, a virtuous girl.
mi'-e-ka'-nis-te, a young woman.
ka-ne-ka'-te, an old woman.
wonder, ba-ra-će-ra'-shik.
wood, ma'-na, ma'-ne, } wood, or a tree.
ma'-ne-a-pe'-ta-ni'-e, leaves falling from the trees.
ma-ne'-sat-siħ, a small strip of wood, a splinter.
ma-ne'-ka, a small piece of wood.
ma-ne'-ba-sa'-bi-sho-shu'-ra-e, a piece of wood with a spear-point in the end, a javelin.
ma'-ne-pi-ru'-pe, a war-club filled with nails.
ma'-ne-sa-će', a forest, or grove of trees.
ma'-ne-ći'-te, green wood.
ma'-ne-će'-se, dry wood.
ma'-ne-u'-she, the root of a tree.
ma'-ne-ho'-pe, a hollow log or tree.
ma'-ne-hi'-te, rotten wood.
ma'-ne-pa'-će, a wooden picket, stake.

ma'-ne-ta'-re, sweet cottonwood.
ma'-ne-a'-ke-de, in the tree.
ma'-ne-sho'-pe, a game with sticks, played by the women.
ma'-na-po'-he, quaking asp.
ma-na'-ke-da, up a tree.
ma'-na-ma'-ta-ta-tsi, scattering trees.
ma-na-kat', the color of wood, wood color.
ma-ni'-ah-e, flood or drift-wood.
mi-mo'-e-ma'-ne, a tree standing in the water.
pe'-ri-čis-ma'-ne, a large willow. *Salix.*

work, i-ba'-di-o, to work.
wound, a-hu'-ra-buh'-e, a fresh wound.
wrist, its-ka'-she.
its-kis'-kip-e, the arm from elbow to wrist.
mih-tse'-mi-tse, a string of beads, used as an ornament for the wrist.

Y.

yawn, mi'-sa-tsih, to yawn, to gape.
yellow, shi'-ri-kat.
ŏk-shi'-re, chrome yellow.
yes, kŏt, to be sure, certainly, yes.
yesterday, hu-raź'.
yonder, i'-e-čěk.
i-eé', yonder it is.
you, di (personal pronoun).
yours, dis (possessive pronoun).

CHAPTER XVIII.

XI. Minnitarees.

ETHNOGRAPHICAL HISTORY.

The Minnitarees, or Gros Ventres as they are called by the traders, formerly inhabited a mud village near the Mandans, when the latter were situated at Fort Clarke, with whom they have always sustained friendly relations. The construction of their houses is the same as that of the Mandans and Arikaras, as also are their usual occupations. Small patches of corn, beans, squashes, pumpkins, and a few other vegetables, have been cultivated by them from the earliest period known, even to the present time.

When living with the Mandans at Fort Clarke they numbered about one hundred and twenty lodges, averaging five souls to a lodge, making an aggregate of six hundred persons, but having suffered by the small-pox at the same time with the Mandans, were reduced to forty lodges, and these thinly peopled and badly provided. In this condition they removed to a large prairie sixty miles above on the opposite side of the river. At this point they now reside, and their village is composed of about eighty huts, which are tolerably well filled with occupants.

The similarity of their language with that of the Crows shows plainly that they were formerly the same people, each being able to talk with and understand each other without much difficulty, though their long separation has caused some variation, as will be seen by comparing the annexed vocabularies. No trace of their origin or migration from other lands is now left, but many traditions are told of their creation, which are reliable only as forming a part of their mythology and affording some index to their intellectual status.

These Indians should not be confounded with the Atsinas or Fall Indians, who inhabit the country of the Blackfeet. The languages of the two tribes are entirely distinct, nor do we know that they have ever held any association with each other whatever, or ever been at war with each other. This is the only tribe in the Northwest to which the name Minnitaree is in any way applicable or proper. Lewis and Clarke present us with a very complete view of the condition of the stationary tribes of the Upper Missouri as they saw them in 1804. In order that we may compare their history and condition at that time with their present state, we will quote the following paragraphs from the excellent Journal of Lewis and Clarke, which, from the well-known character of the travellers, and their advantages for obtaining information, we suppose to be in every way reliable.

"The villages near which we are established are five in number, and are the residence of three distinct nations: the Mandans, the Ahnahaways, and the Minnitarees. The history of the Mandans, as we received it from our interpreters, and from the chiefs themselves, and as it is attested by existing monuments, illustrates, more than that of any other nation, the unsteady movements and the tottering fortunes of the American nations. Within the recollection of living witnesses, the Mandans were settled forty years ago in nine villages, the ruins of which we passed about eighty miles below, and situated seven on the west and two on the east side of the Missouri. The two finding themselves wasting away before the small-pox and the Sioux, united in one village and moved up the river opposite to the Ricaras. The same causes reduced the remaining seven to five villages, till at length they emigrated in a body to the Ricara nation, where they formed themselves into two villages, and joined those of their countrymen who had gone before them. In their new residence they were still insecure, and at length the three villages ascended the Missouri to their present position. The two who had emigrated together still settled in the two villages on the northwest side of the Missouri, while the single village took a position on the southeast side. In this situation they were found by those who visited them in 1796, since which the two villages have united into one. They are now in two villages, one on the southeast of the Missouri, the other on the opposite side, and at the distance of three miles across. The first, in an open plain, contains about forty or fifty lodges, built in the same way as those of the Ricaras; the second the same number; and both may raise about three hundred and fifty men.

"On the same side of the river, and at the distance of four miles from the lower Mandan village, is another, called Mahaha. It is situated on a high plain at the mouth of Knife River, and is the residence of the Ahnahaways. This nation, whose name indicates that they were 'people whose village is on a hill,' formerly resided on the Missouri, about thirty miles below where they now live. The Assiniboins and Sioux forced them to a spot five miles higher, where the greatest part of them were put to death, and the rest emigrated to their present situation, in order to obtain an asylum near the Minnitarees. They are called by the French, Soulier Noir, or Shoe Indians; by the Mandans, Wattasoons, and their whole force is about fifty men.

"On the south side of the same, Knife River, half a mile above the Mahaha, and in the same open plain with it, is a village of Minnitarees surnamed Metaharta, who are about one hundred and fifty men in number. On the opposite side of Knife River, and one and a half miles above this village, is a second village of Minnitarees, who may be considered as the proper Minnitaree nation. It is situated in a beautiful, low plain, and contains four hundred and fifty warriors. The accounts which we received of the Minnitarees were contradictory. The Mandans say that this people came out of the water to the east and settled near them in their former establishment, in nine villages; that they were very numerous, and fixed themselves in one village on the southern side of the Missouri. A quarrel about a buffalo divided the nation, of which two bands went into the plains, and were known by the name of Crow and Paunch Indians, and the rest moved to their present establishment. The Minnitarees proper assert, on the contrary, that they grew where they now live, and will never emigrate from the spot, the Great Spirit having declared that if they moved they would all die. They also say that the Minnitarees Metaharta, that is, Minnitarees of the Willows, whose language, with very little variation, is their own, came many years ago from the plains, and settled near them; and perhaps the two traditions may be reconciled by the natural presumption that these Minnitarees were the tribe known to the Mandans below, and that they ascended the river for the purpose of rejoining the Minnitarees proper. These Minnitarees are part of the great nation called Fall Indians, who occupy the intermediate country between the Missouri and the Saskatchewan, and who are known by the name of Minnitarees of the Missouri, and Minnitarees of Fort de Prairie, that is, residing near, or rather frequenting, the establishment in the prairie on the Saskatchewan. These Minnitarees, indeed, told us that they had relations on the Saskatchewan whom they had never known till they met them in war, and having engaged in the night, were astonished at discovering that they were fighting with men who spoke their own language. The name of Gros Ventres, or Big-bellies, is given to these Minnitarees, as well as to all the Fall Indians. The inhabitants of these five villages, all of which are within the distance of six miles, live in harmony with each other. The Ahnahaways understand in part the language of the Minnitarees; the dialect of the Mandans differs widely from both; but their long residence together has insensibly blended their manners, and occasioned some approximation in language, particularly as to objects of daily occurrence and obvious to the senses."

Brackenridge says that there are remnants of seventeen villages of Mandans and Gros Ventres. They are included in seven villages; five of the Gros Ventres, and two of the Mandans, within a distance of fifteen miles. He says, that though there is not the least affinity in their languages, the Gros Ventres is spoken by all the Mandans.

Morse probably over-estimated the number of the Minnitarees. He observes that they number 3250 persons, have their village on the south side of the Missouri, east of the Little Missouri, about half way between the Mandans and the Yellowstone.

Say, in the account of Long's Expedition to the Rocky Mountains, presents a very interesting account of the customs, habits, and religious opinions of this tribe, but in Prince Neuwied's excellent work, before alluded to, the most minute and accurate description of the Minnitarees is given which can be found in any memoir. He says, however, that the word "Manitarie" was given by the Mandans, and signifies "those who came over the water." From the most reliable information which I could obtain, I am inclined to think that the true meaning is "people of the willows." This opinion is farther strengthened, from the fact that a species of willow, most abundant in the Minnitaree country, is called in their language, min'-i-it-a'-ri, "growing by the water."

The present location of the stationary tribes of the Upper Missouri is as follows. The village of the Minnitarees is situated on the north branch of the Missouri, near latitude 47° 30', and longitude 102°. The village of the Arikaras is located on the south side of the Missouri, at Fort Clarke, in latitude 47°, longitude 101°, and the Mandan village is on the same side of the river, and about four miles above the last.

Several vocabularies of the Minnitaree language have been already published, but the only ones worthy of note are, by Professor T. Say, in Long's "Expedition to the Rocky Mountains," and by Prince Neuwied, in his "Travels in North America." In the Transactions of the American Ethnological Society, Vol. II, Gallatin proved very clearly the affinities of the Minnitaree with the Crow language, and that both of them belonged to the Sioux or Dakota stock.

In treating of the stationary tribes, no mention has been made of the extent of their lands, or of the portion of territory they claim as their own. Properly speaking, they have no land, except their corn-fields, and the prairie immediately around and defended by their village. The moment they leave their huts, they are liable to be attacked and driven back by the Dakotas. The Arikaras, when they leave their homes, hunt in the Dakota country, and by their permission, whilst the Minnitarees depend on their peaceable relations with the Assiniboins when engaged in hunting, as they do annually in the vicinity of the Great Bend. In case of a general war, none of the stationary Indians could leave their village at all. They are too few to contend with the surrounding tribes, and even if united, would not be able to sustain a position in the Dakota country without the shelter of their mud cabins. Still, from Apple River below to the Great Bend of the Missouri above, the country is more hunted by these Indians than by any others, and consequently, it may be called the territory of the three tribes residing in mud villages, though in reality it is neutral ground belonging to particular tribes.

VOCABULARY OF THE MINNITAREE DIALECT OF THE AUH-SA′-RO-KE OR CROW LANGUAGE.

above, ma-ku′-ka.
afraid, bi-di′-tu, I am afraid.
alive, i′-di.
all, huk-a-he′-ta.
ankle, i′-ća-re-shu′-ka.
antelope, ŭh′-i.
arm, a-ra′.
arrow, a-ru′-ti-sha.
autumn, ma-ta′.
axe, bi-ip-sa′.

back, ish-i-te′-ru.
bad, ish-i′-a.
beard, i-ki′.
black, shi-pish′-a.
bladder, u′-shi-ka-ruh′-e.
blood, i′-de.
blue, she-pa′-ći.
boat, ma′-te.
body, a-hu′-a.
bone, ma′-di-ki.
bow, bi-ru′-ha-pa′-ro-wa.
boy, ma-ka-ris′-te-mat′-se, a little boy.
breast, e′-wa-ki.
breechcloth, ma′-i-dip-sha′-ki.
brother, ba′-ta-wa′-će.
bull, ki′-ro-pi.
burn, o′-te, to burn.
by, u-te′-ru.
tut-a′, by and by.

calf, na-ka-ći′-ri.
call, ba-ki-ko′-ha.
chickadee, is-ko-pi′.
chief, bau-tse′-it-se.
coat, ma-i-to′-ke.
cold, ći-di′-a.
cow, bi-ti′-a.
bi-ta-ka′-sha, a young cow.
crow, pe-rit-ska′.
cry, i-bi′.

dance, di′-sha, to dance.
day, ma′-pi.
dead, ta′-ih.
deer, ći-ća′-pi-sha, black-tailed deer.
die, dĕsh.
dog, bi-de′-de.
ći′-pa, prairie dog.
drink, ma-će′-ko-di, to drink.
duck, mi-hah′-a.

ear, a′-pa.
earth, a-wa′.
eating, ba-ru′-te.
enemy, ma-i-ha′.
eye, is-ta′.

face, bi-ta′.
far off, ti′-źi.
father, ta-tish′.
fin, i-to′-i-ka-te.
finger, sha-ki′-nu.
fire, bi′-da.
fish, bu′-a.
bu-a-ka′-te, a catfish.
bu-a-na′-ka, roe of a fish.
bu-a-ća′-she, small fish.
flesh, a-ru′-du.
flint, ba-ći-ka′-sha.
foot, ma′-ći.
forever, ko-ći′-te.
friend, ba-e-ku′-e.
girl, ma-ka-ris′-ti-mi′-a, a little girl.
go, da, to go.
good, sa-ki′.
great, a-ru′-ke-ri′-ći.
green, to-hish′.
gun, o-wut′-se-we-du′-ha.

hail, ma-ka-pit′-a-wi.
hair, a-da′.
hand, sha-ke′.
handsome, sa-ki-ku′-a.
hawk, mu-ki′-ra-ki.
head, a′-tu.
head-dress, ma-i-shu′-a-po-ka.
hear, bi-ke-ku′-a, to hear.
heart, na-ta′.
heaven, a-pah′-e-ru′-she.
heel, i′-će-ki.
hill, it-i′.
hot, bi-ća′-we.
house, a′-ma-ti.
husband (my), ma-ki′-da.

I, bi.
ice, ba-ru′-he.
in, a-ma-hu′-ru.
Indian, hi-na-tsa′.

kettle, bi-duh′-e.
kill, ti′-pe, to kill.
knee, e-re-shu′-ka.
knife, ba-ći′.

lake, bi-di′-ka-ku′-pe.
laugh, ba-ka′.
leg, i-di′-ke.
leggin, hŏp-će′.
light, a-muh′-a-hi.

lightning, ka-di′-ka.
live, i-dits′, to live.
liver, au-pi-sha′.
love, ba-ki-dush′-i.

man, bau-tse′.
ba-shi′, a white man.
mast, ma-re-ko′-peh-e-hūm′-pa.
midday, bi-di-wa′-pa-re-pe′-hi.
midnight, bi-di-i′-nuk-pi.
moon, ma′-ku-mi′-di.
morning, bi-da-ha′-ru-te.
mother, i-kūsh′.
mountain, a-ma-ha′-wi.
mouth, a-pu′-a-te.

nail, sha-kih′-pu.
navel, ma′-i-te-re′-pa.
near, au-tsa-ka′-ti.
neck, am′-pa.
never, huk-a-hi′-ta.
night, o′-ksi.
no, de′-sha.
nose, ma-pa′.
nothing, ba-ru-a-na′-shēsh.

oar, i′-e-ho′-ke.
old, hi′-e.
on, di-ki′-di.
owl, da-ku′-pe.

part, su′-ta.
people, a-ma-she′, people who live in mud houses.
pepper, bi-di-ho′-ha-ta.
perhaps, ha-she-ić′-ki.
pipe, ki′-pi.
plain, a-ma′-ra-su′-ka.
polecat, hu′-ke.

rain, ha′-re.
red, hish′-e.
ring, ma-sha′-ki-o-psa′-ki, brass ring.
river, a′-źe.
a-źe-ka-ris′-ta, a small river.
run, hi-ru′-te.

salt, au′-ma-ho′-ta.
sash, ma′-i-pat-su′-a.
scale, bu-i-shi′-she.
scalp, a′-da-du.
sea, bi-di-ti′-a.
seat, ma-a-shi′-ta-ra-hu′-pi.
see, au-muk′-auk, to see.
sheep, a-shi-ti′-a, big-horn.
shell, o-tish′-ka, shells for ornament.
shoe, bi-di-hōm′-pa.
ba-du-shi′-ish, to untie shoes.
shot-pouch, bi-rut′-se-pi-she.
shoulder, a-ri-ru′.
sinew, bau′-tsu-a.
sing, ma-ke-pa′-hi, to sing.
sister (my), ba-ta-wi′-a.
skin, dah′-pe.
sky, a-pah′-e.
small, ka-rish′-ta.
snipe, a-pit′-sa.
snow, ma′-pi.
something, ma-ho′-a-wi′-tu.
son (my), ba-di-sha′.
sour, a-da′-wi.
speak, ba-de′.
spear, bi-re′-te-ru-te.
spring, ma-ha′ (season).
bi-a-ha′-ku-te, spring, fountain.
squirrel, ko-kōk′-shi, prairie squirrel.
star, i′-ka.
stomach, e′-di.
strike, ma′-di-ki, to strike.
strong, it-ći′-uk.
summer, a-ba′-de.
sun, bi-de-wa′-pi.
sunrise, ma-pa′-wi-di.
sunset, mi-di′-e-wuk′-pi.
swan, bi-da′-tuk-i.
sweet, si-ku′-a.

thigh, ma-na-ta′-ro.
think, ba-ki-ri′-she, to think.
thou, di.
di-he′-di, thou, thyself.
thread, ba-e-ke-ka′-ka, yellow thread.
through, he-ru′-te.
thunder, ta′-ho.
tie, ba-ra-tu′-wi, to tie.
tobacco, o′-pe.
to-day, hi-di-ma′-pe.
toe, i-ći′-pu-wi.
to-morrow, a′-te-rūk.
tongue, de′-źe.
tooth, i′-a.
town, a′-ti.
turkey, si-ah′-ti.

ugly, i-te′-shi-a.
under, bih-ta′-ru.

valley, ta-rūh′-te.
vein, ma-ho′-i-de.

walk, di′-di, to walk.
wampum, ma-ih′-a-ma-ra-ku′-tse.
war-club, mi-re-ku′-tsa.
warrior, bau-tse-i′-di-ki.
water, bi-di′.
weak, ha′-sha.
what, ta′-pa.
ma-ru′-a-ta′-pa, what thing?
which, ta′-pa-tōk, which person or thing?
whiskey, bi-di-a′-ra-wi.
white, ih-o-tuk′-e.
who, tup-e′.
wife (my), ma-ta′-e-wi′-a.
wind, ho′-ći.
windpipe, no′-tish-ka.
wing, ih′-pa.
winter, ma′-na.
wish, hid-ish′, to wish.
within, a-mu-hu′.

without, a-ta-shi'-ku-a.
wood, bat-se-ta'-she, petrified wood.
woodpecker, tŏsh'-ka.
woman, mi'-a.
year, a-ma'-e-ta.
yellow, tsi'-ri.
yes, ko-ush'-ik.
yesterday, hu-ri-shi'-ru.

CHAPTER XIX.

XII. MANDANS.

ETHNOGRAPHICAL HISTORY.

ALTHOUGH one would suppose that all the tribes of the Upper Missouri, being the same barbarous people, accustomed to like occupations, and possessing the same advantages, would exhibit no great national difference, yet each tribe or nation has marked distinctions of character, as much and even more, perhaps, than the several divisions of the European race. This must depend, to a great extent, upon their physical organization, for the pursuits of all Indians inhabiting the plains are or should be radically the same. Hunting and war, amusements and devotion, idleness and activity, divide their time, and would without some peculiarity of constitution lead to a general resemblance of character. The small amount of agricultural labor bestowed upon the soil by the stationary tribes, cannot be reckoned as an item in their national education, or as influencing the conduct of the men, for this is done altogether by the women. The presence of the men is not required in the corn-fields, and if found there, it is from far different purposes than aiding in the work. The question then arises, how it happens that the Arikaras present such grovelling, debased, and mean general features, with scarcely any redeeming qualities, whilst the Mandans, residing but a few miles distant, possess an almost opposite character?

The Mandans, or Mi-ah'ta-nēs, "people on the bank" (of the river), as they call themselves, must have resided on the banks of the Missouri at a very remote period, perhaps not near their present residence, but in several places along the river. It is also probable that if they migrated at all, they came from a southern direction, as the sites of different villages of very ancient date are seen along the Missouri, as low down as the present boundary between the United States and the Dakota country. Some of these antique ruins are said to have been Arikara villages, which is doubtless the case. The fact sought to be established is, that all these stationary tribes migrated in the same direction, from southeast to northwest along this river, which may be inferred from the circumstance, that no remains of their villages are to be seen along any other stream than the Missouri, nor are they found in any place on the plains.

Prior to the visit of Lewis and Clarke in the autumn of 1804, very little information of a reliable character was known in regard to the origin and early history of the Mandans. Col. D. D. Mitchell, in a letter to Mr. H. R. Schoolcraft, published in the third volume of the "History of the Indian Tribes," refers to an early writer by the name of Mackintosh, who it seems was connected with a French trading company as early as 1772. From his own account, he left Montreal in the summer of 1773, crossed over the intervening country, and reached the Mandan villages on Christmas day. He says that at that time, the Mandans occupied nine large towns situated very near each other, and that at short notice they could muster 15,000 warriors. Col. Mitchell is of the opinion that this author exaggerates in his statistics, but that they were a formidable nation, the ruins of numerous villages along both sides of the Missouri bear ample testimony. In 1804, Lewis and Clarke speak of five distinct villages belonging to three distinct nations, viz., Mandans, Ahnahaways, and Minnitarees. They also allude to a lower Mandan village, called "Mahaha." At the present time, the Mandans occupy a small village about three miles above Fort Clarke, and do not number over two hundred and fifty or three hundred souls. The Ahnahaways were undoubtedly a portion of the Mandan nation, but I cannot ascertain that any trace of them exists at this time. In 1833, at the time of the visit of Prince Neuwied to the Upper Missouri, two Mandan villages were standing, the southern village about three hundred paces above Fort Clarke, on the same side of the river, and the other about three miles higher up on the same bank. It is evident that the former is now occupied by the Arikaras, while the latter is in possession of the small remnant of the Mandan nation now living. At the time of the Prince Neuwied's visit, the first village was composed of sixty-five huts, with about one hundred and fifty warriors, and the latter of thirty-eight huts, with eighty-three warriors, both villages, perhaps, possessing nine hundred to one thousand souls.

Our knowledge of this nation, obtained from the American Fur Company, commences in the year 1829, when, through that Company, the fur trade on the Upper Missouri became established on a more solid basis than it had been by the French traders. Anterior to the above date, the latter had been trading with these Indians in their usual way, by building wintering houses, putting therein a trader and a few men, with a small supply of goods, and abandoning the post in the spring, taking with them down the river their returns of furs and skins. At that time the Mandans occupied the same village in which the Arikaras now live, and also had another a few miles up the river. The lower town consisted of two hundred cabins, and the upper of eighty, both built in every respect as described in the chapter relating to the Arikaras, the latter, at that time, occupying their own village near the mouth of Grand River. We thus see that the account given by the American Fur Company of the condition of the Mandans in 1829, does not differ materially from that of the Prince Neuwied, as observed by him in 1834. In the year 1829, the American Fur Company erected Fort Clarke, for the express purpose of trading with the Mandans and Minnitarees, the former nation numbering about six hundred warriors, or eighteen hundred souls, and the latter about half as many.

It is somewhat remarkable that notwithstanding all the misfortunes that have befallen this tribe for so many years, it even to this time preserves its independence and individuality as a nation. Nearly all of the Mandans speak the Minnitaree language, and many of them are familiar with the Dakota and Arikara tongues, but very few if any of the surrounding tribes have acquired that of the Mandans. But one white man has ever learned to speak the language fluently, and he resided among them over twenty years. I cannot ascertain that there are any peculiar difficulties in the sounds or structure of the language, which should prevent individuals of other nations from acquiring it readily; indeed, I think the evidence is quite clear, as suggested by Mr. Gallatin, that it is remotely allied to the Dakota stock, and presents few if any more obstacles to its acquisition than the other dialects of that group.

In the year 1833 these Indians were in their most prosperous state, industrious, well armed, good hunters and good warriors, in the midst of herds of buffalo, mostly within sight of the village, with large corn-fields, and a trading-post, from which they could at all times obtain supplies, and consequently at that time they might have been considered a happy people. In their personal appearance, prior to the ravages of the small-pox, they were not surpassed by any nation in the Northwest. The men were tall and well made, with regular features and a mild expression of countenance, not usually seen amongst Indians. Their complexion also was a shade lighter than that of other tribes, often approaching very near to some European nations, as the Spaniards. Another peculiarity was that some of them had fair hair, and some gray or blue eyes, which are very rarely met with among the other tribes. A majority of the women, particularly the young, were quite handsome, with fair complexions, and modest in their deportment. Instead of the brazen, forward look and manner, customary with females of some of the tribes of the Northwest, they were diffident and shy, avoiding any approaches of strangers or of their own people. They were also noted for their virtue. This was regarded as an honorable and most valuable quality amongst the young women, and each year a ceremony was performed, in the presence of the whole village, at which time all females who had preserved their virginity came forward, struck a post, and challenged the world to say aught derogatory of their character. As this was a religious ceremony, any of those present who could with truth contradict the statement felt bound to do so, and if detected in the deception, the female lost her standing forever afterward among the young of both sexes. In ordeals of this kind, it was remarked that more than two-thirds of the Mandan females came off victorious, which is regarded as a great proportion when the early training and the influences that surround them are taken into consideration. The fact that a ceremony of this kind exists among savages, tending to promote virtue and discourage vice, is of itself sufficient evidence of their mental as well as moral superiority.

Both males and females of every age, especially the young, were very cleanly in their persons and neat in their dress. It was their custom, and still is, growing out of some ancient tradition, to bathe in the river every morning. Even in the winter season they cut holes in the ice, immerse the body, and it is no uncommon thing to see them after taking their cold bath sit naked on the ice, comb their hair, and paint themselves in a snow-storm, the thermometer from 10° to 30° below zero. This constant ablution at all seasons had the effect of inuring the system to cold, for they never shiver, be the weather ever so severe, and sometimes they seem to prolong the making of their toilet in proportion as the air is intensely cold. At all events the practice was a good one for the Indians, inasmuch as it kept their bodies free from most diseases and eruptions incident to their manner of life, and it was remarked that they were uniformly healthy and vigorous. As a general rule the females despised the promiscuous and illicit intercourse with the other sex, so much practised by some of the other tribes, and consequently they were free from syphilitic diseases.

The great object of the young of both sexes was to dress well; and everything they could get was lavished on their persons in clothing and ornament. Some of their dresses were very costly, particularly those of a young brave, the war-eagle feathers of which alone would equal the price of two horses, or one hundred dollars. They were, as a nation, fond of amusements; dances were frequent, and different clans required separate costumes, some of which, although made of skin wrought with figures of beads and porcupine quills, cost six months' labor to complete them. The taking of the war-eagle, whose tail furnishes the most costly ornament of a warrior's dress, requires great patience, and is thus accomplished. About sixty-five or seventy miles above the Mandan village, there is a river called the Little Missouri, which takes its rise in the Black Hills and empties into the Missouri at the lower end of the Great Bend. Along the whole course of this stream the surface is much broken, resembling that described as Mauvaises Terres in the Dakota country. It is a wild region, seldom visited by any persons except passing war-parties, and is the secure abode of the grizzly bear, big-horn, and war-eagle. A Mandan wishing to make an eagle hunt, goes through several days' fasting, offers sacrifices to the Great Spirit, and implores His protection and aid in the success of his expedition. When, by a propitious dream, he believes the time favorable, he proceeds alone to the place above mentioned, killing some animal on his way, the meat of which he will need as bait. When he reaches the wildest and most solitary spot, he digs a hole in the ground large enough to contain his body in an upright position; over this hole is placed a covering of willows, which is overlaid with grass, leaving only a hole large enough for the hand. A stick is then laid over this lid or covering, directly over the hole for the hand, to which the meat or bait is tied. The man descends into the hole, covers it up with the lid, and patiently awaits the approach of the eagle. The eagle, soaring above, sees the bait, and then gradually approaches in circles, and when within a few feet darts down and fastens its claws into the meat, and at the same moment the hunter grasps the bird by the legs, thrusts his knife upwards into its body, and opening the cover draws it in. In this way, during a week or ten days of constant watching, two or three birds are secured, and this is considered a good hunt, though the hunter more frequently returns unsuccessful. The risk attending these solitary hunts in dangerous places, and the rarity of the bird, causes the high value to be set upon the feathers, of which the twelve forming the tail are the only ones used in dress. Two of these tails are sold for a horse, or fifty dollars.

In the palmy days of their national prosperity, when the population comprised six hundred warriors, and as many handsome women very gayly dressed, much time was spent in amusements of every kind. But short intervals clapsed between dances, games, races, and other manly and athletic exercises. One of these was Olympic in its character, and was thus performed. A race-course of three miles on the level prairie was laid off, cleared of every obstruction, and kept in order for the express purpose. Posts were planted to mark the initial and terminating points, and over the track the young men tested the elasticity of their limbs during the fine summer and autumn months, to prepare themselves for the hardships of their winter hunts. On the occasion when races were determined on by the chiefs, the young men were informed by the public crier, and every one who had confidence in his prowess was admitted to the lists. Each of the runners brought the amount of his wager, consisting of blankets, guns, and other property, and sometimes several judges or elderly men were appointed by the chief of the village, whose duty it was to arrange the bets, regulate the starting, and determine the results of the race. As the wagers are handed in, each is tied to or matched with one of equal value, laid aside, and when all have entered, the judges separate, some remaining with the property staked at the beginning of the race-course, and others taking their station at its terminus. Six pairs of runners whose bets have been matched, now start to run the three-mile course, which is to be repeated three times before it can be decided. The ground is laid out in the form of an arc describing two-thirds of a circle, the starting-point and goal being but a few hundred yards distant from each other, the intermediate space being filled up by the young and old of the whole village. The runners are entirely naked, except their moccasins, and their bodies are painted in various ways from head to foot. The first set having accomplished about half the first course, as many more are started, and this is continued as long as any competitors remain, until the entire track is covered with runners, at distances corresponding with their different times of starting, and the judges award the victory to those who come out, by handing each a feather painted red, the first six winning the prize. These, on presenting the feathers to the judges at the starting-point, are handed the property staked against their own. The first and second heats are seldom strongly contested, but on the third every nerve is strained, and great is the excitement of the spectators, who with yells and gestures, encourage their several friends and relations. The whole scene is highly interesting, and often continued for two or three days in succession, to give every one an opportunity to display his abilities. Those who have shown great fleetness and powers of endurance, receive additional reward, in the form of praise by the public crier, who harangues their names through the village for many days afterwards. This is a fine national amusement, and tends much to develope the great muscular strength for which they are remarkable. They also, immediately on finishing the race, in a profuse state of perspiration, throw themselves into the Missouri, and no instance is known where this apparent rashness resulted in any illness.

At all times in fine weather, the Mandan village presents a gay and lively appearance. Ball-playing, horse-racing, and gambling in various ways may be seen going on. These amusements are too numerous to be described in detail here. The dances are of the most brilliant character known among the Indians, displaying a great variety of costumes, adapted to the different occasions, and made of the most gay and costly materials. This is the only nation in which the women are allowed to join the men in their dances. With other tribes, they never mingle, except in the scalp dance, though in one or two medicine ceremonies they perform alone. In admitting women as associates in their amusements, and otherwise treating them with respect, this nation has shown great kindness of disposition. Instead of regarding them in the light of slaves or property, as is the case with other tribes, they never abuse them or impose heavy burdens on them, and this course is rewarded by their usefulness, cheerfulness, and fidelity. Such a thing as divorcing a woman for illicit intercourse is unknown, or at least of very rare occurrence amongst them, and the disgrace and humiliating public ceremony to which female offenders in this way are subject, is worse than death.

The Mandans are a very devotional people. No war excursion is entered upon, corn planted, eagles sought, or any important labors commenced, without propitiating the Great Spirit, in accordance with their traditional customs. Some of these rites consisted merely in sacrifices, accompanied with prayer and fasting, but when a young man is starting out on his first war expedition, or any great benefit is to be derived from supernatural power, they practise self-torturing ceremonies little less severe than those of Hindoo devotees. The place where these religious performances are observed, is back of their village on the prairie, where a post is planted in the ground, and a circle of buffalo-skulls formed round it, about twenty feet in diameter. A young man about commencing his career as a warrior, or a leader on the eve of starting with a party against the enemy, feels bound to undergo the tortures about to be noticed, in order to secure the aid of the Great Spirit in these undertakings. These rites are repeated at different periods when circumstances require their observance. The person under the influence of this superstition, usually prepares himself by three or four days of fasting, lying on the ground without shoes or covering of any kind, without food or water, and without speaking to any one. At the end of this period, he is visited by the medicine-men, who after much incantation, make incisions about three inches long and half an inch deep, lengthwise down the back opposite each shoulder-blade, through which a stout stick is thrust, and a strong cord being attached to the stick, he is drawn up a few feet from the ground by passing the cord through a hole in the top of the post, his entire weight being supported by the skewer in the back. When suspended in this way, the medicine-men take hold of his feet, and running rapidly around, give an impetus to the body so as to wind up the cord, after which the devotee, using his feet, could in the same way unwind himself, and thus keep himself constantly swinging round by striking his feet on the post. Here he hangs for one or two days and nights, until, fainting and exhausted, he is let down by the medicine-men. After being liberated from the post, four or five buffalo-skulls are tied to the end of the cord, the stick still remaining in the incision, and he is obliged to drag these skulls, a weight of fifty or sixty pounds, over the prairie, with the horns ploughing up the ground, and the blood streaming down his back. This is persisted in until the flesh breaks loose, or the person fainting, is carried away by his friends. The ceremony being over, food and drink are given him, and when fully revived, he is considered in a fit state to undertake any dangerous expedition, though he still is compelled to wait, until by favorable dreams he is advised of the proper time. Most warriors of note have passed through this ordeal, and many have repeated the same several times during their lives.

Another and scarcely less painful rite is to burn across the breast with a red-hot iron, making deep sores, about four inches long, six or eight in number, and about an inch apart. Sometimes the burns are made in large circles on the breast, and again on one or both shoulders. This actual cautery is very severe, on account of the slow operation of the medicine-men, who with smoking and invocation require at least an hour to inflict one wound.

In the spring of 1838, that dreaded scourge of the Indians, small-pox, made its appearance among the Mandans. By some accident portions of the clothing belonging to one of the employés of the Fur Company, who had suffered from the disease on the lower part of the Missouri River, were retained on the steamboat, although no appearance of the infection was visible until the boat arrived at Fort Pierre. Here it broke out amongst the voyageurs, and although every precaution was taken in delivering the goods at the different posts, yet it was communicated to the several tribes along the river. All the tribes suffered more or less, but none approached so near extinction as the Mandans. The summer was intensely hot, the disease was general in both villages, and owing to their confined, dark, and ill-ventilated cabins, proved fatal to a degree far beyond that of other nations. It was almost impossible that life could be sustained, on account of the impure state of the air, and the disease usually assuming the confluent form, almost invariably resulted in death. Remedies were tried at first, the principal of which were sweating, cold bathing, and depletion. Of these none succeeded. The first aggravated the fever to delirium, and the sufferers died during the operation. Bleeding produced no more beneficial results, and this, together with all treatment, was soon abandoned, whole families lying helpless, waiting death, in different stages of the disease. The banks of the river were strewn with the dead and blackened carcasses, which were daily pushed into the stream by the traders. The drums and rattles of the medicine-men soon ceased, for they too were overtaken by death. The men committed suicide or murdered their suffering children; the women mourned their fate; and all was misery, despair, and death. The trading-post was closed, the traders confined to their rooms, and the cannon loaded and placed in the bastions, so as to protect them, if need be, against their hitherto most excellent friends. I need not pursue this subject farther than to say, that a period of darkness reigned, in which their fierce passions, being wrought up by disease and frenzy, these Indians committed acts at which the imagination revolts, and which were not witnessed by others than themselves. When the disease had abated, and when the remnant of this once powerful nation had recovered sufficiently to remove the decaying bodies from their cabins, the total number of grown men was twenty-three, of women forty, and of young persons sixty or seventy. These were all that were left of the eighteen hundred souls that composed the nation prior to the advent of that terrific disease, and even those that recovered were so disfigured as scarcely to be recognized.

When the survivors had rallied and recovered, they left the village at the fort, and took up their residence in the other cabins, a few miles above. Here some attempt was made to reorganize their social system, but the race could only be propagated by intermarriage without regard to relationship, unless closely allied. To this they were forced by circumstances. The disease had only left one of a family, here and there, and no choice was offered for new connections. However, they conformed as nearly as practicable to their customary laws, avoiding as well as they were able contracts of marriage with blood relatives, although their condition imposed the necessity of perpetuating their nation by alliances which, had they been differently situated, would not have been resorted to. This appears to be an evil more or less incident to all stationary tribes. Women are very seldom taken from other tribes, for the reason that they usually speak a different language, and the consequence is, that a degree of relationship runs through the whole village, which perhaps is the cause of their living more harmoniously together than the roving tribes. Quarrels very seldom occur, and no great division of feeling or rule is observed, but the ultimate effect of this interconnection is a disregard of the natural barrier of blood relationship, which in its progress, and sanctioned by custom, results in actual incest.

About the time that the Mandans left the lower village, the Arikaras came and took possession, the former readily consenting to this arrangement, because it placed a large body of strangers between them and the Dakotas, with whom, in their now feeble state, they were unable to contend.

The Mandans at this time (1855) number about thirty-five or forty huts, perhaps nearly three hundred souls, raise corn, squashes, beans, &c., same as the Minnitarees and Arikaras, and hunt the buffalo when these animals are near their village. The destroying and humbling effects of the disease referred to could not change their indomitable spirit of pride and independence. They will not join with the other nations near whom they reside, connect themselves with them by marriage, nor practise any customs but those of their ancestors. Their religious rites and ceremonies are preserved entire, and the system of self-inflicting tortures is practised at the present day. Being too few in number to form war-parties, they remain at home and defend themselves.

All of their noted chiefs are dead, and sketches of their lives would be interesting, but will not be related in this place, though they exhibited many amiable features. While living their laws were seldom infringed upon by the claims and pretensions of other aspirants to power. They were respected for their judgment, and loved for the patriarchal care they took in the general welfare, and not feared on account of their personal bravery or extensive relationship, as is the case with the migratory bands. Old age in both sexes is held in veneration and made comfortable. The Mandans deposit their dead on scaffolds near the village, and this also has a tendency to produce diseases in warm weather; but every attempt to induce them to inter the bodies has proven unsuccessful. They cultivate the soil to some extent, raising corn and beans, but seldom more than they need for their own consumption. Their destiny seems tending toward final extinction.

The most complete and accurate history of the Mandans ever published, is given in the excellent work of Prince Neuwied, who spent one winter among them, under the most favorable circumstances for obtaining reliable information. His vocabulary is also quite full, and he has exhibited the grammatical structure with considerable detail. Catlin, also, in his account of the North American Indians, enters quite minutely into their history, manners, and customs, which, though highly colored, are, for the most part, correct. The notion which he entertained that the Mandans are of Welsh origin has been so thoroughly exploded, that it is unnecessary to allude to it farther. His vocabulary of the language, however, is a very excellent one. Schoolcraft also gives a somewhat lengthy vocabulary, derived from Mr. James Kipp, for many years a trader among these Indians. I may as well state here, that not only the information obtained by me in regard to the Mandan language was given by Mr. Kipp, but the same man aided Prince Neuwied and Catlin, so that our present knowledge of the Mandan language has been derived from very nearly the same source. So far as I can learn, the most important contributions to the knowledge of the Mandan language, and the only ones worthy of especial notice, are those of Prince Neuwied, Catlin, and Schoolcraft. That of Prince Neuwied is by far the most important, containing much of the grammatical structure of the language, and, as above observed, it was obtained under circumstances which entitle it to confidence. The latter, though important, are merely lists of words, and convey but a partial idea of the language.

CHAPTER XX.

OBSERVATIONS ON THE GRAMMATICAL STRUCTURE OF THE MANDAN LANGUAGE.

I. Nouns.

1. With few exceptions, Mandan nouns have both a singular and plural form, as is shown by their termination; as, a-pe′, a leaf; a-pīsh′, leaves; ma-he′, a weed; ma-hōsh′, weeds; si, a feather; si′-ish, feathers.

2. The gender of nouns is indicated by the use of different words to express the sex; as, nu′-maŋ-ke, a man; mi′-he, a woman; be′-ro-ke, a bull; p'tīn′-de, a cow; ni′-ka, a calf.

3. The case of a noun is known by its position in a sentence.

II. Adjectives.

4. Adjectives always follow the nouns which they describe; as, mi-he′-shi-na-shūsh, a handsome woman; nat-kan′-ka-sīsh, a hard heart.

5. The numeral adjectives of the cardinal kind are as follows:

one, mah̆′-a-na.
two, nūm′-pa.
three, na′-men-i.
four, to′-pe.
five, keh̆-ūn′.
six, ki′-ma.
seven, kū′-pa.
eight, te-tuk′-e.
nine, mah̆′-pe.
ten, pi′-rah̆.
eleven, a-ga-mah̆′-a-na.
twelve, a-ga-nūm′-pa.
thirteen, a-ga-na′-men-i.
fourteen, a-ga-tōp′.

fifteen, a-ga-hūn′.
sixteen, a-ki′-ma.
seventeen, a-ku′-pa.
eighteen, ak′-te-tuk′-e.
nineteen, a-ga-mah′-pe.
twenty, nūm′-pa-pi-rah′.
twenty-one, nūm′-pa-pi′-ra-ka-ro-mah′-a-na.
thirty, na′-men-i-am-pi′-ra-kōsh.
forty, to′-pa-pi′-ra-kōsh.
fifty, keh-ūn′-am-pi′-ra-kōsh.
sixty, ki-ma′-am-pi′-ra-kōsh.
seventy, ku′-pa-am-pi′-ra-kōsh.
eighty, te-tuk′-e-am-pi′-ra-kōsh.
ninety, mah′-pe-am-pi′-ra-kōsh.
one hundred, i-sūk′-mah-a-na.
one thousand, i-su′-ki-ka-ku′-hi.
one hundred thousand, i-su′-ki-ka-ku′-hi-i-sūk-mah′-a-na.

6. na-ka-mah′-a-na, first one, or first time.
i-ka-ha′-sha-mah′-a-na, last one, or last time.

III. Adverbs.

7. Some of the principal adverbs are as follows: tash-bak′-tōsh, perhaps; ho-ra′-ke-ku′-ser-o, day before yesterday; mat-he-o′-mas-ta, day after to-morrow; tēn′-hash, afar off.

IV. Prepositions.

8. Prepositions follow the nouns which they govern; as, peh′-ti, by; mi-peh′-ti-nak′-ta, sit by me; mun-i-kūsh′-ta, through the water; ti-rōk′-ta, in the house.

V. Conjunctions.

9. ken′-i and ek-tēk′, and; ken′-i-e-pish′, and I said; ken′-i-wa′-ki-wa′-wa-ūsh, and I told him.

VI. Interjections.

10. sha! oh! sha! shi-ni′-hūsh! oh! how cold it is! sha! ma-na′-rūsh! oh! what pain I am in! sha! da′-de-shūsh! oh! how hot it is! i′-na! he′-he-he! i′-he! han′-ta! hark! i-hamp′-ta! hist! hush! ha-nis′-ta! look! behold! wa-he-teh′! you surprise me!

VII. Pronouns.

11. Pronouns are simple or fragmentary. The fragmentary pronouns are used in the declension of nouns and adjectives, and in the conjugation of verbs. The following may be regarded as an example of the intensive form of the simple pronoun:

mi′-o-na, I, myself, or I am.
ni′-o-na, thou, thyself, &c.
i′-o-na, he, himself, &c.
nu′-o-na, we, ourselves, or we are.
ni′-a-o-na, you, yourselves, &c.
i′-a-o-na, they, themselves, &c.

The form of the fragmentary pronouns is shown in the following declensions of nouns and adjectives.

mi-hŭn′-de, my mother.
ni-hŭn′-de, thy mother.
i-hŭn′-de, his mother.

min′-i-ke, my son.
nin′-i-ke, thy son.
i-ko′-ni-ke, his son.
min′-i-kŏsh, my sons.
nin′-i-kŏsh, thy sons.
i-ko′-ni-kŏsh, his sons.

mi-nu′-haŋ-ke, my daughter.
ni-nu′-haŋ-ke, thy daughter.
i-ko-nu′-haŋ-ke, his daughter.
mi-nu′-haŋ-kŏsh, my daughters.
ni-nu′-haŋ-kŏsh, thy daughters.
i-ko-nu′-haŋ-kŏsh, his daughters.
nu-nu′-haŋ-kŏsh, our daughters.
ni-a-nu′-haŋ-kŏsh, your daughters.
i-o-na-nu′-haŋ-kŏsh, their daughters.

mŏŋs, my wife.
nŏŋs, thy wife.
kŏŋs, his wife.
mŏŋ′-ker-ish, my wives.
nŏŋ′-ker-ish, thy wives.
kŏŋ′-ker-ish, his wives.

mi-be′-ro, my husband.
ni-be′-ro, thy husband.
i-be′-ro, her husband.
mi-be′-rŏsh, my husbands.
ni-be′-rŏsh, thy husbands.
i-be′-rŏsh, her husbands.

ma-shish′, I am good.
ni-shish′, thou art good.
iŋ-shish, he is good.
nu-shish′, we are good.
ni-a-shish′, you are good.
i-a-shish′, they are good.

VIII. Verbs.

The following examples show the forms of the verbs so far as determined, though quite incomplete.

i-wa′-sek-ŏsh, I do anything.
i-da′-sek-ŏsh, thou doest anything.
i-i′-sek-ŏsh, he does anything.
nu-i-sek′-ŏsh, we do anything.
ni-i-sek′-ŏsh, you do anything.
i-a-i-sek′-ŏsh, they do anything.
nu-nŏmp′-sha-sek′-ŏsh, we both do anything.

i-wa-sek′-tŏsh, I will do anything.
ni-de-sek′-tŏsh, thou wilt do anything.
i-sek′-tŏsh, he will do anything.
nu-i-sek′-tŏsh, we will do anything.
ni-a-sek′-tŏsh, you will do anything.
i-o-na-sek′-tŏsh, they will do anything.
nu-nŏmp′-sha-sek′-tŏsh, we both will do anything.
ni-a-be′-sek-ta (imp.), do it, all of you.
i-sek′-ta (imp.), do.

wa-dĕk′-tŭsh, } I am going.
wa-de′-hŭsh, }

tha-de′-hŭsh, thou art going.
i-de′-hŭsh, he is going.
nu-de′-hŭsh, we are going.
ni-a-de′-hŭsh, you are going.
i-a-de′-hŭsh, they are going.
nu-nomp′-sha-de′-hŭsh, we both are going.

wa-dĕk-tŭsh′, I will go.
tha-dĕk-tŭsh′, thou wilt go.
iŋ-dĕk-tŭsh′, he will go.
nu-dĕk-tŭsh′, we will go.
ni-tha′-dĕk-tŭsh′, you will go.
iŋ-a-dĕk-tŭsh′, they will go.
nu-nomp′-sha-dĕk-tŭsh′, we both will go.

wa-ki-su′-kŏsh, I go out.
tha-ki-su′-kŏsh, thou dost go out.
iŋ-ki-su′-kŏsh, he goes out.
nu-ki-su′-kŏsh, we go out.
ni-a-ki-su′-kŏsh, you go out.

iŋ-a-ki-su'-kōsh, they go out.
nu-nōmp'-sha-ki-su'-kōsh, we both go out.
ki-sūk'-ta (imp.), go out you.
sūk-ta (imp.), go out.

wa-wa'-ru-tōsh, I eat, or am eating.
tha-wa'-ru-tōsh, thou eatest, &c.
i-wa'-ru-tōsh, he eats, &c.
nu-wa'-ru-tōsh, we eat, &c.
ni-a-tha-wa'-ru-tōsh, you eat, &c.
i-a-wa'-ru-tōsh, they eat, &c.

wa-wa'-rūsh-tōsh, I will eat.
tha-wa'-rūsh-tōsh, thou wilt eat.
i-wa'-rūsh-tōsh, he will eat.
wa-nu'-rūsh-tōsh, we will eat.
ni-wa'-rūsh-tōsh, you will eat.
i-o-na-wa'-rūsh-tōsh, they will eat.

wa-wa'-rūt-wa-ke-he'-rūsh, I have done eating.
ni-wa'-ra-rūt-tha-ke-he'-rūsh, thou hast done eating.
iŋ-wa'-rūt-ke-he'-rūsh, he has done eating.
rūsh'-ta (imp.), eat, used in addressing a woman.
rū-ta'-na (imp.), eat.
wa-rūsh'-ta (imp.), eat on.
ru'-tōsh, eating, to eat.
wa-ra-ru'-tōsh, will you eat?
tash'-ka-ki-wa'-ra-ru-te'-ni-hōsh, what is the reason you do not eat?

wa-wa'-ka-pu-sōsh, I paint or write, or am painting, &c.
tha-ka-pu'-sōsh, thou dost paint or write, &c.
iŋ-ka-pu'-sōsh, he paints or writes, &c.
nu-ka-pu'-sōsh, we paint or write, &c.
ni-a-ka-pu'-sōsh, you paint or write, &c.
i-a-ka-pu'-sōsh, they paint or write, &c.
nu-nomp'-sha-pu'-sōsh, we both paint or write, &c.

wa-ka'-pūs-tōsh, I will paint or write.
tha-ka'-pūs-tōsh, thou wilt paint or write.
iŋ-ka'-pūs-tōsh, he will paint or write.
nu-ka'-pūs-tōsh, we will paint or write.
ni-a-tha-ka'-pūs-tōsh, you will paint or write.
i-a-ka'-pūs-tōsh, they will paint or write.
nu-nōmp'-sha-ka'-pūs-tōsh, we both will paint or write.
wa-ka'-pu-sōsh, to write.
wa-ka'-pu-se, a painting or writing.
ka'-pūs-ta (imp.), write.
a-be-ka'-pūs-ta, write, all of you.

wa-ka-pu'-sa-ma'-mank-a-hōsh, I am painting or writing all the while.
ni-tha-ka'-pu-sa-ma-mank'-a-hōsh, thou art, &c.
iŋ-ka'-pu-sa-ma'-mank-a-hōsh, he is, &c.
nu-a-na-ka-pu'-sa-ma-mank-a-hōsh, we are, &c.
ni-a-tha-ka-pu'-sa-ma-mank-a-hōsh, you are, &c.
i-a-ka-pu'-sa-ma-mank-a-hōsh, they are, &c.
nu-nōmp-shōs-ka-pu'-sa-ma-mank-a-hōsh, we both, &c.

i-wa'-push-i-de'-hūsh, I am thinking.
i-da'-push-i-de'-hūsh, thou art thinking.
iŋ-push-i-de'-hūsh, he is thinking.
nu-i-push-i-de'-hūsh, we are thinking.
ni-a-push-i-de'-hūsh, you are thinking.
i-a-push-i-de'-hūsh, they are thinking.

wa-hu'-na-wa'-kik-a-na'-kōsh, I will come and sit down.
tha-hu'-na-tha'-kik-a-na'-kōsh, thou wilt come, &c.
iŋ-hu'-na-kik-a-na'-kōsh, he will come, &c.
nu-nōmp'-sha-nu-hu'-ni-kik-a-na'-kōsh, we both will come, &c.

kas-ke'-wa-her-i-ki'-tōsh, I will tie.
kas-ke'-tha-her-i-ki'-tōsh, thou wilt tie.
i-kas-ke'-her-i-ki'-tōsh, he will tie.
nu-kas-ke'-her-i-ki'-tōsh, we will tie.
ni-kas-ke'-her-i-ki'-tōsh, you will tie.
i-a-kas-ke'-her-i-ki'-tōsh, they will tie.
nu-nōmp'-sha-kas-ke'-her-i-ki'-tōsh, we both will tie.

kas-ke'-wa-her-ish, I have tied.

wa'-hiŋsh, I have been there.
tha'-hiŋsh, thou hast been there.
i-wa'-hiŋsh, he has been there.
no'-hinsh, we have been there.

ni-a-tha'-hĭnsh, you have been there.
i-a-wa'-hĭnsh, they have been there.

wa-hĕn'-dŭsh, I drink, or am drinking.
tha-hĕn'-dŭsh, thou drinkest.
iŋ-hĕn'-dŭsh, he drinks.
nu-hĕn'-dŭsh, we drink.
ni-a-hĕn'-dŭsh, you drink.
iŋ-a-hĕn'-dŭsh, they drink.

wa-he-na'-ma-ma'-ka-hŏsh, I have been drinking all the while.
tha-he'-na-ma'-ka-hŏsh, thou hast been drinking all the while.
iŋ-hĕn'-da-ma'-ka-hŏsh, he has been drinking all the while.
nu-hĕn'-da-ma'-ka-hŏsh, we have been drinking all the while.
ni-a-hĕn'-da-ma'-ka-hŏsh, you have been drinking all the while.
i-a-hĕn'-da-ma'-ka-hŏsh, they have been drinking all the while.
wa-ra-hĕn'-dŭsh, have you drank?
wa-wa-he'-ni-hŏsh, I have not drank.
tha-hĕn'-tha-ko'-he-rŭsh, you have done drinking.

o-mun'-i-te-o'-wa-hĕ-rish-wa-ru'-he-shŭsh, I cut it off with an axe.
wa-ki-sŭk'-wa-de-i-wa'-ki-su'-kŏsh, I go out anywhere I please.

i-ma'-pot-kik-u'-na-kŏsh, he sits down on the ground.
tev'-e-ti-biŋ'-kŭsh, whose pipe is that?
tev'-e-ta-mi'-ni-swe'-ru-te, whose dog is that?
tev'-e-ta'-o-tĕsh, whose lodge is that?
tev-e-ya'-ki-ta-rŭsh, who are you looking after?
ma-tev'-e-tha-ki'-ta-rŭsh, what are you looking after?
tev'-e-ta-min'-i-skĕ-rish, whose horses are those?
ĭk'-baŋ, laughing.
ĭk-baŋ'-ma-ka-hŏsh, laughing all the while.
ra-tuk-he', crying.
ra-ta'-hŏsh, to cry.
ra-tuk'-he-a-ma'-ka-hŏsh, crying all the while.
nak'-ta (imp.), sit down (to a man).
na'-ka-na (imp.), sit down (to a woman).
ra-ta' (imp.), go.
ra-ha'-na (imp.), go (to a woman).
shi-ha'-ra-ta (imp.), do well.

kap'-kĕsh, it snows.
kap-ke'-kŏsh, it will snow.
kap-ke'-a-maŋ'-ka-hŏsh, it is snowing all the while.
ra-she-de'-hŭsh, it thaws, or melts.
ra-she'-dĕk-tŭsh, it will thaw or melt.
ktaŋ'-hŏsh, it freezes.
ktaŋ'-tŏsh, it will freeze.
ra-pa'-na-rŭsh, it hails.
ra-pa'-nak-tŭsh, it will hail.
he-i'-ni-hŭsh, it thunders.

CHAPTER XXI.

VOCABULARY OF THE MANDAN LANGUAGE.

A.

above, a-ke'-ta.
afar off, tĕŋ-hash'.
affection, pah'-a-de, affection, love.
all, aŋ'-be.
and, ken'-i.
ken'-i-e'-pish, and I said.
ken'-i-wa-ki'-wa, and I told him.
ek'-tĕk, and, also.
ants, ka'-ra-si-sit'-ka.
anything, i'-tas-kash-ka.
arm, a'-de (sing.), a'-rŭsh (pl.), an arm or wing.
arrow, ma-hi'-pe-kŏsh.
autumn, ptan'-de.
axe, o'-ma-na-te.

B.

back, nūp'-h̄e.
bad, h̄e'-kōsh.
beans, o-min'-i-ke.
o-min'-ik-sa'-ni-ker-e, peas.
o-min'-i-ke-h̄ti'-ker-i, potatoes.
bear, ma-to'.
ma-to'-pa, a bear's head.
ma-to'-ker-i, all bears.
ni-shi'-da, a black bear.
beard, hi'-ke-ru'-kis.
bed, o-munk'-e-i-sik-ōsh, to make a bed.
behold, ha-nis'-ta, look! behold!
below, ma-pit'-a.
ma-pit', down, below.
belt, i-ūh'-pa-e-te', a sash or belt.
bird, ma-dēk'-su-ke, a small bird.
bladder, i-dah'-e.
blood, i'-da.
i-de-she'-ro-rūsh, cholera, when the blood turns to water.
blue, to'-he.
boat, mi-na'-ki.
bone, a-hu'-de.
both, nōm'-psha, two, both.
bow, wa-ra'-i-ru'-pa.
box, wi-du'-ke.
ma-ne'-wi-du'-ke, a wooden box.
boy, sūk'-nu-mak, a boy.
breast, tah'-a-rah'-e.
breechcloth, mik'-e.
buffalo, ptīn'-de.
be'-ro-ka, a bull.
be-rūk'-nat-ka, a bull's heart.
burn, rap-tēsh', to burn.
by, peh'-ti.
i-sa'-kaŋ-a-sōsh', by and by, after a while.

C.

call, ru-ker'-ish, to call.
cheat, ma-nōh'-a-ha-rūsh, to cheat any one.
chicken, si-pu'-ska, prairie chicken.
clear, de'-h̄e.
cloud, ha'-a-de.
ha-de-ku'-ta, sky, beyond the clouds.
ha-de'-to-he-kūsh'-ta, in the blue cloud or sky.
coat, i-ma-shu'-te.
cold, shi'-ni-hūsh.
corn, ko-haŋ'-te, corn or grain of any kind.
ma-pe-her'-i, pounded corn or meal.
i-pe'-ke, a mortar for pounding corn.
count, pa-ki'-ri-rūsh, to count.
crow, ho-ki'-h̄a-ka. *Corvus.*
crying, ra-tuh'-e.
ra-tuh'-e-a-ma'-ka-hōsh, crying all the while.

D.

darkness, haŋ-pe'-a-rēsh'-ka.
day, ka-she'-kōsh.
mat-h̄e'-o-nas-ta, day after to-morrow.
deceive, ka-uh'-ash, to deceive.
deer, ma-mo-na'-ku.
ma-mo-na'-ku-dōp'-h̄e, a skin of a deer.
ma-mo-na'-ku-de'-si-ke, the tongue of a deer.
destroy, ki-mih'-er-ēsh, to destroy.
die, te'-rūsh, to die.
dirty, wa-rat'-ker-i, dirty, foul.
dog, men-i-swe'-ru-te, eaters of dung.
door, be-de'-he.
drink, hēŋ-dūsh', to drink.
duck, pa'-to-he.

E.

eagle, ma'-si, war eagle.
ptan'-rūsh, gray eagle.
ear, as'-kash.
eating, ru-tōsh'.
egg, si-ko'-h̄e.
si-ko'-h̄ōsh, (pl.)
elevation, ma-ah'-te.
elk, ōm'-pa.
end, o-na'-ke-o-hank'-ta, the end of all being, the end of the world.
enemy, wi-ra-taŋ'-de.
evening, i-stūn'-de-hūsh, the latter part of the day.
eye, is-ta'.
is-ta-su'-ni-ke, eyes of a cat.

F.

face, is'-ti.
fall, dōp-h̄ēsh', to fall.
ma-pit'-a-dōp-h̄ēsh', to fall down.
father, ratz.
feather, si.
si-ish', (pl.)
wo'-ki-rūsh, a head-dress of feathers.
female, mi'-ka, the female of any animal.
finger, ōŋ-ka'-he, fingers, claws, &c.
fire, wa'-ra-de.
fish, po, a fish.
po-taŋ'-de, a catfish.
po-tuk'-e, a long, slender fish.
pōp-shi'-de, "silver eye," a white, flat fish.
po-su'-nak-er-ish, small fish.
po'-ni-ka, the roe of a fish.
flint, ma-hik'-shu-ke.
flower, o-sed'-e-he.
follow, wah-a-hūsh', to follow.
food, wo-ru'-te, food of any kind.
foot, shi.
fox, i-ru'-te.
o'-h̄a, a prairie fox.
friend, pta-ni'-nah-ah̄.

G.

girl, sūk'-mi-he, a girl.
sūk-ham'-a-he, a little child.
go, de'-hūsh, to go.
good, shēź.
shēź'-ku-shōsh, very good, truly good.
goose, mi'-haŋ.
grass, h̄aŋ-h̄e'.
h̄aŋ-h̄e'-sa-kōsh, dried grass, hay.
h̄aŋ-shi'-h̄e-na, sharp grass, thistles.
grease, i-ker'-i, grease, fat.
great, h̄tēsh, large, great.
gun, wa-ta'-shi-rū'-pa.

H.

hail, ra-ka-nan'-de.
ra-pa'-na-rūsh, it hails.
hair, pa'-h̄i.
hand, oŋ'-ke.
handsome, shi-na'-shūsh.
hark! haŋ'-ta!
hawk, i'-na, and i'-he.
ōm'-psi, a yellow hawk.
head, pa.
hear, wa-ēsh', to hear.
heart, nat'-ka.
nat-kaŋ'-ka-sīsh, a hard heart.
nat-kaŋ'-si-hūsh, a strong heart.
heel, shi-ru'-te.
hereafter, haŋ'-ka, time to come, hereafter.
highlands, ma-hank'-wa'-ko-rōsh, highlands, or hills.
hist! i-hamp'-ta! hist! hush!
hot, da'-de-shūsh.
house, o'-ti, house, or lodge.
ti-rōk'-ta, in the house.
hūsh'-ta, the back part of the house.
hurrah! uk-a-he'! hurrah! all hands!
husband, i'-be-ro.

I.

I, mi.
ice, h̄o'-de.
in, rōk'-ta.
inquire, ki-mah̄'-ēsh, to inquire of any one.
iron, wa-tush'-e-ma'-he.
wa-tush'-o-te, white iron.
wa-tush'-ap-si, black iron.
wa-tush'-sa-ker'-i, red iron, copper.
wa-tush'-se-de, yellow iron, brass.
wa-tush'-i-wi-pu'-shi, a file, or iron whetstone.
wa-tush'-o-du'-ke, a shot-pouch.
island, wit'-ka.

K.

kettle, bi-ru'-h̄e.
kill, te-her'-ūsh, to kill.
knee, iŋ-ta'.
knife, ma-hi'.

L.

land, mah-i-ki', bad land.
laugh, ik-haŋ', ki-ki-da'-shōsh, } to laugh.

leg, do′-ke.
leggin, hŏŋ′-shi.
level, ŏp-shi′-do-shĭsh, a level prairie.
life, i′-ni-hŭsh, alive, health, life.
i′-ni-he, alive.
i′-ni-sĕsh, to live.
light, i-de-aħ′-e.
lodge, o′-ti.
ti-hink′-o-ti, a skin lodge.
long, ba′-ska.

M.

man, nu-mang′-ke.
nu-mang-ka′-ki, the people.
nu-mang-ka′-ħi-kŏsh, a man's acts.
nu-mang-ka′-ke-nat-kaź, a man's heart.
nu-mank′-shi, a chief.
many, hank-tĕsh′, a great many.
meat, mas-kap′-e, meat of all kinds.
moon, i-stŭn′-mi-na′-ke.
morning, mam′-psi-ta.
wa-mam′-psi-ta, early in the morning.
mother, hŭn′-de, and i-hŭn′-de.
mouth, i′-a.
mud, tŭn′-tu-ke.
ma-tŭn′-tu-kŏsh, soft mud.
tŭn′-tu-kŏsh, soft, a bog or marsh.
muskrat, shan-ću′-ke.

N.

nail, ŏŋ-ka′-o-sha-ke.
navel, dŏp′-ta-su.
near, sha′-ha.
neck, i-ta′-o-nu.
night, i-stŭn′.
north, mi-si′-a-hank′-ta.
mi-si-hank′-ta-ro-push′-a-hank′-ta, northeast.
pa-sha-hank′-ta-ro-ta-hank′-ta, southeast.
a-ga-hank′-ta-ro-ta-mi-sa-hank′-ta, northwest.
nose, pa′-ħu, nose, beak of a bird.
pa-ħu-ptap′-taħ, moose, animal with a long nose.
nothing, mĭk′-ska.
now, na-ka′, na-kan′, } now, at this time.

O.

oh, sha!
old, ħi′-hŏsh.
open, rŭp-shuk′-ŏsh, to open.
rŭp-shuk′, opened.
outside, ma-tĭn′-da, out of doors, outside.
owl, iħ-i′-he, large hooting owl. *Bubo Virginianus.*
iħ-ik′-shu-ke, small owl.

P.

paddle, i-pa-ħa′-ka, oar or paddle.
part, o-kup′-e.
perhaps, tush′-hak-tŏsh.
pine, ma-na′-ħo-pin′-i.
pipe, i-hink′-e.
polecat, shŏnk′-te.
poor, a-ka′-ri-he.
pox, ħed′-e-pe, small-pox.
pumpkin, ko′-de.
ko′-de-se-ha′-ru-tŏsh, melons or pumpkins eaten uncooked.
push, put-kĕsh′, to push.

R.

rabbit, maħ-tik′-e. *Lepus campestris.*
maħ-tiħ′-shu-ke, small rabbit. *Lepus artemisia.*
rain, ħai′-dŭsh.
ħai′-i-kŭn′-dŭsh, a rainbow.
raven, ke-ka′.
red, se.
river, pa-sa′-he.
pa-sank′-shu-kŏsh, small rivers, creeks.
robin, ma′-de-kaŋ′-ka. *Turdus migratorius.*
rock, mi-su′-ne-ke-ħtĕsh, a large rock.
mi-su′-ne-ke-ħa-ma′-he-na, a soft rock.
run, pte′-hŭsh, to run.

S.

salt, wa-sku-sho′-te, white sugar.
sandstone, wi-pu′-shi, whetstone, sandstone.
scalp, pa-dŏp′-ħe.
seat, i′-ta.
see, wa-hĕsh′, to see.
shake, ka-tid′-i-ri-sŏsh, to shake.

sheep, aŋ-sah'-te, mountain sheep, big-horn.
shoe, hōm'-pa, shoe, moccasin.
shoulder, a'-kit.
sinew, hi'-se.
sing, wa-ki'-ki-na'-rūsh, to sing.
sister, ta-mi'-he-na.
ptan'-kōsh, elder sister.
skin, dōp-hi'.
small, ham'-o-he.
smooth, saŋ'-sish.
ka-saŋ'-sōsh, to smooth or make smooth.
snow, wa-he'.
soldier, ka-wa'-ka-ra-kah'-a.
something, i-ko-tu'-i.
son, ko'-ni-ke.
sour, ha-rūsh'.
speak, rōt-kish', to speak.
spirit, ma-nah'-i-ke.
spread, phi'-her-ish, to spread.
spring, be'-hi-nūn-de (season).
star, hkik'-e.
hkik'-e-wa-ha-ne-hōsh', the star that does not move, north star.
steal, wa-nūn'-dūsh, to steal.
stone, min'-dēh-tēsh, a large stone or rock.
strike, ro-rūsh', to strike.
strong, si-hūsh'.
summer, ra-ske'-ke.
sun, ma-hamp'-mi-na'-ke.
surprise, wa-he-tēh', you surprise me.
swan, ma-de-hōp'-ni.
sweep, īp-kuk'-i-shūsh, to sweep.
īp-kuk'-i-sha, a broom, or anything to sweep with.
sweet, sku'-hosh.

T.

tail, shōn'-te.
shōn-te-ha'-ska, long tail, a panther.
tallow, sin'-de.
thaw, ra-she'-de-hūsh, it thaws, or melts.
thief, wa-nūn-deh'-te.
thigh, do-kōsh', the thighs.
think, wa-push'-i-de, to think.
this, ant.
an-to-rash', this one, this thing.
ant-wi-do'-ke, this sack.
tie, kas-kēsh', to tie.
toad, hat'-ka.
tobacco, ma-na-she'.
to-day, i-ham'-pe.
toe, shi'-pa, the great toe.
shi-ha'-pa, the second toe.
shi-ni'-ka, the little toe.
to-morrow, mat-he'.
tongue, de'-si-ke.
tooth, hi.
trade, wi-ka'-rūsh, to trade or barter.
tree, ma'-na, wood, or a tree.
ma'-na-i-nin'-dūsh, a tree.
ma-na-a', the bark of trees.
ma-na'-i-ta-hu, an oak tree.
ma-na'-ho-pin-i, a pine tree.
ma-na'-o-ki-saŋ-ka, forks of a tree.
ma-na'-wa-ra-wi-rūsh, elm-wood, of which bows are made.
ma-na-wah'-e, cottonwood.
ma-na-sūk', a shrub or bush.
ma-na-pe', or, a'-pe, a-pish' (pl.), leaves.
ma-na-rōh'-te, a forest.
ma-na-ker'-i, all wood.
ma'-na-i-nin'-de-a-ke'-ta, on the tree.
ma'-na-ka-kin'-he, a wooden wedge.
ma'-na-i-tu-rūk'-shu-ke, a spear or lance.
tremble, ka-tid'-re-kōsh, to tremble, quake.
turkey, ma-ru'-si.
turnip, ma-hōsh'.
turtle, kip-saŋ'-de, turtle or tortoise.
twisted, ka-min'-ish.

U.

ugly, hik'-a-na-shōsh.
upon, a-ki'-a, on or upon.

V.

vein, i'-du-ke, a vein or channel.
i-i'-du-ke, a vein or channel for the blood.
very, ku-shōsh', truly, very.

ku-she'-mi-ka, very good, very true.

village, mi'-ti.

mi-ti'-o-tōsh, with the camp or village.

W.

walk, nin'-dūsh, to walk.

war-club, mih'-a-ske.

warrior, ka-ha'-re-kōsh, a brave or warrior.

water, mun'-i, and men'-i.

men-i-ker'-i, all water, the sea.

men-i-wa'-rat-ker'-ish, dirty water.

men-i-ka-tu'-sōsh, quick or rapid water.

men-i-i-wa'-ka-he, runners on the river shore, plover.

mun-ih'-te, a lake.

mun-i-hin'-i, a spring of water.

mun-i-pu'-shu-hūsh, to swim.

men-i-e'-ha-ka-he, at the water's edge.

men-i-kūsh'-ta, through the water.

we, mi'-o-na.

weak, a-hi'-kōsh.

weed, ma-he'.

what, ta.

ma-tev'-i, what is it?

which, ko-tev'-i, which one?

white, sho'-te.

wa-sku-sho'-te, white sugar, same as salt.

wa-shi', and wa-shi'-ta, a white man.

wa-shi'-psi, a black man.

wa-shi'-ta-ko-haŋ'-te, the white man's corn.

wa-shi'-ta-ptin'-de, the white man's cow.

wa-shi'-ta-ma'-to, the white man's bear, or hog.

wa-shi'-tas-hte, white man's big-horn, sheep.

who, tev'-e.

wife, kōns.

wind, she.

windpipe, i-ni'-he.

wish, i-te'-rūsh, to wish.

with, o-tōsh'.

ko-ke'-ta, within.

kūsh'-ta, under, within.

wolf, she-he'-ke, prairie wolf.

woman, mi'-he-mi-he-shi'-na-shūsh, a handsome woman.

wood, ma'-na.

writing, ka-pu'-se, painting or writing.

Y.

yellow, psi'-de.

yes, hōŋ.

hai'-i, same as Dakota, "how?" "yes," "it is good."

yesterday, ho'-da-ke.

ho-ra-ke'-ku-ser'-o, day before yesterday.

CHAPTER XXII.

XIII. Omahas.—XIV. Iowas, or Otos.

SKETCH OF THE OMAHA, AND IOWA OR OTO INDIANS.

Having made comparatively few observations in person in regard to the Indian tribes of the Lower Missouri, I shall not at this time attempt to present a detailed history of them. It is my intention at some future period to investigate with care all the languages of the Indian tribes now located in the Valley of the Missouri, which have not already been sufficiently studied for ethnological and philological purposes, and to work out the history of their migrations from all the materials within my reach. As I remarked of the tribes previously described, but little information of a reliable character can be obtained from their own traditions farther back than one hundred years. It so happens, however, that most of the Indians at the present time living on the Lower Missouri migrated from the eastward, and were visited and noticed by the earliest explorers of the country. The writings of the Jesuit fathers are invaluable to the student of Indian history. I shall, therefore, content myself with making a few extracts from such of their works as are within my reach, without pretending at this time to exhaust the subject.

That the Iowas migrated from the Mississippi westward to their present location on the Missouri, we have very reliable written evidence. According to Schoolcraft, Father Marquette visited the Iowas as far back as 1673, and records their residence near the mouth of the Des Moines River. Allusion is also made to them in the narrative of the adventures of one of La Salle's party, Father Zenobius Membré, who seems to have visited the different tribes located in the Mississippi Valley in 1680. He remarks that the Kickapoos and the Ainones (Iowas) live on the western side (of Mississippi), and occupy two villages. In Le Sueur's Voyage up the Mississippi, in 1699–1700, several references are made to this tribe, called by him Ayavois. On page 101 of Mr. J. G. Shea's admirable collection of "Early Voyages up and down the Mississippi," Le Sueur says: "At this spot (near Mankato or Blue Earth River, latitude 44° 13′ N.), he met nine Scioux, who told him that this river was the country of the Scioux of the West, of the Ayavois, and the Otoctatas (Otos), a little further; that it was not their custom to hunt on the grounds of others without being invited by those to whom they belonged; that when they should wish to come to the fort to get supplies, they would be exposed to be cut off by their enemies coming up or going down these rivers, which are narrow, and that if he wished to take pity on them, he must settle on the Mississippi, in the neighborhood of the mouth of St. Peter's River, where the Ayavois, the Otoctatas, and the Scioux could come as well as they." It seems also that even at that time, the Iowas as well as the Otos were to some extent an agricultural people. On page 104: "On the 22d, two Canadians were sent out to invite the Ayavois and the Otoctatas to come and make a village near the fort, because these Indians are laborious and accustomed to cultivate the ground, and he hoped to obtain provisions from them, and make them work the mines." Again, we may from Le Sueur's account arrive very nearly at the time when the Iowas and Otos migrated across the country westward to the Missouri. On page 106 of the same work: "On the 16th (of November, 1699), the Scioux returned to the village, and it was ascertained that the Ayavois and Otoctatas had gone to station themselves on the side of the River Missouri, in the neighborhood of the Maha, a nation dwelling in those quarters."

In Alcedo's Spanish Geography, we find the following paragraph in regard to Iowa River: "Which runs southeast into the Mississippi, sixty-one miles above Iowa Rapids, where, on the east side of the river, is Iowa Town, which twenty years ago could furnish three hundred warriors. The upper Iowa town is about fifteen miles below the mouth of the river, on the east side of Mississippi, and could formerly furnish four hundred warriors."

This tribe, which they call Ayauways, seems not to have attracted the special attention of those remarkable travellers and explorers, Lewis and Clarke, yet from incidental allusions to them, we know that they resided on the Missouri near the commencement of the present century. We cannot now attempt to trace out the different villages of the Iowas along the track of their migration, a work which has already been so well done by Mr. Schoolcraft in the third part of his Report. They are at this time located on a reservation on the west side of the Missouri, near latitude 40°. They number about four hundred and fifty persons, have progressed much in the cultivation of the soil, and many of them are partially civilized. Like most of the Indians on the frontier, they seem, however, to contract more readily the vices than adopt the virtues of the white race. Mission schools have been established among them, at which from thirty to fifty scholars are instructed.

The grammatical structure of the Iowa language has been carefully wrought out by those indefatigable missionaries, Messrs. Hamilton and Irvin, and published in several small volumes at the Mission. These books having been prepared especially for the use of the Mission, they have not been circulated to any extent for ethnological and philological purposes. The most important publications on the Iowa language prepared by these gentlemen are,

1st. An Elementary Book of the Iowa Language, with an English translation, by Wm. Hamilton and S. M. Irvin, under the direction of the Board of Foreign Missions of the Presbyterian Church. J. B. Ray, interpreter. Iowa and Sac Mission Press, Indian Territory, 1843. Small octavo; pp. 101.

2d. An Iowa Grammar, illustrating the principles of the Language used by the Iowa, Oto, and Missouri Indians. Prepared and printed by Rev. Wm. Hamilton and Rev. S. M. Irvin, under the direction of the Presbyterian Board of Foreign Missions. Iowa and Sac Mission Press, 1848. Small octavo; pp. 152. There is also a small volume of hymns, but without an English translation.

In the preface to the Grammar, the authors make the following very interesting and truthful remarks:

"The language used by the Iowa and Oto and Missouri tribes is the same; a slight difference is perceptible in their mode of speaking, and a few words are common to one tribe that are not common to the others, yet the difference is not greater than is often found to prevail among the inhabitants of the different States.

"There is so much similarity in the languages of many of the Indian tribes, that it shows them to have had one common origin, while others, again, differ as widely as two languages can differ. This dissimilarity is seen in the Iowa and Sac languages, in which no two words are alike.

"If the language of the Iowa Indians be taken as the starting-point (though tradition says that they, with many other tribes, were originally Winnebagoes), then those of the same family would, as far as has been ascertained, stand related to it in the following order:

1st. Iowa.
Oto.
Missouri.
2d. Winnebago.
3d. Kansas.
Osage.
Inapaw.
Omahaw.
Ponca.

"A number of words are common to all these tribes, and not a few words differ only in the accent and the change of a few letters, indicating a common origin; yet time has produced such a change that in conversing together an interpreter is necessary.

"The barrenness which is supposed to belong to most Indian languages, does not result from the structure or nature of the language, but from the want of ideas in those who use it. So far as they have ideas, they do not lack words to express them, though the mode of expression among them is often as different from that in use among us as their language is from ours."

A few vocabularies of the Iowa language were obtained by early explorers, but they are all superseded by the more complete and accurate works of Messrs. Hamilton and Irvin.

The history of the Otos and Missouris does not differ materially from that of the Iowas just given. By reference to the map it will be seen that they occupy at the present time a reservation on the parallel of 40°, on the Big Blue River, near the head waters of the Big Nemaha River, a portion of their land being included within the boundary of Nebraska and a part in Kansas. They formerly ranged over an extensive area south of the Platte River. They number about six hundred persons of both sexes.

The Omahas formerly ranged over a large area extending from the mouth of the Platte to the Niobrara, on the south side of the Missouri. They are now located on a reservation north of parallel 42°, and bordering upon the river, as indicated on the map accompanying this memoir. A mission school has long been established among them, and their attempts to cultivate the soil have been attended with great success. They number about eight hundred souls.

The Ponkas speak the same language, though forming a distinct tribe, and have their reservation on Ponka River, south of the Niobrara. They make some feeble attempts to cultivate the soil, and obtain thereby a partial support, but they are, for the most part, in their original wild condition, and owing to the almost entire absence of game from their borders, are most of the time in a state bordering on starvation.

A number of vocabularies of the Omaha and Ponka language have been published by various writers, as Long, Prince Neuwied, Gallatin, &c., but no attempt has ever been made to work out its grammatical structure. A small pamphlet of perhaps sixteen pages was prepared some years ago by a gentleman connected with the Mission, containing a few words, phrases, and hymns, in the language, but inasmuch as the English equivalents are not given, it is of no use to the student of general philology.

VOCABULARY OF THE OMAHA LANGUAGE.

A.

above, ma'-shi-a-ta.
alive, ni'-a.
all, waŋ-gi'-re.
ankle, si-taħ'-e.
arm, a.
arrow, ma.
autumn, ta, } dead, it is dead.
tah, }
axe, man'-the-pe.

B.

back, nang'-ka.
bad, pi'-a-źi.
bean, ham'-bre-eŋ-ge.
bear, man'-ću, grizzly bear.
wa-tha'-be, black bear.
beard, i'-hi.
beaver, źa'-be.
bird, wa-źing'-a.
bison, te.
bitter, tōħ'-a.
black, tha'-be.
bladder, neħ'-e, and naħ'-e.
blood, wa'-mi.
blue, to.
boat, man'-de.
ta-de'-i-ga-da, ship drawn by the wind.
body, źu'-ga.
bog, nish-tash'-ta.
bone, wa-hi'.
bow, nan'-de.
boy, nu-shing'-e.
bread, wa-mŭth'-ke.
breast, mang'-e.
brother, wi-shen'-se, my elder brother.
wi-thang'-e, my younger brother.
burns, a'-ne, he burns.
by, ka'-ha.
nīng'-ka-ha, by the shore.
ath-ka'-de, by and by.

C.

call, ba, he calls.
cattle, te-tha'-be, black cattle.
chief, ni'-ka-ka-hi', and nu'-da-ha-ga'.
claw, sha'-ge, hoof, claw.
cloth, źe-a-di-gra', breechcloth.
coat, wo-na'-źi, thin coat.
corn, wa-ta'-the.

wa′-ri-to′-be, corn-meal.
cold, thni.
crow, ka′-he.
cry, ha′-ge.
ha-ga′-i, crying.

D.

dance, nan′-te, he dances.
darkness, o-kah′-na-pa′-zi.
daughter, wi-shang′-e, ni-nis′-i, } my daughter.
day, am′-ba.
deer, tah′-ti.
door, ti′-źe-be′-o-gra, house entrance.
drink, rat′-i, he drinks.
rat′-a, drinking.
duck, nih′-a-shing′-a.

E.

ear, ni′-ta.
earth, tan′-de.
eat, wa′-ra-te, he eats.
wa′-ra-ti, he is eating.
wa′-ra-te, wa′-ra-ta, } eating.
egg, wet-a′.
elk, am′-pa.
embark, man-de′-o-kre, he embarks.
enemy, o-ke′-te.
evening, pa′-ze.
exist, an-go′, we are, exist.
thi-ah′, you are.
e′-ga, he is.

F.

face, en′-de.
far, wi-a-hi′-de, far, far off.
fat, we-hre′.
father, en-da′-de, my father.
fin, we-u-thu′-ka-he.
finger, nam-be′-we-pa′-zu, the forefinger, to point with.
fire, pe′-te.
fish, hu′-hu.
hu′-hu-shing-a, small fish.
we′-to-kre, roe of a fish.
flash, źu.
flint, ma′-hi-si.
flower, źa-hra′.
fly, han′-te-ga.
foot, thi, and si.
forest, hra′-be.
fox, te.
friend, ka′-ge.

G.

ghost, o′-wi-ya′-wa, angel.
girl, mi′-shing-e, a young girl.
go, the, he goes.
good, o′-da, and u′-da.
goose, mih′-e.
mih-a-hi′, goose-hair, feathers.
great, ah′-te.
gun, wa-hut′-a.

H.

hail, ma′-se.
hair, na-źi′-ha.
hand, nam′-be.
handsome, o-ro-kam′-be.
he, e, he or she.
head, pa.
wash′-ki, top of the head.
wa-ra′-ge, head-dress.
hear, wa-na′-e, he hears.
heart, nan′-de.
heel, thi′-re-de.
hill, pa-he′.
horse, shŭn′-ga.
hot, nah′-a-de.
husband, wi-e-krang′-ke, my husband.

I.

I, wi.
ice, nŭh′-e.
in, man′-te.
ti-man′-te, in the house.
ma′-ha-te, in the sky.
infant, shing′-e-shing′-e.

insect, wa-kre', } worm or insect.
wa-gri',
źa-gri'-ska, wood insect, flea.

iron, man'-the.
man-thĕth'-ka, white iron, silver.
man-thĕth'-ka-thi, gold, yellow iron.
man-the'-shi-de, } copper, red iron.
man-the'-shu-de,
man-the'-ma, lead.

island, ni-ran'-da.

K.

kettle, ner'-he, } iron kettle.
ther'-he,

kill, wa-te'-re, } he kills.
wa-na'-a-he'-re,

knee, shi-nan'-de.

knife, ma'-hi.

L.

lake, ne-o-ri'-sha.

late, kan'-te-da.

laugh, ih'-a.

leg, źe'-ga, and źi'-be.

leggin, o-tah'.

life, ta'-źi.

light, o-kam'-be.

lightning, thi-am'-be, and thi-gre'-the.

limb, źa'-ka-ha.

liver, te-ra'-he.

lodge, ti, house or lodge.

log, za, and źa.

love, nit'-a.

M.

man, no, and nu.
ni-a-she'-ge-o-ke'-ni, red man, Indian.

meat, ta.
wash-e', fat meat.

melon, tha'-ka-ra'-te.

midday, mi-ro-mash'-źi.

midnight, ha-ūth-kath'-ka.

mink, to-shing'-e.

moccasin, him'-be.
wa-him'-be, shoe, wooden moccasins.

mole, ma-ni'-gra.

moon, mi-am'-be.

morning, ha'-hi-kat-e.

mother, e-na'-ha, my mother.

mountain, pa-he-mah'-shi.

mouth, i.

N.

nail, sha'-ge.

navel, re'-ta.

near, ash'-ka.

neck, pa'-hi.

never, sha'-sha.

new, te'-ka.

night, ha.

no, ang'-ka-źi.

nose, pa.

nothing, e-da-das'-the-źi.

O.

oats, shang'-e-wa-rat'-e, horse-feed.

old, i-sha'-ke.

on, a-gra'.
hra'-be-a-ga'-ha, on the tree.

otter, nu'-zhra.

P.

paddle, man'-de-o-ro'-ka-hi, oar.

part, do'-pa.

partridge, u-shi-wa'-re.

pepper, we-u-ki'-hi.

pipe, ni'-ni-bah.

plain, tan'-de, prairie.

polecat, man'-ga.

potato, nu, and nu'-tan-ge.

Q.

quill, ma'-sha.

R.

rain, na-źe'.

red, źe'-de.

river, ni.

run, taŋ'-re, he runs.

S.

sail, wah-eh'-a, muslin, cloth.
sash, i-pi'-ra-ge', belt.
scale, shi-she'.
scalp, ni-ka'-na-źi-ha.
seat, nin'-de, rump.
see, tam'-be, he sees.
shirt, wo-na'-źi-bre'-ka.
shot-pouch, ma-u'-źa.
shoulder, eng-ke'-de.
sinew, ta-ka'.
sing, wa-a', he sings.
sister, wi-shan'-se, wi-tang'-e, } younger sister.
skin, nah.
sky, mah'-e, clouds.
smooth, shi'-ah-ći.
snake, wes'-a, and weth'-a.
snow, mas'-he.
something, e-da'-das-the.
son, wi-shing'-e, my son.
soon, oh-re', early.
sour, tha'-re.
speak, i'-e, he speaks.
spear, man'-de-hi.
spirit, wa-kan'-da, Great Spirit.
wa-na-he'-pi-a'-źe, evil spirit.
spring, ni-hang'-a, of water.
me, mme, } a season.
squash, wa'-ta-mo'-he.
squirrel, thin'-ga.
star, mi-ka'-e.
steamboat, pe'-te-man'-de.
stomach, nih'-a.
stone, i'-e.
i-e-tan'-ga, big stone, rock.
stream, wa-te'-ska.
strike, o-ti', he strikes.
strong, a'-wa-źi.
summer, nu'-ge.
sun, mi.
sweet, thi'-re.

T.

that, she.
she'-ta, that man.
she'-ra, that thing.
thigh, ze'-shu.
think, e-re'-ga, he thinks.
this, the.
thou, thi.
throat, we-nam'-bre.
through, a-ku-than'-de.
ni'-a-ku-than'-de, through the water.
thunder, ing-re'-ho-ta.
tie, han'-ta, he ties.
toad, i-haŋ'-gi-ta.
tobacco, ni'-ni.
to-day, am'-ba-de.
toe, si'-pa.
to-morrow, kath'-a-ni.
tongue, re'-ze, and re'-se.
tooth, hi.
tree, hra'-be.
turnip, nu'-kre.
turtle, ke.

U.

ugly, u-kash'-ni-da.
under, ki'-ke.

V.

valley, wōh-mis'-ka.
vein, kah.
village, ta'-we, town.
wa-kan'-da-ta'-we, heaven, God's village.

W.

walk, na-ni', he walks.
wampum, wa-nam'-pi.
war-club, wah-pe'.
warrior, wa-na'-she.
water, ni.
ni-tan'-ga, great water.
we, au'-go.
weak, wa-he'-hi.

weed, ma'-hi.
what? e-da'-da, what is it?
wi'-a-wa'-tha, what thing?
wheat, wa-mŭth'-ka.
white, thka.
who, e'-be.
wife, wi-ha'-he-na, my wife.
wind, te'-de.
wing, a'-hi.
winter, mar'-e.
wish, eth'-ka, he wishes.
within, man'-te.
without, a'-shi.
wolf, shŭn-tan'-ga.
woman, mi-źing'-e, and gath-za'-se.
she'-mi-shing'-e, an unmarried woman.
wood, źa.

Y.

year, o-ma'-re-ka.
yellow, thi.
yes, a-ha'.
yesterday, thi-da'-di.
young, shin'-ga, little.

VOCABULARY OF THE IOWA, OR OTO LANGUAGE.

A.

above, mang'-kri.
i-ro'-ma-ha, above, on a stream.
alive, ih'-a.
all, pro-ke'.
ankle, thi'-ka.
another, o-ki-će'.
ant, na-kan'-yi-ske.
arm, a-kra'-će.
arrow, ma.
ash, ko-hŭn'-ye.
autumn, wa-ha'-he, full harvest.
tan'-yen-ta, falling of leaves, dead leaves.
axe, en'-thwe.

B.

back, nang'-ke.
bad, pĭsh'-kun-yi, not good.
bark, na'-ha.
beak, pa-thŭh'.
bean, ōn'-ye.
bear, man-to', grizzly bear.
mŭn-će', black bear.
beard, i'-hi, hair of the mouth.
beaver, ra-we'.
bird, wa-yeng'-e.
bitter, pa.
black, the'-we, and she'-we.
bladder, će'-ye-he, and wa-će'-ye.
blood, wa-pa'-ke.
blue, to'-ho-će.
boat, pa-će'.
pa-će'-ban-ye, ship, large boat.
ta-će'-re-ta-u'-kra, mast, support for the sail.
body, i'-ro.
bone, wa-hu'.
bow, mah'-tu.
boy, i'-ćin'-to-ing-e.
breast, man'-ge.
breechcloth, de'-ro-ken'-ye.
brother, hi-yi'-na, my elder brother.
burn, ta-ho'-ke, ta-ho'-hi-ka, } he burns.
by, i-ta'-na.
to'-ri-ke-ing'-e, to'-ri-ke, } by and by.

C.

call, wang'-ke, he calls.
ki-wang'-ke, he calls for.
cat, mung'-ka, polecat.
cattle, će, bison.
će-the'-we, black cattle.
ćĕth'-ka, white cattle.
chief, wang'-e-ka-he.
coat, wo-na'-ye.

cold, thni.
corn, wa-tu-će'-di-to-we, cornmeal.
crow, ka'-he.
cry, ha'-ke-ke.
ha'-ki-nang-a-ke, crying.

D.

dance, wa-shi'-ke, će'-ke, } he dances.
darkness, o-han'-the.
day, ha'-we.
dead, će', and će'-ke.
deer, ta.
dog, shŭng'-ko-ken-yi.
drink, ra-tang'-ke, he drinks.
ra-ta'-na, ra-ta'-nang-a-ke, } drinking.

E.

eagle, hra.
ear, nan'-twa.
early, ha'-we-kri, day come.
earth, ma'-ya, ma'-ha, } ground.
eat, ru-će'-ke, he eats.
ru-će'-na, wa-ru'-će-nang-a-ke, } eating.
elk, hu'-ma, and ho'-ma.
elm, e'-hu.
embark, pa-će'-o-mi-na'-re-ke, he went and sat down in a boat to embark.
enemy, wo-re-kĕsh'-kŭn-ye.
evening, pi-hi'-re, sun declines.
exist, ke. re'-ke, } he is.
ni'-ke, a-re'-ke, } to be, to exist.
shni'-ke, you are.
eye, īsh'-ta.

F.

face, en'-će.
far, pa-će'-ma.
ha-re'-ta, far off, at a distance.

father, heng'-ka, my father.
nan-će', your father.
an-će', his father.
feather, mĕh'-e, and mi-ah'-e.
fin, a'-we.
fire, pe'-će.
fish, ho.
pĕh'-e, catfish.
flesh, i'-ro.
flint, me'-thu.
flour, wa-pŭth'-ke-sho'-sho-će.
flower, o-hra'.
fly, pa'-pru-he.
foot, thi.
for, ha'-ri.
forever, i-ya'-mah-ći, and a-mah'-ći.
fox, mĕsh-re'-ke.
friend, i-ta'-ro, and wo-re-ken'-ye.

G.

girl, i-ćeng'-ching-e, and i-ćih'-mi-ing-e.
go, re'-ke, he goes.
good, pi.
pi'-ke, he is good.
goose, meh'-e.
meh'-shing-a, little goose.
meh-ath'-ka-han'-ye, a swan, white goose.
grass, ha'-me, and ha'-će.
ha'-će-pi-the, dry grass.
great, tan'-ra.
green, to.
gun, i-yo-će'.

H.

hail, pa-thu'.
hair, nan'-tu.
hand, na'-we.
na-we'-pa, finger, nose of the hand.
handsome, i-ro'-kam-pi.
hawk, hre'-ta.
head, nan'-thu.
head-dress, wo'-krang-e.
heart, na-će'.
heaven, nang'-kri-nan-ga, above.

heel, thi'-re-će.
hill, a-he'.
a-he'-mak-shi, high hill, mountain.
hog, ko-ko'-tha.
hot, taĥ'-na, and taĥ'-a-na.
house, ći-ro'-ta-ta, in the house.
husband, heng'-kra.

I.

I, men'-re, and mi'-e.
ice, nōĥ'-o.
iron, man'-the.
man-thĕth'-ka, white iron, silver.
island, će-ro-men'-će, and i-ro-man'-će.

K.

kettle, der-he'.
man'-the-der'-he, iron kettle.
kill, će'-hi-ke, he kills.
knee, shas'-ke.
knife, ma'-hi.
ma-thang'-ke, } big knife.
ma'-hi-hau'-ye, }

L.

lake, će-ki'-he, and ni-a-pa'-će.
late, pi-a-hōn'-ye-hu'-ta.
laugh, ik-sha-nang'-a-ke, laughing.
iĥ'-sha-nang-a-ke, he is laughing.
iĥ-sha'-ke, } he laughs.
ik-sha'-ke, }
lead, man'-the-mi.
leaf, na'-we.
leg, hu.
hu'-ro, calf of the leg.
leggin, a-ku'-ta.
life, i'-ha, and iĥ'-a.
light, o'-ha-we.
lightning, ru-kri', and ru-gri'.
liver, pi.
lodge, ći.
ći-ho-the-će', skin tent, log house.
ći'-na, village.
ći-o'-ke, door, house entrance.
log, na'-kri-we.
love, kra'-hi-ke, he loves.

M.

male, wan'-ge.
man, wang'-kwa-sho-she, a brave man.
wa-shi'-ke-shu'-će, } red man, Indian.
wa-shi'-ke-o-ken'-ye, }
meadow, wa-tŭsh'-ra.
midday, hi-mash'-će, warm sun.
midnight, ha-he'-o-ki-nan'-the-te.
mink, tōĥ-shing'-e.
moccasin, a-ku'-će.
moon, pi'-ta-we.
morning, he-ro-taĥ'-ći, and ta-ra-men'-ta.
mother, hi'-na, my mother.
mouth, i.
muskrat, ut-wa'-ke.

N.

nail, sha'-ke.
navel, de'-twa.
near, as'-ke, and as'-ki.
neck, ta'-she.
nettle, han'-to.
never, i-ya'-ha.
night, ha'-he.
no, heng'-e-ko.
nose, pa.
nothing, ta-ku'-pash-kŭn'-ye, and o-ken'-ye.

O.

oak, pu'-tu, and na-pu'-tu.
old, ya'-ke, and sha'-ke.
on, a-ha'-ta-ta.
na-a-hōn'-ye, on the tree.
a-hōn'-ye, to climb.
otter, tŏsh'-nang-e.
owl, mam'-po-ke.

P.

part, to'-he.
o-keth'-ra, half.
partridge, to'-shra-eng-a.
perhaps, as-ku, and a-rĕĥ'-nas-ki.

pigeon, pu-će′-ong-e.
pipe, raȟ′-no-we.
plain, a-prath′-ke, prairie.
poor, wa-hwa′-ta.
post, na-po′-hro-ke.
potato, to-haŋ′-yo.
pumpkin, wat-wa′-ing-e, squash, little pumpkin.
tha-ke-ra′-će, melon, anything eaten uncooked.

R.

rain, ni′-yu.
raven, ka′-he-haŋ′-ye.
red, shu′-će.
river, nĕsh-nang′-a.
rough, ma-ha-i′-yo-yo-ke, a bog.
run, nang′-e-ke, he runs.

S.

sail, ta-ćo′-ro-ta.
salt, nith′-ku, sweet water.
sash, ćo′-hi-i-pi-re.
scale, ki-shu′-we.
scalp, wa-nan′-thu-hu′-ha.
seat, shen′-će, rump.
see, a-ta′-ke, he sees.
she, e-e, he or she.
shirt, wo-na′-ye.
shoe, thi′-re-yo′-ke.
shore, i-ru′-shi-shi′-we-ta, by the shore.
shot-pouch, man′-the-mi-wo′-yu.
shrub, hra′-he, any low bush.
sing, ya-me′-ke, he sings.
sister, he-yu′-na, elder sister.
hen-tan′-ga, younger sister.
skin, ha, and i-hru′-ha.
sky, ko-ra′.
u-hi′-he, in the sky.
slender, thu-eng′-e.
snake, wa-ka′.
snipe, wi-tūh′-e.
snow, pa.
something, ta-ku′-ra-shu.
son, hi-yeng′-e, my son.
di-yeng′-o, your son.
i-yeng′-e, his son.
sour, nath′-ta.
speak, i-će′-ke, i-be′-ta-ke, } he speaks.
spear, wi-yo′-kre.
spirit, wa-kan′-ta, Great Spirit.
wa-kan′-ta-pĭsh′-kūn, evil spirit.
wa-kan′-ta-ći′-na, the Great Spirit's village, heaven.
spring, pe′-ta.
star, pi-ka′-e.
steamboat, pa-će′-ta-ke.
stomach, sho′-ke, and sho′-ku-hōn′-ye.
stone, en′-ro.
en′-ro-haŋ′-ye, big stone, rock.
stream, nesh-nang′-a, nesh-naȟ′-shing, } a small stream.
strike, i-će′, o-ći′-ke, } he strikes.
strong, prĕh′-e.
sucker, kōn′-ye.
summer, to′-ke-ta, wet season.
sun, pi.
sweet, thku.

T.

that, ka′-e.
thigh, re′-ke, and re′-ku-haŋ′-ye.
think, kĕh′-thu-ke, i-ru′-ka-na′-ke, } he thinks.
this, će.
thistle, wĕh′-i.
then, di′-re, and di′-e.
through, wa-he′-će.
thunder, ka.
tie, rūth-ki-će′-ke, i′-re-ske, } he ties.
toad, će-wa′-he.
tobacco, nan′-ye.
to-day, ha′-we-ke.
toe, thi′-ha.
to-morrow, han′-re-ta.
tongue, re′-the.

tooth, hi.
tortoise, ke'-ta.
trout, to'-thi.

U.

ugly, i-ro-kam'-pesh-kūn'-ye, not handsome.
under, ku'-ha.
up, o-me'-si-ta, up the country.

V.

valley, kro'-ke, hollow.
vein, ka.
a'-ka, vein in the arm.
village, ći'-na-pro-ki, the whole village.

W.

walk, man'-ye-ke, he walks.
wampum, u-nam'-pi, beads.
war-club, ma'-ya-ki-ta-wi'-ro-ći.
water, ni.
ni-hūng'-e, through the water.
će'-ta, } great water.
ni'-han-ye, }
we, hi'-e.
weak, pron'-ra-ra.
weasel, hen-thh'-tha.
weather, mash'-će, warm weather.
weed, ha'-će, and ha'-mi.
what, wa-ye'-re-će.
ta-ku'-ra, what is it?
wheat, wa-pūth'-ka.
which, ta'-na-ha.
white, thka.
who, wa-ge'-re.
wife, hen-ta'-mi, my wife.
wind, ta'-će, and tak'-tha-ke.
windpipe, to'-hu-hu.
wing, a'-hu.
winter, pan-ye'-ta, when it snows.
thni'-ta, when it is cold.
wish, kūn'-re-ke.
within, ro'-ta-ta.
without, tan'-gri-ta.
wolf, shūn'-ta.
man-yi-ka', prairie wolf.
woman, i-nūn'-ge, and wa-shi'-ke-mi.
wood, na.
na-pu'-pa-na, pine, sweet-smelling wood.
na-pa-krun'-će, stump, wood cut off.
na-ro-tang'-kre, tree, upright wood.
na-kra'-će, arm of a tree, limb.
pa-će'-hra-we, undergrowth, forest, brush, &c.
hi'-sku, bass-wood.
woodcock, thka'-ge.
woodpecker, to'-kre-kre'-the.
worm, ma-shi'-we.

Y.

ye, di'-re-wi.
year, pa'-yi.
yellow, thi.
yes, hūn'-će.
yesterday, ta'-nan-yi'-ta.
young, shing'-e-ći.

NOTE.

THE materials composing this memoir have been accumulated during several expeditions to the Northwest since 1855. A considerable portion of the information in regard to the history of the Indian tribes was obtained during the years 1854 and '55, while the author was exploring the Valley of the Missouri River, under the patronage and protection of the American Fur Company. The greater part, however, was secured in 1856 and '57, while under the command of Lieut. G. K. Warren, T. E. U. S. A., and in the years 1859 and '60, while attached to the Exploring Expedition to the head waters of the Missouri and Yellowstone, under the command of Capt. William F. Raynolds, T. E. U. S. A. From both Lieut. Warren and Capt. Raynolds, the author cheerfully acknowledges great aid and encouragement in his researches. The results have been prepared and published in their present form by permission of the War Department.

The proof-sheets have been read with great care by a very critical philologist, Mr. Pliny E. Chase, of Philadelphia, and for his kindness and courtesy in this matter, the author gladly acknowledges his indebtedness.

EXPLANATION OF PLATES AND MAP.

The plates of Indian portraits were added to the memoir at the suggestion of an eminent ethnologist after the paper was completed, and this will account for the absence of any allusion to them in the text. It was a favorite design of the late lamented Prof. W. W. Turner, to prepare a work on the Indian languages of America, accompanied with portraits, so far as they could be secured, of the Indians from whom the vocabularies were obtained, showing the mental status of the man, as the representative of his tribe or language. So far as possible I have adopted this plan in the present memoir. The figures on the plates accompanying this work are copied from photographs taken in the Indian country, under the direction of Mr. J. D. Hutton, Topographical Assistant to Capt. William F. Raynolds, T. E., and published by permission of the latter. They are quite characteristic of the tribes they represent.

FIG. 1, Plate I, represents one of the most noted Crow chiefs, who wields great influence in his tribe, is a fine orator, and possessed of strong native talents. From him I obtained much reliable information in regard to the history and the language of the Crow tribe. FIG. 2 is a Shyenne brave, an excellent hunter, with fine natural powers, quick perceptions and intelligence, increased by long association with the whites. He formed the medium through which I obtained all the materials in regard to the Shyennes and their language. He is alluded to in the text under the name of "Rib," on page 276. FIG. 3 is the portrait of "Iron Horn," one of the most noted medicine-men in the Dakota nation. He possesses great influence in his tribe, is a warm friend of the whites, and has done much to harmonize difficulties among his people. He has often acted as guide and hunter to United States Exploring parties in the Dakota country. FIG. 4 represents the daughter of a late chief of one of the principal bands of the Dakota nation, and is now the wife of Mr. Charles E. Galpin, one of the chief partners in the American Fur Company. She is a woman of much intelligence and fine natural capacities, and may be regarded as the highest type of her sex among the Indian tribes of the Northwest.

FIG. 5, Plate II, is a Crow Indian of the more common sort, somewhat below the average grade. FIG. 6 represents one of the most influential chiefs of the Yancton band of the Dakotas, "Smutty Bear," as his Indian name has been interpreted by the traders. He is a fine orator, and manages the affairs of his people with ability and prudence. FIG. 7, *a*, *b*, *c*, are Arapoho chiefs. FIG. 7, *d*, is a tolerably good likeness of "Friday," whose history is given briefly on page 322 of this memoir.

The MAP accompanying this memoir will serve to illustrate the present geographical position of the different Indian tribes inhabiting the Missouri Valley. The discrepancies in the spelling of proper names, which has become so complicated at this time, could not be remedied in the present paper. The names of tribes in large letters indicate their range prior to treaties with the United States. The Reserves on the Lower Missouri are shown by dotted lines.

INDEX.*

GEOGRAPHY.

Blackfoot country, "Bad Lands" of, 250, 251.
Bridger's Pass, 322.
California, 373.
Chagouadmigong Mission, 380.
Coteau de Prairie, 249.
Dakota, Territory of, 364.
English possessions, 240.
Great Bend, 276, 388.
Indian Agency, 322.
Iowa Town, 445.
Mauvaises Terres, or "Bad Lands," notice of, 365, 366.
Minnesota, Territory of, 364.
Miocene Tertiary Period, 367.
Mississippi Valley, 346.
Nebraska, 364.
Northwest Territory, 364.
North Park, 322.
Oregon, 373.
Red Pipestone Quarry, 365.
St. Mary's Valley, 249.
Upper Missouri, 340, 351, 355, 379.

MOUNTAINS.

Alps, 395.
Big-horn, 231.
Black Hills, 274.
Cypress, 237, 346.
Hill of Thunder, 365.
Montagnes des Bois, 237.
Pike's Peak, 321.
Prickly Pear, 236.
Red Buttes, 321.
Rocky, 249, 340, 392.
Slender Butte, 374.
Three Tetons, 322.
Tinder, 237.
Turtle, 239.
Wind River Mountains, 394.
Woody, 236.

RIVERS.

Apple, 364, 365, 375.
Arkansas, 321.
Assiniboin, source of, 239.
Belly, 249.
Big Muddy, 387.
Big Nemaha, 447.
Big Sioux, 364.
Big Snake, 341.
Cannon-ball, 365.
Cimarron, 322.
Columbia, 249.
Deer Creek, 322.
Des Moines, 370.
Grand, 352.
Grand Coulée, 382, 387.
Great Shyenne, North and South Forks, description of, 274.
Green, 276.
Heart, 365.
Illinois, 346.
Iowa, 445.
Iowa Rapids, 445.
James, 364.
Judith, character of, 250.
Knife, 382.
La Riviere aux Souris, 240, 387.
Little Muddy, 382.
Little Shyenne, 275.
Maria, 249.
Mankato, or Blue Earth, 445.
Medicine, 365.
Milk, 251.
Moreau, 365.
Mussel-shell, character of, 250.
Niobrara, 369.
North Platte, 276.
Pembina, source of, 239.
Ponkas, 448.
Porcupine, 382.
Powder, 321.
Quaking Asp, 382.
Red, 239.
Rio del Norte, 321.
Riviere du Parc, 239.
Riviere aux Tremble, or Quaking Asp, 382.
Saskatchewan, 249.
South Platte, 276.
St. Peter's, 379.
Sweet Water, 276.
Teton, 365.
Vermilion, 364.
Wabash, 346.
Washita, 347.
Wash-te'-wak-pa or Good River, 274.
White, 365, 373.
Wolf, or Loup Fork, 346.

LAKES.

Athabasca, 235.
Fresh-water lakes, notice of, 367.
Huron, 236.
Lac du Diable, 375.
Lac de L'Isle Croix, 238.
Lac Qu'appelle, 237.
Lac qui Parle, 364.
Lake of the Woods, 236.
Michigan, 236.
Red Lake, 239.
Slave Lake, 235.
Superior, 236.
Traverse, 239.
Winnipeg and Northern Lakes, 236.

FORTS.

Cassepierre, 239.
Clarke, 352, 356, 423.
Fort de Prairie, 237.
Laramie, on the North Platte, 276, 373.
Pierre, 366, 375.
Union, climate of, 251, 381, 387, 394.

BOTANY.

Amelanchier Canadensis, 370.

* This Index is not intended to be a complete one, but to include only the principal proper names employed in the text.

Apios tuberosa, 369.
Artemisia trifida, 292.
Cornus, osier, 251.
Crategus coccineus, 293.
Grain de bœuf, 370.
Helianthus tuberosus, 369.
Humulus lupulus, var. Americanus, 386.
Indian corn, 353.
Lobelia inflata, Indian tobacco, 273.
Mentha Canadensis, 319.
Opuntia Missouriensis, O. fragilis, 384.
Pomme blanche, or prairie turnip, 280.
Prunus Americana, 370.
Prunus Virginiana, 370.
Prunus pumila, 367.
Psoralea esculenta, "Pomme blanche," 369.
Pumpkins, 353.
"Rose-buds," 370.
Sarcobatus vermicularis, 292.
Squashes, 353.
Yucca angustifolia, 367.

ZOOLOGY.

Arctomys ludovicianus, prairie dog, 368.
Cervus leucurus, 392.
Cervus macrotis, 392.
Dentalium, used as ornaments, 269, 314.
Ovis montana, 366, 392.

ETHNOLOGY.

Ahnahaways, 421.
Arapohos, 232, 231.
Arikaras, 232, 351.
Assinnee-Poetuc, 380.
Assiniboins, 232, 379.
Assinepoils, 380.
Atsinas, 232, 310.
Ayavois, 445.
Big Robber, Crow Chief, 394.
Blackfeet, 232, 248.
Brulées, or Burnt Thighs, 371, 372, 373.
Chippewas, 235, 379.
Clear Blue Earth, 372.
Crows, 232, 391.
Cut-heads, 374.
Dakotas, 352, 364, 379.
Fall, or Big-bellied Indians, Gros Ventres de Prairie, 253.
Flat-heads of St. Mary's Valley, 394.
Foolish People, Arapoho Band, 326.
Friday, Arapoho Interpreter, 322.
Gens des Canots, 387.
Gens du Gauché, 387.
Gens du Nord, 388.
Grand Pawnees, 347.
Ho-ha, or Rebels, 380.
Ho'-he, or Fish-eaters, 381.
Huecos, 347.
Hunk'-pa-pas, 374.
Iroquois, 346.
Issati, 380.
I-ta'-zip-éos, 374.
Kai'-e-na, 256.
Kansas, 232.
Kaskaias, 321.
Killistinoes, 380.
Knisteneaux, or Crees, 232, 239.
Kútonas, 256.
Le Chef du Tonnerre, Cree, 247.
Le Gros Français, 379.
Les Gens des Ruches, 379.
La Lance, 237.
"Le Sonnant," 237.
Mahaha, 421.
Mandans, 232, 426.
Matotantes, 346.
Ma-to'-to-pa, or Four Bears, 374.
Metaharta, 422.
Mexicans, 322.
Mi-nah'-ta-nēs, or Mandans, 426.
Mi-ne-kaŋ-zūs, 374.
Minnitarees of the Missouri, 344.
Minnitarees of the Prairie, 344.
Missouri Dakotas, 371.
Nadowasis, 380.
Nadouessis, or Scioux, 380.
Nandowessie Nation, 380.
Ne'-a-ya-óg, meaning of, 235.
Nehethewas, or Crees, 343.
Ogalálas, 373.
Omahas, 232, 444.
Osages, 232, 346.
Osinipoilles, 380.
Otos, 232, 444.
Pana, 346.
Paneassa, 346.
Panelogo, 346.
Panismahaus, 346.
Paunch, Fall, or Rapid Indians, 343, 422.
Pawnees, 345, 351.
Pawnee Loups, 346.
Pawnee Piets, 347.
Pawnee Republics, 347.
People of the Sage, 321.
Picaneux, 253.
Piegan, 253.
Pickunns, 256.
Plusieurs des Aigles, 237.
Ponkas, 232.
Pine Indians, 374.
Rapid Indians, 254.
Rees, 356.
Rib, Shyenne hunter, 276, 277, 278.
Ricaras, 421.
Sarcees, 256.
Shai-e'la, or Shai-en'-a, 274.
Si'-ha-sa'-pās, 374.
Siksikai, 256.
Sioux, 254.
Small Gulls, 237.
Snake and Nez-Percé Indians, 394.
Soulier Noirs, or Shoe Indians, 422.
Ta-nish' or Sa-nish', "The People," 356.
The Little Eagle, 237.
The Painted Lodge, 237.
Two-Kettle Band, 374.
Wa'-na-ta, 375.
Wattasoons, 422.
Weepers, 380.
Wichitas, 347.
Wo-he-nōm'-pa, 374.
Wolf Pawnees, 346.
Yanctonais, 374.

MYTHOLOGY, CUSTOMS.

Astronomical knowledge of the Crees, 245.
Aurora Borealis, 245.
"Buffalo chips," 388.
Cachés, how used, 353.
Chief's Road, 245.
Great Spirit, 278, 323, 431.
Great Spirit Chief, 245.

Indian paradise, location of, 245.
Milky Way, 245.
Plue, value of, 247.
Polar Star, 245.
Pouderie defined, 360.
Snake Moon, 349.
Sunday, 317.
Ursa Major, 245.
Big Owl Dance, 281.
Buffalo-woman Dance, Arapoho, 326.
Bull-Head Dance, 281.
Dog Dance, 281.
Dog Dance, Arapoho, 325.
Elk Dance, 281.
Foolish Dog's Dance, Arapoho, 326.
Fox Dance, 281.
Little Dog's Dance, Arapoho, 326.
Medicine Dance, 281.
Olympic amusements, 430.
Scalp Dance, 281.
Soldier Dance, 281.
Strong-Heart Dance, 281.
Sun Dance, 280.
War Dance, Arapoho, 325.
White Belt Dance, 281.

AUTHORITIES.

Abert, Lieut., U. S. A., vocabulary taken by, 282.
Alcedo's Spanish Geography, 445.
American Fur Company, 234, 237, 353.
Archæologia Americana, 282, 347.
Bourgmont, visit to Pawnees, 346.
Brackenridge, H. M., Voyage up the Missouri River, in 1811, 254, 343.
Brauninger, Rev. Mr., 231, 395.
Carver, 380.
Catlin, George, "North American Indians," notes on, 254, 356.
Culbertson, Mr. Alexander, 234.
Dakota Grammar, 231, 282.
Dawson, Mr. Andrew, 234, 356.
Denig, Mr. E. T., 234, 381.
De Smet, Father, Travels of, 255.
Dole, Hon. Wm. P., 234.
Doty, Mr. James, 250.
Doway, Father, narrative of, 346.
Dunbar, Rev. Mr., 347.
Emory, Notes, &c., 282.
Ethnological Society, Transactions of, 253, 282.
Fitzpatrick, Mr., 322.
Force, Col. Peter, 234.
Galpin, Mr. C. E., 234, 457.
Gallatin, Hon. Albert, 253, 282, 321, 343, 347, 423, 428.
Hale, Horatio, 254.
Hamilton, Rev. Wm., 347, 447.
Howse, Mr. Joseph, Cree Grammar, 235.
Henry, Prof., 234.
Hudson's Bay Company, 239, 240, 247, 249, 255, 340, 343.
Indian Bureau, United States, 276.
Indian Tribes of the United States, 255.
Kipp, Mr. James, 435.
La Hontan, 380.
La Salle, Voyage, &c., 346.
Le Sueur's Voyage, 235, 445.
Leidy, Prof. Joseph, 367.
Lewis and Clarke's Journal, 253, 346, 379, 421, 446.
Long, Major S. H., 275, 321, 423.
Ludwig, Literature of American Aboriginal Languages, 282.
Maximilian, Prince of Wied, Travels of, 255, 380, 395, 435.
Mackenzie, General History of the Fur Trade, 253, 380.
Meldrum, Mr. Robert, 395.
Pacific Railroad Reports, 250.
Membré, Father Zenobius, 445.
Mitchell, Col. D. D., 255, 427.
Moncrovie, J. B., vocabulary by, 255.
Morse, Rev. J., 254, 276, 321, 343, 423.
Pike, Lieut. Z., 321.
Proceedings of the Academy of Natural Sciences, Philadelphia, 367.
Raynolds, Capt. William F., 276, 322, 457.
Riggs, Mr. S. R., 233.
Say, Prof. T., 423.
Schoolcraft, Mr. H. R., 234.
Shea, J. G., 235, 445.
Smithsonian Institution, 231, 233, 282.
Stevens, Gov. I. I., 250, 344.
Sublette, Mr., 341, 342.
Transactions of the American Antiquarian Society, Vol. II, 254.
Treaty with the Blackfeet in 1855, 252.
Turner, Prof. Wm. W., 233, 457.
Umfreville, 253, 343, 380.
United States Exploring Expedition, Philology of, 254.
Warren, Lieut. G. K., 371, 457.

www.ingramcontent.com/pod-product-compliance
Lightning Source LLC
Chambersburg PA
CBHW030313270326
41926CB00010B/1347

* 9 7 8 3 3 3 7 0 5 7 1 5 2 *